ELEANOR OF AQUITAINE

Alison Weir lives and works in Surrey. Her books include *Britain's Royal Families*, *The Princes in the Tower*, *Children of England*, *Henry VIII: King and Court*, *Mary, Queen of Scots* and most recently, *Katherine Swynford*.

ALISON WEIR

Eleanor of Aquitaine

By the Wrath of God, Queen of England

VINTAGE BOOKS
London

Published by Vintage 2007

8 10 9 7

Copyright © Alison Weir 1999

Alison Weir has asserted her right under the Copyright, Designs and
Patents Act 1988 to be identified as the author of this work

First published in Great Britain by Jonathan Cape Ltd 1999

Vintage
Random House, 20 Vauxhall Bridge Road,
London SW1V 2SA

www.vintage-books.co.uk

Addresses for companies within The Random House Group Limited
can be found at: www.randomhouse.co.uk/offices.htm

The Random House Group Limited Reg. No. 954009

A CIP catalogue record for this book
is available from the British Library

ISBN 9780099523550

The Random House Group Limited supports The Forest Stewardship Council
(FSC®), the leading international forest certification organisation. Our books
carrying the FSC label are printed on FSC® certified paper. FSC is the only forest
certification scheme endorsed by the leading environmental organisations,
including Greenpeace. Our paper procurement policy can be found at
www.randomhouse.co.uk/environment

Printed and bound by CPI Group (UK) Ltd, Croydon, CR0 4YY

THIS BOOK IS DEDICATED

With heartfelt thanks
To my agent,
JULIAN ALEXANDER
and to
JILL BLACK
Who has edited so many of my books

Acknowledgements

I should like to extend very special thanks to my editor, Anthony Whittome, for his creative input and his unflagging enthusiasm for this project, and to my commissioning editor, Will Sulkin, for his tremendous support. Gratitude is also due to Lily Richards for her indefatigable picture research, and to the design team at Jonathan Cape for the jacket design and layout.

As always, I must express my thanks to my agent Julian Alexander, without whom this book would not exist: he kept faith with this project for many years before its acceptance. I am grateful also to his former assistant, Kirstan Romano, for all her kindness. Finally, as ever, thank you, Rankin, my husband, and John and Kate, my children, for putting up with me while this book was in preparation. I could never have done it without you.

Contents

A Note on Names and Spellings

Different variations of the names of people and places occur in twelfth-century sources. For example, the names Matilda, Maud and Mahalde arc interchangeable, as are Alice, Aaliz and Alais.

For the sake of clarity, I have used different spellings of the same name to identify different people. Eleanor's daughter is called Alix, Richard I's betrothed of the same name Alys, and the Lord John's betrothed Alice. All are accurate renderings. A similar differentiation has been used with the name Amaury/Aymer/Aimery. Louis VII's daughter, often called Margaret in other works, is here referred to by the French version of her name, Marguerite.

Eleanor, who would have called herself Aliénore, is referred to by the more familiar anglicised version of her name.

As in many other history books, William the Marshal is throughout referred to as such, even though he did not acquire his office of Marshal until 1199.

Although Eleanor was Countess of Poitou and Duchess of Aquitaine, I have occasionally used the name Aquitaine as a blanket term covering both her domains, although I have tried to differentiate between them wherever possible.

Many place names have changed since the twelfth century, and where appropriate I have given the modern name in parentheses. Some places no longer exist; wherever possible, I have attempted to discover their exact or approximate location.

Illustrations

Effigy of Berengaria of Navarre (detail), after 1230, Le Mans
Cathedral © *Geoffrey Wheeler*
Effigy of King John (detail), c.1225–30, Worcester Cathedral ©
Geoffrey Wheeler
Mural from Sainte-Radegonde, Chinon, c.1196 © *By courtesy of Les
Amis du Vieux Chinon*
Effigy of Isabella of Angoulême (detail), mid 13c., Fontevrault
Abbey © *Geoffrey Wheeler*
Effigy of Eleanor of Aquitaine (detail), c.1204, Fontevrault Abbey ©
AKG London
The tombs of the Plantagenets in the Abbey of Fontevrault ©
Bildarchiv Foto Marburg

Maps

The Angevin Empire in 1154

Europe and the Holy Land in the Twelfth Century

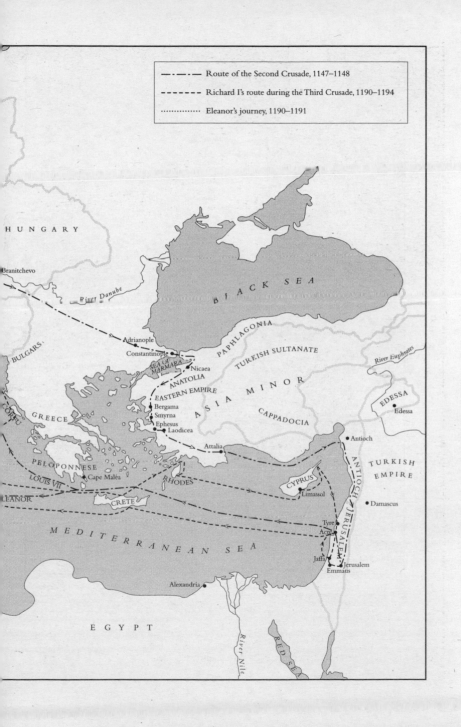

HUNGARY

Branitchevo

River Danube

BLACK SEA

BULGARS

Adrianople

PAPHLAGONIA

Constantinople

TURKISH SULTANATE

River Euphrates

SEA OF MARMARA

Nicaea

ANATOLIA

EASTERN EMPIRE

ASIA MINOR

EDESSA

Edessa

Bergama

Smyrna

CAPPADOCIA

GREECE

Ephesus

Laodicea

Antioch

CORFU

Attalia

TURKISH EMPIRE

PELOPONNESE

RHODES

ANTIOCH

LOUIS VII

Cape Maléa

CYPRUS

Damascus

ELEANOR

CRETE

Limassol

JERUSALEM

Tyre

Acre

MEDITERRANEAN SEA

Jaffa

Jerusalem

Emmaus

Alexandria

EGYPT

River Nile

RED SEA

England in the Twelfth Century

Preface

When, after completing several books on the late medieval and Tudor periods, I suggested writing a biography of Eleanor of Aquitaine, it was put to me that it would be impossible for a biographer to do justice to a woman who lived eight centuries ago: that so few of her utterances or letters have come down to us that I would never be able to bring her to life as a real person to whom my readers could relate.

It was a valid point, because for the earlier medieval period, the sources that so vividly illuminate the characters of the Tudors – diplomatic reports, letters, memoirs, diaries, biographies – rarely survive. And there is a perception, common amongst those who are more familiar with the later period, that such monkish chronicles as we do have are mostly credulous, biased and ill-informed. In some cases, this is indeed so, particularly in respect of the period covering the early years of Henry II's reign, for which there is a paucity of contemporary sources; but there are a considerable number of English chronicles of outstanding quality for the latter part of the twelfth century.

The twelfth century in general is readily accessible to us today because it was an age of burgeoning scholarship that is now regarded as the first Renaissance, an age that gave birth to a succession of outstanding and perceptive chroniclers, whose relatively objective accounts of the personalities and events of their times document a wealth of facts, detail and contemporary opinion.

Many of these writers were eye-witnesses to the events they described; most were well-educated, intelligent men, who were familiar with the court and the great figures of their age. From the pages of their chronicles, as well as from other surviving records, it is possible to garner a considerable amount of material on Eleanor. It is true that there is a lot we still do not know about her – for example, no description of her appearance survives – and that monkish chroniclers in general did not consider women, even queens, sufficiently important to merit much space in their works, but her deeds speak for themselves, as do her surviving charters and letters. I make no apology for quoting two of those letters at length, as they give such insights into Eleanor's character, as well as her state of mind at the time they were written.

There is much that is controversial about Eleanor, yet a great deal of the evidence is independently corroborated by other sources, and while she sometimes remains tantalisingly elusive, due to gaps in that evidence, we know enough of the events surrounding her, and of what her contemporaries thought about her, to draw some conclusions.

We must nevertheless understand that most medieval chronicles were not written primarily as historical narratives or analyses, but as moral tales to illustrate the mysterious workings of God in the events of the time. Almost without exception, chroniclers expected their works to have an improving effect upon their own and later generations, who would benefit spiritually from the lessons to be learned from history.

Many chronicles, such as the *Chronicles of the Counts of Anjou* (dedicated to Henry II and containing a flattering and stirring account of his father, Count Geoffrey), also contain stimulating and popular accounts of mythical or legendary persons and their exploits, making little or no attempt to distinguish between fact and fiction. On occasion, such stories were even fabricated for the enjoyment and edification of a credulous public. Furthermore, there are discrepancies between accounts of real events in the works of different chroniclers, which oblige the historian to seek corroboration from as many sources as possible, where they exist. Often, they do not, and a writer must then use his or her own judgement as to which, on balance, is the most reliable account – never an easy decision, and one that must always take account of what may be inferred from circumstantial evidence. Where this has happened, I have explained in the text or in the notes how I arrived at my conclusions.

Eleanor has been a popular figure with historical biographers for many decades now, and people often react with enthusiasm when her name is mentioned. I realise that I am going to upset some with the theories put forward in this book, but I would point out that these theories have been arrived at only after extensive scrutiny of the evidence and much thought. I have deliberately avoided falling into the romantic mode of some earlier biographies, and have looked afresh at every controversial issue in Eleanor's life, in some cases taking a new approach.

Above all, I have derived great enjoyment from researching and writing this book, although I have to admit that it has felt more like a piece of detective work than a conventional historical biography. I hope that what emerges in the following pages is a credible and balanced account, stripped of the myths, suppositions and misunderstandings that have obscured the real Eleanor of Aquitaine, both in the distant and the recent past.

Alison Weir,
Carshalton, July 1999

Prologue: 18 May 1152

In the Romanesque cathedral of Poitiers a man and a woman stood before the high altar, exchanging wedding vows. It was a simple ceremony. The young man, aged nineteen, was stocky, with red hair, and restless with pent-up energy, knowing he was doing a daring thing. The woman, eleven years his senior and with long auburn locks, was exceptionally beautiful, very sophisticated and a willing accomplice in this furtive ceremony.

Few would have guessed, from the lack of pomp and splendour, that the marriage of this couple was to change the face of Europe. Yet the bridegroom was Henry, later called Plantagenet, Count of Anjou and Duke of Normandy, who had already established a reputation as one of the most formidable princes in Europe. Not only did he hold strategically important domains in what is now France, but he was also the heir to his mother Matilda's claim to the kingdom of England – a claim that few doubted he would prosecute successfully.

Now Henry of Anjou was about to extend his territories even further, by marriage to one of the greatest heiresses of the Middle Ages. The woman who stood beside him was Eleanor, Duchess of Aquitaine and Countess of Poitou in her own right, and former Queen of France. Not only did she own most of the land between the Loire and the Pyrenees, but she was also renowned for her loveliness. In every way, she was a great prize for an aspiring ruler.

However, it was as well that Henry of Anjou was a young man of strong character, since his bride was also headstrong and wilful. Nor had she reached the age of thirty without acquiring a reputation for scandalous behaviour. Rumours of her affairs and unconventional conduct, both in France and during the Second Crusade, were notorious throughout Christendom. Her marriage to Louis VII of

France had recently been annulled, ostensibly on the grounds of consanguinity, but in reality because Eleanor had failed to produce a male heir. In those days, this would have been regarded as entirely the woman's fault, but Eleanor would have had good grounds for disagreeing with that. The evidence suggests, moreover, that it was she, and not Louis, who had been the prime mover in the dissolution of their marriage.

Henry of Anjou was prepared to overlook the shady details of his bride's past so long as he could secure her desirable person and, more importantly, her great inheritance. By marrying her, hastily and without any display of appropriate ceremonial, the young Duke was aware that both he and his bride were defying their common overlord, King Louis of France himself, for neither had sought his permission for their union, as was customary. Nor would it have been forthcoming had they done so, since even the saintly Louis would have foreseen the consequences of such a marriage. Through it, and Henry's subsequent accession to the English throne in 1154, was founded the vast Angevin empire, which comprised England and much of what is now France and stretched from the Scottish border to the Pyrenees. Such an empire would pose a deadly threat to the much smaller kingdom of France.

But when Louis VII found out about the marriage, it was too late: the pattern of western European diplomacy and warfare had been set for the next four centuries, since the rulers of France would henceforth make it their business to divide and conquer the Angevin empire. Thus it was that the marriage of Henry II, the first of the Plantagenet kings of England, and Eleanor of Aquitaine – two very charismatic personalities in their own right – not only had a dramatic impact on the politics of twelfth-century Christendom, but also affected the course of European history over the next 400 years.

This is Eleanor's story.

1

'Opulent Aquitaine'

Eleanor of Aquitaine was born into a Europe dominated by feudalism. In the twelfth century there was no concept of nationhood or patriotism, and subjects owed loyalty to their ruler, rather than the state.

Europe was split into principalities called feudatories, each under the rule of a king, duke or count, and personal allegiance, or fealty, was what counted. This was expressed in the ceremony of homage, in which a kneeling vassal would place his hands between those of his overlord and swear to render him service and obedience.

The most powerful kings and lords could command obedience and aid from lesser rulers; a breach of fealty was generally held to be dishonourable, and although some paid mere lip-service to the ideal, the threat of intervention in a dispute by one's overlord often remained an effective restraint. On the other hand, an overlord was bound to offer protection, friendship and aid to a vassal beset by enemies, so the system had its advantages.

Feudal Europe was essentially a military society. Warfare was the business of kings and noblemen, and to many it was an elaborate game played by the rules of chivalry (a word deriving from the French *chevalerie*, meaning cavalry), a knightly code embodying ideals of courage, loyalty, honesty, courtesy and charity. These rules were often strictly observed, and any breach of them was regarded with opprobrium.

Kings and lords might engage in the most bloody conflicts, but once sieges were broken, castles and territory taken, and a truce signed, it was agreed to be in everyone's best interests for good relations to be restored – until the next conflict broke out. Thus, rulers could be enemies one month, yet swear undying friendship the next, such was the shifting scene of twelfth-century politics. The real victims of war were, of course, the peasants and townsfolk, who served as foot soldiers or were innocent victims of the sacking of towns and villages by mercenaries or the notoriously violent *routiers*, ruthless desperadoes whose lives were dedicated to fighting and plunder. Humble non-combatants often perished in vast numbers at the whim of their rulers – even that of Eleanor herself.

Christianity governed the lives of everyone in feudal Europe. Belief in the Holy Trinity was universal, and any deviation from the accepted doctrines of the Catholic Church – such as the heresies of the Cathars in southern France – was ruthlessly suppressed. Holy Church, presided over by the Pope in Rome, was the ultimate authority for all spiritual and moral matters, and even kings were bound by her decrees.

In this martial world dominated by men, women had little place. The Church's teachings might underpin feudal morality, yet when it came to the practicalities of life, a ruthless pragmatism often came into play. Kings and noblemen married for political advantage, and women rarely had any say in how they or their wealth were to be disposed in marriage. Kings would sell off heiresses or rich widows to the highest bidder, for political or territorial advantage, and those who resisted were heavily fined.

Young girls of good birth were strictly reared, often in convents, and married off at fourteen or even earlier in their parents' or overlord's best interests. The betrothal of infants was not uncommon, despite the Church's disapproval. It was a father's duty to bestow his daughters in marriage; if he was dead, his overlord or the King himself would act for him. Personal choice was rarely an issue.

Upon marriage, a girl's property and rights became invested in her husband, to whom she owed absolute obedience. Every husband had the right to enforce this duty in whichever way he thought fit – as Eleanor was to find out to her cost. Wife-beating was common, although the Church did at this time attempt to restrict the length of the rod that a husband might use.

It is fair to say, however, that there were women who transcended the mores of society and got away with it: the evidence suggests that Eleanor of Aquitaine was one such. There were then, as now, women of strong character who ruled feudal states and kingdoms, as Eleanor did; who took decisions, ran farms and businesses, fought lawsuits and even, by sheer force of personality, dominated their husbands.

It was rare, however, for a woman to exercise political power. Eleanor of Aquitaine and her mother-in-law, the Empress Matilda, were among the few notable exceptions, unique in their time. The fact remained that the social constraints upon women were so rigidly enforced by both Church and state that few women ever thought to question them, but meekly accepted their lot. Eleanor herself caused ripples in twelfth-century society because she was a spirited woman who was determined to do as she pleased.

Eleanor of Aquitaine was heiress to one of the richest domains in mediaeval Europe. In the twelfth century, the county of Poitou and the duchies of Aquitaine and Gascony covered a vast region in the south-west of what is now France, encompassing all the land between the River Loire in the north and the Pyrenees in the south, and between the Rhône valley and the mountains of the Massif Central in the east and the Atlantic Ocean in the west.

In those days, the kingdom of France itself was small, being centred mainly upon Paris and the surrounding area, which was known from the fourteenth century as the Île de France; yet its kings, thanks to the legacy of the Emperor Charlemagne, who had ruled most of northern Europe in the eighth century, were overlords of all the feudatories in an area roughly corresponding to modern France.

Poitou was the most northerly of Eleanor's feudatories: its northern border marched with those of Brittany, Anjou and Touraine, and its chief city was Poitiers. Perched on a cliff, with impressive ramparts, this was the favourite seat of its suzerains. To the east was the county of Berry, and to the south the wide sweep of the duchy of Aquitaine, named 'land of waters' after the great rivers that dissected it: the Garonne, the Charente, the Creuse, the Vienne, the Dordogne and the Vézère. The duchy also incorporated the counties of Saintonge, Angoulême, Périgord, the Limousin, La Marche and the remote region of the Auvergne. In the south, stretching to the Pyrenees, was the wine-producing duchy of Gascony, or Guienne, with its bustling port of Bordeaux, and the Agenais. All these lands comprised Eleanor's inheritance.

It was a rich one indeed, wealthier than the domain of its overlord, the King of France. 'Opulent Aquitaine, sweet as nectar thanks to its vineyards dotted about with forests, overflowing with fruit of every kind, and endowed with a superabundance of pasture land', enthused one chronicler, Heriger of Lobbes. Ralph of Diceto wrote that the duchy 'abounds with riches of many kinds, so excelling other parts of the western world that it is considered by historians one of the most fortunate and prosperous provinces of Gaul'.

The region boasted a temperate climate, and its summers could be very warm. It was a land of small walled cities, fortified keeps, moated castles, wealthy monasteries, sleepy villages and prosperous farms. Its houses were built with white or yellow walls and red-tiled roofs, as many still are today. To the east and south, the land was hilly or mountainous, while fertile plains, high tors and dense woodland were features of Poitou and Aquitaine, and flat sandy wastes and scrubland characterised Gascony.

The people of Aquitaine, who were mostly of Romano-Basque origin, were as diverse as its scenery. In the twelfth century, *The Pilgrim's Book of Compostela* described the Poitevins as handsome, full of life, brave, elegant, witty, hospitable and good soldiers and horsemen, and the natives of Saintonge as uncouth, while the Gascons – although frivolous, garrulous, cynical and promiscuous – were as generous as their poverty permitted. In fact, the whole domain was merely a collection of different lordships and peoples with little in common, apart from their determination to resist interference by their overlord, the Duke.

Most people in Aquitaine spoke the *langue d'oc*, or Provençal, a French dialect that derived from the language spoken by the Roman invaders centuries before, although there were a number of local patois. North of the River Loire, and in Poitou, they spoke the *langue d'oeil*, which to southerners seemed a different language altogether. Eleanor of Aquitaine probably spoke both dialects, although it appears that the *langue d'oc* was her mother tongue.

The Aquitanian lordships and their castles were controlled by often hostile and frequently feuding vassals, who paid mere lip-service to their ducal overlords and were notorious for their propensity to rebel and create disorder. These turbulent nobles enjoyed a luxurious standard of living compared with their unwashed counterparts in northern France, and each competed with his neighbour to establish in his castle a small but magnificent court. Renowned for their elegance, their shaven faces and long hair, the Aquitanian aristocracy were regarded by northerners as soft and idle, whereas in fact they could be fierce and violent when provoked. Self-interest was the dominant theme in their relations with their liege lords: successive dukes had consistently failed to subdue these turbulent lords or establish cohesion within their own domains.

The authority of the dukes of Aquitaine held good, therefore, only in the immediate vicinities of Poitiers, their capital, and Bordeaux. Although they claimed descent from Charlemagne and retained his effigy on the coinage of Poitou, they did not have the wealth or resources to extend their power into the feudal wilderness beyond this region and, since their military strength depended upon knight service from their unruly vassals, they could not rely upon this. Consequently, Aquitaine lagged behind northern France in making political and economic progress.

Nevertheless, the duchy was wealthy, thanks to its lucrative export trade in wine and salt, and it was a land in which the religious life flourished. Its rulers erected and endowed numerous fine churches and abbeys, notably the famous abbey at Cluny – 'a pleasaunce of the angels'[1] – and the Aquitanian Romanesque cathedrals in Poitiers and Angoulême; built in a style typified by elegant archways with radiating decoration and lively but grotesque sculptures of monsters and mythical creatures.

In the first century BC, the Romans had founded Aquitania as a province of Gaul; vestiges of Roman culture and civilisation were still evident in the twelfth century. At the time of the Merovingian kings of France (AD 481–751), Aquitaine became an independent duchy. In 781, Charlemagne had his young son Louis crowned King of Aquitaine by the Pope, and appointed a council of nobles to govern in his name. By 793, the renowned warrior William of Orange, Count of Toulouse, had emerged as their leader, although in that year he was soundly defeated by the Moors of Spain during their last attempt to extend their Moslem empire north of the Pyrenees. A brave and devout man, of whom epic *chansons de geste* (songs of deeds) were written, William retired to the abbey of Gellons near Montpellier, where he later died. In 1066, he was canonised and his burial place was renamed Saint-Guilhelm-le-Désert.

Aquitaine remained a nominal kingdom until 877, but as Charlemagne's empire fragmented, so its status declined, and it was soon the subject of intense rivalry between the counts of Poitiers and Toulouse, who both wished to rule what was now the duchy of Aquitaine. By the middle of the tenth century, Ebalus, Count of Poitou, a distant cousin of William of Orange, had emerged victorious.[2]

Eleanor 'sprang from a noble race'.[3] Ebalus' son, William III (called 'Towhead'), a wealthy, able and devout ruler, was blessed with a capable wife, Adela of Normandy. She was the first of a number of strong-minded women in the ducal family tree. Like his famous namesake, William III also retired to a monastery, dying in 963.

His son, William IV, nicknamed 'Fierebras' or 'Strong Arm', was of a more volatile temperament. Married to another woman of character, the pious Emma, sister of Hugh Capet, King of the Franks, he so offended her sensibilities by over-indulging in hunting and women that she left him twice – but not before wreaking her vengeance on his paramours. Finally bowing to pressure, he withdrew to a monastery around 996, leaving Emma to rule in the name of their son, William V the Great.

Fortunately, William V took after his mother, who remained in power until her death in 1004. Well educated, he was interested in the teachings of scholars from the cathedral schools of Blois, Tours and Chartres; he founded a similar school at Poitiers Cathedral, collected books and promoted learning at his court at Poitiers, already the leading centre of southern culture. He established good relations and alliances with his feudal neighbours and with the Church, and made several pilgrimages to Rome. He, too, married a formidable woman: his third wife, Agnes of Burgundy, was another such as his mother had been.

William V died in 1030. He was succeeded in turn by the three sons of his former wives, William VI (reigned 1030–8), Eudes (reigned 1038–9) and William VII the Brave (reigned 1039–58). The latter was 'truly warlike, second to none in daring, and endowed with foresight and abundant wealth', yet although he was 'eager for praise, pompous in his boastful arrogance' and enjoyed a 'great reputation',[4] he suffered a miserable defeat at the hands of Geoffrey Martel, Count of Anjou in 1042.

William VII was succeeded by his father's son by Agnes of Burgundy, Guy Geoffrey, who took the title William VIII. Despite the fact that she was now married to Geoffrey Martel, Agnes continued to exert her will over her son and his court, until her retirement in 1068 to the nunnery for aristocratic girls that she had founded at Saintes. Yet William VIII was an energetic and dynamic ruler; by 1063, he had annexed Saintonge and Gascony to Aquitaine, thereby increasing the duchy's importance and power in western Europe. It was for a time sufficiently peaceful for its Duke to depart to fight the Moors in Spain. His victory at Babastro was still being celebrated in the *chansons de geste* of the twelfth century.

William's first two wives were barren, so he took a third, Audéarde of Burgundy, twenty-five years his junior and related to him within the forbidden degrees of consanguinity. Their son, William, born in 1071, was not legitimated until his father had personally visited Rome and obtained the Pope's blessing on his marriage.

William VIII died in 1086, when his son was just fifteen. William IX, Eleanor's grandfather, was a handsome and courteous, yet complex and volatile man who is regarded by historians as the first of the troubadours.

Romantic literature flourished in the twelfth century, particularly in Aquitaine and Provence. The *chansons de gestes* tended to celebrate military ideals of courage in battle, loyalty, honour and endurance, as well as legendary heroes such as Charlemagne, Roland and King Arthur, whilst the romantic poems and *lais* (lays) sang of love.

It was the poets of the south, the troubadours, who popularised the concept of courtly love, revolutionary in its day. Drawing on ideas from

Plato and from Arab writers, and influenced by the growing popularity of the cult of the Virgin Mary, these poets composed their lyric poetry and rather complex songs in the mellifluous *langue d'oc* and accompanied them with the music of rebec and viol, fidel and bow, pipe and tabor. They deified women, according them superiority over men, and laid down codes of courtesy, chivalry and gentlemanly conduct. These precepts were to be echoed in the lays of the *trouvères* of northern France, who wrote in the *langue d'oeil*. Thus were born ideals of honour and courtship that in the centuries to come, would permeate European literature and culture to such a degree that their influence is still with us today.

Under the rules of courtly love, the mistress, who is an idealised figure, often high-born and even married, remains unattainable to her humble, worshipping suitor, who must render her homage and prove his devotion and loyalty over a period of time, before his love is even acknowledged. In this aristocratic game – for such it was – the woman always had the upper hand and set the pace and tone of the relationship. Her wishes and decrees were absolute, and any suitor who did not comply with them was deemed unworthy of the honour of her love. There was an underlying eroticism to these precepts, for it was tacitly understood that the persistent lover would one day have his hoped-for reward.

Of course, the ideals of courtly love were at breathtaking variance with contemporary notions of courtship and marriage. In reality, women were rarely consulted in these matters, and there were many – Henry II among them – who regarded these newfangled ideas as subversive and pernicious. They were taken most seriously in the relaxed cultural atmosphere of southern France, where they evolved as an absorbing intellectual pastime of the upper classes, while in the more sober north, courtly love was often seen merely as an excuse for adultery.

The age of the troubadours ended in the early thirteenth century with the vicious persecution of the Cathar heretics in what became known as the Albigensian Crusade. Culminating in the holocaust at Montségur, this left southern France so devastated that its native culture, which had flourished under the auspices of Eleanor of Aquitaine and her forebears, was effectively suppressed and, in many cases, irrevocably lost.

Duke William IX was intelligent and gifted, artistic and idealistic, with an insatiable thirst for sensual passion and adventure. His verses are erotic and occasionally blasphemous, and when coupled with his amoral behaviour, they succeeded – unsurprisingly – in offending the sensibilities of the Church.

He began his reign well enough, quickly establishing himself as a capable and respected ruler and styling himself 'Duke of the Entire Monarchy of the Aquitanians'. In 1088, he married Ermengarde, the beautiful daughter of Fulk IV, Count of Anjou, but it was not long before she began to have violent mood swings and to manifest the symptoms of what was possibly manic depression or schizophrenia. As there were no children of the marriage, William had no difficulty in getting it annulled. Ermengarde then married the Count of Brittany, and William, in 1094, went off to Aragon in serious pursuit of King Sancho Ramirez's nineteen-year-old widow, Philippa.

Philippa was heiress to the county of Toulouse, which bordered Gascony in the south and was regarded by William as a desirable addition to his domains, since within it lay the important trade routes that linked Aquitaine with the Mediterranean. A great-niece of William the Conqueror, King of England, Philippa was a spirited lady in the tradition of the duchesses of Aquitaine: pious, high-minded, strong-willed and of sound political judgement.

Her father, William IV of Toulouse, after bestowing her in marriage, had gone on a pilgrimage to the Holy Land, leaving his brother, Raymond, Count of Saint-Gilles, as regent of his duchy. But when William died five years later, Raymond, ignoring Philippa's right of inheritance, usurped her title. She was therefore anxious to marry a man with the political power and resources to recover Toulouse for her, and she accepted William of Aquitaine with alacrity.

The early mediaeval period was an age of great religious fervour, when thousands of men and women went on long and dangerous pilgrimages to holy shrines, such as that of St James at Compostela, St Peter's in Rome, or even to the Holy Land itself, where was to be found the most sacred shrine of them all, Christ's burial place, the Church of the Holy Sepulchre.

Since AD 640, Palestine had been under Arab rule. In 1095, Pope Urban II preached the First Crusade, in the hope of liberating Jerusalem from the Infidel. William IX considered taking the Cross at this time, but thought better of it. It was Raymond of Toulouse who, in 1096, led an army of 100,000 crusaders to the East, having first renounced his claim to Toulouse in favour of his son Bertrand. In 1098, William marched into Toulouse and successfully laid claim to it, incurring the anger of the Church by violating the Truce of God, which required all Christians to refrain from invading the lands of a crusader during his absence. The intercession of the Bishop of Poitiers successfully averted the threat of excommunication by the Pope,[5] but William's relations with the Church were thereafter strained.

In 1099, Philippa bore a son, called William the Toulousain after the place of his birth, and news of the taking of Jerusalem by the crusaders filtered through to Europe. This set Duke William thinking that perhaps he should have taken the Cross after all, so he mortgaged Toulouse to Bertrand to provide himself with men and funds, left Philippa as regent in Poitiers, and set off for Asia Minor. In 1101, at Heraclea, he watched from a hill, weeping, as his army was cut to pieces by the Turks. After that, he had no choice but to return home, although he lingered on the way to enjoy the exotic delights of the court of Antioch and visit the holy shrines of Jerusalem.

Back in Poitiers, inspired by the culture of the East and the erotic works of Ovid, he began writing poems[6] in the Provençal dialect, with robust, sensual lyrics celebrating female beauty, carnal delights and the pleasures of love. Eleven of his works survive. Some are crude, portraying women as horses to be mounted or as wives chafing at the jealous vigilance of their husbands; others are melancholy. Nothing like them had been written since ancient times, and they caused a predictable stir, not least because William dared assert the unheard-of notion that a man should not demand love from a woman: it should be she who freely bestowed it. Nevertheless, he openly admitted that he usually pursued a woman with only one end in view, and that most of his encounters ended with 'my hands beneath her cloak'.

It was not long before William's court at Poitiers became renowned throughout Europe for this new trend in literature; it was certainly, by the twelfth century, the foremost cultural centre in France.

For the next few years, as his family grew, the Duke remained in his domains, writing poems and fighting useless wars against his unruly vassals, which only served to weaken his position and strengthen theirs. Increasingly self-indulgent, he openly pursued women, even boasting that he would found an abbey for prostitutes near his castle at Niort. He was 'brave and gallant, but too much of a jester', finding 'pleasure only in one nonsense after another, listening to jests with his mouth wide open in a constant guffaw'.[7] Not surprisingly, the Church and many of his more sober contemporaries were outraged by William's behaviour, while his wife maintained a dignified silence and turned increasingly to religion for solace.

Robert d'Arbrissel, founder of the Order of Fontevrault, was a Breton scholar and inspired teacher who wandered the roads of north-western France with his growing band of followers. A large number were women, attracted by his enlightened and sympathetic view of the female sex, and by his compassion for the outcasts of society. His reputation quickly spread, and Pope Urban II recognised him as an apostolic preacher. Nevertheless, there were those who resented his assertion that women were in many respects the superior sex and made better administrators and managers of property than men. To his critics, this sounded like heresy.

Impressed by what she had heard of d'Arbrissel, the Duchess Philippa persuaded her husband to grant him some land in northern Poitou, near the Angevin border, where he could establish a religious community dedicated to the Virgin Mary. In 1100, by a fountain at Fontevrault, near the River Vienne, he founded a double monastery for priests, monks, lay brethren and 300 segregated nuns, all under the rule of an abbess − a revolutionary arrangement for its time. In other respects, the abbey followed the rule of St Benedict. The community was housed in wooden huts and had a simple chapel. In 1119, building commenced on a new stone church, consecrated that year.

The head of the Order was the Abbess of Fontevrault; d'Arbrissel stipulated that she had to be nobly born and a widow, in order to confer prestige on the Order and ensure that it was administered by someone familiar with running a large household. The office was filled by several notable ladies during the twelfth century, among them Isabella of Anjou, the widow of William the Atheling, son and heir of King Henry I of England.

By the time of d'Arbrissel's death in 1117, Fontevrault Abbey had become very popular with aristocratic ladies wishing to retire or temporarily retreat from the world; among them was William IX's first wife, Ermengarde of Anjou, who withdrew there after the death of her second husband. These ladies were accommodated in their own apartments, where they could enjoy worldly status and comforts whilst living in seclusion. The majority of the nuns came from noble families and had lay sisters as maids, but no one, however humble, was turned away. Thanks to the endowments of wealthy benefactors, d'Arbrissel was able to establish daughter-houses and -cells elsewhere. Fontevrault also became a refuge for battered wives and penitent prostitutes, and housed a leper hospital and a home for aged religious. Above all, it quickly earned a reputation for piety and contemplative prayer, and thus fulfilled its founder's aims of enhancing the prestige of women in general and promoting their rights.

Philippa's absorption in what was going on at Fontevrault irritated William of Aquitaine, and he turned elsewhere for female company. He was again at odds with the Church, having once more been threatened with excommunication. But as the Bishop was about to pronounce the sentence of anathema in the cathedral of Saint-Pierre, William charged in with drawn sword, grabbed the startled prelate by the neck and threatened to kill him if he did not absolve him. The Bishop stood his ground, and William backed off. 'I do not love you enough to send you to Paradise,' he sneered.[8]

In 1115, the Duke conceived a violent passion for the wife of his vassal, Aimery I de Rochefoucauld, Viscount of Châtellerault, who was appropriately named Dangerosa. She had been married to Aimery for seven years and had borne him three children: Hugh, his heir, Raoul and Aenor. With no regard to the consequences of his actions, William abducted her from her bedchamber and bore her off to his palace at Poitiers, where he appears to have installed her in the newly built Maubergeonne Tower. Soon the affair became notorious, and Dangerosa was nicknamed La Maubergeonne.[9] Aimery made no recorded protest: he was probably afraid of offending his volatile overlord.

When Philippa returned from a visit to Toulouse, she was shocked at what she found and begged the papal legate, Giraud, to remonstrate with William. But it was useless, for the Duke told the bald legate that curls would grow on his pate before he would part with the Viscountess. Even a renewal of the sentence of excommunication against him had no effect on William.[10] He defiantly had Dangerosa's portrait painted on his shield, saying that 'it was his will to bear her in battle as she had borne him in bed'.[11] A local hermit cursed this sinful union and predicted that neither William nor his descendants would ever know happiness in their children.[12]

Philippa refused to tolerate his behaviour. Before the year was out, she retired in grief to Fontevrault, where she died of unknown causes on 28 November 1118. A year or so later, Dangerosa suggested that William's son and heir marry her daughter Aenor. Their marriage may almost certainly be dated to 1121.

Young William was a reluctant bridegroom. Very tall, broad and robust, with a huge appetite – it was claimed that he ate enough for ten men – and a quarrelsome nature, he had inherited some of the Duke's charm but also his violent temper, and he was very resentful of the way in which his father had betrayed and humiliated his mother. Ralph of Diceto claims that he waged war on William IX for seven years, but dates his rebellion to 1112, before the Duke had even met Dangerosa. His evidence is therefore unreliable.

We know very little about Aenor of Châtellerault, Eleanor's mother. Her position cannot have been an easy one, abandoned by a mother who was branded an adulteress, and then married to a man who did not want her.

Aenor's first child, the daughter who became known to history as Eleanor of Aquitaine, was born in 1122. The exact date is not known, but the year can be determined from evidence of her age at death and from the fact that the lords of Aquitaine swore fealty to her on her fourteenth birthday in 1136. Some chroniclers give 1120 as her birthdate, but her parents cannot have been married until 1121. Eleanor's birthplace was probably either the ducal palace at Poitiers or the Ombrière Palace at Bordeaux, although a local tradition claims that she was born in the château of Belin near Bordeaux, one of her father's residences. She was christened Aliénore, a pun on the Latin *alia-Aenor*, 'the other Eleanor', to differentiate her from her mother,[13] although her name is variously spelled in different sources, and has been anglicised for this text.

Aenor bore William two other children: Petronilla, who is sometimes called Aelith, in c. 1125, and a male heir, William Aigret, around 1126/7.

On 10 February 1127, William IX died, still excommunicate. In 1122, the deceased Count Bertrand's brother, Alfonso Jordan, had taken possession of Toulouse, but William had no longer had the heart or the energy to try to reclaim it. One of his last poems laments the fact that he must soon leave Poitou for the exile that is death; he craves pardon from his friends and from Jesus Christ, and prays for his heir, soon to be left in a world torn by conflict. Yet although he passed on his domains intact to his son, who now became William X, he had been unable to curb the aggression and growing independence of his vassals, with the consequence that ducal authority had been even further undermined.

William X's reign was troubled and brief, marred by strife with his vassals and quarrels with the Church. The court at Poitiers seems to have remained an important cultural centre, for although the new Duke was no poet himself, he patronised the troubadours Marcabru and the Gascon Cercamon, both of whom composed eulogistic laments when he died, and perhaps (according to later sources) also a Welsh fabulator called Bleddri, who may have told the Poitevin court some very early tales of King Arthur. Troubadours from beyond the Pyrenees, from Aragon, Castile, Navarre and Italy, were also welcomed at the ducal court.

In 1130, the Church was rent apart by schism, with rival popes claiming the throne of St Peter. William rashly supported the anti-Pope Anacletus against Innocent II, which led to Innocent excommunicating William and placing Aquitaine under an interdict. In 1135,

William's distant kinsman,[14] the formidable and saintly preacher Bernard of Clairvaux, intervened, venturing into the Duke's domains 'on God's business'[15] and threatening William with divine vengeance if he persisted in his obstinacy. This was too much: as Bernard celebrated mass at Parthenay, William, fully armed, stormed into the church intending to throw him out, but the holy man bore down on him, holding the sacrament aloft. This had such a salutary effect on William that he suffered some kind of seizure or mild stroke and collapsed in fear, foaming at the mouth and unable for a time to move. When he recovered, Bernard attributed it to a miracle, which greatly enhanced his own reputation and left William with no choice but to capitulate. In reparation, he founded a Cistercian abbey at Saintes.

Humiliation was followed by personal tragedy. In March 1130, the Duchess Aenor and her children took up residence at William's hunting lodge at Talmont on the coast of Poitou, north of La Rochelle. Aenor and young William Aigret died there soon afterwards, leaving Eleanor as her father's heiress-presumptive. At eight years of age, she was old enough to realise that she was a very important little girl – indeed, the most important in Christendom.

Despite losing her grandfather, mother and brother at an early age, Eleanor enjoyed a privileged girlhood. Children in those days were required to honour and obey their parents, and any transgressions were usually punished with severe beatings, but the evidence suggests that Eleanor was spoiled. Richard le Poitevin, writing in the 1170s, states that she was 'brought up in delicacy and reared with abundance of all delights, living in the bosom of wealth'.

Like all courts at that time, William X's was itinerant, and Eleanor would have travelled with him from place to place, residing at his castles, palaces and hunting lodges. His favourite seat – and later hers – was the ancient palace at Poitiers, dating from Merovingian times. Sited on the banks of the River Clain, it was surrounded by beautiful gardens. In the tenth century, William V had partially rebuilt it and erected the great hall, which survives today, much altered; known colloquially as the 'hall of lost footsteps', it serves as the antechamber to the Palais de Justice in Poitiers. A more recent addition was the imposing Maubergeonne Tower, in which were situated the ducal apartments. Dangerosa still lived there while Eleanor was a child, but we have no means of knowing how much she influenced her granddaughter.

Another favoured residence was the Ombrière Palace at Bordeaux, a tall keep known as the Crossbowman, which was set in courtyards with tiled fountains and beautiful semi-tropical gardens. Bordeaux itself had been founded by the Romans and the walls they had built to encircle it still stood. Just outside these walls was another property used by the ducal family, the Tutelle Palace.

William X owned a number of other keeps and palaces that would have been visited by Eleanor, including those at Limoges, Niort, Saint-Jean d'Angély, Blaye, Melle and Bayonne. At other times, the court would have stayed in the guest accommodation available in the great abbeys in the region.

Women, as we have seen, played a subordinate role in mediaeval society. During the Dark Ages, when feudal states were being forged out of the ruins of a Roman Empire ravaged by Barbarian invasions, life was brutal and uncertain; might generally prevailed over right; and it was male strength that counted. The weaker sex therefore found itself relegated to subjection, the chief functions of noblewomen being to produce heirs to feudal domains and to act as chatelaines of the castles that were springing up all over Europe. The teachings of the Church Fathers, who followed St Paul in preaching that a woman's role was to learn in silence, and subjection of her husband at home, served to sanctify this masculine domination of society; and although in the twelfth century the parallel codes of chivalry and courtly love would go far towards improving the status of women, they did not seriously challenge their subservient role.

Aquitanian laws, laid down in the years before the Church increased its influence in the ducal domains, were generally favourable to women, ensuring that their status in the duchy was higher than elsewhere in feudal Europe. They could inherit property in their own right and even rule autonomously over lands they inherited. They took a part in public life and, unlike women in northern France, were not kept secluded from men or mainstream society. High-born and wealthy women were renowned for their elegance in dress, yet censured by the Church for their painted cheeks, their charcoal-rimmed eyes and their oriental perfumes, and females of all classes were notorious for their lax attitude towards morality: in the north it was asserted that the whole duchy was no better than a vast brothel. A wife's adultery was not punished, as elsewhere, by imprisonment or execution: Aquitanians took a sanguine view of such matters.

The formal education of women was rarely considered important. Girls of good birth were taught domestic skills at home or in a convent, and rarely learned to read and write, for it was feared that, if they did, they would waste their talents writing love letters or reading romances that led to promiscuity.

Eleanor of Aquitaine was a notable exception. Duke William ensured that his daughter, unusually for the time, received some formal education. She was taught to read in her native tongue; Bertran de Born, who addressed many *chansons* to her, says, 'they were not unknown to her, for she can read'. She was also given instruction in Latin. While she certainly became acquainted with the *gai saber* (joyous art) of the troubadours, there is no evidence that she inherited any of her grandfather's poetic talent, as some writers have claimed. Nevertheless, she shared William IX's enjoyment of romantic literature and poetry, and would in time come to patronise troubadours such as Bernard de Ventadour.

Eleanor grew up to be an energetic and consummate sportswoman. She was certainly taught to ride at an early age, and in later life she enjoyed hawking, and kept some royal gerfalcons at her hunting lodge at Talmont. It is likely that she was also given some tuition in the traditional feminine skills of needlework and household management.

Some biographers have claimed that in later life Eleanor displayed a knowledge of Aristotelian logic, either taught in childhood – which is highly unlikely – or learned in the schools of Paris while she was Queen of France. The letters in which this skill is apparent were in fact composed for Eleanor in 1193 by the accomplished royal secretary, Peter of Blois, and it is far more likely that it was he rather than his royal mistress who was responsible for the Aristotelian arguments so forcefully set out in them.

Eleanor's name first appears in contemporary records in July 1129, when she, her parents and baby brother witnessed a charter granting privileges to the Abbey of Montierneuf in memory of her grandfather, who was buried there. Each inscribed a cross by their names, while the infant made a print with a finger dipped in ink. There is no evidence that Eleanor ever learned to write: princes and nobles in those days customarily employed clerks to serve as secretaries and write their letters for them.

The court in which Eleanor grew up was sophisticated, highly civilised and enjoyed a luxurious standard of living for its time. Richard le Poitevin tells us that Eleanor developed a 'taste for luxury and refinement'. Her patronage of poets and writers in later life suggests that she was captivated early on by the troubadour culture that pervaded aristocratic society in Poitou and Aquitaine. She loved music, delighting in 'the melodies of the flute and rejoicing in the harmonies of the musicians. Her young companions sang their sweet songs to the accompaniment of the tabor [tambourine] and cithara',[16] possibly an early type of lute. Above all, she conceived a great love and loyalty for her ancestral domains: throughout her life Aquitaine would always be her first priority.

These were the years that shaped Eleanor's character. She had inherited many of the characteristics of her forebears, and was energetic, intelligent, sophisticated, headstrong and perhaps lacking in self-discipline. She possessed great vitality and, according to William of Newburgh, a lively mind. Impetuous to a fault, she seems to have cared little in her youth for the conventions of the society in which she lived. Sharing many qualities with that company of ambitious, formidable and strong-minded female ancestors, she was to surpass them all in fame and notoriety.

Eleanor grew up to be very beautiful: all contemporary sources are agreed on this point, and even in an age when chroniclers routinely eulogised royal and noble ladies, their praise of her was undoubtedly sincere. In youth, she was described as *perpulchra* – more than beautiful. Around 1153, the troubadour Bernard de Ventadour called her 'gracious, lovely, the embodiment of charm', referring to her 'lovely eyes and noble countenance' and declaring that she was 'one meet to crown the state of any king'. William of Newburgh emphasised the charms of her person, and even when she was old, Richard of Devizes described her as 'beautiful', while Matthew Paris, in the thirteenth century, recalled her 'admirable beauty'.

No one, however, left a description of Eleanor or even recorded the colour of her hair and eyes. Her tomb effigy shows a tall and large-boned woman, but this may not be an accurate representation. Her seal of c.1152 shows her with a slender figure, but this could in no way be said to be anything other than an impersonal image. However, at the age of fifty-one, she was still slim enough to disguise herself as a man, which suggests that she was reasonably tall, lithe and not too buxom.

The contemporary ideal of beauty was the blue-eyed blonde, and several historians have suggested that the chroniclers would not have been so fulsome in their praises if Eleanor had not conformed to this ideal. However, it is more likely that she had red or auburn hair, since a mural in the church of Sainte-Radegonde in Chinon (see Chapter 19), which almost certainly depicts Eleanor and was painted during her lifetime in a region in which she was well-known, shows a woman with reddish-brown hair.

What is certain is that from an early age Eleanor attracted the attention of men, not only because of her looks but also because of her 'welcoming' manner and inherent flirtatiousness and wit. Gervase of Canterbury described her much later as 'an exceedingly shrewd and clever woman, born of noble stock, but unstable and flighty'.

All the evidence from accounts and chronicles shows that Eleanor enjoyed dressing elegantly in fine clothes, often of silk embroidered in gold thread, and it appears that she became a leader of fashion. She evidently loved jewellery, for she amassed a great many pieces during her life, including jewelled circlets to hold in place the veils that all married women wore in the twelfth century.

Some writers have claimed that Eleanor's uncle, Raymond of Poitiers, her father's younger brother, was close to her as a child. In fact, he had gone to England before her birth as the protégé of King Henry I, who had lost his legitimate sons when the *White Ship* sank in 1120. The landless Raymond was reared and trained for knighthood at the English court, and only left it in 1133 when King Fulk of Jerusalem chose him as ruler of Antioch. He may have visited his native land *en route* for the East, but it is doubtful whether he would have had time to establish a close relationship with his niece.

Beautiful, able and intelligent Eleanor might have been, but she was still a woman, and although contemporary evidence suggests that her father taught her some of the skills of government, it was not considered practicable for a woman to rule a feudal state. To begin with, she would be unable to perform the forty days' annual knight-service required by every overlord from his vassals, and even though she might pay one of her lords to do this for her, it was universally agreed that it was not fitting for a woman to hold dominion over men.

In 1136, William X resolved to provide his subjects with a male heir, and to this end he proposed marriage to Emma, daughter of Viscount Aymer of Limoges and widow of the Lord of Cognac. But Emma's father's friends and allies did not want their Duke extending his authority over the affairs of the Limousin and arranged for Count William of Angoulême to kidnap and marry Emma instead. When their marriage was announced, the Duke took no action, because he was preoccupied elsewhere, having been invited to help his northern neighbour, Count Geoffrey of Anjou, invade and conquer Normandy.

This enterprise lasted a mere four weeks and was abandoned after Count Geoffrey was severely wounded in the foot. William X returned in a deep depression, tormented by nightmares and haunted by memories of the horrors of war. He had never succeeded in subduing his turbulent vassals, and it was now obvious that another rebellion was brewing in the Limousin. But William, with his usual inability to set his priorities in order, decided that he was going on a pilgrimage to the shrine of St James at Compostela (Santiago de Compostela) in north-western Spain, to seek forgiveness for his sins and pray for God's help against his enemies. His hostile vassals, however, believed he was going to seek military aid from his neighbours, to be used against them. The situation in Aquitaine was potentially explosive.

William began to set his affairs in order. Although he intended, after his pilgrimage, to marry and father sons, he realised that he might never return. In that case his vast domains, comprising a quarter of modern France, would pass to a mere girl, his daughter Eleanor, making her the richest and most desirable heiress in Europe. In order to ensure as far as possible her smooth succession, he summoned his vassals and, on Eleanor's fourteenth birthday, commanded them to swear homage to her as the heiress to Poitou, Aquitaine and Gascony.

But this would not be enough to protect her from the ruthless ambition of predatory lords in a land torn by unrest; she would be at the mercy of any fortune-hunter, yet because of her sex there could be no question of her ruling her lands by herself. It was imperative that a strong and powerful husband be found for her, to rule in her name. The Duke therefore made Eleanor a ward of his overlord, Louis VI, King of France, with a view to her marrying the King's son and heir, another Louis. William knew that Louis VI was the only man with the power, status and authority to protect Eleanor's inheritance and safeguard her interests.

The ancient pilgrim route to Compostela passed through William's dominions, and during the Lenten season of 1137 he travelled along it with his daughters as far as Bordeaux, where he left them in the care of the staunchly loyal Geoffrey de Loroux, Archbishop of Bordeaux. He then journeyed south towards Spain, garbed as a pilgrim and attended by only a small retinue of knights and servants. Presently, the little group crossed the Pyrenees via the pass at Roncesvalles, and proceeded across the kingdom of Navarre.

On Good Friday, 9 April 1137, Duke William arrived at Compostela, seriously ill after drinking contaminated water, and collapsed by the wayside. Realising he was dying, he made his will, bequeathing his domains to Eleanor and appointing King Louis her guardian. He made his friends promise to approach Louis and ask him to arrange the marriage of his son to Eleanor without delay. In the meantime, Louis could rule Aquitaine. In order to ensure that his duchy was not swallowed up by the French crown, William further stipulated that Eleanor's domains should not be incorporated into the royal demesne but should remain independent and be inherited by Eleanor's heirs alone. He asked that news of his death be sent in confidence to King Louis and also to the Archbishop of Bordeaux, so that Eleanor could be informed; only then could it be made public.[17]

Near death, the thirty-eight-year-old Duke was carried into the cathedral at Compostela, where he died that same day shortly after receiving Holy Communion. His companions arranged for him to be buried before the high altar next to the shrine of St James the Apostle.[18] When his death was announced in Aquitaine, the chronicler Geoffrey de Vigeois claimed that it had been providential, for it had saved the Limousin from being drenched in blood.

Eleanor, a 'young virgin'[19] of fifteen, was now Countess of Poitou and Duchess of Aquitaine and Gascony in her own right.

2

'A Model of Virtue'

France, according to John of Salisbury, was 'of all nations, the sweetest and most civilised'. The House of Capet had ruled the country since 987, when the feudal lord Hugh Capet had been elected King after the death of Louis V, the last monarch of the Carolingian dynasty, which descended from the Emperor Charlemagne. The surname Capet, which probably means 'cap-wearer' or 'cape-wearer', was not used for Hugh until the thirteenth century, and the dynasty he founded was not described as Capetian until the eighteenth century.

In the early twelfth century, the kingdom of France found itself in a struggle for supremacy with feudal vassals who had extended their territories and become more powerful than the crown, whose own authority held little weight beyond the royal demesne. This comprised the Île de France, a small feudatory that had evolved from the Carolingian county of Paris, as well as Sens, Orléans and part of Berry. The greatest threats to French expansion were posed by the Count of Blois, linked by strong family and political ties to the Count of Champagne; and by the Count of Anjou, who was determined to annex the duchy of Normandy, which he claimed in right of his wife Matilda, heiress of Henry I, King of England. The Norman Conquest of 1066, which made the Dukes of Normandy kings of England, and gave them equal rank with their overlords, had dramatically altered the balance of power in northern France; the separation of Normandy from England would remain the aim of successive French monarchs, who knew all too well that the union of these powerful continental feudatories would encircle and isolate France and prevent her from further extending her territories and influence.

Louis VI was nicknamed 'the Fat'; he was so overweight he could no longer mount a horse or a woman.[1] Yet his contemporaries conceded that he was a man whose spirit was as large as his body,[2] a forceful and generally successful ruler who spent his reign enforcing law and order, promoting religion, curbing the excesses of his barons, encouraging towns to become independent of their feudal lords and thus loyal to the crown, and consolidating and extending the power and territories of the French monarchy. He had been supported latterly in his efforts by his chief administrator, the able and astute Suger, Abbot of Saint-Denis.

Louis was at his hunting lodge at Béthizy, north of Paris, when he learned of Duke William's death and received his last requests. He was so ecstatic at the prospect of marrying his son to Eleanor of Aquitaine, and thereby acquiring the greatest fief in Europe, that he could hardly speak,[3] but some of his advisers expressed concern that Aquitaine would prove too unwieldy and problematical to be successfully ruled and administered from Paris. Suger supported Louis, pointing out that the annexation of so vast and rich a domain to the French crown could only be to France's advantage, for it would give the King equality with his richest and most powerful vassals. One, Count Geoffrey of Anjou, still had greedy eyes on Normandy, and if that duchy was attached to Anjou, which in itself was bigger than the kingdom of France, Louis would potentially have a formidable enemy both to the south and north-west. However, the acquisition of Aquitaine would provide him with twice the amount of land and resources he had at present and would ensure that Geoffrey's fiefs were dwarfed and encircled by the French on both his north-eastern and southern borders. Furthermore, despite Duke William's stipulation, if Eleanor bore young Louis a son, her lands would be absorbed into the royal demesne in perpetuity.

If the question of consanguinity between Louis and Eleanor was raised at this time, it was quickly dismissed, for there is no record of anyone applying to the Pope for any dispensation. The fact remained, however, that the young people were within the prohibited degrees of relationship, being fourth cousins.

His mind made up, the King, who was now so fat and ill he could no longer get out of bed, summoned his son to his couch.[4]

The younger Louis had been born around 1120–21 at Fontainebleau, the second of the six sons of Louis VI and his queen, Adelaide, daughter of Humbert II, Count of Maurienne and Savoy. His older brother Philip was their father's heir, and Louis was destined for the Church, but in 1131, at the age of fifteen, Philip – an insufferably arrogant youth who had been 'a burden to all'[5] – was killed when his horse shied at a runaway pig and threw him. Louis found himself next in line for the throne, and according to Frankish custom, he was crowned King during his father's lifetime, the ceremony being performed by the Pope himself on 25 October 1131, at Rheims.[6]

Until then, Louis had spent most of his childhood as a 'child monk' at the Abbey of Saint-Denis near Paris, where Abbot Suger supervised his education. He was a sweet-tempered, unworldly and pious boy, who would have been ideally suited to the life of the cloister, and he was now reluctant to abandon the religious life; but Louis VI feared that the very qualities that so admirably suited his son for that calling would lead his barons to think that the young King was a weakling. Although he permitted Louis to continue his studies at Saint-Denis, he insisted that the boy learn statecraft by assisting his father in government, and also that he receive instruction in knightly skills.

If the King had hoped by these strategies to make a warlike and authoritarian monarch of his son, in his own mould, he was to be disappointed, for in 1137 sixteen-year-old Louis was as naïve, humble and devout as ever, inclined to burst into tears at the slightest upset and, more disturbingly, occasionally given to irrational and even violent outbursts of temper. It was obvious to all where his true vocation lay.

In appearance and manner, however, he seemed an ideal suitor for the Duchess of Aquitaine, being tall and muscular, with long fair hair, blue eyes, innate courtesy and a disarming smile. Only a large nose marred his looks. He was intelligent, kindly and straightforward, with a sensitive conscience and a well-developed sense of honour. He was incapable of guile or procrastination, and throughout his life retained a childlike air of simplicity.

Like the obedient son he was, Louis did not question his father's choice of bride, and dutifully helped Abbot Suger to make preparations for his departure for Bordeaux. Meanwhile, King Louis had sent the Bishop of Chartres there on a confidential embassy to convey his greetings and condolences to the young Duchess and ensure that she was safe from predatory suitors. The Bishop was able to report that, since learning of her father's death, she had been staying in the Ombrière Palace under strong guard.

In order to ensure that there was no trouble from Eleanor's anarchic vassals, the anxious King summoned 500 knights to escort his son into what would almost certainly be hostile territory, and arranged for Abbot Suger, Count Theobald IV of Champagne and his rival and brother-in-law, Raoul, Count of Vermandois and Seneschal of France (who was also young Louis' cousin) to accompany the boy and act as his advisers. Both counts had been compelled by the King to set aside their differences for the duration of the journey. It was to these three men that Louis VI entrusted the heavy coffers containing the gold that would pay for the wedding trip and enable the new Duke of Aquitaine to make a liberal display and impress his new subjects.[7]

The King instructed Louis to conduct himself with dignity and justice at all times, and to give offence to no one: the people of Aquitaine were not to suffer any financial loss or plunder on account of his presence in their midst; nor was he to billet his men on them, as was his feudal right. Above all, Louis must restrain his temper, even if provoked, and give the volatile southern barons no excuse for using violence against him.

On 18 June, the young King and his escort left Paris in blazing heat. With him, Louis carried his father's blessing and a gift of jewels for his bride. It was so hot that he and his retinue were obliged to travel by night and seek shelter during the day, and many of their food supplies melted.[8] They crossed the Loire near Orléans and on 29 June arrived in Limoges, where, at his father's direction, Louis formally laid claim to the county of Poitou and the duchy of Aquitaine and received the homage of such vassals as had received his summons in time, among them Alfonso Jordan, Count of Toulouse. The next day Louis joined in the celebrations for the feast day of St Martial, the city's patron saint.

Word of Louis' coming and his forthcoming marriage to the Duchess Eleanor had spread rapidly throughout the region, yet there were no adverse demonstrations, and the young King travelled via Périgueux to Bordeaux unobstructed.[9] Arriving there on 11 July, he set up camp outside the city on the east bank of the Garonne, and the next day, escorted by the Archbishop of Bordeaux who had come on the Duchess' behalf to receive him, was ferried across the river to meet his future wife. It took two weeks, however, for Eleanor's vassals to respond to a summons to attend the wedding and pay homage to their new overlord;[10] a few, including the Count of Angoulême, were conspicuous by their absence.

On Sunday, 25 July 1137, Eleanor and Louis were married in the cathedral of Saint-André in Bordeaux;[11] the Archbishop of Bordeaux officiated, and the bride wore a rich gown of scarlet. Almost a thousand guests attended, including most of Eleanor's great vassals, and it would have required 'the tongue of Cicero to do justice to the munificence of the multiform expenditures that had been made, nor could the pen of Seneca fully describe the variety of meats and rare delicacies that were there, nor the richness and variety of these presents and the pomp paraded for these nuptials'.[12]

Louis was now Count of Poitou and Duke of Aquitaine and Gascony, and it was taken for granted by his contemporaries that he would rule those provinces in his wife's name. After the marriage service was concluded, the young couple sat enthroned on a dais in the chancel of the cathedral, both wearing the golden ducal coronets of Aquitaine, which they had received from the Archbishop, and acknowledged the acclaim of their subjects. Then they proceeded through cheering crowds along a street strewn with leaves and past houses hung with tapestries, banners and greenery, to the sound of pipe and tabor and wooden sabots stamping in time to the music.[13] Finally, they arrived at the Ombrière Palace for the wedding banquet. They left Bordeaux immediately afterwards for Poitiers, crossing the River Charente at Saintes and spending their first night together as man and wife at the castle of Taillebourg, owned by Eleanor's loyal and chivalrous vassal, Geoffrey de Rançon.[14] Louis was a virgin when he married, and it was likely that Eleanor, carefully nurtured and guarded as she had been, was too.

The next day they left for Poitiers; they were received in the city on 1 August by a populace in transports of joy[15] and were lodged in the Maubergeonne Tower. Feasting to celebrate the wedding continued for several days, with local lords arriving somewhat reluctantly to pay homage[16] and many gifts being presented to Louis and Eleanor. The celebrations culminated on 8 August with their investiture as Count and Countess of Poitou in Poitiers Cathedral;[17] it was a glittering ceremony, intended by Suger to surpass even the coronations of the kings of France in magnificence and to overawe the Poitevins. Another splendid banquet followed, in the great hall of the ducal palace.

It was probably to commemorate their marriage that Eleanor presented Louis with an exquisite vase made of rock crystal decorated with gold filigree work, pearls and fleur-de-lys, the royal emblem of France. It was typical of Louis that he later donated it to Abbot Suger to adorn the new abbey church of Saint-Denis. The inscription on the vase reads, *Hoc vas sponsa dedit Aanor Regi Ludovico, Mitadolus avo, mihi Rex, sanctisque Sugerus* (Eleanor his wife gave this vase to King Louis, Mitadolus gave it to her grandfather, the King gave it to me, I, Suger, give it to the saints). This vase is the only artefact connected with Eleanor to survive today, and is now on display in the Louvre.

One vassal who had not come to Poitiers to swear allegiance was William de Lézay, castellan of Talmont, the ducal hunting lodge, who had added injury to insult by stealing some of Eleanor's white gerfalcons. When the festivities came to an end, Louis and a party of his knights rode to Talmont to teach de Lézay a lesson and afterwards enjoy some sport. The weather was hot and, being in a holiday mood, they cast aside their chain mail and sent most of their weapons ahead with the baggage carts. Unfortunately, William de Lézay was warned of their coming and conceived a plan to kidnap Louis and hold him to ransom. When the first knights of the young King's party were espied from the castle, they were swiftly taken prisoner. A violent confrontation followed, with Louis – who had never before been involved in an armed conflict – and his men at a distinct disadvantage. They nevertheless gave a good account of themselves and savagely cut down their assailants,[18] Louis personally severing the hands of de Lézay.[19]

On Louis' return, he and the Duchess wasted no time in setting off for Orléans and Paris, Eleanor taking with her her sister Petronilla and her Poitevin household. The extravagance of the latter shocked the French, who disparagingly described them as 'better feeders than fighters'. The people of Aquitaine and Poitou were sad to see their duchess depart, for they would now have an alien overlord who spoke a different language and whose administrators were gradually being installed in key posts throughout the region. The presence of Frenchmen was resented by the fiercely independent indigenous population, and would inevitably cause tension and racial strife in some areas.

And so Eleanor rode to a new life in Paris. On the way, the royal cavalcade was intercepted by a messenger with heart-stopping news: Louis VI had died of dysentery on 1 August, and young Louis and his wife were now King and Queen of France.

Then, as now, Paris wove its spell on people. 'How apt thou art, O Paris, to bewitch and seduce!' wrote Pierre de la Celle, a correspondent of John of Salisbury. 'There was an abundance of men, suave and agreeable, an abundance of all good things, gay streets, rare food, incomparable wine!'

Paris in the twelfth century boasted a population of about 200,000 and was increasing in size and prosperity. The city, which was not recognised as the capital of France until about 1190, had originated as a settlement on an oval island in the Seine, the Île de la Cité, and gradually spread outwards from the banks of the river. On the right bank, still largely rural, was the thriving commercial heart of Paris, the home of merchants and the emerging craft guilds, while on the left bank were to be found the great abbeys of Sainte-Génevieve, Saint-Victor and Saint-Germain-des-Prés, as well as the famous schools of scholarship and debate, which by the middle of the century were pre-eminent in the intellectual life of western Christendom and in the decades to come would evolve into France's first university.

During this period, Europe was witnessing an intellectual revival that flourished in the cathedral schools and emerging universities, and came to have a profound effect on European culture and thought. This movement is now referred to as the Twelfth-Century Renaissance, and much of it was centred upon Paris.

Thanks to the rediscovery of the works of Aristotle, and Greek and Roman writers such as Horace, Ovid, Virgil and Martial, hitherto preserved by the Arabs and disseminated through wider contact with Moorish Spain and the Orient, scholars became reacquainted with classical learning, although this was only through Latin translations; Greek was known only to very few learned men. At Chartres in France, scholars of Plato even began disseminating an early form of humanism.

What was no less than a cultural revolution led to the establishment of famous schools in Paris and other European cities, notably Oxford, which gradually established itself as a university after English students were recalled from Paris in 1167 as a result of Henry II's quarrel with Archbishop Becket. There were also other well-respected English schools at Exeter, Northampton and Lincoln; the university of Cambridge was not founded until the thirteenth century.

In these cathedral schools, outstanding scholars such as Peter Abélard, in Paris – one of whose pupils was the brilliant John of Salisbury – and Franciscus Gratianus, in Bologna, held students spellbound with the breadth of their vision and learning. And from these schools, often held in the open air, evolved universities that would become treasure-houses of scholarship and knowledge.

The Romans had erected the town of Lutetia on the site of a small Gaulish settlement on the Seine, and there remained a number of Roman ruins in the city, including its crumbling wall, while on the Île de la Cité itself, which was linked to the banks by two stone bridges, were two large buildings that towered above the other rooftops[20] – the King's chief residence, the Cité Palace, and the Cathedral of Notre-Dame, both dating from Merovingian times.

In summer, the city was often unbearable, with its stinking, unpaved streets and swarms of black flies, and the king would sometimes be obliged to seek refuge in his hunting lodge at Béthizy. On the outskirts of Paris were also to be found orchards, vineyards and small farms, while on the banks of the Seine there were a number of mill-wheels.

It was to this city that Louis brought his young bride in August 1137. No effort had been spared in affording them a magnificent welcome, and enthusiastic crowds lined a route that ended at the famous tree stump situated beneath an olive tree. This was where the royalty of France customarily dismounted before entering the Cité Palace, which occupied a site where the Palais de Justice now stands, the towers of the Conciergerie being all that remain of it.

The young Queen, used to the luxurious residences of the south, may well have found this palace, which was now to be her chief residence, spartan and unwelcoming. Sited on the western edge of the island, it consisted of a grim, decaying stone tower ventilated only by arrow-slits and accessed by a wide flight of worn marble stairs. Its rooms were small, dark and draughty, and the atmosphere more suited to a monastery than a royal court. It seems likely that Eleanor soon made her dissatisfaction felt, because during the following winter the King ordered that her apartments be enlarged and modernised. Wooden shutters were fitted over the arrow-slits to minimise the draughts, and a very new innovation, a fireplace and chimney, was built into the wall. Eleanor herself commissioned a series of tapestries from the workshops in Bourges.

The palace gardens were more to Eleanor's taste. Enclosed by walls and trellised vines, they had paths bordered with acanthus and shaded by willow, fig, cypress and pear trees; in the flower beds grew roses, lilies and poppies, and there was a herb garden smelling fragrantly of mint, rue, watercress and absinthe.

There was no literary tradition or entertainment at the French court; the slender surviving evidence suggests that Eleanor tried to re-create the ambience in which she had grown up, commissioning plays in Latin and encouraging troubadours and *jongleurs* to visit and entertain her household and guests. The conservative French flinched at the ideals of love expressed in the troubadours' songs, but they could not deny that their new Queen was a civilising influence upon court manners. It was she who insisted upon the boards being laid with tablecloths and napkins, and who commanded the pages to wash their hands before serving at table. After watching the cantor in the Chapel of St Nicholas within the palace, she had him dismissed and replaced with one of her own choice, who was infinitely more talented at conducting a choir.

Court life for a queen of France at that time was, however, stultifyingly routine. Eleanor found that she was expected to be no more than a decorative asset to her husband, the mother of his heirs and the arbiter of good taste and modesty. Her days were an endless round of prayers and trivia. In good weather she and her ladies would sit in the palace gardens or go hawking, which she enjoyed. Sometimes Louis invited the schools to meet in summer in the palace gardens; the brilliant lecturer Peter Abélard claimed that many noble ladies flocked to attend his open-air lectures, but it is nowhere stated that Eleanor was among them.

On wet or cold days, the Queen and her ladies were confined to their apartments where they spent their hours playing chess, singing, recounting stories, telling riddles or idly conversing. It was a suffocating existence for a girl of Eleanor's intelligence and independent spirit, and it is not surprising that she tried to circumvent custom and tradition by indulging in unconventional pursuits of her own that disturbed and sometimes shocked Louis' courtiers, who were already grumbling at the expense and size of the Queen's household.

There can have been no doubt in Eleanor's mind as to what was expected of her as a wife. In her day, women were supposed to be chaste both inside and outside marriage, virginity and celibacy being highly prized states. When it came to fornication, women were usually apportioned the blame, because they were the descendants of Eve who had tempted Adam in the Garden of Eden with such dire consequences. Women, the Church taught, were the weaker vessel, the gateway to the Devil, and therefore the source of all lechery. The great scholar and preacher St Bernard of Clairvaux wrote: 'To live with a woman without danger is more difficult than raising the dead to life.' Noblewomen, he felt, were the most dangerous of all. Women were therefore kept firmly in their place in order to prevent them from luring men away from the paths of righteousness.

Promiscuity, and its often inevitable consequence, illicit pregnancy, brought great shame upon a woman and her family, and was punished by fines, social ostracism and even, in the case of aristocratic and royal women, execution. Unmarried women who indulged in fornication devalued themselves on the marriage market, for no one wanted to take soiled goods. In England, women who were sexually experienced were not permitted to accuse men of rape in the King's courts. Female adultery was seen as a particularly serious offence, since it jeopardised the laws of inheritance.

Men, however, often got away with casual sex and adultery with impunity. Because the virtue of high-born women was jealously guarded, many men sought sexual adventures with lower-class women, who had a reputation for being freer with their favours. Prostitution was common and official brothels were licensed and subject to inspection in many urban areas. There was no effective contraception apart from withdrawal, and the Church frowned upon that anyway: this was why so many aristocratic and royal bastards were born during this period. Bastardy carried a social stigma and was a barrier, in common law, to inheritance. Although the Church did have the power to legitimate bastards, this was rarely exercised, for it was generally agreed that illegitimate offspring should bear the consequences of their parents' sin.

Divorce was unknown, but marriages could be annulled (or declared invalid) by the Church on a number of grounds: consanguinity – strictly speaking, close cousins were not allowed to marry, although dispensations were granted in certain circumstances; the existence of a former pre-contract – a betrothal was considered as binding as a marriage; impotence or non-consummation – because there had to be proof of this, which was often intrusive and embarrassing, few cases ever reached the Church courts; and lack of consent to the marriage – the Church considered mutual consent to be an essential element of the marriage contract. Eleanor and Louis had freely consented to theirs, and expected to be bound together for life. Yet the seeds of future discord had already been sown.

The indications that there would be problems ahead within the royal marriage were evident from the start. The young couple came from strikingly different backgrounds, had divergent interests and were very unalike in temperament.

Suger described the new King as 'a child in the flower of his age, and of great sweetness of temper, the hope of the good and the terror of the wicked'. According to his secretary, later on his chaplain, Odo de Deuil, Louis VII was a prince 'whose entire life is a model of virtue, for when, a mere boy, he began to reign, worldly glory did not cause him sensual delight'. He continued his studies at nearby Notre-Dame, beautified the royal chapels, assisted at mass, joined in the singing of the cathedral choir, kept the vigils each day, fasted with the monks on bread and water every Friday, and was assiduous at his private devotions. He was often to be seen at the heels of the Bishop, taking care in his humility not to inconvenience anyone at worship.[21] He dressed more like a humble clerk than a king, and disliked rich robes, pomp and ceremony.

As a ruler, Louis allowed himself to be governed too much by his feelings and ideals and made many ill-judged decisions, some of which rebounded on him with disastrous consequences. 'He was a man of warm devotion to God and of extraordinary lenity to his subjects and of notable reverence for the clergy, but he was rather more credulous than befits a king and prone to listen to advice that was unworthy of him,' observed William of Newburgh. Yet when it came to matters of principle he could be inflexible. 'Because he was gentle in manner and kind-hearted, unaffectedly simple toward men of any rank, he seemed to some lacking in force,' wrote Walter Map, 'yet he was the strictest judge, and even when it cost him tears, he meted justice with even hand to meek and arrogant alike.' However, his rare but savage outbursts of temper sometimes provoked him to rash acts.

Louis carried on his father's policy of reaffirming the rights of the crown, extending the royal demesne and curbing the ambitions of his vassals. Additionally, he took steps to ensure that the royal administration became more efficient. He saw himself as God's vice-regent on Earth, and was so sincere in his convictions that few doubted his integrity. His admirable sense of honour was on occasions a serious disadvantage when it came to dealing with more wily and pragmatic princes. Over the years, however, Louis came to be recognised as a man who, in many respects, fulfilled the knightly ideal, and he earned international respect and prestige for his personal qualities.

There is no doubt about Louis' feelings for Eleanor: 'he loved the Queen almost beyond reason,' John of Salisbury observed in 1149, commenting that the King's immoderate affection was 'almost puerile'. Although Louis was Eleanor's senior by a year or two, he was immature for his age and perhaps somewhat overawed by this forceful, sophisticated beauty. He showed his devotion by allowing her to have her way in most things, and by showering her with extravagant gifts: she took her pick from luxury goods brought to the palace by merchants trading with the Orient.

Yet Louis did not visit his wife's bed very often,[22] and then only in accordance with the teachings of the Church, which decreed that sex was to be indulged in solely for the purpose of procreation, and not for pleasure, even within marriage. A husband or wife did not have the right either to demand sex from their spouse or to refuse it, and there was a catalogue of forbidden sexual practices, notably homosexuality, bestiality, certain sexual positions, masturbation, the use of aphrodisiacs and oral sex, which could incur a penance of three years' duration. Nor were people supposed to make love on Sundays, Holy Days or Feast Days, or during Lent, pregnancy or menstruation. If these rules were disobeyed, people believed that deformed children or lepers might result.

Unfortunately, Louis' conjugal visits were not frequent enough to fulfil their purpose, and apart from the Queen suffering a miscarriage during the first or second year of her marriage,[23] the hoped-for heir to France and Aquitaine showed no sign of making his appearance. It became apparent only much later how deeply this sexual neglect affected the more worldly and passionate Eleanor.

Yet sex was not the only problem within the royal marriage. To Louis, it seemed natural to turn to Abbot Suger, his former teacher and his father's chief adviser, for help in governing his realm. He himself was, after all, young and inexperienced, and relied heavily on the older man's wisdom, statecraft and excellent memory – the Abbot knew the Bible almost by heart.

Suger was now fifty-six; born a serf, he was a gifted and

compassionate man who had risen through the ranks of the Church by virtue of his own abilities, and become Abbot of Saint-Denis in 1122. He was utterly devoted to the French monarchy, and dedicated his life to enhancing its power and prestige. It was Suger who underlined the sacred nature and function of kingship by insisting that its rituals and ceremonials be rigorously and splendidly observed. At the same time, he was practical, energetic and cautious, and had sound financial sense. His life's great project was the rebuilding of the abbey church of Saint-Denis for centuries the mausoleum of the kings of France − in the new Gothic style, with soaring stained-glass windows and sumptuous ornamentation. Bernard of Clairvaux had once criticised Suger for his love of worldly luxuries; the Abbot had taken his words to heart and now lived an ascetic life in a tiny, bare cell at Saint-Denis.

The headstrong Eleanor thought it was equally natural for Louis to seek advice from her. What she lacked in judgement she more than compensated for in enthusiasm and impetuosity, and many older people at court looked on in alarm as it became evident how much influence she exerted on her idealistic young husband. She seems from the first to have resented Suger, Odo de Deuil and the other austere ecclesiastics who controlled the King and the government, and to have insisted that Louis make his own decisions without reference to them. She also asserted that she was better qualified than Louis' ministers to advise on Aquitainian affairs. Suger testifies that a number of the King's clerical advisers were dismissed after the marriage, while those that remained had no choice but to acclimatise themselves to the changes that the Queen was determined to force on a hitherto sober court.

After this, however, either Louis or his ministers, or more probably Abbot Suger − who felt that both Louis and Eleanor were too young and immature to exercise power with responsibility − took steps to ensure that Eleanor's influence was confined to the domestic sphere, leaving the way clear for Suger himself to teach the King the art of wise government. The Abbot could not, however, control what went on between Louis and Eleanor in the privacy of their apartments, nor did he attempt to come between husband and wife, being committed to the success of their marriage for the sake of Eleanor's inheritance.

This decision to curb the Queen's power represented a break with tradition and had far-reaching consequences. Louis VI's wife and other French consorts had played an active political role, being consulted by their husbands on matters of policy and openly sharing in the decision-making process. If Louis consulted Eleanor − and there is reason to believe he did, and that she exerted her influence in the only way in which she was able to − it was in private, for during the first decade of the reign she played no more than a ceremonial role in public life and there is no record of her presence in the King's court, nor does her name appear on many of his charters. These changes in the fundamental role of the queen consort, which came about purely as a response to concern over Eleanor's influence, set a precedent for future queens of France, who mostly found themselves without power or political influence.

Naturally, Eleanor made enemies. The French nobility in general were wary of her, but they may simply have been prejudiced against southerners, particularly southern women, who were supposed to be promiscuous and flighty. The French still shuddered at the memory of Constance of Arles, third queen of Robert II, who had been notorious for her indiscreet dress and foul language.

Eleanor's first clash was with her mother-in-law, Adelaide of Maurienne, who is said by most of Eleanor's biographers to have taken a dislike to her daughter-in-law from the very first, and to have criticised whatever she did or failed to do: her attire, her profligate spending on silks and jewellery, her extravagant hospitality at the expense of the royal treasury, her singing, her use of cosmetics, her lack of piety and her lack of interest in learning the *langue d'oeil*. What is more likely is that Adelaide's resentment arose out of being deprived of her marriage portion, which was apparently transferred to Eleanor. Moreover, Adelaide, supported by Raoul of Vermandois, had for years been engaged in her own power struggle with Suger, who, like Louis, was unwilling to listen to her complaints and may well have seized upon them as an excuse to be rid of her. Whatever the reason, she either chose to leave court soon after Eleanor's arrival, or was compelled to, possibly with a view to freeing accommodation for the younger Queen's large household.

After the Queen Dowager had left court, she resided on her dower lands at Compiègne. Within the year, she remarried; her new husband was an obscure seigneur, Matthew de Montmorency. She died in 1154.

One person certainly did criticise Eleanor's mode of dress, and that was Bernard of Clairvaux. He was one of the most influential and admired figures of the twelfth century, and was largely responsible for the rapid growth of the austere Cistercian Order of white monks. When he joined the Order in 1113, it had one house; thanks to his inspirational teaching and international prestige, by the time of his death in 1153 there were 350, and thousands had followed him into their cloisters. His influence was felt through the numerous letters he sent from his cell at the Abbey of Clairvaux, in which he pronounced his considered views on virtually every topical issue of the age, and through his gift of oratory.

He was the typical ascetic: tall, skeletally thin, with transparent skin and white hair. The rigours of his austere existence had made him old before his time, and an aura of sanctity clung to him. He had no time for the new Gothic cathedrals with their stained glass and gilded decoration; his faith was one of simplicity and contemplation, and he preached that God was a benevolent and loving father – a revolutionary view in an age when people were taught to fear the Deity and heed His commandments if they wished to avoid the horrors of Hell.

Bernard showed surprising toleration on some issues, condemning the persecution of Jews and doing his best to love his enemies. But he could be ruthless to the latter when they expressed unorthodox views that challenged what he believed to be the will of God, as expressed in his own teachings. He had such a forceful and magnetic personality, and such deeply held convictions, that the very sight of him or sound of his voice was enough to silence the most vociferous of his opponents, and kings and senior churchmen went in awe of him.

One of Bernard's chief opponents was the respected lecturer Peter Abélard. As a young man, Abélard had seduced the beautiful Héloïse, niece of a canon of Notre-Dame; their love affair resulted in a secret marriage and the birth of a son. The canon found out and, at his instigation, a gang of ruffians broke into Abélard's lodging and castrated him. In grief, Héloïse retired to a convent, while Abélard devoted his life to teaching rationalist theory and promulgating his controversial views on the Holy Trinity. Bernard, who preached the triumph of faith over reason, was one of Abélard's fiercest critics. In 1136, Abélard had been accused by the Church of heresy, and in 1140, his case still unresolved, he was summoned to a public debate with Bernard at a council held at Sens, which Louis and Eleanor attended, and which resulted in Abélard being condemned and his theories discredited.

It was at Sens that Bernard saw Eleanor for probably the first time, and his reaction was stiff disapproval. Writing later to a maiden called Sophia, he described the Queen and her ladies so that his young correspondent 'may never sully her virginity but attain its reward'. Fortunately for the modern historian, his diatribe includes a detailed description of the dress worn by Eleanor and her noble companions:

> The garments of court ladies are fashioned from the finest tissues of wool or silk. A costly fur between two layers of rich stuffs forms the lining and border of their cloaks. Their arms are loaded with bracelets; from their ears hang pendants, enshrining precious

stones. For head-dress they have a kerchief of fine linen which they drape about their neck and shoulders, allowing one corner to fall over the left arm. This is the wimple, ordinarily fastened to their brows by a chaplet, a filet or a circle of wrought gold.

His description tallies with one by Geoffrey de Vigeois, who also condemned the outlandish French court fashions of the period:

They have clothes fashioned of rich and precious stuffs, in colours to suit their humour. They snip out the cloth in rings and long slashes to show the lining beneath, and the borders of the clothes are cut into little balls and pointed tongues, so that they look like the devils in paintings. They slash their mantles, and their sleeves flow like those of hermits. Youths affect long hair and shoes with pointed toes.

As for the ladies, 'you might think them adders, if you judged by the tails they drag after them'.

Bernard was shocked by such extravagance, and was at a loss to understand how Christian women could borrow the skins of squirrels and the labour of silkworms to lend themselves merely superficial beauty: 'Fie on a beauty that is put on in the morning and laid aside at night! The ornaments of a queen have no beauty like to the blushes of natural modesty which colour the cheeks of a virgin. Silk, purple and paint have their own beauty, but they do not make the body beautiful.' He likened Eleanor to:

one of those daughters of Belial who, got up in this way, put on airs, walk with heads high and mincing steps, their necks thrust forward, and, furnished and adorned as only temples should be, they drag after them trains of precious material that makes a cloud of dust. Some you see are not so much adorned as loaded down with ornaments of gold, silver and precious stones, and all the raiment of a court, indeed with everything that pertains to queenly splendour.

After Eleanor's departure, the unrest in her domains had grown worse. The Poitevins in particular objected to French rule, and late in 1137 the citizens of Poitiers formally repudiated Louis' authority and declared themselves a commune. Probably at Eleanor's urging, Louis immediately descended on the city with an army and occupied it without a blow being struck.

Everyone expected the King to dissolve the commune, but he did not. Instead, he demanded that the sons and daughters of the chief burghers return with him to France as hostages for their fathers' good behaviour. This provoked an outcry, and Suger, receiving complaints in Paris from horrified Poitevins, hastened to Poitiers, where he found wailing children and loaded baggage carts in the square before the ducal palace, ready to depart, their anguished parents looking on. In response to Suger's urgings, Louis rescinded his order and returned to France, having displayed appalling lack of judgement and achieved nothing beyond arousing the resentment and fear of the Poitevins and the anger of his wife. Eleanor accused him of weakness in bowing to pressure from Suger and demanded that in future he listen to her instead, for she knew her people better than anyone else. As a result, Suger's moderating influence was eclipsed for some time,[24] while Louis bowed to the private dictates of his domineering and somewhat irresponsible wife.

Shortly after this episode, on Christmas Day, Eleanor was crowned Queen of France at Bourges. Louis, it will be remembered, had already been crowned in his father's lifetime, and it appears that he simply had the royal diadem ceremonially placed on his head on this occasion.

After his initial attempt to subdue Eleanor's vassals, the King maintained a low profile in Aquitaine. His officials were administering the duchy and his soldiers garrisoning the ducal castles, but he did not have the resources to enforce his authority, which meant that the lords of the region were able to enjoy greater autonomy than ever before. Eleanor visited her fiefs occasionally, the first time being in September 1138, when she attended the Festival of Our Lady at Puy l'Evêque in neighbouring Quercy. Sometimes Louis accompanied her; more often than not it was her sister Petronilla who rode at her side. All the evidence suggests that the sisters were very close to each other. In fact, it was Eleanor's loyalty to Petronilla that was largely responsible for the first major conflict of the reign, sparking a chain of events that were to culminate in a tragedy that would have an indelible effect on Louis VII.

3

'Counsel of the Devil'

Early in 1141, Louis VII decided to lay claim to Toulouse in his wife's name; it is likely that his interest was prompted by Eleanor, who was determined to recover a territory she believed was rightfully hers, by virtue of her descent from its heiress, her grandmother, Philippa of Toulouse.

For the past twenty years, Toulouse had been ruled by Count Alfonso Jordan. Louis saw its acquisition as a means to extend his own domains almost as far as the Mediterranean and enhance his personal prestige. Fired with enthusiasm for the project, he drew up strategies for his campaign without consulting Suger or his chief vassals, with the result that some – among them the powerful Count Theobald IV of Champagne – refused him their support. Nor did the Count fulfil his feudal obligation to send Louis knights and soldiers, and when the King and Queen departed for the south on 24 June, Louis was seething with anger against Theobald.

Leaving Eleanor in Poitiers, where she seems to have remained for the duration of the campaign, Louis marched his army through Aquitaine, intending to take the city of Toulouse by surprise. Confident of his success, he had not thought it necessary to take with him many siege engines. Nor was he a very competent commander: his men were poorly organised and ill-disciplined.

When he arrived before Toulouse, the King saw to his dismay that Alfonso Jordan had been warned of his coming and that formidable defences were in place. Realising that he had no hope of taking the city, Louis retreated in undignified haste via Angoulême to Poitiers, where he was obliged to confess his failure to Eleanor.[1]

The King and Queen remained in Poitou throughout the summer, with Eleanor's sister Petronilla in attendance.[2] Together, they all went on a progress through Eleanor's domains, visiting the monastery of Neuil-sur-l'Autise and the abbey of Millezais, where Eleanor's aunt Agnes was Abbess, and to which Louis now granted certain privileges. Then the court enjoyed the hunting at Talmont for several days before returning to Paris in the early autumn.

It was during this summer that sixteen-year-old Petronilla became involved in an adulterous affair with Count Raoul of Vermandois, Seneschal of France, who was about thirty-five years her senior and was married to Eleanor, sister of Count Theobald of Champagne. Raoul, who was a cousin of the King, held wide estates to the north of France, between Flanders and Normandy; Petronilla was a very desirable bride, for she had been granted estates in Normandy and Burgundy for her dower, although she had so far refused all offers of marriage. Now she wanted only Raoul, while he, according to John of Salisbury, 'was always dominated by lust'. Eleanor seems to have supported the lovers from the first; she wanted to indulge her sister's desire to marry Raoul and encouraged him to have his existing marriage annulled. The Queen had no love for Theobald of Champagne, who had long been Raoul's enemy and had so recently failed to honour his feudal obligations to Louis, and she doubtless relished the prospect of his anger at this insult to his sister. In the meantime, she herself brought pressure to bear on Louis.

Soon after his return to France, it was brought to Louis' notice that the archbishopric of Bourges had fallen vacant. Bourges was an important city, being situated near the border with Poitou, and therefore a convenient place for Louis and Eleanor to hold court for their vassals. The canons of Bourges had put forward their own candidate, Pierre de la Châtre, a Clunaic monk, to fill the vacancy, but the King nominated instead the rather less suitable Carduc, his own Chancellor, to this politically significant office. The cathedral chapter wisely but provocatively opted for Pierre de la Châtre. Louis vetoed their choice, but Pierre was already in Rome, where Pope Innocent II confirmed his appointment and duly consecrated him Archbishop of Bourges.

Louis exploded in fury on learning of this and had the gates of Bourges closed to Pierre upon his return, whereupon the Archbishop complained to the Pope, who in turn voiced the suspicion that it was Eleanor rather than Louis who was opposed to Pierre's appointment, although there is no proof of the Queen's involvement. Presumably Innocent felt that she was following in a family tradition of anticlericalism. As for Louis, the Pontiff warned the King's ministers that he was a mere child who needed to be taught good manners, and exhorted them to make him stop 'behaving like a foolish schoolboy': those with any influence on him should ensure that he did not in future meddle in what was clearly not his business. Innocent's rebuke was reported to the King, who was deeply insulted and retaliated by swearing, on holy relics, that while there was breath in his body, Archbishop Pierre should never again set foot in Bourges.[3]

Furious, Innocent threatened to excommunicate Louis, but the King defied him, declaring that he would not renounce a vow he had sworn directly to God with his hand on holy relics. The Pope decided instead to place the royal household under an interdict, effectively excluding its members from the sacraments of the Church – a terrible punishment for one so devout as Louis, and one that horrified his advisers. Yet even now the King would not give way, and his fury was further fuelled by reports that Archbishop Peter had been granted asylum by Count Theobald of Champagne.

Enticed by the prospect of marriage to the Queen's sister, with whom he seems to have begun cohabiting, Raoul of Vermandois had now deserted his wife and had finally decided to have his marriage annulled. At the end of 1141, Louis, who was almost certainly pressurised by Eleanor, found three compliant bishops – Raoul's own brother, the Bishop of Noyon, and the Bishops of Laon and Senlis – who heard the case and willingly granted the Count of Vermandois an annulment on the grounds of consanguinity. Early in 1142, these same bishops officiated, with the King's approval, at the nuptials of Raoul and Petronilla.

At the Church's behest, an enraged Count Theobald took under his protection his abandoned sister Eleanor and her children, and, heeding her pleas, protested forcefully to the Pope, to whom he sent documents drawn up by himself proving that both the annulment and Raoul's remarriage were invalid. He argued that Raoul had not sought the Pope's consent before proceeding with his case, and that there was clear evidence that the bishops had been suborned by Louis, who was not qualified to interfere in what was entirely a matter for the Church. Briefed by Theobald, a shocked Bernard of Clairvaux also wrote to the Pope, expressing in the most vigorous terms his disapproval of this outrage against the House of Champagne and the sacrament of marriage itself.

In June 1142, Innocent arranged for a Church council to meet at Lagny-sur-Marne in Champagne; here, on the Pope's express instructions, the papal legate, Cardinal Yves, excommunicated the Bishop of Noyon, suspended the other two bishops and ordered Raoul of

Vermandois to return to his wife; when Raoul refused, he and Petronilla were excommunicated and their lands placed under an interdict.[4] An indignant King Louis, still smarting because of the interdict on his household and angry with Theobald for harbouring Pierre de la Châtre, immediately sprang to Raoul's defence: he refused to acknowledge the legate's sentence, which he interpreted as a direct attack on his regal authority, and began plotting war on Theobald, whom he blamed for these developments. While Louis was thus occupied, Geoffrey of Anjou seized his opportunity and invaded Normandy.

Louis, his patience exhausted, sent an army into Champagne, intending to bring Theobald to submission by punishing his people. For several months his soldiers laid waste the countryside, burning crops, looting churches and homes, killing men, women and children indiscriminately and, according to most chroniclers, committing unspeakable atrocities.

Theobald remained inflexible, and in January 1143, leaving Eleanor in Paris, the King himself led a force of mercenaries and *routiers* into Champagne and laid siege to the small town of Vitry-sur-Marne (sometimes known as Vitry-en-Perthois), which clustered around one of the Count's castles, which Louis intended to occupy. Local people, terrified of a fresh French onslaught, had sought safety within the town's walls, and now had no way of retreat from the encircling enemy.

From his camp on the La Fourche hills, the King directed an assault on the castle, which was built of wood. As his men advanced, they were met with a hail of bowshot from the keep, but the royal forces retaliated with a more deadly weapon, launching flaming arrows at the wooden edifice, which was soon ablaze. With its defenders either engulfed in flames or intent on putting the fire out, there was no one to prevent the royal mercenaries from swarming into the town, brandishing swords and torches, and the people ran from their houses in terror. In vain did their commanders try to curb the bloodlust of the soldiers, who threw their torches into the doorways of houses and fired their thatched roofs, careless of whether there was anyone within.

Soon the whole town seemed to be ablaze, and its panic-stricken inhabitants fled to the sanctuary of the cathedral; estimates vary, but between 1,000 and 1,500 people took refuge there that day, among them women, children, the old and the sick. But the wind was against them: as the conflagration spread, the cathedral itself was engulfed in flames, its roof caved in and every soul trapped within its walls perished.[5]

From his position overlooking the inferno, Louis heard the screams of the dying and smelt their burning flesh; he shed tears of horror and remorse,[6] and when his captains came to him for further orders, they found him shaking and unable to speak, his face ashen and his teeth chattering. He appeared to be in a trance, and seemed unaware of their presence. Concerned for his health, his officers helped him to his tent, where he lay in the same state for two days, refusing to speak or take nourishment.

When he emerged, he was a changed man, weighed down by guilt. Although he had not ordered the sacking of the town – which was known for hundreds of years thereafter as Vitry-le-Brûlé – he castigated himself ceaselessly for having caused the deaths of its people, whose cries haunted his days and nights. He either suffered terrifying nightmares or lay sleepless, weeping into his pillows. Not only did his physical health suffer, but he felt he had been cast spiritually adrift, and that his soul was forever damned.

Broken in spirit, the King returned to Paris, having lost his appetite for war. In fact, his armies had overrun most of Champagne and he was now in a strong position to dictate terms. He therefore offered to make peace with Count Theobald, on condition that the latter use his influence to have the sentence of excommunication on the Count and Countess of Vermandois lifted. Bernard of Clairvaux suggested that Pope Innocent lift the ban, but only until Louis had restored Theobald's lands to him, and the Pope readily complied.

After Louis had ordered a general retreat of his forces, Innocent ordered Raoul one final time to renounce Petronilla. Raoul refused, and found himself and his wife excommunicated a second time. Anger roused Louis out of his deep depression, and he stormed back into Champagne at the head of his army, wreaking a terrible vengeance on the land and its people.

Public opinion in France had turned against the war. From Clairvaux, Abbot Bernard dispatched a stream of thunderous letters to the King, condemning his aggression towards Theobald and accusing Louis, amongst other things, of 'slaying, burning, tearing down churches, driving poor men from their dwelling places and consorting with bandits and robbers'. The Abbot warned Louis that he was imperilling his immortal soul and provoking the terrible wrath of God. 'Do not, my King,' he begged, 'lift your hand with rash audacity against the terrible Lord who takes away the breath of kings.' Finally, he asked: 'From whom but the Devil did this advice come under which you are acting? Those who are urging you to repeat your former wrongdoings against an innocent person are seeking in this not your honour but their own convenience. They are clearly the enemies of your crown and the disturbers of your realm.'

Since Louis had for some time ceased to heed the warnings of Suger and his other advisers, there can be little doubt that the mentors referred to so scathingly in Bernard's letter were Eleanor, her sister and Raoul of Vermandois, who had probably urged the King to return to Champagne and pursue the war to its inevitable bitter end.

Bernard wrote also to Suger and other royal advisers, criticising them for failing to give the King sound advice. At Suger's invitation, he visited Louis at Corbeil and harangued him in person before his court. The interview ended badly, with the King exploding in a fit of temper at a baron's suggestion that Raoul had led him by the nose, but the Abbot's rebuke had its effect. After Bernard had left, Louis was visibly shaken and once more overwhelmed by guilt.[7] The horror he had felt at Vitry returned in full force and so consumed him that he suffered a form of breakdown, which affected his health so badly that his doctors feared he would die. Cut off from the sacraments, thanks to the interdict on his household, he was convinced that he was irrevocably damned, and his mental agony was unbearable.[8]

On 24 September, Pope Innocent died. His successor, Celestine II, was informed by Bernard of Clairvaux of the spiritual malaise that affected the King of France, and out of compassion lifted the interdict. Louis, however, was too sunk in dejection for this news to cheer him. He believed that nothing could avert the divine punishment that awaited him. When he arose from his sickbed, he was a changed man. He cut off his long hair and was shorn like a monk; he took to wearing the monastic's coarse grey gown and sandals; he spent hours at prayer, begging God for forgiveness, and was even more rigorous than before in his religious observances and fasts. He resolved to heed once more the injunctions of Abbot Suger and his other ecclesiastical advisers, who urged Louis to make peace with Count Theobald.

The effect of these changes on Eleanor is not recorded, nor do we know how she dealt with Louis' guilt. There is no doubt, however, that he remained a fond and even foolish husband; nowhere is there any suggestion that he blamed her for what had happened in Champagne.

It was during 1143 that the validity of the marriage of Louis and Eleanor was first questioned. The Bishop of Laon had drawn up a pedigree that exposed the consanguinous affinity between the royal couple, then Bernard of Clairvaux raised the matter twice. He asked why Louis should disapprove of the consanguinous relationship between Raoul of Vermandois and his first wife, when he himself was related to Queen Eleanor within the forbidden degrees. Later, when Theobald of Champagne sought to gain support against the French by marrying two of his heirs to the King's powerful vassals, and Louis forbade the marriages on the grounds of consanguinity, Bernard asked, 'How is it that the King is so scrupulous about consanguinity in the case of Theobald's heirs, when everyone knows that he himself has married his cousin in the fourth degree?' Louis chose to ignore these censures, but it is clear, from what was to come, that Eleanor took them more seriously.

On Saturday, 10 June 1144, Louis, Eleanor and the dowager Queen Adelaide joined the throngs of pilgrims and sightseers travelling from Paris to Saint-Denis for the consecration of Suger's new abbey church. The King hastened to spend the night keeping vigil with the monks before the altar, while Eleanor and her mother-in-law were escorted by Suger through cheering crowds to the abbey's guest house. The monastery precincts were congested with visitors, and many people were obliged to camp out in the fields.

On Sunday, the Feast Day of St Barnabas, Suger's life's work reached its culmination in the dedication of the church to Saint-Denis in the presence of the King and Queen. The finished church was the first truly Gothic masterpiece in Europe, boasting no fewer than twenty altars, and possessing many sacramental vessels of gold and silver decorated with precious gems. Its arched windows were glazed in a blaze of coloured glass, and on the high altar stood a crucifix twenty feet tall. Among its newly acquired treasures were gifts from every feudal lord in France, including the crystal vase that Eleanor had given to Louis on their marriage. For the next 300 years, the Oriflamme, the sacred banner of St Denis and standard of the kings of France, would be kept on the high altar.

Saint-Denis was that day filled to capacity with thousands of guests and pilgrims, among them Bernard of Clairvaux and Theobald of Champagne, both present in the interests of peace. The heat was so stifling that both queens nearly fainted. King Louis' attire drew some adverse comment from several onlookers, for while Eleanor wore a pearl-encrusted diadem and a robe of damask in honour of the occasion, Louis was clothed in the drab gown and sandals of a penitent. Others were impressed by the change in him: 'No one would have taken the King for that scourge of war who had lately destroyed so many towns, burned so many churches, shed so much blood. The spirit of penitence shone in his whole aspect.'[9]

Bearing on his shoulder the new solid-silver reliquary containing the bones of the martyred St Denis the Areopagite, patron saint of France, which had hitherto rested in the crypt of the old church, the King led the clergy in procession round the great edifice and placed the relics reverently in their new bejewelled shrine of blue and gold marble in the choir. Louis was greatly moved by the ceremony of dedication, as was

Bernard of Clairvaux, and after it had ended the two men exchanged friendly greetings, with no trace of their former contention. Bernard exhorted the King not to give way to despair and reminded him of God's goodness, mercy and forgiveness.[10]

After the dedication, Eleanor saw Bernard privately, probably at her own request. He came prepared to offer more spiritual comfort, thinking that she too might be suffering qualms of conscience over Vitry, but he was surprised to learn that she was not. Nevertheless, several matters were indeed troubling her, not least the problems of her sister. She asked him to use his influence with the Pope to have the excommunication on Raoul and Petronilla lifted and their marriage recognised by the Church. In return, she would persuade Louis to make peace with Theobald of Champagne and recognise Pierre de la Châtre as Archbishop of Bourges.

Bernard was appalled at her brazen candour. In his opinion, these affairs were no business of a twenty-two-year-old woman. He was, in fact, terrified of women and their possible effect on him. As an adolescent, first experiencing physical desire for a young girl, he had been so filled with self-disgust that he had jumped into a freezing cold pond and remained there until his erection subsided. He strongly disapproved of his sister, who had married a rich man; because she enjoyed her wealth, he thought of her as a whore, spawned by Satan to lure her husband from the paths of righteousness, and refused to have anything to do with her. Nor would he allow his monks any contact with their female relatives.

Now there stood before him the young, worldly and disturbingly beautiful Queen of France, intent upon meddling in matters that were not her concern. Bernard's worst suspicions were confirmed: here, beyond doubt, was the source of that 'counsel of the Devil' that had urged the King on to disaster and plunged him into sin and guilt. All was now made clear, and Bernard could only reproach himself for having been blind to what was going on. His immediate reaction was to admonish Eleanor severely.

'Put an end to your interference with affairs of state,' he ordered her in the voice that was capable of quelling the opposition of kings. So sternly did he reprove her that she burst into tears and revealed that she had interfered in politics because her life was empty and bitter, since 'during all the seven years she had lived with the King, she had remained barren, apart from one hope in the early days, which had been quickly dashed. She despaired of ever having the longed-for child', although she had prayed many times to the Virgin to grant her wish.

Could God, the healer of the lame, the blind and the deaf, move Heaven to bestow on her the gift of motherhood?[11]

Gratified to hear such proper womanly sentiments and moved by Eleanor's obvious distress, Bernard took compassion on her, but he still could not resist the opportunity to deliver a little homily.

'My child,' he said, in a more gentle tone, 'seek those things which make for peace. Cease to stir up the King against the Church and urge him to a better course of action. If you will promise to do this, I in my turn promise to entreat the merciful Lord to grant you offspring.'[12]

Later that day, thanks to the intervention of Bernard and Abbot Suger, a treaty of peace was concluded between Louis and Theobald. As a result, the King returned to Count Theobald all the territory he had wrested from him during the recent war, renounced the oath he had sworn on holy relics and confirmed Pierre de la Châtre as Archbishop of Bourges.

Wisely, Louis meddled no further in the matter of the Vermandois marriage. The Pope eventually recognised their union as valid, although Bernard warned that they would not enjoy each other for long, nor would their children be fruitful. Their only son, Ralph, died a leper, and their two daughters – Elizabeth, who married Philip of Alsace, later Count of Flanders, and Eleanor, who married Matthew, Count of Beaumont – both died childless. Raoul lived until 1151; Petronilla's date of death is not recorded.

Louis had now done everything he could to make reparation for his great sin, yet still he was weighed down by guilt. He began privately to consider fulfilling the vow he had made in childhood, on behalf of his dead brother Philip, to take the Oriflamme of France on a pilgrimage to Christ's tomb in the Church of the Holy Sepulchre in Jerusalem.[13] Yet events were moving in such a way as to afford him a more satisfactory means of expiation.

The First Crusade to capture the Holy Land from the Turks, in 1096–9, had been a marked success, and had resulted in the establishment of four crusader states dominated by the Latin kingdom of Jerusalem. These states, ruled mainly by Normans and Frenchmen, were collectively known to Europeans as Outremer.

The need to maintain a military presence to guard the holy places in Palestine against the Turks and protect pilgrims had brought into being two crusading orders of knights under monastic vows. These were the Knights of the Order of the Hospital of St John of Jerusalem (Knights Hospitaller), founded in 1099, and their rivals, the exceptionally wealthy Poor Knights of Christ and the Temple of Solomon (Knights Templar), founded around 1118. Both guarded and protected pilgrims to the Holy Land, but the powerful Templars, whose headquarters were in Jerusalem itself, now also acted as bankers to the kings of Europe.

But on 24 December 1144, the security of the Christian kingdoms in Outremer was threatened when the city of Edessa, capital of the first crusader state, which was founded in 1098, was occupied by Saracen Turks led by the formidable Zengi, Governor of the Islamic states of Mosul and Aleppo. With Edessa fallen, the way lay clear for the Infidel to march against and occupy the vulnerable neighbouring principality of Antioch and, beyond that, the Latin kingdom of Jerusalem itself and its holy Christian shrines.

In February 1145, a new Pope, Eugenius III, was elected, but although he had received pleas for help from the beleaguered states of Outremer, he was too preoccupied with the schism within the Church to be able to respond; thanks to the presence of an anti-pope, he was barred from entering Rome and had had to establish his exiled court in Viterbo. The catastrophic news nevertheless provoked widespread alarm throughout Christendom, for it was quickly understood that the hard-won and greatly prized conquests of the First Crusade were in jeopardy.[14]

Launching a crusade against the Turks was an enterprise dear to the King's heart, and he considered it seriously, realising that it presented him with the ideal opportunity to make reparation for Vitry and restore his international prestige. So weighed down with guilt was he that his chief interest in the venture was the spiritual relief he hoped to gain by making the pilgrimage to Jerusalem. He was now weak from fasting for three days each week, and had taken to wearing a hair-shirt beneath his outer garments in order to mortify his flesh. He had also sent aid to Vitry to enable the town to be rebuilt and relief given to those who had lost relatives in the holocaust. But none of this was sufficient to relieve his feelings of self-loathing or avert his fear of damnation.

It seems that Eleanor had taken the admonitions of Bernard of Clairvaux to heart, for from now on she appears to have ceased to meddle in politics, leaving Louis to heed the wise advice of Abbot Suger, now fully restored to favour as his chief counsellor. Perhaps the Queen's prayers, and those of Bernard, had been efficacious, or perhaps Louis had been more attentive in bed, for during 1145 – the exact date is not recorded – she bore a daughter, who was named Marie in honour of the Virgin. If the infant was not the male heir to France so desired by the King – the Salic law forbade the succession of females to the throne – her arrival encouraged the royal parents to hope for a son in the future.

Relationships between aristocratic parents and children were rarely close. Queens and noblewomen did not nurse their own babies, but handed them over at birth into the care of wet-nurses, leaving themselves free to become pregnant again. It was customary for sons to be sent away to another noble household to be trained for knighthood, and for daughters to be reared in convents until the time came for them to marry. Royal children were often given their own households, and contact with their frequently busy or absent parents was at the mercy of circumstances. Virtually nothing is recorded of the Princess Marie's childhood, yet the course of events suggests that Eleanor was a distant mother.

Louis' love for his wife was undimmed, but he was perturbed by the effect that her beauty and charm had on others, and around this time, perhaps after the birth of Marie, he found himself suffering the unfamiliar pangs of jealousy. Earlier, Eleanor had invited the Gascon troubadour Marcabru to Paris. She had known him as a girl, for her father had been his patron and he had often displayed his poetic talents at the court of Poitiers. Since then, his fame had spread throughout Aquitaine and the south, and the Queen must have been delighted when the renowned troubadour accepted her invitation.

It was not long, however, before Marcabru overstepped the bounds of propriety. It was expected that he would write impassioned verses in honour of his unattainable patroness, but it soon became apparent to Louis that the poet, whose lyrics were generally derogatory to women, was showing an unacceptable degree of familiarity in his addresses to Eleanor. There is no hint that she returned his interest, and it is possible that Louis did not appreciate the more relaxed social customs of the south and completely misinterpreted the situation. Nevertheless, his outrage was deeply felt, and he banished Marcabru from his court. Eleanor's reaction is not recorded.

In September, Zengi died, but this was hardly comforting news to the beset crusader states, since his son, Nureddin, was a ruthless warrior and religious fanatic, who was determined to carry on his father's plans for a Moslem reconquest.

Louis' tentative plans for a crusade had to be set aside during the autumn, when he had to mount a punitive expedition against his wife's disputatious vassals in Aquitaine. On his return, he received the Bishop of Djebail and other messengers sent by Eleanor's uncle, Raymond of Poitiers, Prince of Antioch, with an appeal for aid against the threat posed by Nureddin; they brought 'noble gifts and treasures of great price in the hope of winning favour'.[15] At this time also, Queen Melisende of Jerusalem sent a forceful plea to the Pope at Viterbo, urging him to preach a new crusade. On 1 December, Eugenius published a papal Bull exhorting King Louis and all the faithful Christians of France to muster their resources and deliver the states of Outremer from the Infidel; in return, all who joined the new crusade would receive remission for their sins. A similar Bull was later sent to the German Emperor, Conrad III.

Louis and Eleanor held their Christmas court at Bourges that year, and it was here that the Pope's appeal reached them.[16] Their response was immediate and enthusiastic; according to Odo de Deuil, Louis' heart burned at the prospect of leading a crusade to Jerusalem, and he believed that such a mission was divinely appointed. Without consulting his advisers, he wrote to Eugenius, expressing his zeal for the crusade and declaring his intention of committing himself fully to its successful outcome.

On Christmas Day the King disclosed 'the secret in his heart' and announced to the assembled vassals of France and Aquitaine, who were present to renew their allegiance to their sovereign,[17] that he intended to take the Cross and launch a Second Crusade in order to liberate Edessa from the Turks.[18]

His announcement did not receive unanimous approval. The barons of France and Aquitaine were generally lukewarm in their response, many suspecting that Louis' priority was penance rather than reconquest. Eleanor's vassals recalled that 70,000 of their countrymen had perished during William IX's ill-fated venture into the Holy Land, while the French lords were jealous of their richer countrymen in Outremer, and thought them more than capable of protecting themselves. Most thought that Louis was asking a great deal of them: thousands of Frenchmen had also died fighting in the First Crusade, and the long journey to the Holy Land was fraught with dangers.

Even the pious Suger urged the King to reconsider, declaring that God would be better served by Louis remaining in France, maintaining peace and governing his kingdom wisely; the Abbot voiced fears that unrest and disorder might well result from the King being absent for at least a year.

Suger became even more alarmed when Eleanor announced her intention of taking the Cross too and accompanying her husband on the crusade. Given the fact that she was potentially able to muster a vast following of her vassals, it was unlikely that Louis would gainsay her. Moreover, according to William of Newburgh, writing half a century later, the Queen had so bedazzled her husband with her beauty that, fearing out of jealousy to leave her behind, he felt compelled to take her with him. Suger therefore pointed out that Louis had little experience of military leadership and that his previous campaigns had ended in disaster.

He warned that it would be foolhardy for the King to leave France without first siring a male heir, for if he did not return, the succession would undoubtedly be disputed. He urged the royal couple to reconsider their decision, in the interests of France.[19]

His pleas fell on deaf ears, for Louis and Eleanor were, for different reasons, so eager and determined to implement their plans that they were unwilling to listen to dissenting voices. Eleanor seems to have viewed the crusade as an opportunity to escape the boring routine of the court in favour of adventure and the chance to make a pilgrimage to Jerusalem and see her uncle in Antioch. She would have been a cold wife indeed, had she not wished to see her husband's peace of mind restored and, like most people in Europe at that time, she was undoubtedly inspired by the desire to protect from the Infidel the holy places associated with Christ.

During that Christmas season, Eleanor set to work on her vassals, and her enthusiasm was such that before long several lords of Aquitaine were declaring themselves keen to take the Cross, among them her loyal Geoffrey de Rançon, Lord of Taillebourg, her constable, Saldebreuil of Sanzay, and two notoriously volatile lords of the Limousin, Hugh de Lusignan and Guy of Thouars; but there were many more to win over. As the court prepared to leave Bourges, it was still uncertain whether there was enough support to enable the crusade to go ahead. Suger advised that the decision therefore be postponed until Louis could summon a full council of his barons and bishops. It was arranged that this should take place at the end of March at Vézelay in Burgundy. Suger thought that might be the end of the matter, but when he learned that the Pope, with Louis' support, had enlisted Bernard of Clairvaux to preach the crusade at Vézelay, he knew with mounting despair that it would not be. And his chances of prevailing on the King seemed even more remote when in March 1146 Louis received a letter from the Pope bestowing his blessing on the crusade and warmly praising Louis' valour.

At Easter 1146, in good weather, vast crowds converged on the new Romanesque abbey of St Mary Magdalene on its hilltop at Vézelay to hear Bernard of Clairvaux preach the new crusade. There were too many people to fit into the church, so on Easter Day, 31 March, the frail Abbot mounted an open-air platform in a field and delivered an inspirational sermon to the assembled multitudes. Apart from his reiteration of the papal Bull and its promise of salvation to all who took the Cross, his words are not recorded,[20] but they inspired great fervour and deeply moved his listeners, not least Louis and Eleanor, who, shriven of their sins, sat enthroned behind the Abbot, surrounded by their chief vassals and bishops.

Amidst shouts of 'To Jerusalem!', the King went first, weeping with emotion, to take the Cross blessed for him by the Pope, prostrating himself in front of Bernard,[21] who attached it to the shoulder of Louis' mantle. Eleanor followed, falling to her knees before the Abbot and vowing to take her vassals with her to the Holy Land. It had been by no means unusual for women to accompany their husbands on the First Crusade, and there is no contemporary evidence that Eleanor's decision provoked adverse comment. It was only fifty years later, when Eleanor's reputation had suffered, that chroniclers such as William of Newburgh asserted that the motives of these female crusaders were anything but spiritual; he complained that their presence in the army was disruptive and attracted women of dubious morals, who diverted many of the men from their holy purpose. 'In that Christian camp, where chastity should have prevailed, a horde of women was milling about. This in particular brought scandal upon our army.'[22]

The chroniclers did not have space to list all the other noble ladies who followed the Queen's example,[23] but among them were those who were to be her personal companions: Mamille of Roucy, Sybilla of Anjou, Countess of Flanders, Florine of Burgundy, Torqueri of Bouillon and Faydide of Toulouse. Three hundred humbler women volunteered to go and nurse the wounded. It took some courage for these women to take the Cross, for during the previous crusade many of their sex had suffered extreme hardship or even death, or had been captured by the Turks and sold as slaves.

Gervase of Canterbury states that, after receiving their crosses, Eleanor and these other ladies withdrew, dressed themselves as Penthesilea and her Amazon warriors in white tunics emblazoned with red crosses, plumes, white buskins and cherry-red boots, and galloped on white horses through the crowds on the hillside, brandishing banners and swords, calling upon knights and nobles to heed the summons of Almighty God, and tossing spindles and distaffs to those faint-hearts who held back from making a final commitment.[24] Most historians dismiss this tale as pure legend, because there are no contemporary accounts of it, but it is in keeping with what we know of Eleanor's character, and was believed credible by some who knew her in her later years. The tale may have originated from the eye-witness account of a Greek observer, who described Eleanor and her ladies as being dressed as Amazons on their way to the Holy Land.[25] Ordericus Vitalis tells a similar story of Isabella of Anjou, who retired to Fontevrault after riding armed into battle like an Amazon.

It is perhaps significant that when, probably a decade or so later, Benoît de Saint-Maure dedicated his *Roman de Troie* to Eleanor, he dwelt at some length upon Penthesilea and her Amazons, describing the warrior Queen as riding into battle on a fine Spanish horse caparisoned with 'a hundred tiny golden twinkling bells' and armed with 'a hauberk whiter than snow', a sword, a lance and a golden shield bordered with rubies and emeralds. She and her Amazons let 'their lovely hair hang free'. This description tallies with the Greek account of the noble ladies in the crusading army, and Benoît may have intended to recall Eleanor's already fabled exploits during the crusade.

Whether or not the story is true, thousands of people came forward, all eager to receive their crusaders' emblems from Bernard himself. Great lords shouted, 'Crosses! Give us crosses!' and their cry was taken up by humbler folk. 'It is God's will!' they chanted. Soon, the Abbot ran out of crosses and was obliged to cut strips from his white wool choir mantle. He was still distributing them when darkness fell.[26] For once, the turbulent barons of Aquitaine set aside their private feuds and united in a common enterprise with their French counterparts. Among them were Count Theobald's heir, Henry; Count Alfonso Jordan of Toulouse; Louis' brother Robert, Count of Dreux; and Thierry of Alsace, Count of Flanders.

All France, it seemed, was afire with crusading fervour, which soon spread north across the Rhine and south across the Pyrenees. A triumphant Bernard informed the Pope: 'You ordered, and I obeyed. I opened my mouth and spoke, and the crusaders at once multiplied into infinity. Villages and towns are deserted, and you will scarcely find one man for every seven women.'

It was decided that the crusaders should set out in the spring of 1147; the marathon of planning and organisation that had to be completed beforehand precluded an earlier departure. Louis imposed a heavy tax on his subjects, which caused great hardship and provoked many complaints, while the royal administrators in Aquitaine were ruthless in raising money and supplies. The churches donated their treasure and the Jews were mulcted of the profits of usury. Armourers busily made chain mail and weapons, lords mortgaged their estates in order to finance the journey, and the poor forgot the miseries caused by a famine that had blighted their lives for five years.[27]

At Étampes in February, the King, now in much better spirits, consulted his vassals and deliberated as to which route to travel on to Outremer. It was decided that an overland route via Constantinople, whose Emperor had offered his support, would be safer and more economic.[28] Louis then chose his personal entourage. While Suger remained in France, governing in the King's name, Louis' secretary and chaplain, Odo de Deuil, was to be his chief adviser, who would share the King's tent at night and write an official account of the crusade.[29] A Templar, the eunuch Thierry Galan, was given charge of the coffers containing the money raised for the enterprise, and was also instructed to keep fortune-seekers and sycophants at a distance from his master,[30] an order that he seems to have interpreted as including Eleanor. Louis also visited abbeys and leper hospitals, distributing alms in return for prayers of intercession.

Eleanor immersed herself with zest in the preparations. She toured her domains, whipping up support amongst her vassals for the crusade. She recruited troops, held tournaments to attract the interest of the knightly classes, helped to organise supplies for the vast army, and granted or renewed privileges to religious houses in exchange for financial and spiritual support. She also made her first recorded visit and gift to the abbey of Fontevrault, where she confirmed a donation made by Louis just after he had taken the Cross and pledged the nuns a profit of 500 sous from each fair held in Poitou on the eve of her departure for the East. In return, they promised to pray for her soul if she died on crusade. She had made a similar arrangement with other abbeys, notably those at Montierneuf and La Grâce-Dieu. Thanks to her efforts, the larger part of the crusading army comprised her own vassals. Even the troubadours played their part: the exiled Marcabru composed crusading songs, whilst others, including Joffré Rudel, who perished in the Holy Land, vowed to fight the Infidel.

In the autumn of 1146, Bernard had gone to Germany to preach the crusade. The Emperor Conrad, insecure on his throne, was reluctant to take the Cross, but at Christmas – after having great pressure brought to bear on him by a persistent Bernard – he was shamed into capitulating. Bernard continued to travel about preaching the crusade until the spring of 1147, when he returned to Clairvaux.

Suger was still concerned about the risk of Louis leaving his kingdom without a male heir, and both he and the King were perturbed by the ambition of Count Geoffrey of Anjou. In 1144, after a three-year campaign, Geoffrey had conquered Normandy, and Louis, as its overlord, had confirmed him as its duke. Geoffrey was politically astute. Five years earlier, his wife Matilda had unsuccessfully prosecuted her claim to the English throne, which had been usurped by her cousin, Stephen of Blois. Geoffrey had not embroiled himself in that war, since his ambitions were focused on the continent, and he now sought to extend his influence to France itself; he had been appointed seneschal of

Poitou by Louis. He therefore proposed to the King that his son Henry, then aged thirteen, marry Louis' infant daughter Marie. The Salic Law prevented Marie's accession, but it is possible that Geoffrey felt himself powerful enough to circumvent this in the event of the King dying whilst on crusade. Although Henry of Anjou was undoubtedly a suitable match for his daughter, Louis prevaricated. Then Geoffrey began to put pressure on him.

While Louis was considering the proposal, Bernard of Clairvaux got to hear of it, and wrote at once to the King to express his disapproval:

> I have heard that the Count of Anjou is pressing to bind you under oath respecting the proposed marriage between his son and your daughter. This is something not merely inadvisable but also unlawful, because apart from other reasons, it is barred by the impediment of consanguinity. I have learned on trustworthy evidence that the mothers of the Queen and this boy are related in the third degree. Have nothing whatever to do with the matter.

Armed with Bernard's letter, Louis turned down Geoffrey's proposal, and the matter was dropped.

It was later asserted by Giraldus Cambrensis, in his *De Principis Instructione*, that 'Count Geoffrey of Anjou, when he was Seneschal of France [*sic*], had carnally known Queen Eleanor' and that the Count later confessed this to his son. It is not known exactly when Geoffrey was seneschal of Poitou (not of France, as Giraldus asserts), but it was probably during the years before the crusade; his tenure of the office appears to have ceased some time before 1151. He was an extremely handsome man trapped in a tempestuous marriage, and several bastards testified to his various extra-marital affairs.

After Louis confirmed him as duke of Normandy, Geoffrey was on friendly terms with the King, but their relations may have cooled when Geoffrey declined to accompany the crusade in order to protect his own interests in Normandy. As Geoffrey's half-brother Baldwin was King of Jerusalem, Louis may have felt that the Count was ducking both his spiritual and his familial obligations.

Giraldus claimed that he had heard about Eleanor's adultery with Geoffrey from the saintly Bishop Hugh of Lincoln, who had learned of it from Henry II of England, Geoffrey's son and Eleanor's second husband. Eleanor was estranged from Henry at the time Giraldus was writing, and the King was trying to secure an annulment of their marriage from the Pope. It would have been to his advantage to declare her an adulterous wife who had had carnal relations with his father, for that in itself would have rendered their marriage incestuous and would have provided prima-facie grounds for its dissolution. Indeed, the grounds on which Henry sought an annulment were shrouded in secrecy, which may in itself have been significant. It seems likely that he alleged consanguinity, which could have embraced either his genetic affinity with Eleanor or her possible affair with his father. The incestuous nature of such a connection would alone have ensured confidentiality.

It is unlikely that Henry would have lied about the affair to the respected Bishop Hugh, who would surely have protested at being named as the source for such a calumny if it were untrue.

It has been stated, with some truth, that at the time he was writing, Giraldus was antagonistic towards Henry II for blocking his election to the See of St David's; his text is hostile and sometimes scathing. Even so, it is hardly likely that he would have written something so prejudicial to the King's honour and to the legitimacy of his heirs without reliable evidence. It is true that Giraldus did not like or approve of Eleanor, but it is also fair to say that he must have had some grounds for his disapproval, very probably Eleanor's own conduct.

On balance, therefore, it seems likely that she did indeed have an affair with Count Geoffrey, which they managed to keep secret from Louis and the rest of the world. It probably happened on impulse and was of brief duration, and it may have flourished during one of the Queen's visits to Poitou, possibly the one she made in the autumn of 1146. By then, it is likely that she may have been having doubts about the validity of her marriage.

After Giraldus wrote his account, discretion appears to have been maintained. Walter Map, a trusted royal secretary, justice and confidant, would say only that the Queen 'was secretly reputed to have shared the couch of Louis with Geoffrey'. It was for this reason that Map and others believed that the offspring of Henry and Eleanor were 'tainted at the source'. How, Giraldus asked, could happy issue stem from such a union?

By the second week of May, 1147, everything was ready for the crusade. The army and royal retinues were assembled and the baggage carts packed; Eleanor's luggage filled a good many of them, for she was determined not to travel without the courtly comforts and luxuries to which she was accustomed. Her luggage included clothes, furs, tents, saddles, harnesses, household plate, jewellery, veils, pallet beds, goblets, washbasins, soap and food. Other ladies followed suit, and they and the Queen were criticised for taking so much unnecessary gear as well as an excessive number of tirewomen, which would be encumbrances that the crusaders could well do without.

The King and Queen, accompanied by the Queen Adelaide, then went to Saint-Denis, where they lodged on the night of 7 June. That evening, Louis dined in the refectory with the monks, while Eleanor and her mother-in-law ate in private in the guest house.

On 8 June, clad in a black pilgrim's tunic emblazoned with a red cross, the King entered the abbey church, which was hung with banners and illuminated by thousands of candles. In the presence of the Pope, he committed his kingdom to the safe-keeping of Abbot Suger. Eugenius then delivered to him the red and gold silk Oriflamme of St Denis to take to the Holy Land. As Louis grasped its gilded pole, the congregation burst out cheering and Queen Eleanor wept with emotion. Finally, Eugenius gave Louis his blessing and handed him the traditional pilgrim's staff and wallet.

It was now time for the departing crusaders to say farewell to their loved ones, many of whom had come to see them off. 'The crowds and the King's wife and his mother, who nearly perished because of their tears and the heat, could not endure the delay; but to wish to depict the grief and wailing which occurred is impossible'.[31] Then the army, which numbered around 100,000 persons – 'an immense multitude from every part of France'[32] – set off, ahead of the King, for Metz in Germany, where Louis had arranged to rendezvous with the Emperor Conrad.

Louis had decided to defer his own departure until 11 June, the feast day of St Denis, in order to invoke the saint's protection, but on that day the press of people around the abbey was still so great that the front door was blocked and the King and Queen were obliged to leave Saint-Denis via the monks' dorter. Then, with Eleanor and her entourage going on ahead of Louis, with her unwieldy baggage train, the royal couple left for Metz on the first stage of their long journey to the Holy Land.

4

'To Jerusalem!'

After traversing Champagne, King Louis met up with the Emperor Conrad at Metz on the banks of the Mosel. In the middle of June 1147, amidst cheering crowds and the pealing of bells, the two armies left for the Holy Land, Eleanor looking resplendent in a robe embroidered with the lilies of France and riding a proud horse with a silver saddle and plaited mane; some noble ladies in her entourage carried falcons on their wrists, while a number of lords and knights bore swords with fragments of the True Cross set into their hilts. Marching at a brisk pace, the two armies set off on their separate courses, the French making for Ratisbon (Regensburg) in Bavaria, whence they would follow the course of the River Danube through Hungary and Bulgaria, covering between ten and twenty miles a day. 'Anyone seeing these columns with their helmets and buckles shining in the sun, with their banners streaming in the breeze, would have been certain that they were about to triumph over all the enemies of the Cross and reduce to submission all the countries of the Orient.'[1]

Eleanor and Louis travelled with their separate retinues, the King bringing up the rear. He heard mass every morning, and at night Odo de Deuil and Thierry Galan, who acted as the King's bodyguard and was not allowed out of his sight, shared his tent, while Eleanor was relegated to the company of her noblewomen and vassals. Odo praises Louis for the purity of his designs, and it seems likely that, for pious reasons, the King had resolved to abstain from sexual relations. Doubtless he had also taken practical as well as spiritual considerations into account, for if Eleanor became pregnant there would be unnecessary complications.

It was asserted by many later historians that the Queen and her ladies behaved as if they were on a pleasure trip, distracting their male companions from their holy purpose and causing general mayhem, but in fact there is very little contemporary evidence attesting to Eleanor's activities on the journey. Odo de Deuil, for example, does not refer to her at all in the passages of his work covering the first weeks, and thereafter makes only four brief references to her. Some modern historians suggest that his work has been censored by later writers, but there is no real proof of this. Probably Odo did not consider women worthy of much mention.

The King had given express orders commanding his soldiers to behave in a godly manner, but at Worms these were already being flouted:[2] a merchant who protested at crusaders plundering food was murdered. After that, it became clear that Louis was ineffective at maintaining discipline, and some of his men even began to desert.

At Ratisbon, Louis was met by two emissaries of the Byzantine Emperor, Manuel Comnenus,[3] who, while outwardly committed to supporting the crusade, was nevertheless alarmed at the prospect of such a vast host converging on Constantinople. In particular, he was nervous about the presence of so many Poitevins, for he and Raymond of Antioch had been deadly enemies since Manuel's brother, the late Emperor John, had established Byzantine suzerainty over Antioch and been savagely treated by Raymond in return. The Emperor therefore asked for guarantees that Louis came in friendship and would not attempt to take any cities or towns belonging to Manuel, and also that he would surrender to Manuel all the territory he took from the Turks. Louis agreed to the two former demands, but not to the latter, saying that he would discuss this with the Emperor when they met.

In Hungary, food was plentiful and spirits were high. Eleanor received letters from Manuel's wife, the Empress Irene, in joyful anticipation of her visit to Constantinople.[4]

'The Lord is aiding us at every turn,' Louis wrote to Suger, but he had spoken too soon.

The Imperial army, 10,000 strong, led by Conrad, had marched ahead through Greece, where the German soldiers had plundered, looted, burned, raped and murdered without check, and had so alienated the local people that they had butchered any stragglers from the ranks. The situation had become so fraught that the Emperor Manuel thought it fit to send a large force to escort the Germans to his capital and prevent them from committing any more violent acts. Conrad took exception to this and quarrelled with Manuel, and when he and his leaders arrived in Constantinople, they deliberately vandalised the quarters they were assigned in Manuel's hunting lodge, the Philopation, located outside the city walls.

The French, having crossed the Danube at Branitchevo, followed through Greece towards Adrianople in September, finding towns and cities closed to them, and such food as the hostile Greeks were willing to sell excessively dear. The decomposing bodies of the Germans still lay unburied and, according to Odo de Deuil, 'polluted all things, so that to the Franks less harm arose from the armed Greeks than from the dead Germans'. Louis, who wrote complaining to Suger of the 'intolerable hardships and infinite dangers' of this stage of the journey, was shocked to receive news that the Emperor Manuel had just concluded a twelve-year truce with the Turks. Many of his advisers feared treachery and urged the King to lay siege to Constantinople, but he refused to consider it, asserting that he had not come to make war on Christian princes but to liberate the Holy Land from the Turks.

On 3 October, a few days after Conrad and his army had left Byzantium for Asia Minor, the French crusaders approached the double walls of the fabled city of Constantinople, capital of the Byzantine Empire, centre of the Eastern Orthodox Church and guardian of much of the tradition and culture of the ancient Roman Empire. Louis was welcomed by dignitaries sent by Manuel, who, the following day, escorted the King and his advisers to the Boukoleon Palace on the Golden Horn. Here the Emperor, clad in purple and gold, was waiting to receive them and give them the kiss of peace.[5] Odo was overawed by the magnificence of the palace, which was 'throughout elaborately decorated with gold and a great variety of colours, with marble floors'.

Eleanor was not present, but a Greek chronicler, Niketas Choniates, writing about fifty years later, has left what was probably an eye-witness description of the women in the army as they arrived at Constantinople. He marvelled that:

> even women travelled in the ranks of the crusaders, boldly sitting astride in their saddles as men do, dressed as men and armed with lance and battle axe. They kept a martial mien, bold as Amazons. At the head of these was one in particular, richly-dressed, who, because of the gold embroidery on the hem of her dress, was nicknamed Chrysopus [Golden Foot]. The elegance of her bearing and the freedom of her movements recalled Penthesilea, the celebrated leader of the Amazons.

This was almost certainly Eleanor, who would not have been allowed to dress in men's clothes, and it may be that the so-called legends of her dressing up as an Amazon are really based on fact.

Manuel Comnenus was a highly intelligent man in his late twenties, who was renowned for his knowledge of medicine. He extended an outwardly warm welcome to the French, then had Louis and Eleanor escorted to their lodgings, which were either in the opulent Blachernae Palace, Manuel's second residence, which overlooked the Golden Horn, or more probably in the hastily refurbished Philopation, so recently pillaged by Conrad and his men. Here they were to reside during their twelve-day stay at Constantinople. At the insistence of the Emperor, the huge army was confined to its camp outside the city walls.

During the visit, the Emperor royally entertained Louis and his nobles. There was a solemn service in the domed basilica of St Sophia, followed by a sumptuous reception and banquet in the hall of the palace. At the banquet, the guests were served artichokes, stuffed kid, fried frogs, caviare and sauces flavoured with expensive spices, such as cinammon, pepper, coriander and sugar. The food was served in silver dishes, the wine in glasses, and forks (unknown in the West) were used to eat with. The floor was a bed of rose petals, and sweet music played throughout the meal; afterwards, the guests were entertained by dancers, jugglers and mime-artists.

There were hunting expeditions with tame leopards and a day spent watching the races at the Hippodrome. Constantinople, built like Rome on seven hills and surrounded on three sides by water, was a wondrous city, quite unlike anything the French had ever seen, with its spacious squares, fountains, wide streets and piped water system. Louis was escorted by Manuel to several shrines and shown the sacred relics, claimed by the Byzantines to be authentic, kept in the ancient palace of Constantine: the lance that had pierced Christ's side, the Crown of Thorns, part of the True Cross, a nail that had held Jesus to the Cross, and the stone from His tomb.

We know little of Eleanor's stay in Constantinople. Women in the Eastern Empire were generally kept secluded in the oriental manner, and there is no mention of the Queen accompanying her husband on his public forays. She seems to have been privately entertained by the Empress Irene, formerly Bertha of Sulzbach, a Bavarian noblewoman whose sister was married to the Emperor Conrad III, and who now lived a gilded but restricted existence waited on by slaves and eunuchs.

The common soldiers, confined to their camp, soon became restive and unmanageable, and Louis was forced to resort to stern measures to control them. 'The King frequently punished offenders by cutting off their ears, hands and feet, yet he could not check the folly of the whole group.'[6]

Manuel had his own hidden political agenda. His empire had suffered from the inroads of the Turks and he had spent years playing their leaders off one against the other in order to deflect them from further attempts at conquest. It was clear to him that the western princes had little understanding of Middle Eastern politics, and that their crusade, which had already provoked the warring Turkish factions to unite against the West, might further jeopardise the already crumbling Eastern Empire. Manuel was also at war with Sicily, and had no intention of involving himself in another conflict, especially when it might prove so damaging to himself. He therefore resolved to be rid of Louis and his army as soon as possible, in the hope that the crusaders and the Turks might destroy each other and so leave him in peace.

To Manuel's relief, the King was eager to press on to Jerusalem. On 16 October, rather than follow the overland route through the mountains, which Conrad had taken, Louis sent his army south across the Bosphorus and along the western coast of Asia Minor. He and Eleanor lingered in Constantinople for five days, awaiting the arrival of a supplementary force from Italy, headed by Louis' uncle, the Count of Maurienne and the Marquess of Montferrat. The royal couple then joined the main army at Chalcedon (Kadikoy) on the coast, where the King wasted five more days deliberating on whether he should press on to rendezvous with Conrad or wait for news of him. It was a fatal delay, for the army was rapidly consuming its food supplies, and those sent begrudgingly by Manuel were insufficient to replace them.

On 26 October, as an eclipse of the sun darkened the sky – a phenomenon interpreted by many as an evil omen – the King gave orders for the crusaders to resume their march south, although he himself returned to Constantinople. Here Manuel, dismayed to see him again and doubtless concerned that he would never get rid of this importunate guest, informed Louis he had received word that the Emperor Conrad had won a great victory at Anatolia (Anadolu), annihilating 14,000 Turks. Exhilarated by this news, Louis left the same day to rejoin his army at Nicaea (Izmit) on the Marmara Sea. Manuel had offered to send some guides, or dragomans, to take the crusaders through the inhospitable territory that lay inland, but they never materialised. He had, however, sent guides with Conrad, and some of them arrived in the French camp at Nicaea, bringing further news of the German victory.

At the end of October, the crusaders continued their march south along the coastal lowlands. A day or so later, they met up with several hundred men from Conrad's army, most of them starving, wounded or dying. They revealed that they were all that was left of the imperial army and that, far from gaining a victory over the Turks, they had suffered a devastating defeat, with more than nine-tenths of their number being slaughtered.[7] They warned that the Turks were now lying in wait for the French.

Louis was 'stupefied with grief',[8] not only at the loss of life but also at Manuel's perfidy, for it was now clear that he had abandoned the crusaders to the enemy for purely selfish reasons, and that his guides had deliberately led the Germans into danger. The King ordered the army to march on, in the hope of finding more survivors, and on 2 or 3 November he finally met up with Conrad, who had suffered a serious head wound, the sight of which made Louis burst into tears.[9]

The two leaders called their captains to a council of war and debated on the safest route to the Holy Land. They abandoned their original plan to travel through the mountains of Cappadocia in favour of two other options: either they could take the longer way around the coast, most of which was in Byzantine territory, or they could opt for the shorter and more dangerous route overland, through mountainous country infested by Turks. Their food supplies were dwindling, and it was felt that they would have a better chance of replenishing them along the coastal route, and be within reach of the ports.

Throughout November and December, the crusaders moved south via the ancient towns of Pergamus (Bergama), Smyrna (Izmir) and Ephesus (nowadays a ruin), which they reached in time for Christmas. Their journey took them through often inhospitable territory, riven with canyons and gorges, and they tried in vain to discover shortcuts to avoid these obstacles; Louis was lost for three days searching for one, and had to be guided back to camp by 'rustics'.[10] Inevitably, supplies were lost along the way, and some of the ladies' gear had to be traded for food, which was scarce. As morale sank lower, discipline slipped and it became obvious that Louis had lost interest in trying to control his unruly troops, some of whom had deserted. The Emperor Conrad was appalled at this, and 'found the arrogance of the Franks unendurable'.[11]

At Ephesus, where the crusaders set up camp on the banks of the River Maeander, it became clear that Conrad was too ill to go further, and he and his barons took a boat back to Constantinople, to take issue with Manuel. Manuel, however, ended up personally nursing Conrad back to health; by then most of the German crusaders had gone home. Meanwhile, on Christmas Eve, the Christians were victorious in their first skirmish with the Turks, cutting down many, driving the rest into the hills, and raiding their deserted camp for gold and food.

On Christmas Day and for the next four days there was torrential rain and sleet, and the river flooded its banks. Gale-force winds wrecked the crusaders' camp, many men and horses were drowned or battered to death on the rocks, and vital food stores and equipment were lost.[12]

Surveying the devastation, Louis decided that they had no choice but to press on to Antioch without delay, taking the most direct route over the Phrygian mountains to Laodicea and Attalia (Antalya). As they had no guides, they would have to rely on the sun and the stars for directions. It was no easy journey, for the weather was rough and Turkish raiding parties on fast ponies continually harassed the crusaders, shooting them with bows and arrows or cutting them down with deadly sabres. 'The road had become so rugged that sometimes the helmets of the knights touched the sky, while sometimes their horses' hooves trod the very floor of hell.'[13] For safety, and protection against the weather, Eleanor and her ladies now travelled in horse-drawn litters with closed leather curtains. At night, they were among the few who were sheltered by the remaining tents, sleeping on painted beds.

In January 1148, as the crusaders were crossing table-land on Mount Cadmos in the mountains of Paphlagonia, Louis sent ahead Eleanor's vassal, Geoffrey de Rançon, with the Count of Maurienne, the Queen and her ladies and the vanguard of the army, to set up camp on the bare plateau before the next mountain pass. However, when he found the chosen terrain to be flat and windswept, Geoffrey, taking the advice of the Count and probably that of Eleanor, as his suzerain, ignored his sovereign's orders and pushed on through the rocky pass, beyond which he found a sheltered and well-irrigated valley, which he considered a much more suitable site for a camp.[14]

When the main army arrived at the appointed place, they found it deserted. Louis, bringing up the rear, did not arrive until later, his progress impeded by the sheer unwieldiness of his wife's excessive baggage, and was alarmed to discover that Eleanor and the vanguard were nowhere to be seen. He therefore sent his scouts ahead in the hope that they would catch up with de Rançon's party.[15]

The Turks, however, were lying in wait at the pass. Having allowed the unsuspecting vanguard to pass, they swooped on the main army and cut it to pieces; many men and horses, attempting to flee, plunged down a ravine to their deaths.[16] Geoffrey de Rançon, not being where he was supposed to be, was unaware of what was going on and therefore unable to help. Not only are the Turks said to have killed 7,000 crusaders, but they also ransacked the baggage train and made off with valuable supplies and most of the women's gear. Louis, whose horse was killed beneath him, barely escaped with his life. After his bodyguards had been slain, 'he nimbly and bravely scaled a rock' by grabbing hold of tree roots, and held off the Turks with his back to the mountain.[17] Soon, darkness fell on the terrible scene of carnage, and the enemy retreated.

Midnight approached, and Odo de Deuil, espying the distant fires of de Rançon's camp, rode towards it. As the evening had worn on, and the main body of the army failed to appear, Geoffrey and his party had grown anxious and sent a party of knights to make a search. They came upon the scene of slaughter and encountered some survivors, covered in blood and faint from exhaustion, wandering towards the pass. When they revealed what had happened, there was much weeping and wailing.

As dawn broke, Louis, also blood-smeared and half-dead with fatigue, arrived in de Rançon's camp, his borrowed horse guided by a monk. Despite his relief at being reunited with Eleanor, he was furious to find her and his vanguard in a vulnerable and exposed position below hills from which the enemy could swoop down at any time. Although he rejected suggestions that Geoffrey de Rançon be hanged for treason, he castigated him severely and, refusing to listen to his excuses, sent him back to Poitou in disgrace. Because it was Eleanor's vassal who had disobeyed orders, many people believed – perhaps with justification – that he had done so at her instigation, or at least with her approval, and there was so much bitter feeling against her that her fame was irrevocably tarnished.[18] There is no record, however, of Louis reproaching her for what had happened.

Fearing that the Turks were still lurking in the mountains, the King decided that the crusaders should make for the nearest port and complete their journey by sea. Guided by the Knights Templar, the tattered remnants of the army now descended to the port of Attalia, harassed by the Turks and so short of food that they were obliged to kill and eat their horses, a practice normally forbidden to Christians. Nevertheless, 'even the wealthy were satisfied with this food'.[19]

On 20 January, they reached Attalia, where they would stay for five weeks while their leaders tried to find ships to transport them to Antioch, one of the four crusader states established after the First Crusade. Most of those in the army were in a sorry state, starved and dirty. The ladies had lost most of their clothes, and some bishops went barefoot, having lost their shoes. Many horses had perished and a great deal of equipment was lost. But there was little relief to be found in the town, for the surrounding countryside, which was normally well cultivated, had suffered from Turkish aggression, and its people were short of food themselves. Such food as they had was shipped in, and they would only sell it to the crusaders at a very high price.

Louis was told that the local Greeks were prepared to ferry the army to Antioch – a voyage that usually lasted three days – but only at a cost of four silver marks per passenger. The alternative was a forty-day march over hostile and difficult country, but Louis was reluctant to pay so much money. While he haggled, conditions in the crusaders' camp worsened, with wind and rain battering the tents, men and horses dying of starvation and many people falling sick.

The King insisted they must 'follow the route of our fathers, whose incomparable valour ensured them renown on Earth and glory in Heaven',[20] but when plague broke out in the camp and the crusaders began to die at an alarming rate, his chief vassals forced him to hire the ships, saying that those who wished to go with him would pay for themselves. There were many without the means to do so, and 7,000 unfortunate souls were left behind to starve or die of plague; more than 3,000, enticed by offers of food from the Turks, converted to the Moslem faith.[21]

On 19 March, after a stormy and perilous voyage lasting an incredible three weeks, Louis and Eleanor disembarked at the port of St Simeon in northern Antioch to the sound of a choir singing the Te Deum. Waiting on the quayside was a great concourse of cheering people, headed by a reception committee sent by the Prince of Antioch and led by its Patriarch, Aimery of Limoges, who gave the crusaders his blessing. Soon afterwards, Raymond himself appeared, having sailed with his courtiers ten miles down the Orontes River from the city of Antioch to meet his niece and her royal husband and escort them to his capital.[22]

Odo de Deuil informed Suger:

> The King has reached Antioch only at the end of immense danger. We now know that he can take care of himself and meet reverses with firmness and courage. He thinks only of the misfortunes of others and has done his utmost to relieve them. He is in good health and keeps up his religious observances. He has never gone against the enemy without receiving the Sacrament, and at his return he recites Vespers and Compline. God is the Alpha and Omega of his enterprise.

Although its official language was the *langue d'oc*, Antioch was a curious mix of eastern and western cultures, and had once been the third most important city in the Roman Empire. Built on terraces on the slopes of Mount Silpius, it boasted beautiful hanging gardens, pine groves and orchards, colonnaded villas, public baths, amphitheatres and streets paved with marble. Yet despite the huge encircling walls intersected by no fewer than 360 towers, Antioch's great prosperity and high standard of living were under threat from Nureddin of Aleppo.[23]

Now aged around thirty-six, the ruler of Antioch, Raymond of
Poitiers, was 'taller, better built and more handsome than any man of his
time; he surpassed all others as warrior and horseman'.[24] He loved
hunting and gambling and possessed extraordinary physical strength,
being able to halt his mighty destrier merely by clenching his thighs, or
bend an iron bar with his bare hands. Because of this his friends called
him Hercules. Although he could neither read nor write, Raymond was
an accomplished conversationalist who was familiar with the troubadour
culture of Aquitaine, and in some respects his court resembled that of
Poitiers. Whilst he was a popular, pragmatic and able ruler, he was also
impulsive, subject to sudden, terrifying outbursts of rage, and at times
rather lazy, although no one doubted his courage. Abstemious in his
habits, he was not given to gluttony, drunkenness or debauchery.[25]

Raymond had spent his youth at the court of Henry I of England,
where he had been knighted and treated by the King as a son. He had
arrived in Outremer around 1134, at the invitation of King Fulk of
Jerusalem, who, after King Bohemond II of Antioch was killed by the
Turks, had 'sustained the principality'[26] against the Moslem threat and
now wished to appoint an independent ruler. Bohemond's widow Alice
was acting as regent for his only daughter and heiress, nine-year-old
Constance, and Fulk hoped that the landless but nobly born Raymond
would prove a suitable husband for Constance. Alice, however, wanted
to rule Antioch herself, and pre-empted the King's plan by offering the
hand of Constance to the Emperor Manuel Comnenus. When
Raymond arrived in Antioch, having travelled disguised as a pedlar in
order to avoid the hostility of the predatory King of Sicily, he paid court
to Alice and asked her to marry him. Succumbing to his undoubted
charm, she accepted, but while she was making arrangements for their
wedding, he secretly married her daughter with the connivance of the
Patriarch. Thus, by devious means, did he establish himself as sovereign
prince of Antioch.

Raymond was relieved to see the arrival of the crusading army,
anticipating that its coming heralded the recovery of Edessa and the
removal of the Turkish threat to Antioch, and he extended a lavish
welcome to Eleanor and Louis, sparing no expense. He threw banquets
and tournaments in their honour, presented them with jewels, lucky
charms and relics, and had them served wine chilled with mountain
snow. They were lodged in his own palace on Mount Silpius, which
had such luxuries as glass windows and running water and was lit by
perfumed candles. There were also new silk gowns for Eleanor. The
Prince 'handled everything with the greatest magnificence'.[27]

Raymond also spent a noticeable amount of time alone with Eleanor, with whom he struck up an instant rapport. It was to be asserted, however, that their relationship quickly developed into something beyond that of uncle and niece. John of Salisbury, who in 1149 was a secretary in the papal curia and must have learned the details from Pope Eugenius (in whom Louis and Eleanor confided that year), states that 'the attentions paid by the Prince to the Queen and his constant, indeed almost continuous conversation with her aroused the King's suspicions'.[28]

William of Tyre, writing thirty years later, says that Raymond's ultimate ambition was to extend his territory, and to this end 'he counted greatly on the interest of the Queen with the Lord King'. In fact, like Manuel Comnenus, Raymond had a greater understanding of the politics of Outremer than Louis. He wanted the crusading army to first distract Nureddin by attacking Aleppo and then go on to recapture Edessa and reinforce the defences of Antioch against the Turks,[29] and it appears that he managed to convince Eleanor of the wisdom of this. But Louis, suspecting that there was a degree of self interest in Raymond's schemes, made it clear that he was more interested in pressing on to Jerusalem than in recovering Edessa and assisting Antioch. This made Raymond exceedingly angry, and:

> his attitude changed. Frustrated in his ambitious designs, he began to hate the King's ways. He openly plotted against him and took means to do him injury. He resolved to deprive him of his wife, either by force or by secret intrigue. The Queen readily assented to this design, for she was a foolish woman. Her conduct before and after this time showed her to be far from circumspect. Contrary to her royal dignity, she disregarded her marriage vows and was unfaithful to her husband.[30]

Gervase of Canterbury stated that he thought it best to remain silent about matters best left unspoken. Giraldus Cambrensis gleefully reiterated the rumours concerning Eleanor's conduct in Antioch, while Richard of Devizes, writing around 1192, commented cryptically, 'Many know what I wish none of us knew. This very Queen was at Jerusalem in the time of her first husband – let none speak more thereof, though I know it well. Keep silent.' Odo de Deuil did remain silent on the matter, since neither he nor Louis would have wished the official account of the crusade to be sullied by the sordid tale of the Queen's disloyalty. Diplomatically, he ended his history with the King's departure from Attalia.

The Poitevin troubadour Cercamon, in a song thought to have been composed during the crusade, made what some historians believe to be an oblique reference to Eleanor: deploring the conduct of a woman who lies with more than one man, he says, 'Better for her never to have been born than to have committed the fault that will be talked about from here to Poitou.'[31] This would appear to refer to the rumours that were rampant at the time and for years afterwards – rumours that would hardly have been so widespread, or so durable, had they concerned any lesser woman than Eleanor.

Other, later writers would tell even wilder stories. Around 1260, the anonymous Minstrel of Rheims, in a highly fanciful account, claimed that Eleanor was 'a very evil woman' who carried on a love affair by letter with the future Turkish Emir Saladin, and tried to elope with him on a galley at Tyre, but that the King seized her at the jetty and forced her to return to the palace with him. 'You are not worth a rotten pear!' she is said to have screamed at him. The Minstrel omitted to say that Saladin was no more than thirteen at the time. This tale is typical of the legends circulating about Eleanor after her death, legends that doubtless originated in contemporary reports and rumours. Such was her reputation in the thirteenth century that most people would have believed anything said of her.

In the face of all the reliable contemporary evidence, it is puzzling to find that most of Eleanor's modern biographers do not accept that she had an adulterous affair with Raymond, when in fact the sources make it clear that she had tired of Louis and begun to seek emotional – and possibly sexual – satisfaction elsewhere. Although there was a social taboo against relationships between uncle and niece, which were regarded as incestuous, and Raymond was reputedly faithful to his wife and no womaniser, Louis seems, with some justification, to have feared that the Prince was exercising a subversive influence over Eleanor, both politically and personally. Indeed, the relationship between them provoked such an enduring scandal, and so upset the King, that it is entirely credible that there was a degree of sexual involvement. What is certain is that the possibility of an annulment had been on Eleanor's mind for some time.

Louis remained obdurate in his refusal to comply with Raymond's plans, and a very public row ensued; the King's barons supported him, much to Raymond's incomprehension and disgust, but Eleanor intervened and warned her husband that, if he did not attack Edessa first, she would stay in Antioch with her vassals. According to John of Salisbury, 'the Queen wished to remain behind, and the Prince made every effort to keep her, if the King would give his consent'. Both she and Louis knew that for her to remain in Antioch with her vassals would cripple the crusaders' chances of success in the Holy Land. However, the King, who was surprised, chagrined and very hurt,[32] would not let her dictate terms to him and threatened 'to tear her away'[33] from Antioch by force, as was his marital right. His reaction suggests he suspected that something more than political intrigue was going on between his wife and the Prince.

In retaliation, Eleanor dropped her bombshell. 'She mentioned their kinship, saying it was not lawful for them to remain together as man and wife, since they were related into the fourth and fifth degrees.'[34] She said 'she would not live as the wife of a man whom she had discovered was her cousin';[35] it was her belief that her failure to bear a son was due to God's displeasure. For the safety of both their souls, she wanted an annulment. She would then relinquish her crown, resume her title of Duchess of Aquitaine and remain for the time being in Antioch, under Raymond's protection.[36]

Louis was 'deeply moved', for he still loved Eleanor 'almost beyond reason',[37] and did not wish to lose either her or her lands. But seeing her so determined, 'he consented to divorce her if his counsellors and the French nobility would allow it'.[38]

In grief, Louis confided in Thierry Galan. Eleanor 'had always hated him', probably because 'he had the King's ear';[39] there had been no love lost between them since she had publicly ridiculed him for the loss of his manhood. Thierry now took his revenge and:

> boldly persuaded the King not to suffer her to dally longer at Antioch, because guilt under kinship's guise could lie concealed, and because it would be a lasting shame to the kingdom of the Franks if, in addition to all the other disasters, it was reported that the King had been deserted by his wife, or robbed of her. So he argued, either because he hated the Queen or because he really believed it, moved perchance by widespread rumour.

Louis reluctantly agreed and gave orders that Eleanor be 'torn away and forced to leave for Jerusalem with him'.[40]

The French were no longer welcome anyway in Antioch and made secret preparations for their departure. At midnight on 28 March, Eleanor was rudely awakened and summarily arrested by soldiers, who bundled her unceremoniously into a waiting litter and stole away with her through St Paul's Gate, giving her no chance to bid farewell to Raymond. Outside Antioch, the King and his army were waiting, ready to march south to Tripoli and Jerusalem. 'His departure was ignominious,' wrote William of Tyre, and there was no concealing the fact that the Queen was in disgrace.

Louis' actions caused a bitter rift between the royal couple. 'Their mutual anger growing greater, the wound remained, hide it as best they might'.[41] In despair, a distracted Louis wrote to Suger,[42] telling him how Eleanor had behaved and asking if his marriage was indeed consanguinous. Suger, who believed that an annulment of the royal marriage would have disastrous consequences for France, and who felt that the crusade should be Louis' priority at present, replied: 'Concerning the Queen your wife, conceal your rancour of spirit, if there is any, until such time as you both shall have returned to your own estates, when this grievance and other matters may be attended to.'

Louis heeded Suger's advice, but also saw to it that Eleanor maintained a low public profile in the Holy Land. Although it pained him to do so, he kept his distance from her, and it became clear to all his advisers that her much-resented influence over him was at an end.

In May 1148, the crusaders had their first glimpse of the Roman walls of Jerusalem in the distance.[43] They were ecstatic with joy, falling on their knees in prayer, with tears running down their faces. No one could sleep, and the whole army kept vigil that night. Many, including Louis, fasted. The next day they proceeded across a narrow ridge known as the Pilgrims' Ladder, and so came to the Jaffa Gate of the Holy City.

Here, Louis was received as a hero, being welcomed 'as an angel of the Lord' by the entire population, who had been led to the gate by Queen Melisende, with her son, young King Baldwin III, Foulques, Patriarch of Jerusalem, the Emperor Conrad (now recovered and recently arrived from Constantinople) and a delegation of the Knights Templar. There was music and cheering, and many people carried banners or olive branches. The King, however, would not acknowledge the acclaim until he had accomplished his pilgrimage, and was taken in procession through festively bedecked streets to the Church of the Holy Sepulchre in order to fulfil his pilgrim's vow and be purged of all his sins. Profoundly moved to find himself on the site of the rock of Calvary and the tomb of Jesus, he reverently laid the Oriflamme of France on the altar and received the long-awaited absolution. He and his lords were then taken to other shrines and holy places in Jerusalem, before being conducted to their lodgings in the Tower of David. Only then did the King feel free to break his fast and turn his attention to more practical matters.[44]

The chroniclers are silent regarding Eleanor's whereabouts on this joyful day. Had she been at Louis' side she would no doubt have warranted a mention, so it seems likely that she was still in disgrace.

On 24 June, a conference was held at Acre (Akko), a seaport to the north of Jerusalem. Here, the crusader leaders met: King Louis, the Emperor Conrad, Queen Melisende and the barons of Jerusalem, France and Germany.[45] Eleanor was not present. Opinion was divided as to what to do next. Raymond of Antioch had made it clear that he would do nothing further to support the crusade, whilst Raymond, Count of Tripoli, was under suspicion of causing the death by poison of Alfonso Jordan, Count of Toulouse, and boycotted the conference in self-righteous indignation. Joscelin, Count of Edessa, dared not leave his domains for fear of Turkish incursions.

It was becoming alarmingly plain to Louis that few people in Jerusalem shared his pious objectives. Many were purely concerned with material gain, whilst others resented foreign interference. The King could not begin to understand the extent of corruption and intrigue within the kingdom, and he was woefully ignorant of local politics.

'Wishing to restore his reputation',[46] he favoured the suggestion of an assault on the Turkish emirate of Damascus, a strategic enterprise supported by the Emperor Conrad and the Knights Templar, but the ensuing siege was a fatal mistake, since Damascus had hitherto been a friendly neighbour. On 28 July, after an assault lasting only only four days, the attempt ended in humiliating failure as the Emir sent a plea to Nureddin for aid and the Christians were forced to retreat with considerable loss of life.[47] There was talk amongst the crusaders that either the Emir of Damascus or the Prince of Antioch had bribed the treacherous lords of Jerusalem to go away,[48] but, whatever the truth of this, the defeat signalled the end of the crusade. The French had made themselves a laughing stock in the eyes of the Moslem world and their reputation lay in the dust. Money and resources were running out, morale was low and Louis, who had been dogged by disaster throughout, seems to have lost his enthusiasm for the military aspects of the venture, as had the other leaders.

Contemporaries were appalled by the failure of the crusade. Henry of Huntingdon gave voice to public opinion by attributing it to the displeasure of the Almighty, 'for [the crusaders] abandoned themselves to open fornication and to adulteries hateful to God, and to robbery and every sort of wickedness'.

As autumn approached, the French army began to disintegrate, as men 'impelled by want'[49] demanded to go home or deserted. Louis gave orders that those remaining be given money for their passage, but he himself made no move to leave, despite receiving several urgent pleas from Abbot Suger, begging him to return to France. His realm needed him; there was great sadness and anger at the failure of the crusade. Louis ignored these pleas: he wanted to celebrate Easter in the Holy City before departing.

The King arranged for his brother, the Count of Dreux, to escort his barons and prelates back to France. Then, on 8 September, the Emperor left by ship for Constantinople, whence he would travel to Germany.

At Christmas, Louis and Eleanor were still in Jerusalem and still estranged. Louis, feeling the situation was hopeless, had again written to Suger, declaring that he would have his marriage dissolved when he returned to France. Alarmed, Suger wrote reminding him of what he stood to lose – 'the great Provence dower' – and warned Louis that, should Eleanor remarry and have sons, Princess Marie would be deprived of her inheritance. Louis saw the sense of this and occupied his mind by making plans for another crusade, which never came to fruition.

We know nothing of Eleanor's activities during the eleven months she spent in Jerusalem: the contemporary chroniclers do not mention her, and stories of her deeds and pilgrimages there belong to later romances; one legend claims that she brought back from the Holy Land the *gallica* rose, a distant forebear of the red damask rose, later used to represent the royal House of Lancaster. Another credits her with introducing silkworms from the Orient into Aquitaine, and the mulberry trees whose leaves they ate. There may be a modicum of truth in these tales, for her experiences of life in the Holy Land must have had tremendous significance for her and left their mark in many ways, even though she had no obvious public role to play.

After celebrating the Easter of 1149 in Jerusalem, the King and Queen, attended by a retinue reduced to 300 persons, sailed from Acre in two Sicilian vessels bound for Calabria in southern Italy. Louis, Odo de Deuil and Thierry Galan were in one ship, Eleanor and her ladies in the other.

Unfortunately, Sicily and Byzantium were at war. After passing Cyprus, Rhodes and the Aegean Isles without incident, the two ships skirted the Peloponnese coast, where, perhaps near Cape Maléa, they were suddenly confronted by Byzantine ships intent on hostile action. The King gave orders that the fleur-de-lys banner of France be hoisted up the mast of his ship, but this did not impress the enemy, who had been ordered by the Emperor Manuel to kidnap Louis and Eleanor and return them as hostages to Constantinople. Eleanor's ship was actually captured and turned towards Greece, but fortuitously a fleet of Sicilian galleys was in the area and came to the rescue, driving off the Greeks and enabling Louis and Eleanor to continue their voyage towards Italy.[50]

Their troubles were by no means over. A violent storm separated the ships, and the one bearing the Queen was blown off-course. Eleanor's whereabouts before it was brought finally to harbour at Palermo in Sicily are still a mystery. For two months there was no word of her as she made a 'circuit of land and sea', possibly even seeking refuge on the African shores of the Mediterranean.

Louis, who had also been feared lost at sea, arrived in Calabria, possibly at Brindisi, on 29 July. Soon afterwards he informed Suger that he had no idea whether or not Eleanor was still alive. He was shortly relieved to learn from messengers sent by Roger, the Norman King of Sicily, that the Queen's ship had been driven by adverse winds towards 'the coast of Barbary' (North Africa), but 'by the mercy of God' had been intercepted by his own navy and had lately arrived at Palermo.

When Eleanor disembarked, she was very ill indeed, possibly due to exhaustion, and had to rest awhile, cared for by attendants sent by King Roger. Louis told Suger he anxiously 'awaited the arrival of the Queen for almost three weeks', and, relieved when Eleanor was at last strong enough to join him in Calabria, was moved to reveal to the Abbot that she had 'hurried to us with all safety and joy'. Clearly, four months of separation had wrought some benefits. Although Louis informed Suger of 'the very serious illness of the Bishop of Langres', he did not refer to Eleanor's sickness, an omission that suggests she had apparently regained her usual good health.

The royal party then began to make its way back overland to France, travelling west to Potenza, where they were warmly received by Roger, whose court resembled that of an oriental potentate. Here, Eleanor received news that on 29 June Raymond of Antioch had been killed in an ill-advised skirmish with Nureddin,[51] who sent his head in a silver case as a trophy to the Caliph of Baghdad, who had it displayed over the city gate. The Queen gave money for perpetual masses to be said for the soul of her uncle.

Leaving Potenza, Louis and Eleanor set off northwards towards Rome, with an escort provided by King Roger. They did not get very far: Louis was soon writing to Suger that Eleanor had again fallen 'seriously ill'.[52] Whether her malady was physical or mental is not specified, nor do we know if it was precipitated by the news of Raymond's terrible fate or whether it was a recurrence of her earlier illness. She seems to have continued the journey in slow stages, making frequent stops. On 4 October, the royal party stayed at the hilltop abbey of Monte Cassino, founded by St Benedict in the sixth century. Here,

Eleanor rested for three days, while Louis received a civic deputation come to offer him the freedom of Rome.

Pope Eugenius, meanwhile, had been informed of the approach of the King and Queen, and invited them to stay with him in his palace at Tusculum (Frascati), south of Rome. Eleanor was now recovering and able to make the two-day journey.

They arrived on 9 October; Eugenius welcomed Louis 'with such tenderness and reverence that one would have said he was welcoming an angel of the Lord rather than a mortal man'.[53] This was heartening for the King, for he was painfully aware that most of the princes of Europe held him responsible for the ignominious end of the crusade.

During their visit, both Louis and Eleanor separately confided in the Pope about their marital problems, with which he had already been acquainted by Suger. Louis made it clear 'he loved the Queen passionately, in an almost childish way'.[54] Having heard Eleanor's doubts about the validity of the marriage, and learned that sexual relations between the couple had ceased,[55] the Pope adamantly refused to consider an annulment, but blessed the marriage and confirmed it, both in person and in writing, and 'commanded under pain of anathema that no word should be spoken against it and that it should not be dissolved under any pretext whatever'.[56]

The normally reserved Eugenius,[57] who belonged to the austere Cistercian Order, also took practical measures to bring about a reconciliation between the King and Queen. He delivered an ongoing homily on the duties of marriage and endeavoured 'by friendly converse to restore love between them'. He even 'made them sleep in the same bed', leading them to a sumptuous room draped with silken hangings from his own chamber and furnished with a double bed embellished with valuable ornaments, and ordering them to make good use of it. This was all very pleasing to Louis, who made demonstrations of love towards his wife 'in an almost puerile fashion',[58] while Eleanor submitted dutifully.

The next day, the royal couple prepared to leave for Rome with an escort of cardinals provided by Eugenius for his 'dear children. When they took their leave, the Pope, for all his sternness, could not restrain his tears. On their departure he blessed them and the kingdom of France'.[59] It shortly appeared that God had approved of his strategies, for Eleanor became pregnant again.

The King and Queen, having been presented with the keys of Rome, spent a whole day touring the city's shrines, as nuns and street urchins cried with one voice, 'Blessed is he that cometh in the name of the Lord!' The royal couple left Rome the next morning and, after taking their leave of the cardinals at the border of the papal domains, travelled north via Acquapendente and crossed the Jural Alpine Pass into France.

After riding through Burgundy, the King and Queen were welcomed at Auxerre by Abbot Suger, who had been summoned by Louis to give an account of his stewardship and the state of the realm. The King was aware that his brother, the Count of Dreux, had been plotting to usurp the throne, and was gratified to learn that Suger had deftly put paid to his treacherous schemes.

Around 11 November, Louis and Eleanor returned to Paris, after an absence of nearly two and a half years. It was the eve of the Feast of St Martin, and the citizens received them with demonstrations of joy. Two medals were struck to commemorate the crusade, one embossed with a relief of Louis standing victorious in a chariot.[60] Yet there was no mistaking the people's underlying disappointment and discontent at the humiliating failure of the enterprise. Devout Christians could not understand it. 'No one may question the acts of God, for all His works are just and right,' commented William of Tyre, 'but it remains a mystery to the feeble judgement of mankind why Our Lord should suffer the French, who of all the people in the world have the deepest faith and most honour Him, to be destroyed by the enemies of religion.'

During the months to come, as scapegoats were sought, the blame would be laid mainly at Louis' door. Nor was Eleanor considered entirely blameless: her rumoured responsibility for the disastrous episodes on Mount Cadmos and in Antioch would never be forgotten.

5

'A Righteous Annulment'

The winter of 1149–50 was bitterly cold;[1] rivers iced over and roads became impassable. Suger had undertaken repairs and improvements to the Cité Palace against the King's return, but the old building was freezing. Nor was the atmosphere between Louis and Eleanor much warmer, for after their return, when life resumed its normal routine, 'there arose discord between them concerning certain things which happened on the crusade, which are best passed over in silence.'[2] William of Newburgh states that the affection in the marriage was largely on Louis' side, and that Eleanor found his ascetic habits increasingly hard to live with. There were many quarrels; Eleanor 'was greatly offended with the King's conduct, even pleading that she had married a monk, not a king.'[3]

Abbot Suger, who along with everybody else was fervently hoping that the Queen would soon give birth to the long-awaited male heir, made it his business to bring about a reconciliation, and used his influence with Louis to this end. But there were others, Thierry Galan among them, who must have feared a resurgence of the Queen's influence as mother of the King's son, and who may well have tried to undermine Suger's conciliatory policy.

That winter Louis revisited Vitry, where he planted cypress trees brought specially from the Holy Land; their descendants may still be seen there today.

During the latter half of 1150[4] Eleanor gave birth to a second daughter, who was named Alix.[5] Her sex was a bitter disappointment to Louis, who was now approaching thirty and still had no heir to succeed him, a situation that had never yet occurred in the Capetian royal line. It now seemed to him that God did not, after all, approve of his marriage, and that both Bernard and Eleanor had been right to call its validity into question. This was the view of the barons of France, who now began to urge Louis to set aside the Queen and marry someone less controversial, who could give him sons. Not only was his present union consanguinous, but the Queen was still the subject of defamatory rumours.[6]

Suger, however, took a longer view and urged caution. Through Eleanor, Louis had acquired vast domains which, should the couple have no son – and there was still time for that – would be the inheritance of their eldest daughter Marie. But if the royal couple's marriage was dissolved, Louis would lose Eleanor's inheritance, which would then pass to whoever else she married, and the chances were that she might choose someone hostile to French interests. Her duchy, on her death, would be inherited by her eldest son of her second marriage, and Marie would be deprived of her inheritance. Suger was committed to the eventual permanent absorption of Aquitaine into the French royal demesne, despite the administrative problems of maintaining royal authority over such a vast area, and he now tried harder than ever to revive the failing marriage and restore amicable relations between the King and Queen.

At this time Louis had other worries to preoccupy him. Around January 1150, Count Geoffrey of Anjou had ceded the duchy of Normandy to his son Henry. In Henry, young as he was, Louis perceived the greatest threat to his crown and the welfare of his realm. For Henry of Anjou planned to unite Normandy, Anjou and England into one vast domain, and for Louis that prospect was alarming in the extreme.

Bernard of Clairvaux distrusted Geoffrey of Anjou, and when he first saw Geoffrey's young son Henry, he knew a moment of terrible foreboding. 'From the Devil they came and to the Devil they will return,' he announced.[7] He was referring, of course, to the notorious legend of the diabolical ancestress of the House of Anjou, a tale often fondly repeated by its members: Henry II and Richard I were both apt to make disconcerting jokes about it.[8] One of the early counts – it is not clear whom – was said to have returned from a journey with a new wife, a beautiful woman called Melusine. She bore him four children and was satisfactory in every way except one: she could not be prevailed upon to remain in church for the sacrament of the mass. This troubled her husband, who secretly arranged for four knights to stand upon her cloak and prevent her from leaving the service. The knights did as they were bid but, just as the priest prepared to elevate the Host, Melusine tore away from them and flew shrieking out of a window, taking two of her children with her and leaving two behind. She was never seen again, and it was generally concluded that she had been the Devil's own daughter, who could not bear to look upon the Body of Christ. By the twelfth century, this tale was very well known, and it was generally believed that the Counts of Anjou were descended from Melusine. Similar legends had attached themselves to other noble families, notably the House of Lusignan, but this was the most famous.

The true history of the Angevin line was less fantastic, but just as remarkable. Anjou was a rich and fertile territory on the River Loire. Its capital was Angers. Around 1200, Ralph of Diceto wrote:

> The industry of the early Angevins caused this city to be sited in a commanding position. Its ancient walls are a glorious testament to its founders. The south-eastern quarter is dominated by a great house, which is indeed worthy to be called a palace. For, not long ago, vast chambers were constructed, laid out and adorned in a luxurious manner, entirely worthy of a king. Such is the extent of this great house that on the one side it looks out over the river [Maine] flowing past, and on the other towards the vine-clad hills.[9] It would be difficult to find another place so abounding in religious houses, endowed by the generosity of princes.

Tours, the capital of Touraine, which was also Angevin territory, was another fine city, where most main roads merged for the Loire crossing. This made the county of Anjou of great strategic importance in western Europe. To the west was the county of Brittany, to the north the duchy of Normandy, to the east the counties of Blois and Champagne and the kingdom of France, and to the south Poitou and Aquitaine.

Anjou was largely a wine-producing area, lying in a fertile valley and enjoying a warm southern climate fanned by cool breezes from the ocean; it was popularly known as the Garden of France, because of the many varieties of fruit and flora that grew there, including palm trees, camellias, oaks, cedars, broom and fig trees. Yet its inhabitants were perceived by their neighbours, particularly the hostile Normans, as savages who desecrated churches, murdered priests and had disgusting table manners. There had been little love lost between the Normans and Angevins since the time of the Norman Conquest of England in 1066, when the hitherto impoverished Normans had gained ascendancy in northern Europe by the acquisition of a whole kingdom, much to the chagrin of their neighbours.

The Counts of Anjou were usually little better than their people, being 'a ferocious and warlike race'.[10] Henry of Huntingdon, writing in 1154, observed, 'It is well-known that the Angevin race has flourished under high-spirited and warlike rulers, and that they have dominated the people surrounding them with terror. No one questions the fact that they wrought all the destruction within their power upon their neighbours, and subjugated the lands around.' The Angevin greed for land and power was notorious.

The Angevin counts were renowned for their hot temper, voracious energy, military genius, political acumen, engaging charm and robust constitution; the spectacular Angevin temper, characteristic violent behaviour and a tendency to go to extremes were all attributed to their demonaic ancestry. It was no surprise to their contemporaries that they were often at loggerheads with the Church, although many of them were notable for their generosity towards it. It was rare for a count of Anjou to be renowned for piety, as in the case of Fulk II the Good (d. 960/1), who was a saintly pacifist. Most counts were known for their cruelties, their irregular matrimonial affairs – Fulk IV Rechin (the Quarrelsome, d. 1109) married five times – and their debaucheries, as well as for their family feuds. Several were intelligent, cultivated and surprisingly literate men; Fulk the Good had told Louis IV of France that 'an unlettered king is a crowned ass'. Most of these qualities and failings would be evident in the Angevin men associated with Eleanor of Aquitaine.

The Angevins were a good-looking race. Many were of impressive stature, with a strong physique and red-gold hair, and most bore themselves like royalty, commanding considerable respect from their peers and vassals. They were in the main dynamic and capable rulers, and in time would provide England with a dynasty of remarkable kings, the Plantagenets, which would rule the land for 331 years.

Emerging in the ninth century from an obscure past that would later be embellished by fantastic legends,[11] the rulers of Anjou, who were originally castellans in the Loire valley, were first styled count in the tenth century. Thereafter they steadily increased in fortune, territory and power by virtue of brilliant diplomacy and a series of advantageous marriages with the heiresses of neighbouring domains, including Amboise, Vendôme and Maine. Other castles and lands were acquired by conquest, such as Chinon in 987, Saumur in 1026 and Touraine, to the south-east, in 1044. Many of the early castles built to defend this expanding territory – among them Montbazon, Langeais and Loches – remain standing today; they are some of the earliest stone castles to survive from the Middle Ages.

Fulk V, Count of Anjou from 1109, was by his first wife, Aremburga, heiress of Maine, the father of Count Geoffrey the Fair. Fulk 'led an honourable life, ruling his territory wisely'. He was 'an upright and vigorous man of orthodox faith [who] achieved a glorious and excellent reputation that was second to none'.[12] According to William of Tyre, Fulk was 'a ruddy man, faithful and gentle, affable and kind, a powerful prince, and very successful in ruling his own people; an experienced warrior full of patience and wisdom in military affairs'. In 1128, at the request of Baldwin II, King of Jerusalem, Louis VI of France chose Fulk as the most suitable husband for Baldwin's only daughter Melisende, who was heiress to the crusader kingdom of Jerusalem; the following year, Fulk resigned Anjou to his son Geoffrey and travelled to Outremer. In 1131, on the death of Baldwin II, Fulk became King of Jerusalem. After successfully defending his kingdom against the Turks, he died in 1143, leaving a young son, Baldwin III, for whom Melisende was to act as regent.

Before leaving for the East, Fulk had knighted his son Geoffrey, invested him with the county of Anjou and arranged a brilliant marriage for him with Matilda, only daughter and heiress of Henry I, King of England, and widow of the German Emperor Henry V. The marriage took place in the spring of 1128, when Matilda was twenty-six and Geoffrey not quite fifteen. It was not a success.

Born on 24 August 1113, Geoffrey was early on nicknamed 'le Bel' (the Fair); he grew up to be an exceptionally good-looking and graceful man, who embodied many early ideals of chivalry. 'Tall in stature, handsome and red-headed', he had many

> outstanding, praiseworthy qualities. As a soldier he attained the greatest glory, dedicating himself to the defence of the community and to the liberal arts. He strove to be loved and was honourable to his friends; he was more trustworthy than the rest. His words were always good-humoured and his principles admirable. This man was an energetic soldier and most shrewd in his upright dealings. He was meticulous in his justice and of strong character. He did not allow himself to be corrupted by excess or sloth, but spent his time riding about the country and performing illustrious feats. By such acts he endeared himself to all, and smote fear into the hearts of his enemies. He was unusually affable and jovial to all, especially soldiers.[13]

The charm, however, concealed a cold, shallow and selfish character.[14]

Geoffrey was nicknamed Plantagenet on account of the sprig of broom flower (Latin: *planta genista*) that he wore in his hat. Although the dynasty founded by his son is referred to as the Plantagenet dynasty – a term coined by Shakespeare – the name was not used again by

Geoffrey's descendants until Richard, Duke of York adopted it around 1460 in order to emphasise his claim to the throne.

Geoffrey also carried a shield emblazoned with golden lions, given to him by his future father-in-law, Henry I of England, on the occasion of Geoffrey's knighthood at the King's hands in c.1127. Henry I is thought to have used the symbol of a lion as his personal badge; during his reign the first lion ever seen in England was displayed in the royal menagerie at Woodstock, and this may have been the inspiration for the device. Certainly, Henry was known as the Lion of Justice, which may allude to his badge. Geoffrey's shield is evident in the enamelled picture of him on his tomb, and is the earliest known example of what was probably an hereditary blazon. It was almost certainly one of the devices on which the heraldic trio of leopards, later adopted by the Plantagenets and still used in the royal coat-of-arms today, was based.

Geoffrey's marriage was a stormy one, with no love on either side. According to her biographer, Arnulf of Lisieux,[15] Matilda was 'a woman who had nothing of the woman in her'. Henry of Huntingdon also speaks of her 'masculine firmness', which seemed out of place in an age when women were expected to be subordinate to men. A complex character, Matilda 'resembled her father in fortitude and her mother in sanctity',[16] but she had none of the gentleness of the latter, Matilda of Scotland, being 'always superior to feminine softness and with a spirit steeled and unbroken in adversity'.[17]

Born in 1102 and christened Adelaide (she took the name Matilda on her first marriage), she became Henry I's sole heir when her brothers were drowned in 1120 in the *White Ship* disaster. By then, Matilda had been married for six years to the Emperor Henry V, who was thirty years her senior. The marriage was childless and he died in 1125. In 1121, Henry I had taken a second wife, but she also failed to bear him any children and he was obliged, on three separate occasions, to make his barons recognise Matilda as his heir. This they did reluctantly, since there was no precedent for a woman ruler, either in England or Normandy.

The Empress was a handsome and learned woman but insufferably arrogant and haughty – William of Malmesbury calls her 'a virago' – and she despised her new young husband for being merely the son of a count and unworthy of her. Geoffrey, in turn, resented and disliked Matilda, and took his pleasure from mistresses. As we have seen, Eleanor of Aquitaine may have been one of them.

Although incompatible, Geoffrey and Matilda nevertheless realised that it was in their own interests for their marriage to survive, and produced three sons to continue their line: Henry, born on 5 March

1133 at Le Mans, capital of Maine; Geoffrey, born on 1 June 1134 at Rouen or Argentan in Normandy (he was created Count of Nantes in c. 1150); and William, born in the summer of 1136 at Argentan or Angers.

Matilda and Geoffrey were at least united in desiring the best education for their sons, but it was mainly Geoffrey who arranged it. He himself was 'exceedingly well educated',[18] a cultivated man who could converse in Latin and took an interest in art and literature; he was passionately interested in military history, 'possessed a thorough knowledge of antiquity',[19] and never went to war without a scholar riding by his side to advise him on strategies that had worked in the past. The Count was praised by his son's tutor, William of Conches, for the care he took in raising his children and providing them with a good education.[20] Even his bastards benefited from this: a daughter, Marie, became Abbess of Shaftesbury in Dorset, and may perhaps be identified with the mysterious Marie de France, famous for her lays (songs) and translations. Matilda was rarely around to supervise her sons' education; in 1139 she sailed to England, intent upon claiming the throne that was hers by right.

When Henry I of England died in 1135, his barons broke their sworn promise to ensure Matilda's smooth succession, and crowned her cousin Stephen of Blois, son of the Conqueror's daughter Adela, as King of England. Stephen, who proved a weak and ineffectual ruler, also inherited Normandy, but Geoffrey immediately claimed it in right of his wife and proceeded to take it by force, thus initiating a war that was to last for the best part of a decade.

Matilda was determined to wrest the other half of her inheritance from Stephen. Supported by her half-brother, Robert, Earl of Gloucester (one of Henry I's twenty or more bastards), she invaded England in 1139 and launched a civil war, but at first met with little success. In 1141, however, after steadily gaining support, she emerged victorious and was recognised by the Great Council at Winchester as Lady of England and Normandy. In triumph, she went to London, where she was well received, 'but she was swollen with insufferable pride by her success in war, and alienated the affections of nearly everyone. She was driven out of London'.[21] After that, it was easy for Stephen to regain the advantage, and by 1142, when she was obliged to escape from Oxford Castle in a blizzard, camouflaged in a white cloak, it was apparent that Matilda's cause was hopeless. Nevertheless, she was to continue the struggle for another six years.

In 1142, Geoffrey of Anjou sent his nine-year-old son, who would from now on be known as Henry FitzEmpress, to England, hoping that his presence would inspire Matilda's disillusioned supporters to rally once more to her banner. The ploy did not work, and after a year Henry was sent home.

England had now descended into anarchy as unscrupulous barons took advantage of the weakness of Stephen's rule, and his preoccupation with the war with Matilda, to devastate the land, building unlicensed castles and engaging in private feuds and wars. The Scots and Welsh rampaged unchecked and committed atrocities against English border-ers, while foreign mercenaries seized and tortured innocent civilians to extort booty from them. Famine only added to the people's miseries. As the years passed, the situation grew steadily worse, and men said that during Stephen's reign, 'Christ and His saints slept'.[22] Not for nothing was this period of English history called the Anarchy.

By 1144, when the capital city of Rouen fell, Geoffrey had conquered most of Normandy, and in January that year he was invested with the ducal crown in Rouen Castle. The following year, Geoffrey's overlord, Louis VII, acknowledged him as Duke of Normandy. Although Geoffrey made it clear he was not interested in ruling England, his conquest of Normandy was a dreadful blow to King Stephen and greatly helped the Angevin cause in England, for many English barons held land on both sides of the Channel and realised that it was in their interests to stay friendly with the man whose son might well be their future king. Many anticipated that, before long, Henry of Anjou would use Normandy as a bridgehead from which to invade England, and most were eager to see Normandy and England reunited. For this reason, the English barons were reluctant to accept Stephen's son Eustace, Count of Boulogne, as the heir to England.

In 1148, relinquishing her cause and her claim to England in favour of her son Henry, the Empress retired from the fray and settled in Rouen, where she devoted herself to spiritual matters and good works. Her experiences had belatedly taught her wisdom, shrewdness and humility, and in the years to come her opinions would be respected by many. Henry would often seek his mother's advice; indeed, she was the only woman able to influence him.

The following year, Henry, now sixteen and a force to be reckoned with, returned to England, determined to enforce his claim to the throne. At Carlisle, he was knighted by his great-uncle, King David I of Scotland, and then proceeded to rally men to his cause. Evading Stephen's efforts to defeat and capture him, he returned to the continent, where, on an unspecified date between November 1149 and March 1150, Count Geoffrey made him Duke of Normandy.

By this time, the lords of England were heartily sick of civil war and anarchy, and eager to reach some kind of settlement or compromise over the succession. They, and the oppressed English people, wanted a ruler who would govern firmly and wisely and maintain the peace, as Henry I had, and they now looked to Henry's grandson as their hope for the future.

Henry of Anjou was to play a role of paramount importance, not only in the life of Eleanor of Aquitaine, but also in the history of Europe. In appearance, he had a lion-like face and cropped red hair; 'his countenance was one upon which a man might gaze a thousand times, yet still feel drawn to return to gaze upon again'.[23] He was 'of middle height, reddish, freckled complexion, with a large round head, grey eyes which glowed fiercely and grew bloodshot in anger, a fiery countenance and a harsh, cracked voice'. His bull-like neck 'was somewhat thrust forward from his shoulders, his chest was broad and square, his arms strong and powerful. His frame was stocky with a pronounced tendency to corpulence, which he tempered by exercise'.[24] Throughout his life he was obsessed with keeping his weight down, through rigorous diets, fasting or punishing sporting activity. 'In agility of limb he was second to none, failing in no feat which anyone else could perform.'[25]

He cared little for ceremony or the trappings of rank and dressed carelessly, often in hunting gear; his clothes were nevertheless clean and made from fine fabrics. If they were torn, he would mend them himself with a needle and thread. His hands were rough and horny because he refused to wear gloves, except when hawking. He was not a pretentious man, and did 'nothing in a proud or overbearing fashion'.[26] He was 'liberal in public, frugal in private',[27] and abstemious in his consumption of food and drink. According to Walter Map, 'he does not take upon himself to think high thoughts; his tongue never swells with elated language; he does not magnify himself as more than man; but there is always in his speech that cleanness which is seen in his dress. He comes nearer to admitting himself to be despicable than to making himself a despiser'.

Henry was renowned for his formidable and forceful personality. He was self-assured, articulate, intelligent and, unusually for a twelfth-century ruler, literate: Giraldus Cambrensis claims he was 'remarkably polished in letters', although Walter Map may be nearer the truth when he says that Henry 'had skill of letters so far as was fitting or practically useful'. As a child, he had been taught by the brilliant academic, Peter of Saintes. During his first year in England he lived at Bristol under the rule of the renowned Master Matthew of Loudun,[28] a tutor chosen for him by his uncle, Earl Robert of Gloucester, whose circle included such scholars as Adelard of Bath (who dedicated his treatise on the astrolabe to young Henry) and Geoffrey of Monmouth; it may have been the latter's *History of the Kings of Britain* that inspired in Henry a lifelong fascination with the Arthurian legends. After returning from England, the boy completed his education at Angers and in Normandy under William of Conches, an eminent Norman grammarian who taught his pupil letters and manners and, around 1150, dedicated to Henry his *De honesto et utili*, a treatise on moral philosophy.

As an adult, Henry was able to hold his own in the company of scholars and was voracious in his desire for knowledge: 'anything he had once heard worthy of remembrance he could never obliterate from his mind. So he had at his fingers' end a ready knowledge of nearly the whole of history and a great store of practical wisdom';[29] he was particularly well informed on the history of his own family. He would often withdraw into his private chamber to indulge his pleasure in reading works of literature, and he also 'had a knowledge of all the languages from the French sea to the Jordan, but spoke only Latin and French'.[30] His memory was excellent, especially when it came to recalling names and faces.

Henry's character was complex and unpredictable. A wary man, he kept his own counsel, never revealed his motives, preferred to do things himself rather than delegate, and was firm and decisive: he had a will of iron and 'was never one to procrastinate'.[31] Once he had conceived a liking or loathing for someone, he was slow to change his views.[32] Hugh of Avalon, Bishop of Lincoln, thought Henry volatile, crafty and unfathomable. Only in his small circle of intimates did he relax his guard.

Both Walter Map and Giraldus Cambrensis speak of his courtesy: Map calls Henry 'a treasure house of politeness', while Giraldus says that he was 'second to none in politeness'. Map also states that Henry was infinitely patient and 'exceedingly good and lovable', and that, when he was in a good mood, no one compared with him for 'good temper and affability'. 'In stress of evil circumstances no one could be kinder; when fortune smiled again, no one more unbending.' In general, he was 'affable, sober, modest, pious, trustworthy and careful, generous and successful, and ready to honour the deserving; when oppressed by importunate complaints or provoked by abuse, he bore it all in silence'.[33]

However, 'he readily broke his word',[34] and would later be described by Thomas Becket as a Proteus in slipperiness. He could also be caustic and cynical, and 'answered roughly on every occasion',[35] often resorting to his favourite oath, 'By the eyes of God',[36] which was considered blasphemous in the extreme. He was eloquent in argument, had a sharp wit[37] and particularly enjoyed a joke at someone else's expense.

Henry's temper was truly spectacular, and needed little provocation. His normally benign expression would suddenly change dramatically as his face became empurpled with fury. When in a rage, he would often throw himself on the ground, roll yelling on the floor or grind his teeth on the rushes. On one occasion, he fell screaming with anger out of bed, gouged the stuffing out of his mattress, and crammed it into his mouth. When angry, he could be vindictive.

Henry was an able soldier and a competent general, but he did not love war for its own sake, and would avoid it if he could reach a settlement by diplomatic means. He was not, by nature, a cruel man, as his Norman predecessors had been; both Giraldus Cambrensis and Peter of Blois testify to the fact that he despised violence and hated war.

Although he 'loved quiet', Henry was a restless and impatient soul. He 'detested delay above all things',[38] could not bear to stay still for long, and remained continually active. 'Except when riding a horse or eating a meal, he never sits.'[39] Even at mealtimes, he often stood, consuming his food with no apparent pleasure, and finishing his dinner within five minutes. He transacted all business standing up, pacing back and forth on his muscular, bowed legs, or discussing matters of state whilst cleaning or repairing his hunting gear. His big, coarse hands were never idle, and he was forever fiddling with his bow, book, falcon, hunting spear, armour or clothing. Even at mass, which he attended daily, although scarcely for an hour, he fidgeted, glanced this way and that, plucked his neighbour's sleeve, whispered, scratched himself, doodled, scribbled orders, notes and messages, and even strode up and down impatiently.[40] When talking or listening to others, his eyes and hands were incessantly moving.

He was immensely hard-working and possessed of prodigious energy. He was never tired, and 'shunned regular hours like poison'.[41] He would invariably rise before cock-crow, then 'at crack of dawn he was off on horseback, traversing wastelands, penetrating forests and climbing the mountain-tops, and so he passed his restless days. At evening, on his return home, he was rarely seen to sit down, either before or after supper. And despite such tremendous exertions, he would wear out the whole court by remaining on his feet'.[42] 'There are times when he rides four or five times the distance which most men cover in a day.'[43] It was not unusual for him to walk so far that his feet were sore and blistered. Even so, he would stay up until the small hours, talking and arguing with his friends. Sometimes he would attend to business throughout the night. He excelled at all athletics, and had an immoderate love of the chase: he would happily spend all the hours of daylight in the saddle, hunting at a killing pace; some chroniclers believed he did so to dissipate his sexual energy, but Henry himself insisted he was trying to lose weight. 'He was addicted to hunting beyond measure', delighting 'in birds of prey, especially when in flight, and in hounds pursuing wild beasts by their keen scent. Would he had given himself as much to his devotions as he did to the chase!'[44]

Henry chased women too, with the same kind of fervour. Throughout his life, his vigorous sexual appetite would draw comment and fuel gossip. An aggressively virile man, he had numerous casual encounters with women and several enduring affairs. Quite a few of these liaisons produced bastard children.

Walter Map attributes Henry's worst character traits to his mother's influence, but also makes it clear that he acquired much of his statecraft from her. She passed on her hard-won knowledge of how to deal with his vassals: 'Dangle the prize before their eyes, but be sure to withdraw it again before they taste it. Then you will keep them in eager and find them devoted when you need them.' He should avoid hangers-on and during his leisure seek the company of wise men and scholars.[45] 'Be free in bed, infrequent in business,' she told her son, a saying he was fond of repeating.[46] It is clear that he inherited both good and bad qualities from both parents. Fortunately, he had none of his mother's arrogance and poor judgement.

By 1150, Henry of Anjou's reputation was formidable. Given the aggressive independence and increasingly threatening power of the House of Anjou, it was hardly surprising that, when Henry pointedly failed to pay homage to his overlord King Louis for Normandy, Louis refused to confirm him as its duke. Instead, he allied himself that summer with King Stephen's son, Eustace – who was married to Louis' sister Constance – in an abortive attempt to wrest the duchy from the Angevins. Despite encroaching age and ill health, Suger intervened and arranged a truce, and Louis withdrew his army from the Norman border without ever having confronted Henry.

Suger's death on 13 January 1151 removed the last obstacle to an annulment of the marriage of Louis and Eleanor. Whilst his mentor lived, the King had a powerful advocate for retaining Aquitaine within his grasp, but with the man whom Louis now affectionately referred to as the father of the country gone, dissenting voices made themselves heard, and doubtless Eleanor's was prominent amongst them. When Bernard of Clairvaux again voiced his doubts about the legality of the marriage, and urged Louis to have it declared invalid, the King paid heed; he was, after all, very concerned about his lack of the heir who was essential to the survival of his dynasty. By the summer, it appears that he was beginning to reconcile himself to an annulment. All that remained was to sort out the administrative and legal processes by which the marriage would be dismantled.

First, however, there was the problem of Henry of Anjou to be solved. In August 1151, Louis advanced with a large army down the Seine, to where Geoffrey and Henry waited defiantly with their forces on the Norman border. A violent conflict seemed unavoidable, but Louis fell ill with a fever and hastened back to Paris, where he took to his bed, leaving Bernard of Clairvaux, now old and infirm, to mediate in the hope of securing a peace. Geoffrey and Henry were summoned to Paris, but when Geoffrey, blaspheming, refused to comply with Bernard's terms, the old Abbot predicted that he would be dead within a month.[47] Although outwardly nonchalant about this, Geoffrey, after a few days, astonished everyone by advising young Henry to offer the King the Norman part of the Vexin, a much disputed strip of land on the north-eastern Norman-French border,[48] in return for recognition as Duke.

Both Henry and Louis were agreeable to this, and a peace was concluded. Henry paid homage to Louis for Normandy, was formally invested with the duchy, and received the kiss of peace.[49]

While Henry was in Paris, he met Queen Eleanor, who at twenty-nine was eleven years his senior, although still very beautiful. The evidence suggests that they felt an immediate mutual attraction. Walter Map was of the opinion that it was in Paris that Henry first cast lustful eyes on Eleanor, and that she, in response, 'cast her unchaste eyes' at him. Giraldus Cambrensis, in his *De Principis Instructione*, states that Geoffrey, seeing this, 'frequently forewarned his son' about Eleanor, 'forbidding him in any wise to touch her, both because she was the wife of his lord and because he had known her himself'. According to Giraldus, Henry chose to ignore this: 'It is related that Henry presumed to sleep adulterously with the Queen of France, taking her from his own lord and marrying her himself. How could anything fortunate, I ask, emerge from these copulations?'

As for Eleanor, she seems to have decided very soon that she wanted Henry of Anjou to be her second husband, although she kept this a secret from Louis. According to William of Newburgh, 'It is said that while she was still married to the King of the Franks, she had aspired to marriage with the Norman duke, whose manner of life suited better with her own, and for this reason she desired and procured a divorce'.

Walter Map supports this, claiming that it was Eleanor who 'contrived a righteous annulment and married him'.

The prospect of a marriage between Eleanor and Henry made sound political sense for both. Once free of Louis, Eleanor – as the greatest heiress in the known world – would become the prey of land-hungry lords; not only would she need a powerful protector, but she also wished to marry a man with whom she was compatible, as William of Newburgh makes clear. Henry, she knew, had the strength, vigour and expertise to govern her unruly vassals, whilst she would bring to the marriage her vast inheritance to add to Henry's already considerable domains, along with men, money and resources to support his claim to England. The acquisition of such a bride would make him the greatest prince in Europe and leave his rival Louis politically and geographically isolated.

It is possible, indeed likely, that before Henry left Paris, he and Eleanor had reached a secret understanding that they would marry as soon as her marriage to Louis was dissolved. It has also been suggested by several modern historians that Geoffrey knew of this understanding and that it was the reason for his otherwise inexplicable change of heart towards Louis.

Early in September, Geoffrey and his son travelled homewards to Anjou along the Loire. Henry was planning a final assault on England, and had summoned his Norman barons to a consultation at Angers on 14 September. On 4 September, since the weather was exceptionally hot, Geoffrey cooled down by swimming in a small tributary of the river at Château du Loir. That night, lodged perhaps at the nearby castle of Le Lude, he developed a raging fever, and over the next two days it became clear that Bernard's chilling prophecy was about to come true, for no physician could do anything for him.[50]

As Geoffrey lay *in extremis*, 'he forbade Henry his heir to introduce the customs of Normandy or England into his own county',[51] and gave instructions that his body was not to be buried until Henry had sworn that, if and when he became King of England, he would hand over Anjou and Maine to his younger brother Geoffrey. Henry, however, refused to swear away an inheritance that was his by right of birth, and so, after Geoffrey 'paid the debt to nature'[52] on 7 September, his body lay unburied. Pressured by his companions, who warned him it would be a disgrace if he permitted his father's corpse to lie rotting and be denied a Christian burial, Henry capitulated and, weeping with frustration, made a solemn vow that he had no intention of keeping. He then proceeded at once to Anjou, where he made arrangements for his father to be laid to rest with great ceremony in the abbey of Saint-Julien in Le Mans (now the cathedral); later, Bishop William of Le Mans would build 'a most noble tomb' adorned by 'a venerable likeness of the Count', fashioned of enamel and 'suitably ornamented with gold and precious stones'.[53]

After Geoffrey's burial, Henry took firm possession of Anjou and Maine, and then set about securing the allegiance of his vassals. For the moment, England would have to wait.

Not suspecting what Eleanor had in mind, Louis finally capitulated in the face of her renewed pleas for an annulment, and agreed to initiate proceedings.

Towards the end of September 1151, the King and Queen commenced what would be their final tour together of Aquitaine, taking with them two large retinues; Eleanor's comprised her own lords, relations and prelates, among them the Counts of Châtellerault and Angoulême, Geoffrey de Rançon, the Bishops of Poitiers and Saintes, and the Archbishop of Bordeaux, who had kept a watchful eye on the affairs of Aquitaine during the absence of the Duchess. The purpose of the tour was to oversee the smooth and peaceful transference of the administration of Eleanor's domains from royal officials to her own liegemen, and to arrange for the withdrawal by Christmas of all the French garrisons, and the dismantling of alien fortifications.[54]

At Christmas, the King and Queen held court together at Limoges, and in January 1152 progressed south to Bordeaux, where they took steps to quell minor local disturbances. On 2 February, they and the Archbishop of Bordeaux presided over a plenary Candlemas court at the abbey of Saint-Jean d'Angély. In northern Poitou, at the end of February, the King and Queen took their leave of each other, Louis returning to Paris, while Eleanor probably retired to Poitiers.

On 11 March 1152, a synod of bishops summoned by Archbishop Hugh of Sens, Primate of France, assembled at the royal castle of Beaugency on the Loire, just south-west of Orléans, for the purpose of dissolving the marriage of the King and Queen of France. Archbishop Hugh presided, and both Louis and Eleanor were present, as were the Archbishops of Bordeaux and Rouen, their suffragans and many lords; Archbishop Samson of Rheims acted as cautioner for the Queen, who did not contest the action.

On 21 March, the Friday before Palm Sunday, with the approval of Pope Eugenius, solicited perhaps by Bernard of Clairvaux, the four archbishops granted an annulment on a plea of consanguinity within the fourth degree; Eleanor herself, in a charter to the Abbey of Fontevrault, later confirmed that she had separated 'for reasons of kinship from my lord, Louis'. However, before the end of the twelfth century, particularly in France, where Eleanor's reputation was ruined as a result of the annulment, rumour would assert that the King had repudiated her because of her adultery.[55] There is no contemporary evidence to support this assertion; indeed, the King himself brought witnesses to testify to the affinity between himself and Eleanor. Likewise, the romantic fabrications of the seventeenth-century historian Jean Bouchet, which depict Eleanor as fainting and distraught at being cast off by her husband, have no basis in fact.[56]

The terms of the settlement had obviously been agreed upon beforehand. Archbishop Samson received assurances from Louis that Eleanor's lands would be restored to her as she had possessed them prior to her marriage, and pronounced that both parties were free to remarry without hindrance, so long as Eleanor preserved her allegiance to Louis as her overlord. Because their marriage had been entered into in good faith, their daughters, the Princesses Marie and Alix, were declared legitimate, and custody of them was awarded to King Louis. Once these matters had been resolved, a decree of separation was granted.

When the proceedings were over, Louis and Eleanor took their leave of each other; Eleanor had probably said farewell to her daughters when she left Paris the previous September. It is unlikely that she was close to them. Royal mothers normally lived their lives at some distance from their children, and Eleanor had seemingly suffered no qualms at leaving Marie for two and a half years to go on crusade. She seems, at this time, to have been more preoccupied with her own immediate future than with the children she was leaving behind in France.

The King now returned north, having willingly renounced more than half his domains, an act of folly that would lead to a disastrous disturbance of the balance of power in France, and to more than 300 years of conflict with England. As the Minstrel of Rheims was to comment, a century later, 'Far better had it served him to have immured the Queen' for adultery, for 'then had her vast lands remained to him during his lifetime.' But that would have precluded either of them remarrying, and for Louis, the need for a son far outweighed the desirability of retaining Eleanor's inheritance, which had proved virtually impossible to govern and administer properly with the limited resources at his disposal. A last resort would have been for him to have Eleanor condemned to death for adultery – then a capital crime on the part of a queen – and sequester her lands, but that would have resulted in a fearful reaction on the part of her outraged vassals, with whom she was very popular, and it is almost certain that the King would have been personally reluctant to take such a drastic and cruel measure. He also had his own reputation to consider.

Eleanor, meanwhile, with an escort of her vassals, had taken the road to Poitiers, her capital, a free woman. She would never meet Louis again.

6

'A Happy Issue'

It soon became very clear to Eleanor that, while she remained single, she would be at the mercy of fortune-hunters. Twice, as she was making her way to Poitiers, would-be suitors, with covetous eyes on her vast inheritance, attempted to abduct her. At Blois, the future Count Theobald V was plotting to seize her on the night of 21 March 1152; forewarned in time, and protected by her escort, she was forced to flee under cover of darkness, taking a barge along the Loire towards Tours. Further south, at Port des Piles, near the River Creuse, where she intended to make a crossing, Geoffrey of Anjou, younger brother of Henry, lay in wait for her. Again, she received a warning from 'her good angel' – possibly a member of her escort – and narrowly evaded capture,[1] swinging south to where she could ford the River Vienne and, avoiding the main roads, make a dash 'by another way' for Poitiers.[2]

Clearly, her marriage to Henry of Anjou had to be arranged without delay, or it might never take place at all. As soon as she arrived in her capital, in time for Easter, Eleanor sent envoys to Henry, asking him to come at once and marry her;[3] this was not necessarily a proposal, as some writers have inferred, for it is possible that the couple had already agreed to marry. Then Eleanor informed her chief vassals of the annulment and summoned them to renew their allegiance to her as Duchess of Aquitaine and, no doubt, to approve her choice of husband. Eleanor also underlined her autonomy by annulling all acts and decrees made by Louis in Aquitaine, and by issuing charters in her own name and renewing grants and privileges to religious houses within her domains. The surviving documents from this period testify to her industrious attention to the business of ruling, which suggests that she was enjoying her independence. In France, she had been relegated to a subordinate role, which must have been stifling for a woman of her intelligence, energy and ability. Now she was free and able to make her own choices, but, with remarriage on her agenda, she must have known that her brief autonomy would soon be curbed, even if Henry proved an indulgent husband.

In March, a delegation from England had visited Henry in Normandy and begged him to delay no longer, as his supporters were losing patience. On 6 April, Henry met his Norman barons at Lisieux. Although they discussed the planned invasion of England, the Duke's priority was now marriage with Eleanor, and he took counsel of his vassals, seeking their approval of the match. Having obtained this, he set his affairs in order and left with a small escort for Poitiers, arriving in the middle of May.

On Whit Sunday, 18 May, Henry and Eleanor were married quietly in the eleventh-century cathedral of Saint-Pierre at Poitiers 'without the pomp and ceremony that befitted their rank'.[4] Although there existed between them the same degree of affinity as there had been between Eleanor and Louis, there is no record of a dispensation being sought.

By all the laws of protocol and courtesy, Henry and Eleanor should have sought King Louis' permission before marrying; they were after all his two greatest vassals, and Eleanor, being without a male protector, was legally his ward. But both of them knew that Louis would certainly forbid an alliance between them; he already feared Henry's power and regarded him as his foremost enemy, and the prospect of Aquitaine being annexed to Henry's already considerable European domains would horrify him. Therefore, although marrying without his consent was an act of the greatest provocation, not to mention discourtesy, Henry and Eleanor had decided to risk the consequences rather than abandon their alliance.

Not only had Eleanor failed to obtain Louis' consent to her marriage, but she had also allied herself with his arch-rival, a man who was as closely related to her as he was and who had been forbidden to marry her daughter on grounds of consanguinity. Eleanor must have known that she could have done nothing much worse than this to injure her former husband; indeed, there may have been an element of revenge in her defiance.

So as not to alert Louis to what was afoot, Henry and Eleanor had gone to great lengths to keep their marriage negotiations secret – they were so successful in this that no documentation survives and few of their contemporaries ever found out how their union had come about. Robert of Torigni, for one, was not sure whether Henry had entered into the marriage 'on impulse, or by premeditated design'. Yet although most people were taken by surprise, the evidence suggests that the couple had decided to marry the previous August.

Eleanor was now, at thirty, Duchess of Aquitaine and Normandy and Countess of Poitou and Anjou, whilst Henry had acquired by marriage almost half of what is now modern France – more than doubling his continental possessions and gaining handsomely in status, power, wealth and resources, as well as acquiring cities and castles of great strategic importance. He was now master of a vast tract of land stretching from the English Channel to the Pyrenees, a domain that was ten times as large as the royal demesne of France. Through marrying Eleanor, he had founded an Angevin empire and established himself, at the age of nineteen, as potentially the most powerful ruler in Europe.

Naturally, the acquisition of such an inheritance carried risks. Aquitaine was notoriously difficult to govern, outsiders being resented, and Henry might have expected to find that his newly won men and resources were being diverted from his cherished enterprise in England to resolve petty disputes between his turbulent southern vassals. This, however, presented the kind of challenge that Henry relished, and he was confident of his ability to do better than Louis had; moreover, he could not have left Eleanor free to marry anyone else, for that might have resulted in another enemy threatening his southern border.

A further risk was the chance that Eleanor might not bear him a son to succeed to his empire; in fifteen years of marriage to Louis, she had produced only two daughters. Yet this does not seem to have put Henry off. Eleanor must have confided to him that Louis had come infrequently to her bed and, as a true child of his age, he would have accepted her view that God had withheld a son because the marriage was invalid and therefore unsanctified.

Eleanor did not allow her marriage to disrupt her official duties, and was soon busy granting honours and privileges to favoured vassals, among them Saldebreuil of Sanzay, Constable of Aquitaine, whom she made her seneschal, and her uncle, Raoul de Faye. She also continued to make generous gifts to monasteries.

On 26 May, less than a week after her wedding, the Duchess visited Montierneuf Abbey, where, styling herself 'Eleanor, by the grace of God, Duchess of Aquitaine and Normandy, united with the Duke of Normandy, Henry of Anjou', she confirmed all the privileges granted by 'my great-grandfather, my grandfather and my father'. On the following day she was at the nearby abbey of Saint-Maixent, in response to a plea from Abbot Peter to restore a tract of woodland that had been granted by Louis but taken back by Eleanor immediately after her return to Poitiers. 'This gift which I at first made reluctantly, I have now renewed with a glad heart, now that I am joined in wedlock to Henry, Duke of Normandy and Count of Anjou,' she declared in the charter restoring the woodland to the abbey.[5]

Early in June 1152, Eleanor made a pilgrimage to Fontevrault, where she was received by the Abbess Isabella, Henry's aunt, to whom Eleanor would afterwards refer as 'my aunt'. The Duchess's affection and reverence for this place, which had held such significance for her family, comes across in the wording of the new charter she granted at this time to the abbey:

> After being joined to my very noble lord Henry, most noble Count of the Angevins, by the bond of matrimony, divine inspiration led me to want to visit the sacred congregation of the virgins of Fontevrault, and by the grace of God I have been able to realise this intention. Thus have I come to Fontevrault, guided by God. I have crossed the threshold where the sisters are gathered, and here, with heart-felt emotion, I have approved, conceded and affirmed all that my father and forebears have given to God and to the church of Fontevrault, and in particular this gift of 500 sous in the coinage of Poitou, made by myself and my lord Louis, King of France, in the days when he was my husband.

Attached to the charter was Eleanor's newly-made seal as Duchess of Aquitaine and Normandy, which survives in the Archives of France and, although in poor condition, bears a worn image of a slender woman in a long, fitted gown with tight sleeves, wearing a veil and cloak and holding in her outstretched hands a flower – thought to be a fleur-de-lys – and either a hawk or a bird perched upon a cross (then a symbol denoting sovereignty).

The buoyant tone of these charters suggests that Eleanor was happy in her new marriage. What was to become one of the most turbulent royal marriages in history seems to have begun well. Although little is known of the state of the marriage before 1173, much may be inferred from circumstantial evidence. Henry and Eleanor had a great deal in common: they were both strong, dynamic characters with forceful personalities and boundless energy. Both were intelligent, sharing cultural interests, and both had a strong sex-drive. Gervase of Canterbury, writing many decades later, implies that there was a strong mutual attraction, if not love, between Henry and Eleanor, and there was certainly a high degree of shared ambition and self-interest. Like many marriages of the period, it was a business arrangement between feudal magnates, with both partners committed to safeguarding their own interests, which they knew would of necessity entail long periods of separation. Such separations may well have helped the marriage to survive for as long as it did. When they were together, Henry and Eleanor presided together over their court, travelled together on progress through their domains and slept together regularly.

Naturally, Henry was the dominant partner, and he soon made it clear that he expected Eleanor to be submissive to his will and to confine her influence and ambition to the domestic sphere. While he allowed her a certain degree of autonomy with regard to her own lands – in so far as this served his own purposes – he kept a tight rein on her, rarely seeking her advice or allowing her to interfere in politics.

Nor did he remain faithful to her. Giraldus says that 'in domestic matters he was hard to deal with. He was an open adulterer.' Henry took his sexual pleasure wherever he found it, with whores, women he picked up on his travels and the 'court prostitutes' who regularly infiltrated his household. Eleanor, of course, was expected not only to turn a blind eye to these infidelities, but to remain faithful herself, so as not to jeopardise the succession. However, she now had no cause to complain of a lack of husbandly attention: the evidence shows that, for the first fifteen years of their marriage, Henry was a regular visitor to her bed.

William of Newburgh states that Henry did not commit adultery until Eleanor was past childbearing age, which became apparent around 1167–8, but this is unlikely, given the evidence of other chroniclers. It is possible that the amorous excesses referred to by the chroniclers were confined mainly to Henry's youth or his later years, but it is improbable. Well before 1167, he indulged in a passionate affair with Rohese, Countess of Lincoln and sister of Roger de Clare, Earl of Hertford, who was said to be the most beautiful woman in England. Another mistress was Avice de Stafford.

Henry's extra-marital encounters produced a number of known bastards and doubtless others who were never acknowledged. The most famous of these bastards, Geoffrey, was probably born before Henry's marriage to Eleanor, during one of his early sojourns in England. His mother was Ykenai, who was described by Walter Map as 'a base-born, common harlot who stooped to all uncleanness'.[6] After his accession to the English throne, Henry acknowledged Geoffrey as his own, against the advice of his counsellors and 'without reason and with too little discernment', according to Map, who obviously believed that the King had been hoodwinked into accepting another man's bastard. Henry, however, was devoted to Geoffrey, who reciprocated his affection, and always behaved as if Geoffrey were his true son, bringing him up initially in his own household with his children by Eleanor – whose views on this arrangement are not recorded – and then sending him to be educated in the schools at Northampton and Tours, with a view to him entering the Church. While still 'a mere boy', and certainly before 1170, Geoffrey took minor orders and was appointed Archdeacon of Lincoln.

Geoffrey had a brother called Peter, but he is nowhere referred to in the records as Henry's son and was probably sired by another of Ykenai's clients. Amongst Henry's other known bastards was William, later nicknamed 'Longsword', a name used in the tenth century by one of the dukes of Normandy. William's date of birth is unknown – he is not mentioned in the records until 1188 – as is the name of his mother. It is possible that she was also Ykenai, because in later life William asserted his right to inherit the estates of one Roger of Akeny. If Akeny is to be identified with Ykenai, then Henry's mistress was less common than Walter Map suggests, although he was probably referring to her trade and her morals rather than her lineage. It is also fair to say that, if Ykenai bore Henry two children, their affair was more than a casual encounter and may have been going on during the early years of Henry's marriage to Eleanor.

William Longsword became Earl of Salisbury by right of his marriage to Ela, heiress of William FitzPatrick, Earl of Salisbury, in 1198. He was a faithful servant of Henry and his successors, received many honours and offices and died in 1226. His tomb effigy may still be seen in Salisbury Cathedral.

Henry had another son, Morgan, by a noble Welshwoman called Nesta, the wife of Sir Ralph Bloet, a northern knight who had settled on the Welsh marches and who probably brought up Morgan in his own household; Morgan became Provost of Beverley Minster in 1201 and Bishop-Elect of Durham in 1213. The Pope refused to confirm his election unless Morgan declared that he was Ralph Bloet's son; legitimacy was, strictly speaking, a requirement for episcopal office, although sometimes a pope might be prevailed upon to issue a dispensation to waive it. This Pope, however, the zealous Innocent III, was inflexible on such issues, and when Morgan loyally declared it unthinkable that he should deny his father the King, the bishopric was withheld.

Matilda, Abbess of Barking in Essex, was reputedly a bastard daughter of Henry, and it has even been suggested, without the slightest shred of evidence, that Hugh of Avalon, Bishop of Lincoln, was his son, which has been inferred purely from the affection in which Henry held the future saint. Yet there were others, born later on in the reign, in the darkest of circumstances, who were almost certainly the King's bastard children, as we shall see.

In commemoration of their marriage, Henry and Eleanor commissioned a stained-glass window for Poitiers Cathedral, which may still be seen today and depicts them kneeling, donating the window to St Pierre. This is perhaps the earliest surviving representation of Eleanor. Several biographers have suggested that one or more pairs of the lifelike statues of the kings and queens of Judah on the west porch and façade of Chartres Cathedral, completed around 1150, may be likenesses of Eleanor and Louis, but there is no evidence for this, although it is true that the face of one Queen of Judah – although slimmer, younger and with plumper cheeks – resembles the face on Eleanor's tomb effigy. Certainly these figures wear the kind of queenly robes that she would have worn, and as she was Queen of France at the time they were sculpted, she may well have been the inspiration behind them.

As we have seen, there was a very limited concept of portraiture in the early Middle Ages, so none of the few surviving representations of Eleanor – except, perhaps, for her tomb effigy, which will be discussed later – can be described as a true likeness. They are purely images of a queen. For example, twin Romanesque corbel heads thought to be Henry and Eleanor, now in the Cloisters Collection in the Metropolitan Museum of Art in New York, but originally in the church of Notre-Dame-du-Bourg at Langon near Bordeaux, and probably carved around 1152 at the time of the couple's nuptial progress through Aquitaine, are identical with each other, and no attempt has been made to portray a true likeness. Similar representational heads may be seen in the church of Saint-André near Bordeaux, the church of Chaniers near Saintes, the church at Sharnford, Lincolnshire, and in Oakham Castle in Rutland, but those in the Cloisters Collection are the finest surviving examples.

According to Henry of Huntingdon, the marriage of Henry and Eleanor 'was the cause and promoter of great hatred and discord between the King of France and the Duke'. News of the wedding soon reached Louis, who was shocked and angered by it. Convening a council of his outraged barons, he complained that Henry had breached feudal law by having 'basely stolen' his wife;[7] it was now clear to him why Eleanor had been so eager to have their marriage annulled. Some lords urged Louis to revoke the terms of the annulment,[8] or even the annulment itself;[9] others even demanded that the guilty pair be excommunicated. But before Louis would consider that, he summoned Henry and Eleanor to his court to account for their treasonable conduct. When there was no response, he felt fully justified in going to war.

Others who believed that they had a legitimate grievance against Henry, among them Eustace of Boulogne and Geoffrey of Anjou, offered Louis their support. They were joined by Henry of Blois, who had recently succeeded his father as Count of Champagne; his betrothal to Marie of France had just been solemnised and he faced losing her inheritance if Eleanor bore Henry a son.[10] His brother Theobald, now Count of Blois, who had so recently tried to abduct and marry Eleanor, was now betrothed to her daughter Alix, Marie's little sister; he also hastened to ally himself to Louis.

Even the rumblings of armed conflict did not shake Henry's defiance. In June, Louis led an army into Normandy, determined to assert his authority and seize his rebellious vassal's lands, including those acquired by marriage, which would then be divided between the King and his allies.[11] Henry, who barely a month after their marriage had left Eleanor in Poitiers and was preparing to sail from Barfleur to England with an invasion force,[12] was forced once again to abandon his plans, and advanced upon Louis with such speed that several horses collapsed and died on the road.

Bypassing the royal army, which was beating a hasty retreat, Henry laid waste the Vexin and the domain of Robert of Dreux, Louis' brother. He then marched west to Touraine and effortlessly took two of the three castles that had been left to his brother Geoffrey by their father. Louis, meanwhile, suffering from a fever, had fallen back upon Geoffrey's remaining stronghold, Montsoreau on the Loire, which was the next castle to be besieged by his impudent young rival. When it fell, Geoffrey lost his nerve and begged his brother for forgiveness, while Louis, still laid low by sickness, gave up his cause as lost, agreed to the Church's demands for a long truce and returned to Paris.[13] The triumphant victor, who within six weeks had gained the advantage,[14] and who was not unaware of the significance of his success, which firmly established him as the dominant power in western Europe, blithely resumed his preparations for invading England.

Late in August, when Henry returned to Eleanor in Poitiers, they set out on a progress through her domains, visiting Poitou, the Limousin, Les Landes in Gascony, the salt flats of Saintonge and the Talmont. The purpose of the tour, which lasted four months, was to introduce the new Duke of Aquitaine to his vassals, but their reception of him was cool. Always fiercely independent and, in the opinion of many, ungovernable, they had resented French interference in the duchy, but Henry represented a far more potent threat to their autonomy than his predecessor had done. They were deeply suspicious of his aspiration to be king of England, and feared that he would milk the duchy dry to achieve this, then use the vast resources at his disposal as a sovereign ruler to force his will upon them. Some lords, although they were devoted and loyal to their Duchess, categorically informed her that they owed Henry no allegiance, save as her husband.

The Duke and Duchess were initially well received at Limoges, having pitched their tents outside the city walls, but at dinner on the first night, Eleanor's cook complained that the burghers of Limoges had failed to provide the royal kitchens with the customary supplies. Glowering at the sparse fare, Henry demanded to know why – to which the haughty Abbot of Saint-Martial explained disdainfully that supplies were delivered only when the Duchess lodged within the city walls. His insolence provoked an outburst of the already notorious Angevin temper: full of 'black bile',[15] Henry gave orders for the walls of Limoges, so recently rebuilt, to be razed to the ground. In future, he declared, no Abbot would be able to use them as an excuse to withhold from their Duke his just and reasonable dues.

After that, the sullen vassals of the south held their peace, and the progress proceeded without further incident. In Gascony, Henry was able to recruit men for his invasion force, gather some supplies and charter ships from the ports.

In December, Eleanor returned to Poitiers while Henry travelled to Normandy, where his invasion fleet was waiting to sail. Before embarking, he went to Rouen to visit his mother, the Empress Matilda, who lent him money to help finance his expedition. There is no record of Eleanor meeting Matilda during the first months of her marriage, nor might either have relished such a prospect: Matilda may well have been reluctant to receive the woman whom rumour accused of having had an adulterous affair with her own husband, while Eleanor may have resented the Empress's influence over her son and the fact that it was she whom he consulted on political matters, rather than his wife.

In January 1153, Henry sailed from Barfleur for England with a fleet of twenty-six ships[16] and an army of 3,000 foot and 140 horse, intending to bring King Stephen to submission. He left Normandy in the care of the Empress Matilda, and Anjou and Aquitaine in the custody of Eleanor, who shortly after his departure seems to have taken up residence at Angers,[17] leaving her maternal uncle, Raoul de Faye, as her deputy in Aquitaine. By the spring, Eleanor knew that she was pregnant.

It was perhaps at around this time that the celebrated troubadour Bernard de Ventadour presented himself at Eleanor's court. According to a biography of him written in the thirteenth century,[18] Bernard, who

was blessed with good looks and a fine singing voice, was the son of a
kitchen maid in the household of Eble II, Viscount of Ventadour in the
Limousin. The Viscount, who came from a family with a tradition of
patronising troubadours, realised that the boy had talent and tutored him
in the arts of poetry and composition. But when, on reaching maturity,
Bernard repaid his noble patron by attempting to seduce Alaiz, his wife,
he was thrown out of the household at Ventadour, while his hapless
paramour was locked up by her enraged husband and had her marriage
annulled.

The account continues:

> Bernard left and went to the Duchess of Normandy, who was
> young and of great worth, and she had understanding of matters of
> valour, honour and fine flattery, and liked songs in praise of her.
> Bernard's voice and songs pleased her greatly, and she received
> him as her guest with a warm welcome. He was at her court for a
> long time and fell in love with her, and she with him, and he
> composed many excellent songs for her. While he was with her,
> King Henry of England made her his wife and took her from
> Normandy to England.

There are obvious inaccuracies in this story: Eleanor was not Duchess of
Normandy until she married Henry, an event that took place before he
became King of England, but such errors are inevitable in a work
written a century after the events it describes. There is nevertheless
much evidence in Bernard's surviving verses, which are written in
Provençal and are very moving, that he was at Eleanor's court and was,
indeed, somewhat in love with her. His lyrics express this love and
eulogise the object of it in the conventional courtly manner. One reads:

> When the sweet breeze
> Blows hither from your dwelling
> Methinks I feel
> A breath of Paradise.

Elsewhere, addressing Eleanor as 'my comfort' or 'my magnet', Bernard
refers to her as 'noble and sweet . . . faithful and loyal . . . gracious,
lovely, the embodiment of charm', indeed, 'one meet to crown the state
of any king'. When she looked at him with eyes full of fire and
eloquence, he felt the joy normally associated with a festival such as
Christmas. 'You have been the first among all my joys and you shall be
the last, so long as there is life in me.' Of all women, Eleanor was the

most beautiful, and he would not have traded her charms for even the wealthy city of Pisa. Delighted that she was able to read, Bernard wrote poems intended for her eyes alone, in which he inserted secret messages that he hoped she would understand. Tristan, he declared, never suffered such woe for the fair Yseult as he, Bernard, suffered for his chosen lady. When he was in her presence, he trembled like an aspen, his wits fled and he had 'no more sense than a child, so overcome by love was I.' Everything he wrote, he wrote for Eleanor:

> I am not one to scorn
> The boon God granted me.
> She said, in accents clear,
> Before I did depart,
> 'Your songs they please me well.'
> I would each Christian soul
> Could know my rapture then.
> For all I write and sing
> Is meant for her delight.

How deeply these feelings went, and whether or not Eleanor reciprocated them, is not clear, although the indications are that Bernard's passion went unrequited. Looking back on the episode in later life, he wrote, 'I was like a man beyond hope, sighing in such a state of love, though I would come to realise that I had been a madman.'

The dating of this episode is problematical: Bernard may have joined Eleanor's household at any time during the period from March 1152 to early 1154; as we are told that he was at her court for a long time, it cannot have been much later.

As far as Eleanor was concerned, it was perfectly normal for troubadours to express passionate devotion to a high-born lady such as herself, and everything we know about her suggests that she enjoyed being the object of such reverence and probably expected and encouraged it. As Henry was away in England, these games of courtly love provided her with a welcome diversion. It did not occur to her that her husband might disapprove of them.

When, after a stormy crossing, Henry arrived on the south coast of England on 6 January, 'the earth quivered with sudden rumours like reeds shaken in the wind'.[19] When the Duke went into a church to hear mass, he heard the priest declare, 'Behold, the Lord the ruler cometh, and the kingdom is in His hand.' Interpreting this as a good omen, he pressed on in buoyant mood, deciding that his first objective must be to relieve his chief supporters, who were under siege at Wallingford Castle.

'God Himself appeared to fight for the Duke':[20] after months of skirmishing, during which he took many towns and castles, among them Malmesbury and Warwick, and earned an impressive reputation for bravery and military skill, Henry at last confronted Stephen's forces before Wallingford in July.[21] The war-weary English barons and bishops, prominent amongst them Archbishop Theobald of Canterbury, urged the two leaders to negotiate; many felt that Stephen should acknowledge Henry as his heir.[22]

The King's son, Eustace, however, was determined to assert his rights, and in an attempt to force a military confrontation, began laying waste East Anglia. His sudden death, probably from food-poisoning, on 17 August at Bury St Edmunds was regarded as divine vengeance for sacking the property of the abbey there.[23] On that very day, in far-off Poitiers, seemingly as a further token of God's approval of Henry's cause, Eleanor bore a son and heir, who was baptised William in the time-honoured tradition of the dukes of Aquitaine, and styled Count of Poitiers.[24]

The removal of Eustace from the political arena simplified matters. Although he had a younger son,[25] an exhausted and demoralised King Stephen lost the will to fight on, and the mediators seized this opportunity to bring about a peaceful settlement. In November, Stephen was persuaded to meet Henry at Winchester and thrash out terms. A peace was quickly agreed upon, with the King accepting that Henry had an hereditary right to the throne and acknowledging him as his heir. In turn, 'the Duke generously conceded that the King should hold the kingdom for the rest of his life', provided that he swore on oath that Henry should succeed 'peacefully and without denial' upon his death.[26]

This agreement was enshrined in a treaty drawn up by Archbishop Theobald and ratified at Westminster at Christmas 1153. By the terms of this treaty, which was witnessed by fourteen bishops and eleven earls, Stephen not only made Henry his heir, but adopted him as his son and agreed 'that in all the business of the kingdom I will act with the advice of the Duke'. Henry, in turn, would do homage to Stephen, their supporters would swear to make peace and the bishops would ensure that the terms of the treaty were adhered to.[27]

'So God granted a happy issue and peace shone forth,' wrote Henry of Huntingdon. 'What boundless joy! What a happy day!'

From Winchester, Stephen took Henry to London, 'where he was received with joy by enormous crowds and splendid processions. Thus, by God's mercy, peace dawned on the ruined realm of England, putting an end to its troubled night.'[28]

Henry had kept in regular touch with Eleanor during his sojourn in England, and also with his vassals on the continent. It was probably through them that he learned of Bernard de Ventadour's passionate addresses to his wife, and, being unfamiliar with the troubadour culture and its games of courtly love, was alarmed at what he heard. He may also have remembered that Eleanor had been free with her favours in the past, spurning her marriage vows, not only with his father but also with himself. Now that she was his wife and the mother of his heir, no breath of scandal must touch her, so Henry diplomatically summoned Bernard to England, claiming that he had need of him to compose martial tunes upon his lyre.

Reluctantly, Bernard complied. When he arrived it was still winter, and in his verses he says that, whenever he thought of the Duchess, his heart was so filled with joy that everything in Nature seemed altered: even the snow on the banks of the Thames seemed to bloom with 'red, white and yellow flowers'. Miserable in his exile, he begged leave to return to Eleanor's court, once more to mingle with 'ladies and chevaliers, fair and courteous'. At length, he did go back, apparently without first obtaining Henry's permission: when the Duke sent a further summons, he managed to ignore it.

In the spring of 1154, Henry 'returned triumphantly' to Rouen in Normandy, where 'he was duly received with joy and honour by his mother Matilda, his brothers, and all the people of Normandy, Anjou, Maine and Poitou'.[29] Soon, Eleanor joined him to celebrate Easter, bringing with her their eight-month-old son and heir, William. The family was lodged in the palace built by Henry I beside the church of Notre-Dame-des-Prés, just outside the city walls, which was now Matilda's chief residence. This was the first recorded occasion on which the Duchess met her formidable mother-in-law. Shortly afterwards, Henry made a brief visit to Eleanor's domains to suppress a minor rebellion; by the end of June, he was back in Rouen. Two months later, Eleanor was able to tell him that she was again pregnant.

During that year, Louis VII of France remarried. In the summer, he went to the shrine of St James at Compostela in Spain, ostensibly on a pilgrimage, but in reality to assess the suitability of Constance, daughter of Alfonso VII, King of Castile, as a future bride. Impressed by her modesty and demeanour, he arranged their betrothal with her father, then returned to Paris, travelling by way of Toulouse and Montpellier so as to avoid passing through Eleanor's domains. His marriage to Constance took place soon afterwards, at Orléans. His subjects were of the opinion that he was 'better married than he had been'. In consequence of his marriage, he relinquished the title Duke of Aquitaine and made overtures of friendship to Henry. At a meeting in August, the two were finally reconciled.

An illness in September laid Henry low, and there were fears that he might die, but by early October he was recovered and fit enough to lead a campaign against some rebellious Norman vassals in the Vexin. Eleanor remained with Matilda in Rouen, and it was she who, on 26 October, received a messenger with important news from Archbishop Theobald in England.

On 25 October, the 'nineteen long winters'[30] of Stephen's reign had come to an end with the King's death. News of his passing reached Henry early in November, just as he was besieging a rebel castle. Neither the news that he was to be a king,[31] nor a plea for him to 'come without delay and take possession of the kingdom'[32] deterred him from his purpose, and he calmly reduced the castle, took counsel of his mother the Empress, then set about putting his affairs in Normandy in order before joining Eleanor in a flurry of preparations for their departure for England. Amongst the items packed in Eleanor's baggage were forty-two gowns of silk, linen and wool, many richly embroidered, fourteen pairs of shoes, six of them embroidered with gold thread, five mantles of various colours furred with ermine, a great quantity of veils and ten warm undershirts.

Henry, meanwhile, took just two weeks to assemble an escort sufficiently imposing to impress his new subjects.[33] It included, amongst a host of magnates and bishops, his brother Geoffrey and Eleanor's widowed sister Petronilla. He also decided that the Empress should remain in Normandy to keep the peace whilst he was in England.

Henry now seized the opportunity of ridding himself of the irritating Bernard de Ventadour, who 'remained behind, full of grief and sorrow, then went to the good Count Raymond of Toulouse, with whom he remained until his death. Because of his grief, he entered the Order of Dalon, where he ended his days',[34] renowned as perhaps the greatest troubadour of all. In fact, far from being grief-stricken, he in the meantime found another patroness. In a poem probably written soon after Eleanor's departure for England, he claims that it was because of her that he was forced to leave the King's service; he also begs a messenger to go on his behalf and sing this song to 'the Queen of the Normans'.[35] There is no record of Eleanor having any further dealings with him, and a reference by Bernard to her 'fair disdain' indicates that she had lost interest in his courtly addresses.

Although Henry, Eleanor, young William (who was to travel with them) and their retinue were ready to leave in good time, heavy storms, gales and sleet delayed their departure, and it was 7 December before Henry was able to sail from Barfleur to take possession of his kingdom. Even then, they had to brave a tempest and the violent sea, but despite the risks and the fact that Eleanor was seven months pregnant, Henry would delay no longer. England had been without a king for six weeks; nevertheless, with Archbishop Theobald in charge, no one had dared to dispute the succession and the realm had remained at peace 'for love of the king to come'.[36] Such was Henry's reputation that 'no man dared do other than good, for he was held in great awe'.[37]

On 8 December, after a storm-tossed voyage lasting twenty-four hours, in which some of their vessels were scattered, the royal party landed safely in a harbour south of the New Forest[38] – probably Osterham near Southampton. They rode straight for Winchester so that Henry could take possession of the royal treasury[39] and receive the homage of the English barons, who, summoned by Archbishop Theobald, were 'quaking like a bed of reeds in the wind for fear and anxiety', thunderstruck at learning that their formidable new ruler had, with almost superhuman courage, defied the storms and gales to come to England.[40]

Then, with the royal entourage increasingly augmented by English lords and prelates, it was on to London, where the people received their new sovereign 'with transports of joy',[41] acclaiming him as 'Henry the Peacemaker'.[42] It was probably at this time that the English bestowed on him the nickname Curtmantle, on account of the short French cloak he wore.

Since the palace of Westminster was in a badly dilapidated state, having been vandalised by Stephen's supporters, the royal couple were lodged in the old Saxon palace at Bermondsey,[43] situated on the Surrey shore of the Thames opposite the Tower of London, just below London Bridge. Nearby stood the newly built abbey of Bermondsey.

On Sunday, 19 December, Henry and Eleanor were 'crowned and consecrated with becoming pomp and splendour'[44] in Westminster Abbey by Archbishop Theobald. The crown used was that commissioned by William the Conqueror in imitation of the imperial crown of Charlemagne, and the officiating clergy wore splendid vestments of silk, such as had never before been seen in England, while the royal couple and their barons were attired in robes of silk, brocade and gauze. It was a very moving occasion: Henry was 'blessed as king with great joy and many crying for happiness, and splendidly enthroned'.[45] Afterwards, as the new King and Queen rode in procession along the Strand, the citizens ran alongside to catch a glimpse of them, crying, '*Waes hael!*' and '*Vivat Rex!*'[46]

Thus Henry 'took possession of his hereditary kingdom to the acclaim of all, while throughout England the people shouted, "Long live the King!" So many evils had sprung up in the previous reign that the people hoped for better things from the new monarch, especially when they saw he possessed remarkable prudence, constancy and zeal for justice, and at the very outset already manifested the likeness of a great prince'.[47]

The long rule of the Plantagenets had begun.

7

'All the Business of the Kingdom'

The realm of which Eleanor of Aquitaine became Queen was, like most European kingdoms, a feudal society. The land was fertile and its people were growing ever more prosperous. In 1066, William the Conqueror had successfully prosecuted his claim to the throne of England and established an alien monarchy in the realm of the Anglo-Saxon people. He had also imposed the hierarchical feudal system of land tenure upon his kingdom, reformed its Church along sterner, more disciplined Norman lines, and laid an iron hand of justice on his new subjects with such success that, after his death in 1087, it was said that 'a man could travel unmolested throughout the country with his bosom full of gold'.[1]

Norman England was a rural society based on the village as an economic unit. From the few records that survive, it is estimated that the rising population numbered around two and a half million by 1200. Life expectancy was short, thanks to plague, famine and insanitary living conditions. Most people lived and worked on the land, and only a tiny proportion of the population lived in towns. The Norman kings distributed land to their earls, barons and bishops, who became tenants-in-chief owing fealty and military service to the sovereign. They in turn had their own tenants, barons and knights, who would preside as lords of the manor over the lower echelons of the social pyramid, the villeins and serfs. These last were bondmen, tied to the land that they worked for themselves and their lords, and unable to leave their manors without permission. All overlords had a duty to protect their vassals, and all subjects owed fealty to the King as well as to their immediate overlord, if they had one.

By the mid-twelfth century, the indigenous Saxon population had come reluctantly to accept the Norman yoke. Henry I had attempted to ease relations with the conquered people by marrying a princess of the deposed Saxon line in 1100, only to suffer the disparaging jeers of his barons for doing so. There was no mistaking the demarcation line that ran through English society: Norman magnates held most of the land, most Saxon earls having been ousted, Norman laws held sway, and Norman-French was to remain the language of the court, the upper ranks of the hierarchy and the law courts until the late fourteenth century. Latin was from 1066 the official language of government. Only the native population spoke what is now called Middle English, although there is some evidence that their masters made some attempt to learn it. Yet it was not until the fourteenth century that important works of literature would be written in the vernacular and English would emerge as the dominant tongue. The Norman conqueror had been nothing if not thorough.

During Eleanor's time, however, there were signs that the two races were beginning to intermingle. Where once English kings had addressed their subjects as 'French and English', by the thirteenth century they were referring to them as purely 'English'.

The King was the supreme power in feudal England, answerable only to God. There was no parliament, and government was essentially carried out personally by the King and his Great Council of lords, both spiritual and temporal, on whose loyalty he relied. The personality and abilities of a king were of crucial importance to the welfare of his kingdom.

It was taken for granted that the crown would pass from one member of the ruling family to another, but despite the efforts of Henry II, the law of primogeniture – succession of the first-born – was not properly established until the thirteenth century. Prior to that, the candidate nominated by his predecessor usually succeeded, his accession being confirmed by popular election (in theory at least), an essential part of the coronation rite.

A king was deemed to rule 'by the grace of God', whom he was legally deemed to represent on Earth. The ceremony of crowning, established in recognisably its present form in the reign of Edgar during the tenth century and based on the rituals used by the Pope to crown the Holy Roman Emperor Charlemagne in 800, conferred sanctity and a form of priesthood upon a king. Hitherto, he had been styled merely 'lord', but once crowned and anointed he was invested with divine authority to rule and could begin his reign proper. Until the time of Edward I (ruled 1272–1307), regnal years were always dated from the day of the King's coronation. It was to underline the sacred nature of their kingship that the early mediaeval sovereigns held ceremonial

crown-wearings at Easter, Whitsuntide and Christmas, at which the
Litany was recited and there was great feasting and solemnity.

The sanctity of monarchy was universally accepted throughout
Christendom. Kings from Henry I onwards laid hands on their
scrofulous subjects in the firm conviction that the royal touch could
effect a cure. Yet despite their semi-divinity, kings had obligations to
their subjects, which they were bound to honour by the terms of their
coronation oath: to keep the peace in Church and state, to forbid
violence and wrongdoing, and to show equity and mercy in all their
judgements. How they went about this was very much a matter of
personal interpretation, however. 'The prince is controlled by the
judgement of his mind alone,' commented John of Salisbury, one of the
finest scholars and political observers of the age.

John also believed that a king should be able to read and write, so that
he could read about the law of God and 'think about it every day'.
Furthermore, a king 'must not plead ignorance of the law of God by
reason of his military duties'.

The King was the fount of justice. Lords who administered their own
courts held their authority from him. William I and his successors had
adopted and in some cases revised the laws of the Saxon kings, and
Henry II insisted that his Constitutions of Clarendon (1164) merely
restated the laws and customs of his grandfather Henry I's time, which
was not strictly true. In an age that saw the codifying of canon and civil
law throughout Europe, Henry was responsible for several significant
changes in the common law and the administration of justice.

It was the King's business to appoint the chief officers of Church and
state, to determine foreign policy, to make war or peace, and to act as
supreme commander of his armies, which he would often lead in
person. To finance all this, he drew revenues from his crown lands,
collected his feudal dues and imposed taxes as he thought necessary. As
the fount of justice, he promulgated and maintained law and order and
presided, often in person and always in spirit, over the supreme court in
the land, the *curia regis* or King's Court.

By 1135, London was eclipsing Winchester as the metropolis and
chief city of the whole kingdom – it would be recognised as the capital
by the end of the century – yet England had, at this time, no central seat
of government. The royal court was itinerant, moving from castle to
castle, and most of the chief departments of state travelled with it.
During his reign, Henry II established these departments at Westminster, which became the centre of royal bureaucracy and justice.
Simultaneously, Westminster Abbey, built by Edward the Confessor in

1065, and the Palace of Westminster, dating from Saxon times, became the focus for royal ritual and ceremonial, as they still are today.

The chief minister of the early Angevin kings was the justiciar, who exercised judicial and political power and often acted as regent in the King's absence. The justiciar was head of the Court of the Exchequer, which controlled the royal finances. The Exchequer was responsible for collecting royal revenues, for adjudicating on cases connected with them, and for auditing the royal accounts. The royal treasure was stored in the Lower Exchequer, under strong guard, whilst in the Upper Exchequer officials would convene around the Board of the Exchequer, a table spread with a chequered cloth, its design incorporating an abacus that was used to check returns made by sheriffs. Sums received would be recorded by means of notches on wooden tally sticks, and transactions of the Exchequer were listed on long parchment scrolls stored in pipes – the Pipe Rolls.

The King's second minister was the chancellor, who headed the Chancery, the royal secretariat, which issued in the King's name writs concerning administrative and legal matters. Because the chancellor also served as the King's chaplain and head of the royal chapel, he was always in holy orders. The chancellor was not only the monarch's spiritual adviser, but also his personal assistant and keeper of the King's seal; royal seals had been used to authenticate documents from the time of Edward the Confessor (1042–66), since not every sovereign at this period could write his name. The chancellor attended meetings of the Exchequer and took charge of the administrative work of the royal household. The Chancery was also responsible for the issue of charters conferring privileges and land grants, Letters Patent making temporary grants, and Letters Close, which contained secret orders for royal officials. From 1199, the issue of these letters was recorded on long rolls known as Patent Rolls and Close Rolls.

The King ruled in consultation with his chief nobles, who formed the nucleus of what was in effect a military aristocracy, whose power was centred on the castles they built to subdue and dominate the land. Introduced after the Norman Conquest, castles were originally simple affairs consisting of a wooden tower known as a keep or donjon, which would house the great hall and lord's solar, where he and his family slept: privacy was a privilege only of those of high rank, and everyone else bedded down on pallets in the hall. The tower would be built on an earthen mound (the motte) surrounded by a wooden palisade and moat. Within the palisade was the bailey, an open area housing workshops, stables and a kitchen; the latter was always built separately because of the risk of fire. In uncertain times, the villagers, who looked to their lord for protection against invaders, could take refuge in the bailey with their livestock until the danger had passed.

During the twelfth century, many timber castles were rebuilt in stone with square keeps, which made them better able to resist a siege. The walls of these newer castles were very thick and had only arrow-slits for windows. Often draughty and damp, with unpaved earthen floors strewn with rushes, they were heated by open fires in the central hearth of the great hall, the smoke escaping through a vent in the ceiling, or by braziers in the smaller rooms. Built-in fireplaces were rare in England at this period, since the design of keeps could not easily accommodate chimneys, yet we know that Queen Eleanor had one installed at Winchester.

Each castle was under the control of a constable, who was entrusted to keep the peace in the region during his lord's absence. When the lord was in residence, however, he would hold court, attend to local affairs, dispense justice and oversee administration.

Knights, who fought on horseback, belonged to the lower ranks of the military élite, and often found warfare a lucrative business. Their daily rate of pay rose steadily in the twelfth century: by 1189, it was one shilling (5p). On top of that, they could expect to profit from taking enemy knights for ransom or from sharing the spoils of war. The rituals of conferring knighthood were varied and became increasingly elaborate as time passed. There were around 7,000 knights in England at this time.

One of the most favoured knightly pursuits was the tournament, which became popular in France in the eleventh century but was not legalised in England until 1194 by Richard I. Early tournaments were merely occasions for brutal battle practice; they began with single combats called jousts and ended with a violent mêlée over a wide area. Deaths and injuries were commonplace; Eleanor herself was to lose one of her sons in a tournament. Nevertheless, knights could earn rich prizes and good money at tournaments, and they became popular social gatherings. It was only in the thirteenth century, with the growing concept of chivalry, that they began to be better regulated and governed by an ever-stricter code of etiquette. It was for the identification of participants at tournaments that the code of heraldry developed in the late twelfth century.

England was divided into shires, each under the control of a sheriff (shire-reeve). He represented the King and was supposed to safeguard the crown's interests in the shire, which was divided into administrative divisions called hundreds. The sheriff enforced the King's justice in the shire courts, and ensured that royal revenues and debts were collected.

His was a lucrative office and its holders were never very popular: witness the sheriff of Nottingham, of Robin Hood fame. Until the time of Henry II, the magnates had often extended their influence by appropriating shrievalties for themselves, but Henry replaced them with professional administrators and made them more accountable for their actions and finances.

There was a high incidence of violent crime during this period. There was, of course, no police force, and local enforcement of law and order was left to the sheriffs, lords of the manor and local communities. Every so often, the King's itinerant justices would visit each shire in turn, to hear all pleas at the shire court. The King himself and the judges who followed his court would hear individual cases as they travelled around the kingdom. Later, it became customary for the royal justices to sit on the King's Bench at Westminster and hear civil and criminal cases.

Although the crime rate was high, convictions were hard to secure because the machinery of justice was often inadequate. If they witnessed a crime, ordinary people could raise the hue and cry, inciting everyone to chase after a wrongdoer. A felon might claim sanctuary in a church, usually for no longer than a fortnight; if he escaped, he risked being declared an outlaw.

There were several ways of determining a person's guilt. The Normans had introduced two procedures invoking divine judgement: trial by ordeal – either by water or fire – which was commonly resorted to up until Henry II's reign, and trial by combat; if the loser was not killed, he would be hanged. Finally, there was trial by jury, an old Anglo-Saxon process, which became the accepted procedure from the time of Henry II.

Punishments were severe. William I had abolished capital punishment, preferring the very efficacious deterrent of mutilation, but it had been restored by Henry I, although the royal courts were judicious in its use. Male murderers were hanged, females burned to death; rapists were castrated, arsonists burned at the stake. For slander or false accusation, a man could have his tongue cut out. The most common punishment was a fine, which hit poor felons hardest.

The Church administered its own courts, presided over by archdeacons or bishops, which adjudicated on matters such as heresy, annulment, sexual misconduct, disputes over wills and other cases touching the cure of souls. Ecclesiastical courts also dealt with offenders in holy orders who had committed civil crimes, usually imposing more lenient sentences. Even the lowliest clerks could claim this 'benefit of clergy', which Henry II thought to be unfair: his attempt to reform the system was one of the major causes of his quarrel with Thomas Becket.

Much of England was then covered by forests. During the Middle Ages, the continual clearance of forest areas was so commonplace as to merit little mention in the records, yet at this period the forest was regarded chiefly as 'the sanctuary and special delight of kings, where, laying aside their care, they withdraw to refresh themselves with a little hunting. There, away from the turmoils inherent in a court, they breathe the pleasure of natural freedom'.[2] So seriously did the early mediaeval kings take the sport of hunting that they set aside vast acres of land for their own use, built numerous hunting lodges in the royal forests (of which the most notable was the spacious palace of Clarendon, near Salisbury, recently excavated) and introduced a series of savage forest laws designed to prevent the King's subjects from poaching his game, a hazardous business at the best of times since predatory wolves still roamed the forests of England in the twelfth century. The Norman kings had executed or mutilated those who transgressed these laws, but Henry II and his successors preferred to punish them with imprisonment or a fine.

In England, as elsewhere, the feasts of the Church, her holy days and saints' days, governed the Christian's year, and the parish church was the focal point of social life in every village. Shrines to the Virgin Mary and the saints, many containing holy relics, were to be found everywhere and were the objects of special veneration and pilgrimages. In every city and town, and throughout the countryside, men raised the most beautiful churches to the glory of God.

The Archbishops of Canterbury and York were rivals for the primacy of England until the fourteenth century. The ultimate ecclesiastical authority was the Pope, who was regarded as the successor to St Peter, but the Church was mainly run by bishops, and bishops in the twelfth century were chiefly politicians, businessmen and administrators. Some, such as Hugh of Avalon, Bishop of Lincoln, had a genuine aura of sanctity, but they were the exception rather than the rule, most preferring to seek high office and influence in the service of the King. Most of the great offices of state were filled by bishops, some of whom were even appointed sheriffs. Thus did the Church spread its influence over secular affairs. Indeed, many bishops were very worldly men, who lived like princes and spent more time indulging themselves with hunting, entertaining, building projects and the acquisition of wealth than they did on their spiritual and pastoral duties.

At the other end of the scale, a village priest, living on his glebeland and caring for the souls of his flock, often earned a mere pittance, for he was required to rely on tithes imposed on the parish, which were usually paid in kind, and he often had a family to support. William I had forbidden English priests to marry, on penalty of a heavy fine, but even as late as the reign of Henry II it was common for a priest to keep 'a hearth girl in his house who kindled his fire but extinguished his virtue. His miserable house [was] often cluttered with small infants, cradles, midwives and nurses.'³ It was not until 1181 that this practice was forbidden by the Archbishop of Canterbury.

There were 9,000 parishes in England. Many parish priests were sincere men, who carried out their duties with simple faith and humanity, but there were many more who were often drunk, lax or so illiterate that they could not properly read or fully interpret for their flock the offices and services of the Church, which were all in Latin, its universal language. Many priests, and even some of the higher clergy, preferred to preach in English.

The twelfth century witnessed a great monastic revival, with the founding of several new orders with stricter rules: the Cistercians, white monks who built their abbeys in the northern wildernesses laid waste by William I, reclaimed the land for sheep-farming and became England's foremost wool producers; the Augustinian canons, whose double houses admitted both men and women in holy orders; the Carthusians, who lived under an austere rule requiring them to embrace a life of solitude and silence; and the Order of Fontevrault, especially dear to Eleanor of Aquitaine and her family.

In England, a programme of monastic reform had been imposed by William I. Most of the Norman kings founded abbeys in England, such as those at Reading and Faversham, whose respective founders Henry I and King Stephen were buried in the churches they had endowed. William I and his queen, Matilda of Flanders, founded or endowed several abbeys in Normandy, notably at Caen, where they were entombed.

The religious houses were not just the refuge of those who wished to retreat from the world and live lives dedicated to God. They fed and cared for the poor, healed the sick, dispensed alms and gave shelter to travellers. Many were cradles of learning, preserving in their libraries ancient books, documents and manuscripts, and training their monks in the arts of illumination and calligraphy so that they could produce Bibles and devotional works glorifying God – most books were about religious subjects – or new chronicles and annals recording the history of their house or of England itself. The Church therefore enjoyed a monopoly over the written word.

The expensive art of illumination had been imported from Byzantium, thanks to the expansion of trade with the Eastern Empire, and there are some exquisite English examples from this period, notably the Byzantine-influenced Winchester Bible. Manuscripts were written mainly in the rounded Carolingian minuscule script, which had not yet given way to Gothic lettering. Most books were bound with leather-covered oak boards, but some were lavishly adorned with gold or metal filigree work, ivory reliefs or precious stones.

Monks were not universally popular. Enclosed in their communities, and undertaking no pastoral works outside those walls, they were often perceived as idle troublemakers who led promiscuous lives and were over-critical of those who remained in the world. 'From the malice of monks, O Lord deliver us!' wrote Giraldus Cambrensis with feeling. By the end of the twelfth century, religious rules were being subverted by softer living conditions, and the decline of monasticism had set in.

Education was then dominated by the Church, which used it as a means of training those who were destined for holy orders. All schools had to be licensed by bishops: many were grammar schools, attached to cathedrals and monasteries. Only boys were admitted. They studied the trivium (grammar, rhetoric and dialectic) and the quadrivium (mathematics, music, geography and astronomy). All lessons were in Latin and discipline was strict. Nevertheless, there was no prejudice against a bright boy from a poor background gaining acceptance in these schools and by the benefits of his education rising through the ranks of the Church to high office. In fact, it was the peasant classes who seemed to care most about education, for they 'vied with each other in bringing up their ignoble and degenerate offspring to the liberal arts'.[4] The nobility, on the other hand, were often 'too proud or too lazy to put their children to learning'.[5] Upper-class boys were more likely to be taught the manly arts of warfare, preferably in another noble household, where they would be sent initially as pages, in the hope that their hosts would secure future honours and advantages for them. It would appear therefore that it was mainly the peasant, merchant and artisan classes who sent their sons to the schools and universities. Relatively few lay people, however, learned to read and write: literacy was chiefly the preserve of those in holy orders.

Music, sacred or otherwise, pervaded every walk of twelfth-century life, although very little survives, and that which does is so poorly annotated that we can only guess at how it should be played. Nevertheless, we have examples of the hymns that were sung in churches, the songs that were sung by soldiers, and the part-songs that originated in Wales and were sung for pleasure in castles and manor houses. Carols had not yet become associated purely with Christmas, but were sung and danced in a ring to celebrate a variety of holy days and even the coming of spring. *Sirventes* were songs of a satirical nature, often only of topical interest, which is why they were rarely written down, but they were highly popular.

Life in mediaeval castles was lived communally, and during the evenings everyone would gather in the great hall of the keep to eat supper and take their leisure by the light of torches and candles in the wall-sconces. If they were lucky they might be entertained by minstrels, clowns, acrobats, Morris dancers, mummers, mime artists and jesters (joculators). Kings and lords would keep their own jesters; Rahere, founder of St Bartholemew's Church and Hospital, was Henry I's jester, and had a special talent for mimicry. The repertoire performed by these artistes, who were usually of lowly birth and disreputable reputation, was often coarse and bawdy, punctuated by swearing and obscenities. Satirical humour was popular, then as now, and slapstick drew much merriment.

Christmas was marked by twelve days of religious offices and revelry, and every English king held a special court in honour of the occasion. The Church itself entered into the spirit of frivolity, appointing Boy Bishops for the duration and holding a Feast of Fools, to the hilarity of beholders, but it was stern in condemning jollifications at any rite that had obvious pagan origins. Thus May Day rituals and observation of the Summer and Winter Solstices were either prohibited or somehow incorporated into the Christian calendar.

In order to spread the Word of God, the Church sanctioned the performance of miracle plays or tableaux of scenes from the Bible, which had become very popular by the end of the twelfth century. They were at first performed in churches, and later on colourful stages set up in market places. Many of these early plays were in the vernacular, so that the common folk could understand them.

During the twelfth century, English towns flourished and grew, thanks to the development of trade and commerce. Several new towns were founded by kings and noblemen, and some villages received charters conferring township status. Conscious attempts at town planning were made in new urban developments, such as Leeds and Liverpool, which were constructed on a grid system.

Towns were known as boroughs, from the Saxon word *burh*, and were centres of trade; the merchants who lived in a borough were known as burgesses. Towns would have walls built around them for protection, which often meant that, with the expansion of their trade and population, too many people were crowded together in houses crammed into narrow streets. As the century progressed and society became less militaristic in its outlook, suburbs grew up outside town walls.

Some towns and cities were communes, which meant that they had secured the right to self-government by elected aldermen, often in the face of opposition from kings like Henry II, who disapproved of towns being independent from the crown. Kings and lords would also grant charters licensing the holding of fairs and markets, invariably a lucrative source of profit for themselves.

London, with an estimated population of 35,000, was by far the biggest and most important city. Its chief citizens were known as barons. They were a politically acute clique who wielded considerable influence, and by the end of the century they had wrested their independence from the crown, declared themselves a commune and in 1191 elected their first mayor, Henry FitzAilwin. Many citizens were bilingual, speaking both Norman-French and English, or a curious combination of the two. Intermarriage between those of Norman and Saxon origin was common.

We are fortunate that, around 1180, the chronicler William FitzStephen wrote a description of London as a preface to his biography of Thomas Becket, who was born in the city. Thus we have at first hand a picture of the London Eleanor knew.

London had occupied its 326-acre site on the banks of the Thames since Roman times, and its landward boundaries were protected by a high stone wall with towers and seven double gates: Bishopsgate, Cripplegate, Moorgate, Aldgate, Aldersgate, Ludgate and Billingsgate. The city was dominated by three fortresses: the White Tower, built by William the Conqueror, and Baynard's Castle and Montfichet Castle, where the city garrisons were housed. Between 1176 and 1209, a strong stone bridge was built to replace the old wooden structure that connected the city to the Surrey shore. Within the city walls, the ordinary houses were built of wood and gaily painted red, blue and black. Because there were so many timber buildings, there were frequent fires: one in 1135 destroyed St Paul's Cathedral and a wide area around it.

By 1180, the city was bustling and prosperous, boasting a fine stone cathedral, thirteen religious houses, 126 parish churches, lordly residences, guildhalls and schools. London was a great centre for trade, and had streets of shops displaying a variety of luxury goods, including silks from Damascus and enamels from Limoges. There were also markets where merchants would come from all over Europe to sell their goods, and numerous stalls and booths. There was even a cook shop by the river serving ready-made meals to take away. The city's population was growing and suburbs such as Smithfield, where there was a horse fair every Saturday, were by now springing up beyond the walls. In these suburbs, the richer citizens had fine timber-framed houses set in beautiful gardens planted with trees. Nearby were 'excellent suburban wells with sweet, wholesome, clear water', such as Clerkenwell, Holy Well and St Clement's Well. Beyond these suburbs lay pleasant meadows and mill-streams, and forests where the Londoners would go with their merlins, falcons and dogs to hunt stags, deer, boar and even bulls. They also had the right to hunt further afield in the Chiltern Hills.

There was much to do in London. Annual carnivals took place, and the people regularly participated in bull- or bear-baiting, cock-fighting, horse-racing, archery and wrestling. Boys and youths enjoyed football – then a much more violent game than it is now – and their fathers and the city elders often came on horseback to watch. During Lent, there were tournaments every Sunday, and at Easter 'naval tourneys' on the Thames. In winter, people made skates out of animal bones and whizzed across the frozen marshes north of the city. For refreshment, there were many inns and taverns, identified by the bunches of greenery hanging above their doors.

FitzStephen described London as a beautiful and splendid city, 'known for its healthy air and honest, Christian burghers', but Richard of Devizes stated that, compared with Winchester, it was a cynical, terrifying and evil place. The murder rate was high, and it was dangerous to venture out on the streets after curfew because of predatory street gangs. The worst areas for crime were actually across the bridge on the Surrey shore, particularly between the Bishop of Winchester's palace in Southwark and the Archbishop of Canterbury's palace at Lambeth, which was the equivalent of a modern red-light district.

Other cities and towns were far smaller than London, often not much bigger than a large modern village. Winchester, York, Lincoln and Norwich boasted fewer than 10,000 citizens each, while Oxford and several other cities had not yet fully recovered from being sacked by the Conqueror's troops after refusing to submit to him.

Ecclesiastical architecture flourished at this time. By the end of the century, nearly every English cathedral and monastic church had been rebuilt in stone in the Norman style known as Romanesque. This was characterised by a massive barrel vault supported by thick columns and rounded arches, often decorated with geometric or zigzag chevron patterns. Most churches had very long naves and imposing towers over the crossing with the transepts, and were furnished with several altars to meet the high demand for masses. Durham Cathedral is the finest of the few remaining examples of English Romanesque architecture.

Towards the end of the century, after the development of the pointed arch in Burgundy and France, Gothic architecture became fashionable. In England, this style is known as Early English, and an outstanding example is the choir of Canterbury Cathedral, built by William of Sens. This set a new trend in church building and was soon followed at Lincoln, Wells and other cathedrals. Twelfth-century churches were rich in carvings – a visual aid for the faithful – and covered in instructive and decorative wall-paintings depicting biblical scenes, saints, doom-paintings, allegories, floral patterns and even battles, as at Kempsley Church, Gloucestershire. Most were whitewashed over at the Reformation, yet a few have been restored, giving us some idea of how colourful mediaeval churches were.

In the early twelfth century, church windows were small and filled with clear glass. Shortly, glass stained in grey and black and known as grisaille appeared. Then, as the development of the Gothic arch facilitated larger windows, coloured stained glass was introduced into the first French Gothic cathedrals. It began to appear in English churches only towards the end of the century, and very little survives from that time, that in the choir at Canterbury being one of the best extant examples.

Sculpture was primitive, ill proportioned and crude, although there were some talented craftsmen at work in this field, as is evident from the stone sculptures at Chartres Cathedral and Cluny Abbey in Burgundy. Most sculpture was brightly painted, even if it adorned the outside of a church. Tomb effigies were rare, and those of the Plantagenets at Fontevrault are of unusually good quality. Opinions differ as to whether these were genuine attempts at portraiture, but their very diversity implies that perhaps they were. Portraiture as an art form did not exist – people had only a rudimentary knowledge of anatomy – and such paintings as survive are murals or manuscript illustrations that display little attempt at realism.

England was rich in natural resources. Her coal seams were not mined until the thirteenth century, but iron, lead, silver and charcoal were, and in Devon and Cornwall tin was becoming the major industry. Staffordshire was already known for its pottery, although much of what was produced was primitive in design and execution. The major industry was the production of wool, which became the basis of England's wealth from the twelfth century onwards. Trade was not yet dominated by craft guilds: the weavers' guild was the only one of any significance in this period.

There was a variety of fabrics on sale, many of them home-produced, particularly in Lincolnshire. Velvet would not be invented until the fifteenth century, and the finest cloth available was that dyed scarlet, which was made almost exclusively for Henry II and his family at 6s 8d (33p) an ell (a measure laid down in Henry I's reign and equal to the length of the King's right arm). Green say cost half that: it had a more delicate texture, but the colour was not as fashionable. Then there was a striped fabric called ray and the coarse white blanchet cloth worn by Cistercian monks and poorer folk. Linen was woven in Wiltshire and was used for women's head-dresses and for undergarments for both sexes.

Money was coming into more general use, replacing the system of barter or payment in kind that had sufficed in early feudal times. The only currency in England in the twelfth century was the silver penny. Money was counted in units known as shillings (12d, or 5p), marks (13s 4d, or 67p) pounds (240d, or £1), and gold marks (£6), but there were no actual coins of these denominations. In the interests of trade, upon which England's burgeoning prosperity depended, Henry II took measures to ensure that the coins bearing his image, which continued to be issued throughout the reigns of his sons, were accepted as sound currency throughout Christendom. Nevertheless, there were many clipped or debased coins in circulation.

A labourer earned roughly one shilling a day, a thatcher one penny and a plumber three pence, while a miller received as an annual stipend five shillings and a chaplain around forty shillings. There was chronic inflation and prices were constantly rising.

Trade, of course, was largely dependent on communications. It is a misconception that people rarely ventured out of their villages or towns at this period. In fact, royalty, nobles, knights, merchants, craftsmen, pilgrims and a host of others were constantly on the move, by land or water. Not that travel was always easy. Some Roman roads, notably Watling Street, Ermine Street and the Fosse Way, remained in use, as did the prehistoric Icknield Way: all were designated royal roads in the twelfth century, and were under the King's protection. By law, they had to be wide enough to allow two wagons to pass each other or sixteen armed knights to ride side by side. The surfaces of these royal roads were 'metalled' and paved. Most people travelled on horseback or by horse-drawn carts and covered wagons.

There were other main roads, known as the King's Highways, but they were often mere dirt tracks, which frequently became muddy and waterlogged. For this reason many goods, and people, were transported by river on barges. Towns that were sited by major rivers, such as York, Gloucester and Norwich, grew rapidly in prosperity.

Most seafarers travelled in round cogs with a single mast, a square, coloured sail and elevated castles at each end. Sailings were frequently delayed by inclement weather, and ships were often blown off course. It could take several days to cross the English Channel, and in all seas there were hazards such as shipwreck or pirates to be braved.

England enjoyed a lively foreign trade with France, Italy and other Mediterranean states, Flanders, Hainault, Scandinavia and the German principalities bordering the Rhine. Gold was even imported from Arabia. The Thames was constantly thronged with ships, and the wharves of London 'packed with the goods of merchants coming from all countries',[6] who imported timber, furs, gold, silver, gems, fabric, chain mail and even gerfalcons, those hunting birds used only by royalty. France's principal export to England was wine, chiefly from Poitou, Gascony and Auxerre, although Rhenish wine was also favoured. The marriage of Eleanor of Aquitaine and Henry II gave a great boost to the wine trade.

The diet of the English was more varied than we today might imagine. The fertile soil allowed several types of crop to be grown, whilst wild herbs, often used in cooking, were to be found in the meadows. Fruits and berries grew on trees and bushes, and a wide variety of birds were killed for the table. In the towns and markets, spices imported from the Orient, such as ginger, nutmeg, cloves and cinammon, could be purchased, at a price. Meat was a staple, but it could only be eaten fresh in the summer, because all livestock were slaughtered in the autumn, there being no means of feeding them through the winter, and their meat was smoked or salted down for the colder months. Stuffings, marinades and rich sauces, often flavoured with garlic, were used to disguise the taste and smell of rancid meat that had in many cases gone green. The poor kept pigs, whilst the rich hunted for game such as venison, wild boar, swans, hares and even peacocks.

Great varieties of fish were also eaten in large quantities, it being mandatory to do so on Fridays and also during Lent, when the devout were expected to give up meat. Most manors and monasteries had their own fish ponds or streams, and castle moats were often stocked with fish.

Many recipes known today, such as *coq au vin*, *boeuf bourguignon* and *bouillabaisse*, date from the twelfth century. Herb-flavoured omelettes were popular, as were stews and pies. There were no potatoes, and most meats were served upon thick trenchers of bread. Only the better off used plates, and these were usually shared between two people, a gentleman always inviting his lady to take the tastiest morsels. Sweets and desserts were popular, and might include dried fruits, compotes, jellies, biscuits, tarts, waffles, fritters, gingerbread or macaroons.

The staple drink of all classes was ale or 'home brew', which was consumed in huge quantities in leather or pottery tankards or jugs – 'the whole land was filled with drink and drinkers'.[7] Thin red and white wines were also home-produced in vineyards near Bedford, Tewkesbury and York, but they were so poor in quality that they had to be drunk with closed eyes and clenched teeth.[8] The best wines came from abroad and were drunk in the households of the upper classes and used at communion. These fine wines cost up to 34s (£1.70) a cask in 1184, and were often drunk from silver goblets. Wines could be spiced with cloves or sweetened with fruit such as pears. Cider and mead were also popular.

The main meal of the day was eaten between nine o'clock and noon, depending on the season. In castles and manor houses it was served with elaborate ceremony in the great hall, where the lord and his family would sit at the high table. This would be laid with a cloth, and ewers, basins and towels would be brought so that the diners could wash their hands. Knives and spoons were used as eating utensils, but forks had not yet been invented. Salt – then an expensive luxury – would be placed in cellars on the table, along with goblets, tankards and jugs of wine. Each course would be brought in by servants, whilst the company – which included guests, travellers and retainers – would enjoy lively conversation or transact business. Sometimes music would accompany the meal.

Bad harvests were often followed by winters of famine, which was greatly feared, for it was not uncommon for poorer people literally to starve to death once their supplies of food had been exhausted. Farming was carried out by manual methods, the only technological aids being the water-mill, for grinding corn, and the plough. The chief crops were wheat, barley, oats and vegetables. Because most manors were divided into strips, and because one field in three was often left fallow for a year, the yield could be poor, leading to a dearth.

Science made some advances at this time, thanks to the rediscovery of classical works, particularly on medicine, preserved by the Arabs. The study of astronomy was very popular, whilst in 1145 the Arab system of algebra was first introduced into Europe by Robert of Chester. It was either he or the great scientist Adelard of Bath who first used Arabic numerals in Europe, although these would not replace the old Roman numeral system until the sixteenth century.

Medicine was rudimentary and crude. Diseases and their causes were not properly understood, and physicians often found it hard to reach an accurate diagnosis. Even when they did, there was little they could do for the patient beyond prescribing baths or offering herbal remedies or infusions, some of which were efficacious. Badly wounded limbs were usually amputated with an axe without benefit of anaesthetic, often with fatal results, and it was some time before the Arab practice of dressing wounds was followed in the West.

Life in twelfth-century England was often short and hard and it was universally believed that, whilst the wicked who had committed mortal sins would be consigned after death to the flames and tortures of Hell, those who had striven for goodness in this life would receive their reward in Heaven. However, in order to avoid a sojourn in purgatory beforehand to expiate lesser sins, it was common for men and women to invest their life savings so that perpetual alms could be distributed for the safety of their souls.

8

'Eleanor, by the Grace of God, Queen of England'

At Christmas 1154, King Henry II and Queen Eleanor presided over a great court at Westminster,[1] which was attended by the chief barons and prelates of England. With their assistance, Henry immediately set to work to tackle the evils and decay that beset his kingdom and to establish well-organised government. He began by ordering the expulsion of Stephen's Flemish mercenaries, the destruction of 1,100 unlicensed castles, and the resumption of royal castles and alienated crown lands,[2] acts that 'earned the praise and thanksgiving of peace-loving men'.[3]

Henry was passionate about justice, paid 'due regard to public order, and was at great pains to revive the vigour of the laws of England, which had seemed under King Stephen to be dead and buried. Throughout the realm he appointed judges and legal officials to curb the audacity of wicked men and dispense justice to litigants.'[4] In his coronation charter, Henry made no mention of Stephen's reign, but referred frequently to the laws and customs of Henry I, which he was determined to restore and enforce. In fact, as his reign progressed, he would not slavishly follow his grandfather's policies, but would introduce new and sometimes radical legislative reforms of his own.

He divided the country into administrative regions, and instituted legal circuits, whereby his justices would visit each region to ensure that the King's Peace was being kept and administer justice through assize courts. Whilst on his travels through his kingdom, Henry himself would preside over these courts, and his judgements were reputed to be so just that anyone with a sound case was anxious to have it heard by him, while those with dubious cases would not come before him unless they were dragged into court.[5] Another change was the gradual replacement of trial by ordeal with trial by jury. It was due to these dramatic reforms that, during Henry II's reign, the foundations of English common law were laid down.

Henry also 'jealously watched over the royal interests',[6] judiciously increasing the wealth and prestige of the crown whilst curbing the power of his barons.

What made all this possible was the strong desire of the English aristocracy and people for peace after the terrible anarchy of Stephen's reign, which Henry exploited to the full in order to press on with his reforms. He knew that it was essential to restore public confidence in the monarchy and the government, and by quickly establishing a strong grip on affairs and learning to control his barons and make them co-operate, he succeeded in achieving this. Gradually, he established the supremacy of the royal court – the *curia regis* – over the feudal courts of his vassals, and improved local government by dismissing corrupt or inept sheriffs. There was no aspect of national or local government that escaped his attention, and soon after his accession, it was said that a virgin could walk from one end of the realm to the other with her bosom full of gold and suffer no harm, and that evil barons had vanished like phantoms.[7]

The King also took steps to reorganise and improve the royal finances, which were in chaos. He levied new taxes, minted a purer coinage and ensured that all royal revenues were collected by the Exchequer, which had been vigorously reorganised by 1158. This policy was highly successful: royal income, which was £22,000 in 1154, had increased to £48,000 by the end of the reign.[8] Out of this, Henry had to maintain not only himself and his household, but also the royal estates and castles, and finance the government of the realm. His careful housekeeping benefited not only himself, but England too, for it led to a boom in trade and prosperity, which in turn resulted in increased royal revenues.

By the summer of 1155, thanks to Henry II's genius for good government, order had been re-established within the kingdom, with such thoroughness that it would remain at peace for nearly two decades.

Even after he became King, Henry II disdained the trappings of sovereignty. He did not need them anyway, for his very presence was enough to quell those who would have opposed him and reduce mighty lords to servility. He was a despot, both as a ruler and as the head of his family, and one of the most able and gifted rulers to sit on the throne of England: his contemporaries accounted him 'the greatest of earthly princes'.[9]

He nevertheless remained the most affable of monarchs, although no one ever mistook his geniality for a want of sovereign authority.[10] 'He was expansive towards strangers and prodigal in public,' wrote Giraldus. When assailed and jostled by a crowd of clamorous suitors, he would remain even-tempered and endeavour to give each one a hearing.[11] Few, however, got what they wanted, for Henry had

> a fault which he contracted from his mother's teaching: he is wasteful of time over the affairs of his people, and so it comes about that many die before they get their matter settled, or leave the court depressed and penniless, driven by hunger.
>
> Another fault is that when he makes a stay anywhere, which rarely occurs, he does not allow himself to be seen, but shuts himself up within and is only accessible to those who seem unworthy of such ready access.[12]

In a crisis, Henry usually stayed calm and decisive, and his sense of humour often served him well. Once, after a stormy clash with the King, Hugh of Avalon, Bishop of Lincoln approached him with trepidation as Henry sat on the ground in the forest with his courtiers in a circle around him. Since Henry had forbidden anyone to acknowledge Hugh's presence, no one rose to greet him, 'but Bishop Hugh, undaunted, eased an earl out of his place beside the King and sat down. There was a long, brooding silence, finally broken by Henry who, unable to do nothing, called for needle and thread and began to stitch up a leather bandage on an injured finger. Again, there was a heavy silence until Bishop Hugh casually remarked, "How like your cousins of Falaise you look"' – a droll reference to William the Conqueror's mother, who had been a tanner's daughter from Falaise. 'At this, the King's anger fled from him and he burst into laughter which sent him rolling on the ground. Many were amazed at the Bishop's temerity, others puzzled, until the King, recovering his composure, explained the gibe to them.'[13]

For all his geniality, Henry's rage could be terrible when his will was flouted, his authority undermined or his trust betrayed. Generally, however, 'he possessed remarkable prudence, constancy and zeal for justice',[14] and knew when to be merciful. When Ralph d'Albini flung a stone at the King at Bedford Castle – a gross insult – the King merely confiscated one of his estates.[15]

Henry could be kind and generous towards his servants[16] and those hit by misfortune. Walter Map recalled how, 'although he was not obliged to do so, and the cost was high', he had made good the losses of some seamen when their ships, which they had 'provided as a service to the Cinque Ports without cost to the crown', were wrecked during a storm.

In 1176, when there was terrible famine in Anjou and Maine, the King emptied his private stores to succour the poor.[17] His laws displayed concern for the needs of his humbler subjects,[18] and he was 'more and more anxious about the common welfare [and] most intent on showing justice to everyone'.[19]

Walter Map stated that Henry was generous with almsgiving, but 'in secret, lest it should be known to his left hand what his right hand gave'. Map also claimed that the King was a pious man, but Giraldus insisted that he could see no sign of personal devotion in him. William of Newburgh criticised Henry to his face for leaving bishoprics vacant so that he could appropriate their revenues, but the King merely retorted that it was better that the wealth of the Church be spent to the benefit of the realm than on the pleasure of bishops, which Newburgh thought shocking. Indeed, Henry's open anti-clericalism prejudiced many chroniclers against him, notably Ralph Niger and Gervase of Canterbury, although Adam of Eynsham, the biographer of St Hugh of Lincoln, testifies to the King holding truly devout men in high regard, and Walter Map tells of him tactfully averting his eyes and making no comment when a monk's habit blew up and exposed his bare buttocks.

Giraldus Cambrensis deplored the way in which Henry sometimes ridiculed the clergy, as well as his frequent blasphemies, which were as offensive then as four-lettered words are today. Comparing him unfavourably with Louis VII, he wrote that Louis did not, like some princes he could mention, swear by the eyes, the feet, the teeth or the throat of God, and that his device was not bears, leopards or lions, but the simple lily. The reference to leopards and lions may allude to the developing royal arms: Henry had perhaps inherited one lion from his father; the second he probably acquired on his marriage, for the device of Eleanor of Aquitaine was a golden lion on a red background. These two lions appear quartered on a shield of the Duke of Saxony and Brunswick, who later married Henry's daughter. Not until the reign of Henry's son would the Plantagenet arms featuring three lions or leopards evolve.

Henry's benefactions to the Church were lavish. He and Eleanor endowed many leper hospitals, including those at Caen, Angers and Le Mans. He directed his almoner to give to the destitute one-tenth of all the food and drink that was purveyed by or given to the royal household. The bequests in his will were exclusively for religious houses. He gave generously to the abbeys of Fontevrault, Reading (where Henry I lay buried) and Grandmont in the Limousin. Henry had a great attachment to the austere Order of Grandmont, visited it frequently, founded several cells and in 1170 expressed a wish to be buried in the stark abbey church. This horrified his barons, who felt that such a resting place would be inconsistent with his dignity as king. Henry also had a deep respect for the even more ascetic Carthusian Order, and founded their first house in England at Witham, Somerset.

For a man of his time, Henry could be surprisingly tolerant. Unlike other Christian rulers, he refused to persecute the Jews, and he offered asylum to Albigensian heretics who had fled from persecution in the south of France. Yet, like most people of his time, he regarded homosexuality as an offence against God, and authorised the torture of some Templars who had been arrested on suspicion of that and other unnatural practices; they confessed and were severely punished. This was the first time that torture was used under royal warrant in England.

Inheriting the crown of England placed Henry, at the age of just twenty-one, on an equal footing with his rival, King Louis, yet he was by far the richer of the two in lands and resources, for his empire now extended from the Scottish border to the Pyrenees. Nevertheless, he remained Louis' vassal for his lands in France, which meant that from time to time he would have to bow the knee to him in homage. Both were aware, however, that Henry was the more powerful monarch, and Louis both feared and distrusted him, even while extending the hand of friendship. Thus France was always a potential enemy.

Although Henry worked hard and efficiently to establish his authority in England, his chief interests lay on the continent. However, he found his continental domains far more difficult to govern than his kingdom – especially Aquitaine, where his rule was never popular and which remained in a state of almost constant revolt against him. Governing such far-flung territories presented many practical difficulties in an age of poor communications, but with his tremendous energy Henry strove to overcome them, keeping in constant touch with the affairs of each domain by messenger, letter and personal visits. His understanding of languages was an asset, but from now on virtually his whole life would be lived on the move, as he enforced his authority in his various territories. The chronicler Herbert of Bosham described him as a human chariot who drew all behind him, while King Louis was astonished at the pace of Henry's travels: 'Now in Ireland, now in England, now in Normandy, he must fly rather than travel by horse or ship!' he exclaimed.[20]

Henry also facilitated efficient rule by centralising the administration of his territories at Westminster and Rouen. All his orders were processed centrally through his secretariat, the Chancery, which travelled with his court; these orders, or writs, were renowned for their

clarity and could be understood everywhere in his empire. This helped
to establish a degree of uniformity throughout dominions that had no
common language, laws, customs or currency.

Despite these measures, Henry was almost constantly at war, either
with France, or subduing rebellious vassals, or keeping his borders secure
from attack. Yet 'above everything in the world, he labours for peace;
all that he thinks, all that he says, all that he does, is directed to this end:
that his people may have tranquil days'.[21]

By the time she became Queen of England, at thirty-two, Eleanor was
already something of a legend. In Germany, her beauty was lauded in
the contemporary collection of anonymous student songs known as the
Carmina Burana:

> If all the world were mine
> From the seashore to the Rhine,
> That price were not too high
> To have England's Queen lie
> Close in my arms.[22]

Another German *minnesinger* – the equivalent of a troubadour – wrote:

> The sweet young Queen
> Draws the thoughts of all upon her
> As sirens lure the witless mariners
> Upon the reef.

This is also thought to refer to Eleanor. The likelihood is that these
poets had not even seen her, but had relied upon reports of her looks
and her reputation. In England and France, her praises were sung in a
more conventional manner, as in this tribute by Benoît de Sainte-Maure
in his *Roman de Troie*:

> For my presumption, shall I be chid
> By her whose kindness knows no bounds?
> Highborn lady, excellent and valiant,
> True, understanding, noble,
> Ruled by right and justice,
> Queen of beauty and largesse,
> By whose example many ladies
> Are upheld in emulous right-doing;
> In whom all learning lodges,

Whose equal in no peer is found.
Rich lady of the wealthy King,
No ill, no ire, no sadness
Mars your goodly reign.
May all your days be joy.

In the introduction to his Bestiary, formerly dedicated to Adeliza of Louvain, second queen of Henry I, and now reissued in the hope of acquiring a new patroness, the writer Philippe de Thaün takes a similar laudatory approach:

God save Lady Eleanor,
Queen, who is the arbiter
Of honour, wit and beauty,
Of largesse and loyalty.
Lady, born were you in a happy hour
And wed to Henry, King.

Yet for all her fame, throughout the thirty-five years of Henry's reign, the chroniclers rarely mention Eleanor, unless it is to record her presence by the King's side on various occasions, or the births of her children, through which she was fulfilling her prime function as queen. Most of her modern biographers therefore conclude that she enjoyed little political power as queen, and that Henry saw to it that her role was purely dynastic and ceremonial. Yet there is evidence in official documents that she was allowed a certain autonomy in decision-making and considerable responsibility for administrative matters, especially during Henry's frequent absences abroad, although naturally she did not make major decisions affecting policy. Nor were English queens in the twelfth century expected to be entirely subservient to their husbands: they were '*regalis imperii participes*' – sharers in the imperial kingship. It may therefore be concluded that, because of the prejudices against her sex, and the fact that her role was completely overshadowed by Henry's deeds and achievements, Eleanor's activities were not considered worthy of mention.

The few observations that the chroniclers do make about Eleanor are perceptive. While Thomas Agnell, Archdeacon of Wells, called her 'a woman of great discernment', referring perhaps to her taste rather than her judgement, Gervase of Canterbury described her as 'an exceedingly shrewd woman, sprung from noble stock, but fickle'.

For the first few years of the reign, when Henry was away on the continent, Eleanor acted as regent of England. She dealt with routine business, implemented orders sent by the King from abroad, approved all the acts of his ministers, arbitrated in disputes and supervised the accounts of, for example, the market at Oxford, the tin mines of Cornwall and her mill at Woodstock.[23] Until 1163, she issued official documents or writs under her own name and seal,[24] which were attested by her own chancellor. Often, she was co-regent with the justiciar and acted in association with him; and occasionally she is recorded as having presided over courts and dispensed justice at Westminster, Cherbourg, Falaise, Bayeux or Bordeaux. Her rulings were drawn up by her clerk, Master Matthew, and her letters, dictated to her clerks and written in Latin, were signed 'Eleanor, by the grace of God, Queen of England', although not in her own hand; the earliest extant signature of an English queen is that of Joanna of Navarre in the fifteenth century.

The sparse surviving evidence indicates that Eleanor was zealous in upholding her husband's policies. This is clear from two extant letters recording her intervention in disputes. One is to John FitzRalph, a baron of London:

> I have received a complaint from the monks of Reading to the effect that they have been unjustly dispossessed of certain lands in London which were bestowed on them by Richard FitzB—when he became a monk. I command you to look into this without delay and, should it be true, to ensure that these lands are returned to the monks without delay, so that in future I shall hear no more complaints about deficiencies in law and justice. I will not tolerate their being unjustly deprived of anything that belongs to them. Greetings.

The second letter was sent to the tenants of Abingdon Abbey:

> To the knights and men holding lands and tenures from Abingdon Abbey, greetings. I command that in all equity, and without delay, you provide Vauquelin, Abbot of Abingdon, with those same services which your ancestors provided in the days of King Henry, grandfather of our sovereign lord; and if you do not do so, then the King's justice and my own will make you do so.

This is not the tone of a woman conscious of the narrow parameters of her authority. This is an imperious, dictatorial ruler confident in her power to enforce her decrees, whilst remaining aware that her husband retained ultimate control over affairs. Moreover, her actions during the reigns of her sons prove that she had gained considerable political experience, both in England and on her travels; and also through having known personally many of the great figures of the age, and by administering her own lands, a task for which she had been groomed since childhood. Eleanor would also have been conscious that, through Henry's marriage to her, England was enjoying increased prosperity, largely due to an expansion of the wine trade with Gascony and the import of silk, both of which brought great wealth to London and its merchants. In addition England enjoyed beneficial cultural links with Aquitaine as a result of the marriage; many English churches of the period display southern influence in their architecture.

Like Henry, Eleanor was constantly on the move, travelling throughout England, Normandy, Anjou and Aquitaine. Often, she accompanied the King and his court, but on many occasions she travelled alone, with an escort, apparently unfazed by stormy seas or the dangers that sometimes lurked on the roads.

When the King and Queen were in England, they followed a tradition set by the Conqueror, by ceremonially wearing their crowns at special courts held at Christmas, Easter and Whitsun, either at Westminster or at Winchester, the old Saxon capital. On these occasions there would be formal processions and church services at which the royal couple made offerings and took communion, all with great ceremony.

As queen, Eleanor was very rich, although her wealth did not come from conventional sources. On his accession, Henry endowed her with numerous manors. The precise details have not survived: the earliest extant charter for an English queen's dower is that of Isabella of Angoulême, wife of King John, which dates from May, 1204 and states that Isabella's assignment was identical to Eleanor's. According to Roger of Hoveden, Eleanor held the same lands as had been assigned to the queens of Henry I and Stephen.

Her dower manors should have provided Eleanor with substantial revenues in the form of annual rents, taxes and yields, and houses in which to lodge whilst on her travels. However, it is clear from the records that Eleanor did not gain control of her dower until Henry's death, and that during his lifetime all her revenues went to the Exchequer, although she was at liberty to visit her manors.

Her income came from two sources. Although little documentation exists, it is almost certain that Eleanor was the first English queen granted the right to claim queen-gold, an additional tenth payable to her on any voluntary fine over the value of ten marks, made in exchange for a licence or pardon from the crown, and on taxes on Jews; the first reference to queen-gold dates from Henry II's reign. It was paid direct to a clerk of the Exchequer appointed by the Queen, who had a thankless task collecting it, for it was very unpopular. Eleanor was also paid dues by the sheriffs in whose bailiwicks she resided. These payments were authorised by the King.

It may be inferred from these arrangements that Henry wished to retain control over her finances. In the 1180s, Eleanor attempted to increase her revenue from queen-gold by extending the range of fines on which it was levied, which suggests that she was finding Henry's constraints unwelcome.

In fact, the financial independence of earlier queen consorts had been much eroded before Eleanor's time. In the eleventh century and earlier, queens had managed not only the royal household but also the royal treasure, which made them both influential and wealthy. By 1135, however, the supervision of the household and treasury had been delegated to officials, diminishing the importance of the Queen's role. However, Henry's constraints upon Eleanor's finances probably had little to do with this trend and everything to do with his determination to limit her powers of patronage and prevent her from alienating crown lands. Not until the mid-thirteenth century were queens of England allowed to administer their own estates and income.

It was Henry, therefore, who paid the running costs of Eleanor's household and the salaries of the officials who administered her estates and of her personal servants. If she needed money for private expenditure, the Keeper of the Royal Wardrobe provided it.

Eleanor was a pious woman and, like her husband, a great benefactor of religious institutions, especially in Poitou and Aquitaine. With Henry, she helped to fund the rebuilding of the church of Notre-Dame-la-Grande at Poitiers in the Gothic style, a project she instigated herself and which would take a century to complete; with Henry, also, she once made a pilgrimage, bearing rich gifts, to the heights of Rocamadour, to visit the oldest shrine to the Virgin in France. In 1190, she gave to the Knights Hospitaller the port of Le Perrot.

Eleanor is also said to have built the tiny church of Saint-Pierre de Mons, near Belin, to which a curious legend attaches: in the twelfth century and later, local annalists claimed that she buried her 'numerous bastards' in its churchyard. Considering that her life was lived on so public a stage, it is hardly likely that she could have produced one bastard, let alone several, without the more veracious chroniclers of the age recording the fact.

Naturally, it was the abbey of Fontevrault that benefited most from the Queen's patronage and generous endowments, made over a period of nearly sixty years. In 1170, for example, she granted lands to the

Order, with the right to take timber and firewood from one of her forests, the charter being witnessed by Saldebreuil of Sanzay, Raoul de Faye, Eleanor's chaplain Peter, and Jordan, her clerk. She built a great octagonal kitchen for the nuns, which boasted five fireplaces and twenty chimneys, and which still stands today. When, in later years, her granddaughter, the daughter of Alix of France and Theobald of Blois, entered Fontevrault, Eleanor was lavish in her gifts to the girl.

Thanks to Eleanor's patronage, Fontevrault's prestige increased, and it was transformed from being a house offering a refuge to women of all classes, including prostitutes, into an aristocratic institution fashionable with the daughters of kings and nobles.

In England, Eleanor was responsible for the spread of the Order of Fontevrault, founding cells at Eaton and Westwood; in 1177, Henry II, himself a generous patron of Fontevrault, also founded a cell, at Amesbury in Wiltshire. Eleanor founded a chapel dedicated to St Nicholas in Tickhill Castle, Yorkshire, and endowed it, providing a warden and four chaplains. She and Henry also befriended the future saint, Gilbert of Sempringham, founder of the Gilbertine Order of nuns and canons. In the 1160s, when his lay-brothers, irked by their poverty, accused the nuns and canons of fornication, the King and Queen rallied to Gilbert's side and five bishops declared the charges unfounded.

All mediaeval queens gave alms for the expiation of their sins and, as was customary, Eleanor employed an almoner to distribute charity on her behalf, although details of her donations have not survived.

Henry II was said to have had more learning than any other European monarch of the age, and to have constantly increased his store of knowledge. 'With the King, there is school every day, constant conversation with the best scholars, and discussion of intellectual problems,' wrote Peter of Blois. When the King had leisure, 'he occupies himself with private reading or takes great pains in working out some knotty question among his clerks'.[25] Yet Eleanor also wielded considerable intellectual influence over the cultural life of the court and, indeed, of the twelfth century in general, because her patronage of troubadours and other literary figures facilitated the spread of sophisti-cated southern cultural traditions throughout the Angevin empire and later, through the marriages of her children, into other parts of Europe.

Many writers and poets dedicated their works to Eleanor, among them the Norman Robert Wace, a native of Jersey, who presented his translation into French of Geoffrey of Monmouth's *History of the Kings of Britain* to her around 1155–7,[26] saluting 'noble Eleanor' as being 'wise and of great virtue'. Henry II also liked Wace's works and made him official court reader; in 1160 he asked Wace to compile a metrical history of the dukes of Normandy, *Le roman de Rou* (Rou being Rollo, first Duke of Normandy and direct ancestor of William the Conqueror). Most of the books commissioned by Henry or dedicated to him are of an historical nature, reflecting his interest in his forebears.

Since the appearance of Geoffrey of Monmouth's *Historia Regum Britanniae* around 1135, the Arthurian legends had rapidly acquired popularity in England as well as in France, where Chrétien de Troyes and Marie de France developed the tradition at a highly sophisticated level. In no time at all, King Arthur had come to embody every contemporary ideal of knighthood and kingship. Many stories were told of him, most of them mythical, but in their day they were accepted as historical fact and eagerly retold and embellished by writers and poets. Only a few scholars, notably Ailred of Rievaulx and William of Newburgh, dared to question the veracity of Geoffrey's history.

Both Henry and Eleanor were fascinated by the legends of King Arthur, or the 'Matter of Britain', as they were then known. Henry had been taught them in childhood, whilst Eleanor had long been familiar with the romance of Tristan and Yseult; in one of his poems, Bernard de Ventadour had compared his love for her with that of the doomed lovers. Later, one of Henry and Eleanor's grandsons would be called Arthur.

Whilst Geoffrey of Monmouth had collected old Celtic legends and written the first popular account of King Arthur, Wace was the first writer to mention the Round Table, where no one knight had precedence. Prior to 1173, the poet Thomas wrote a romance of Tristan and Yseult, which survives only in part and was probably dedicated to the King and Queen. Marie de France, reputedly Henry's half-sister, wrote five lays of King Arthur and Tristan and Yseult, while Eleanor's daughter, Marie, Countess of Champagne, was the patron of Chrétien de Troyes, who wrote at least five poems based on the Arthurian legends, including 'Perceval' and 'Lancelot', and was the first to set them at Camelot and to recount the doomed romance of Lancelot and Guinevere. It has been suggested that Eleanor of Aquitaine may have been the inspiration behind some of the later legends surrounding Guinevere, but, although possible, this supposition rests only on very slender evidence.[27]

By the 1170s, as a result of royal interest, the Arthurian legends had become enormously popular, both at court and throughout England, and indeed throughout all Christendom – even as far away as Constantinople and Alexandria – and it became fashionable for knights and ladies to emulate the chief characters, whose chivalric ethic reflected the aristocratic values of the twelfth century. Already, people were flocking to sites associated with Arthur, such as Caerleon on the Welsh River Usk[28] and Glastonbury in Somerset, which Henry and Eleanor themselves visited. Indeed, there was so much speculation that Arthur would one day return to his kingdom that a disconcerted Henry II instituted a search for the hero-king's grave at Glastonbury.[29] In 1190, bones believed to be those of Arthur and Guinevere were exhumed there, along with a leaden cross inscribed 'Here lies Arthur, the famous king, in the Island of Avalon'. Thanks to this find, the Isle of Avalon has ever since been identified with Glastonbury. The bones were reburied with great ceremony in the abbey church.[30]

Other works dedicated to Queen Eleanor include romances of Oedipus and Aeneas, and we know that she enjoyed performances of mystery and miracle plays, from a letter written by Peter of Blois, in which he congratulates his brother, Abbot William of Blois, on his tragedy *Flora and Marcus*, which had been played before the Queen, either at Westminster or Winchester.

Cultivated it may have been, but Henry II's court was no haven for those with a taste for luxurious living. It was a hive of frenetic activity, which revolved around the ever-moving person of the King. Like all mediaeval courts, it was nomadic, staying at a succession of castles, palaces, abbeys, manor houses and hunting lodges, and rarely remaining in one place for more than a few weeks or, in some cases, a few days. These frequent moves were made in order to serve the interests of the state, or to facilitate the King's hunting expeditions or enable a vacated residence to be cleaned: twelfth-century sanitation left a lot to be desired, being limited to primitive garderobes or chamber-pots, and when 250 people had been staying in a house for any length of time, the stink could become unbearable, especially in summer.

Henry II, more than any other contemporary monarch, was, as Walter Map complained, 'forever on his travels, covering distances in unbearably long stages, like a courier, and in this respect merciless beyond measure to his household'. 'He does not linger in his palaces like other kings, but hunts through the provinces, inquiring into everyone's doing, and especially judges those whom he has made judges of others.'[31] His companions moaned about 'the miseries of court life':[32] Walter Map grumbled that 'we wear out our garments, break our bodies and our beasts, and never find a moment for the cure of our sick souls', yet the King did not seem to notice and 'suffered patiently the discomforts of dust and mud'.[33]

When it came to making travelling arrangements, Henry was

notoriously unpredictable. 'If the King has said he will remain in a place for a day – and particularly if he has announced his intention publicly by the mouth of a herald – he is sure to upset all the arrangements by departing early in the morning. And then you see men dashing around as if they were mad, beating packhorses, running carts into one another – in short, giving a lively imitation of Hell.' Even those who had been bled or had taken laxatives were ordered to move or be left behind. Yet 'if, on the one hand, the King orders an early start, he is sure to change his mind, and you can take it for granted that he will sleep until midday. Then you will see the packhorses loaded and waiting, the carts prepared, the courtiers dozing, traders fretting and everyone grumbling.'[34] Often, the maids and doorkeepers knew more about the King's plans than the great lords and councillors.[35]

The court on the move resembled a straggling procession of horses, wagons, baggage carts and pack-animals, including oxen, which were laden with all kinds of luggage. The Queen and other ladies either rode on horseback or in brightly painted but unsprung barrel-shaped wagons with leather roofs.

When Henry II travelled, he took with him some of the royal treasure (leaving the bulk in the treasury at Winchester) and the chief departments of state, accompanied by the justiciar, the chancellor and the Lord President of the Council, with their officials and all the paraphernalia of their work, such as parchments, documents, barrels of coins and boxes of jewels. Most items were packed in chests, sacks, leather bags or pouches.

In addition, there was the royal household, which numbered around 200 persons and provided for the domestic needs of the King and his court. The household had its own departments, headed by the steward, who had charge of the hall, kitchen, pantry and larder; the chamberlain, who presided over the chamber (which comprised the royal apartments and was also a secretarial and accountancy office, and would later evolve into the presence and privy chambers); the treasurer, who looked after the royal treasure, which was kept in a chest in the King's bedroom; the Lord High Constable, who was in charge of the outdoor servants and the stables; and the King's Marshal, who was responsible for maintaining order and discipline within the court and, with the constable, for organising the royal sports and supervising the archers who formed the King's personal bodyguard; finally there were the keepers of the seals. All of these officers enjoyed specific allowances of food, wine, candles and other perquisites.[36]

Then there were the officers of the Queen's household, whose names are known mainly from the charters they witnessed. They comprised her treasurer, chancellor, attorneys and clerks, who administered her estates (which were run by her stewards and baillifs), and her personal servants, such as her chamberlain, knights, esquires, chaplains, ladies and Master of the Horse.

The household included a great army of servants: cooks, bakers, confectioners, cellarers, fruiterers and poulterers, all of whom either purveyed or prepared food; the chief butler and his staff, who were responsible for the provision of wine; and keepers of the cups, who served it. Other kitchen and pantry officials included the usher of the spirit house, the keeper of the dishes, the master steward of the larder and the workmen of the buttery. The numbers of royal servants were augmented by chaplains, clerks, painters (limners), ushers, huntsmen, horn-blowers, watchmen, guards, archers, men-at-arms, cat-hunters, wolf-catchers, keepers of the hounds, keepers of the royal mews, keepers of the tents, the chamberlain of the candles, the bearer of the King's bed, the King's tailor, laundresses, including the King's personal washerwoman, and a ewerer, who dried his clothes and prepared the royal bath.[37] It is not known how often Henry used this, and we may surmise that it was not very often; King John prompted astonished reactions in 1209 when he had eight baths in six months.

These hordes of servants required even more piles of baggage, for they needed to transport kitchen equipment, hunting spears, weapons, altar cloths, communion vessels and plate, tables, chairs, feather beds, pillows, sheets, coverlets, hangings, napery, chamber pots, cosmetics and clothing.[38]

The royal retinue would also include scholars, artists, 'actors, singers, dicers, gamblers, buffoons and barbers'[39], as well as mimers, jugglers, conjurers, magicians, fortune tellers[40] and a host of whores and pimps. Not for nothing did John of Salisbury and Walter Map write disparagingly of Henry's court as a hotbed of scandal and frivolity. John of Salisbury, who compared the court to ancient Babylon, particularly condemned the effeminate garments of the fashion-conscious nobles and gallants, the polyphonic music that kindled all kinds of licentiousness, the widespread indulgence in love-making that would once have been described by serious men as depraved, the dancing, the sport and the gambling – all done to excess; and he was scathing about the hangers-on, the wheedlers and flatterers who thought they could fawn their way to favour and advancement. Worst of all were the coarse mimes and bawdy dramas, with their extravagant acting and gross buffoonery, that were staged at court: John thought that all involved in them should be excommunicated for so corrupting their audiences.

Once the court was on the move, messengers would be sent speeding ahead to warn the King's tenants or hosts that he was about to descend on them, and bid them prepare accommodation and ensure they had sufficient provisions for his retinue. In addition, hosts were required to provide one night's entertainment for the court. It was often a condition of land tenure that royal tenants provide these services, although many abbots and secular hosts were financially ruined through so doing. The King also had a habit of making sudden appearances. Peter of Blois tells us that Henry enjoyed vexing his stewards with the uncertainty of his plans: many a time he would announce his destination, 'and we would be comforted by the prospect of good lodgings'. But at the end of a long day's ride, 'the King would turn aside to some other place where he had, it might be, just a single dwelling with accommodation for himself and no one else. I hardly dare say it, but I believe he took a delight in seeing what a fix he put us in.' A royal visit was therefore a prospect that filled most people with dread.

One thing that Henry always looked for was good hunting, a pleasure he indulged in wherever he went. Map states he was 'a great connoisseur of hounds and hawks, and most greedy of that vain sport'.

Even when it was settled in one place, the court was chaotic, disorganised and noisy. Walter Map complained that, although Henry was a friend to scholars and loved learning, the Muses flourished less at his court than at any other, 'since the worry of it would not allow an interval for rest sufficient for sleep, let alone study'.

The food was appalling, and so was the wine, despite hundreds of barrels of it being regularly imported from Gascony, Poitou and Burgundy and brought directly to the royal palaces and hunting lodges. Peter of Blois recorded:

> At mealtimes or out riding, or during the long evenings, there is no order or restraint. The clerks and knights feed on poor, ill-fermented, unkneaded, unleavened and unbaked barley loaves, made of the dregs of beer, full of bran and heavy as lead. To drink, they are given a tainted, murky, thick, rank, flavourless wine, greasy and rancid and tasting of pitch. I have seen wine set before persons of eminent rank which was so thick that to get it down a man had to close his eyes, clench his teeth and sift it rather than drink it, grimacing with horror. The ale tastes horrible and looks filthy.
>
> On account of the great demand, cattle are sold to the court whether they are healthy or diseased, meat is sold whether it be fresh or not, and fish – four days old – is no cheaper for being putrid or foul-smelling. We have to fill our bellies with carrion and

become graves for sundry corpses. The servants care nothing whatever whether the unlucky guests become ill or die, provided they load their master's table with dishes. Indeed, the tables are sometimes filled with rotting food, and were it not for the fact that those who eat it indulge in powerful exercise, many more deaths would result from it.'

Nothing was ever done to rectify these shortcomings because food was not important to the King. When the monks of St Swithun at Winchester complained, weeping, to him that their bishop allowed them only ten courses at meals, Henry was not impressed.

'In my court, I am satisfied with three,' he snapped. 'Perish your bishop if he doesn't cut your dishes down to the same.'[41]

It was only on the three great religious festivals that the court ceased being a strictly functional institution and became a theatre of ceremony. Henry commonly kept Easter at Winchester or Windsor, Pentecost at Westminster, and Christmas at Gloucester or Windsor, and all these feasts were marked by solemn religious observances and feasting. There was as yet no concept of the court as a regular forum for aristocratic pleasures, as in Tudor times, yet it formed a centre of patronage to which suitors flocked.

Henry II was aware of the political value of royal display, and although fine clothes, luxury and personal comforts meant little to him, his accounts include payments for rich furs, silken robes, plate and jewels,[42] which must have been purchased for great ceremonial occasions. Even King Louis commented on the relative magnificence of his rival, telling Walter Map: 'Your King, the lord of England, has men and horses, gold and silk and jewels and fruits, game and everything else, while we in France have nothing but bread and wine and gaiety.'

Queen Eleanor also exercised a degree of patronage, mainly in cultural matters, yet her role in the court was chiefly decorative and ceremonial. She was often present at the King's side when he received important visitors or envoys, who came from all over Europe, and at royal banquets, religious ceremonies and state occasions.

As we have seen, the Queen had her own household and her own officers and personal attendants. She was waited on by the wives and daughters of the nobility, all of whom were paid, some receiving salaries and others occasional gifts: the records of these payments contain the first references to ladies-in-waiting in England. The pattern of payments suggests that unmarried girls were expected to attend the Queen on a regular basis, whilst married ladies waited upon her for part of the time and spent the rest on their husbands' estates or bearing children.

For all her experience at the civilised and orderly courts of Aquitaine and France, Eleanor seems to have made little attempt to impose more sophisticated standards upon Henry's court. She did lay down some rules of courtesy, insisting for example that no man appear before her with unkempt hair, unless he wished to be promptly ejected from her presence, but the evidence suggests that she was unable to enforce more stringent reforms. Instead, she appears to have resigned herself to enjoying, in the privacy of her apartments only, a higher standard of living than the rest of the court, achieved through importing many luxury items from abroad; these included gold for plates and goblets, regular shipments of spices, her favourite wine from La Rochelle, and incense for her chapel and to disguise the smell of the London fog.[43] We know that Eleanor's private bowers boasted the very latest in decoration, including tiled floors, glazed windows, silken hangings and carpets imported from the Orient, and that she always took tapestries and cushions with her on her travels.[44]

The Pipe Rolls also record purchases for the Queen of 'oil for her lamps', wine, flour, linen for tablecloths, brass bowls and sweet-scented rushes for the floor, all of which give a clearer picture of the comfort in which she lived. However, we have no way of knowing how Eleanor occupied her time, although we may surmise that, when she was not attending to her state and administrative duties, she read books and poetry, listened to music, spent a part of each day at her devotions, attended to household and family matters, and perhaps undertook some sewing and embroidery, those age-old pastimes of queens.

During Henry II's reign, the crown owned perhaps sixty castles and a number of hunting lodges. It was customary for apartments to be kept ready for the King and Queen at most of these residences, in case they chose to pay a visit or demanded a night's lodging whilst on their travels.

Of the chief royal residences of Eleanor's day, three are still in use today: the Palace of Westminster, the Tower of London and Windsor Castle. Other important castles, such as those at Winchester, Nottingham, Ludgershall, Gloucester and Marlborough, are now ruins.

King Edward the Confessor had had a Thames-side residence at Westminster in the eleventh century, but this had been replaced by a palace built by William Rufus, who also erected the vast New Hall, completed around 1099–1100, which still stands today (although with a fourteenth-century hammerbeam roof) and is now known as Westminster Hall. From the time of Henry II, the King's judges sat here to dispense justice. Nothing else survives of the Norman palace, although we do have William FitzStephen's description of how it appeared in

Henry II's reign: 'Upstream, to the west, a royal palace rises high above the river, an incomparable building ringed by an outwork and bastions, two miles from the City and joined thereto by a populous suburb.'

In 1153, King Stephen built a new wing of the palace, which was surrounded by orchards and woodlands, extending down to the river bank. In this wing were the royal apartments that were found to have been vandalised on Henry II's accession. The older palace lay to the south, and was used to house the various departments of state and provide accommodation for courtiers. It was a sparsely furnished and strictly functional building.

William the Conqueror's priority had been to strengthen the defences of London, and in 1067 he had begun building fortifications on what is now Tower Hill, on the site of an ancient Roman stronghold on the banks of the River Thames. Around 1078, he ordered the building of the White Tower, which was completed in 1097 and remained unchanged until 1190, when the building of two curtain walls, bisected by towers, began. William FitzStephen refers to the Tower as the Palatine Castle, stating that it was 'very great and strong with walls rising from very deep foundations, their mortar being mixed with the blood of beasts'.

The White Tower, so named because of the regular coats of whitewash applied to it, stood ninety feet high, with walls eleven feet thick. It was a rectangular building with turrets at each corner, one housing a spiral staircase. Access was through a doorway set high above the ground, reached by an external staircase, and the walls were pierced with arrow-slits, which were not converted into windows until 1715.

In each of the royal residences, the King's apartments were divided into hall, chamber and chapel, which together formed the substance of his household. On the upper floors of the Tower were to be found a galleried great hall and chamber, each two storeys high, the royal apartments and a Norman chapel dedicated to St John the Evangelist, constructed of Caen stone with rounded Romanesque arches and brightly painted stonework. It is still in use today. The ground floor provided quarters for the Constable of the Tower, and in the basement there were storerooms and a well. There is no evidence of an indoor kitchen, and it was probably housed in a separate building in the bailey.

The Tower dominated London. It was not only a fortress and palace but also a state prison, garrison, arsenal, armoury, mint, wardrobe and treasure house: the crown jewels were always kept here. There was even a small menagerie. Even by King Stephen's reign, it was famous as one of the chief residences of the kings of England.

In 1070–80, in order to complete his ring of fortresses around

London, built to control the south-east of England, William the Conqueror had erected a defensive wooden castle on top of a steep earthwork at Windsor, in the parish of Clewer, not far from Edward the Confessor's palace at Old Windsor. The castle overlooked the River Thames, had far-reaching views across a wide area, and was surrounded by forests and heathland offering excellent hunting grounds. The Conqueror and his sons had enclosed much of Windsor Forest for their own use and built kennels for their hounds and a royal mews.

The Conqueror's tower had been built, in Norman fashion, on the summit of the earthwork, with courtyards known as the Lower Ward and Upper Ward on either side of it; the whole area was surrounded by a wooden palisade and a ditch. The entrance was via a drawbridge and gate in the Lower Ward. Within the courtyards were huts for the garrison, stables, cages for prisoners and access to secret subterranean tunnels for emergency use when the castle was under siege. The later Norman kings had added a range of royal apartments, a great hall, a kitchen and a chapel dedicated to St Edward the Confessor.

Around 1166–70, Henry II ordered that Windsor Castle be rebuilt in stone. The work took several years to complete, and entailed transporting blocks of heath-stone from quarries near Bagshot and lead for the roofs from Cumberland in the north. The palisade was replaced by half a mile of massive stone walls, and the tower – rebuilt in 1180 and thereafter known as the Round Tower – and other buildings were also rebuilt in stone; these included the private royal apartments in the Upper Ward (on the site of the present state apartments) and an official royal residence with a great hall, known as the Winchester Tower, in the Lower Ward. On the slopes of the escarpment on which the castle was built, a vineyard was planted, although its yield was never plentiful.

Very few of Henry II's buildings survive today, having either been demolished, rebuilt by later sovereigns or disguised during the early nineteenth century, when Jeffrey Wyatville remodelled the castle for George IV. The earliest surviving room at Windsor is a thirteenth-century dungeon. Nevertheless, the size and form of the original mediaeval buildings may still be seen, and because of the dirt-repellent properties of heath-stone, the twelfth-century walls at Windsor still look as pristine as they did eight centuries ago.

William the Conqueror also built the royal castle known as the King's Castle at Winchester, although hardly anything remains after its demolition by Cromwell's men in the seventeenth century, and the surviving great hall dates only from 1235. We know from the Pipe Rolls and other sources, however, that the castle boasted a painted chamber in Eleanor's time.

In Oxford, around 1130, Henry I had built the King's House, later known as Beaumont Palace. A complex of massive wooden and stone buildings, it was surrounded by a defensive wall, had a great chamber, in which Henry II held court, a great hall adorned with mural paintings, two chapels, a cloister and private quarters for the use of the Queen, the royal chaplains and other officials. Two of Eleanor's children were to be born here. The palace was later converted into the church of the White Friars, which became in turn a workhouse; in the nineteenth century, a crumbling, roofless chamber with the remains of a fireplace was pointed out as the birthplace of King Richard the Lionheart.

Nearby was the royal hunting lodge at Woodstock, built by Henry I on the site of a Saxon manor house. It stood in the middle of a forest and was surrounded by a well-stocked deer park. Here, Henry II founded the first royal menagerie in order to house the animals sent to him as gifts by foreign rulers. They included lions, leopards, lynxes, camels and a porcupine; later, Richard I housed a crocodile there. Although Woodstock was used chiefly as a hunting lodge, Henry also held meetings of the Great Council there.

Another important hunting lodge, particularly favoured by Henry II, was situated at Clarendon in the New Forest, near Salisbury. Around 1176, the King ordered it to be rebuilt in palatial style with a magnificent hall, marble pillars and a large wine cellar, and for the next two centuries it remained in constant use by his successors. Although the site is now overgrown, its partial excavation in 1978 revealed much valuable information about what life was like in a twelfth-century palace.

9

'The King Has Wrought a Miracle'

During the Christmas court and afterwards there was a constant stream of magnates arriving at Bermondsey to discuss with the King 'the state of the realm and the restoration of peace'. They brought with them so many pet dogs, monkeys, parrots and hawks that the great hall resembled a menagerie rather than a palace.[1]

The King wasted no time in appointing his chief officers of state. The capable and trustworthy Richard de Lucy was made justiciar in association with Robert de Beaumont, Earl of Leicester, who had served Stephen loyally, yet worked tirelessly to secure Henry's succession. Nigel, Bishop of Ely, was made treasurer.

It was probably during the Christmas court that Archbishop Theobald presented his most promising clerk, Thomas Becket, to the King, and warmly recommended him as an excellent candidate for the office of chancellor. Henry took an instant liking to Becket and agreed to the appointment without hesitation. Thus began one of the most famous friendships in history, a friendship that was to have far-reaching consequences for both men.

Becket, who was of middle-class Norman parentage, had been born in London in 1118.[2] His father was a wealthy merchant who arranged for young Thomas to be educated at Merton Priory and a London grammar school, before being sent to the schools of Paris, Bologna and Auxerre to study law. Despite this very comprehensive education, Becket was no academic and never fully mastered Latin. A family friend who held the office of justiciar of London taught him business skills and accountancy, and in 1143 other influential friends, recognising his talent as an administrator, secured him an appointment as a clerk in the household of Archbishop Theobald, which entailed taking minor orders in the Church.

The Archbishop soon recognised Becket's intelligence and adminis- trative ability and earmarked him for promotion. Before long, he was being sent on successful diplomatic missions to Rome and elsewhere, and by 1154 was the holder of several parishes and benefices and had been appointed Provost of Beverley and ordained Archdeacon of Canterbury. It seems, however, that he was now resting on his laurels, for he grew over-worldly and lax in his duties, and was threatened by Theobald with excommunication if he did not improve.

A spell abroad allowed tempers to cool, and when Becket returned, good relations were restored. By the time of Henry's accession, the Archbishop was convinced that Becket would not only make a good chancellor but would also be a loyal champion of the Church. Initially disappointed in this hope, for Becket proceeded to immerse himself wholeheartedly in secretariat matters and affairs of state, Theobald did not live to see how dramatically it would later be fulfilled.

Becket was very tall and slim with dark hair, finely chiselled features, an aquiline nose and rather effeminate, tapering hands. He was a good conversationalist, despite a slight stutter, and had great charm of manner. Like Henry, he was a man of enormous energy and versatile talent, whose chief pleasures were hunting, hawking and chess, although unlike Henry he avoided encounters with women, having taken a vow of chastity in his youth. He was elegant, witty, generous, vain and ambitious, and thrived on the public role that went with his promotion to chancellor, 'throwing off the deacon' and indulging his love of display in magnificent clothes and an extravagant standard of living. He was the perfect courtier. However, he also took things to extremes, being self- willed, obstinate, manipulative and uncompromising, and, as a consum- mate actor, was well able to play the martyr in order to get what he wanted.

His friendship with the King was unusually close, although no one has ever suggested that there was anything unnatural about it; contemporaries observed that Becket stood with the King as Joseph did with Pharaoh. Henry, who was fifteen years younger, knew Becket's worth, and Becket in turn served him faithfully and efficiently as chancellor. 'A man of diligence and industry, experienced in many and great affairs, he discharged the onerous duties of his office to the praise of God and the well-being of the whole realm.'[3] When it pleased him, the King could now relax and leave affairs in Becket's capable hands: 'All things were entrusted to Thomas; while the King gave himself up to youthful pursuits, Thomas governed the whole realm according to his will.'[4]

As chancellor, Becket maintained a splendid household in London, which was paid for by his master and said to outshine the King's in splendour. It came to outrival the court as a forum for ambitious men and a school for the sons of the nobility. This did not bother Henry, who was rather amused by it, but it aroused the envy of his courtiers, who felt themselves displaced. Yet Henry, who was bored by pomp and ceremony, and had little time for impressive displays, was happy to allow Becket to indulge his passion for such things, knowing that it would reflect well upon the wealth and status of his royal master. Therefore he denied him nothing. 'The King bestowed upon him many revenues and received him so much into his esteem and familiarity that throughout the kingdom there was none his equal save the King alone.'[5]

The King and the chancellor greatly enjoyed each other's company and spent whole days together, hunting, feasting, discussing state affairs or enjoying witty conversation.[6] 'The King and Becket played together like little boys of the same age, at the court, in church, in assemblies, in riding.'[7] Becket was occasionally the butt of Henry's practical jokes. Once, riding together through London in the depths of winter, they espied a beggar, shivering in the cold.

'Would it not be a meritorious act to give that poor old man a warm cloak?' asked the King.

Becket concurred.

'Yours be the merit then!' cried his master, whipping off Becket's cloak and, foiling his attempts to recover it, tossing it to the beggar.[8]

History does not record what Queen Eleanor thought of this friendship during these early years, although several historians have perceptively suggested that it relegated her to the side-lines of affairs and undermined her influence with the King. When Henry was abroad, it was Becket, rather than Eleanor, who dispensed patronage on Henry's behalf and received important visitors to England. Nor do we know Becket's opinion of Eleanor, although he was a close friend and colleague of John of Salisbury, whom he had met when both were in the service of Archbishop Theobald, and John could have told him several interesting – and politically sensitive – things about Eleanor's past. If so, he kept them to himself. There is no evidence that the Queen slighted Becket or bore him any malice during the period of his chancellorship. It may even have humoured her to take an opposite stance to her mother-in-law, the Empress Matilda, who disapproved of Becket and made no bones about saying so. Yet this was one issue on which Henry ignored his mother's otherwise welcome advice.

The evidence for Eleanor's life as Henry's queen is at first sight fragmentary, yet when all the fragments are put together, a rounder picture emerges. Sometimes all we have is an itinerary, and an incomplete one at that, yet the surviving official documents give intriguing insights into different aspects of Eleanor's existence, offering clues as to what she was really like. What follows in this and the next few chapters is an attempt to reconstruct this period of her life from these few precious sources.

Feeling that he could safely leave the administration of his realm in the hands of his chancellor and justiciars, Henry left London at the end of January 1155 to establish his authority in other areas of his realm. Marching through East Anglia to York, he besieged several castles and crushed attempts at resistance by a few stubbornly rebellious barons.

On Monday, 28 February 1155, Eleanor, who had remained at Bermondsey, gave birth to a second son. The infant was baptised Henry by Richard de Belmeis, Bishop of London.[9] About a month later, the King returned victorious, to greet the new arrival. Charters issued by him at this time to the canons of Holy Trinity and Christ Church were witnessed by Eleanor, Becket and Richard de Lucy.

The King intended that young Henry should succeed to Anjou.[10] In April, with Eleanor, he travelled to Wallingford to present both princes to the barons and clergy and to command them to swear allegiance to his elder son, William, as the heir to England and, perhaps, Normandy; then, in the event of William's early death, to young Henry as his successor.[11] Since William was styled Count of Poitiers, it appears that he had been designated his mother's heir. It was probably at around this time that Henry acknowledged his bastard son Geoffrey and took him into his household to be brought up with his legitimate sons.

During the spring, Eleanor prevailed upon Henry to undertake repairs to the Palace of Westminster, his chief residence. At Easter, he delegated responsibility for the work to Becket, who undertook it with such energy and enthusiasm that the palace was ready for occupation by Whitsun: a veritable army of workmen had accomplished in fifty days what would, in the normal run of things, have taken a year at least, although the noise they had made had been deafening.[12]

Early in June, Eleanor took up residence at Westminster, but she was not there for long, since she accompanied the King on a tour through his now peaceful realm, visiting important castles and cities.[13] It may have been at around this time that she commissioned the building of her own dock in Thames Street, known as Queenhithe. It was here, in a basin cut into the river bank next to Vintners' Quay, that ships from Aquitaine would in future find moorings. The entrance to the dock was by a great gatehouse, which remained for centuries one of the sights of London.

In September, Eleanor moved with her household to Winchester to be reunited with Henry, who had spent some weeks hunting with Becket in the New Forest. On 29 September, the barons attended a Michaelmas council to discuss the King's projected invasion of Ireland, of which he had been named overlord by Pope Adrian IV, the only Englishman ever to occupy the throne of St Peter. Ireland was then in chaos, torn by wars between feuding chieftains, and the Pope believed that Henry II was the only man who could bring it to order.

Henry was enthusiastic at the prospect of conquering Ireland, and spoke of giving it to his youngest brother William, but the Empress Matilda, learning of his plans, was horrified, and came in haste to England to oppose them. Ireland, she told the council, was a poor land, full of barbarians, which would not be worth the trouble it would bring the King. When she revealed that her middle son, Geoffrey, was taking up arms to enforce his claim to Anjou and Maine, which his father had meant Henry to cede to him once he became king, Henry's interest in Ireland was immediately shelved and he began making plans to deal with Geoffrey.

Henry and Eleanor remained at Winchester throughout the autumn; by the time they celebrated Christmas there, Eleanor knew she was pregnant again.

On 10 January 1156, having spent more than a year in England, Henry crossed from Dover to Wissant and returned to Normandy to attend to the affairs of his continental fiefs, leaving Richard de Lucy as regent and placing Eleanor and their children under the guardianship of Archbishop Theobald and John of Salisbury; the Pipe Rolls show that the Queen was paid allowances for the two boys, and also record that she was supporting in her household her sister Petronilla and their two bastard brothers, William and Joscelin. During the period 1154–8, there are thirty-six entries relating to Exchequer payments to William, as well as regular payments of generous sums for wine for Petronilla.

On 5 February, Henry met King Louis on the Norman border and finally paid him homage for Normandy, Anjou and Aquitaine.[14] He spent the next few months bringing Geoffrey to submission, and in the summer managed to buy him off with an annuity – which he failed to pay in full – and the castle of Loudun. Shortly afterwards, the lords of Nantes and southern Brittany, who had been warring over the Breton succession since the death of Count Conan III in 1148, offered Geoffrey the comital circlet, but he did not live long to enjoy it, dying at Nantes on 26 July 1158.

During the spring, Eleanor travelled widely about the realm, running up a high expenditure of £350.[15] Although she was not officially associated with Richard de Lucy in the regency, the numerous writs issued in her name at this time attest to the fact that she was actively involved in government.

In April or June (sources differ), Eleanor's eldest son, William, who was not quite three years old, died at Wallingford Castle.[16] The circumstances and cause of his death are unknown. He was buried at the feet of his great-grandfather, Henry I, in Reading Abbey.

The grief that Henry and Eleanor felt at losing their son may have been somewhat mitigated by the birth of a daughter in June, either in London or, less probably, at Windsor Castle. The baby, who was baptised by Archbishop Theobald in the church of the Holy Trinity at Aldgate,[17] was named Matilda in honour of the Empress. The Pipe Rolls record the purchase of a baby carriage for her.

Late in July, Eleanor drew funds from the Exchequer and crossed the Channel with the new baby and the Lord Henry, and by 29 August had been reunited with the King at Saumur in Anjou. In October, the family travelled south to Aquitaine, where they undertook a progress, receiving homage from Eleanor's vassals and taking hostages to ensure they did not break their oaths.[18] At Limoges, in order to underline his authority, Henry made the young Viscount his ward and installed Norman officials to administer the county. One baron who had caused trouble for Eleanor in the past was the Viscount of Thouars,[19] who had supported Geoffrey of Anjou in his recent conflict with his royal brother. Henry's vengeance was swift and thorough: he expelled the Viscount from his lands in Poitou and destroyed all his castles.

Henry and Eleanor held their Christmas court at Bordeaux. By the end of February 1157, Eleanor was back in London with her children, leaving Henry to conclude his business on the continent. Soon after her return, she realised that another baby was on the way. Around 8 April, Henry followed her back to England, and at Whitsun they were at Bury St Edmunds for a ceremonial crown-wearing.

After Easter, the King had begun planning a campaign against Owain Gwynedd, Prince of North Wales, who was threatening to take the city of Chester. When, at the end of July, he set out at the head of his army, Eleanor acted as regent. Henry did not fare well in Wales: he was unused to the guerrilla tactics employed by his opponents, who paid no heed to the normal rules of chivalry and routinely decapitated their enemies. During an early skirmish, Owain's men fell upon the English with such savagery that the royal standard was cast into the dust and the King was believed killed. Indeed, he barely escaped with his life, leaving many of his men dead in the field. At Rhuddlan, defeated, he negotiated a truce with Owain and returned to Chester.[20] From there, he embarked on a progress that would take him the length and breadth of England.

Thomas Becket, Richard de Lucy and Robert de Beaumont were all summoned north to join the King, but Eleanor, because of her advancing pregnancy, was obliged to remain at Westminster. In early August, Henry swept south through Warwickshire to Malmesbury, Windsor, Woodstock and Oxford, where Eleanor was able to join him. There, in the King's House (later Beaumont Palace) on 8 September 1157, she gave birth to their third son. The Pipe Rolls record a payment of twenty shillings to cover the expenses of the confinement.

The boy was christened Richard[21] and was given into the care of a nurse, Hodierna of St Albans, whose own son, Alexander Nequam, had been born the same night; this boy, Richard's foster-brother, grew up to be one of the greatest scientists of the age, the author of a treatise on natural history and the first European to study magnetism. Hodierna took care of Richard during his early years. As he grew, he became attached to her and years later, when he became king, he rewarded her for her care of him with a large pension. The old name for West Knoyle in Wiltshire, Knoyle Odierne, suggests that she may have retired there.

It seems likely that Richard was designated the heir to Poitou and Aquitaine, in place of his deceased brother William. Ralph of Diceto implies that this son was special to Eleanor from birth, recalling one of the ancient prophecies of Merlin, which in the twelfth century were widely believed to apply to Henry II and his family: 'The eagle of the broken covenant shall rejoice in her third nesting.' Eleanor was the eagle, the broken covenant the dissolution of her marriage to Louis, and the third nesting was the birth of her third son, Richard.

Once she was over her confinement, Eleanor joined Henry on his great progress, which initially took them to the north of England, where Malcolm IV of Scotland acknowledged the English King as his overlord and paid homage to him. Over the course of the next year, Henry travelled a staggering 3,500 miles, and for much of that time, if not all, Eleanor was with him.

The Christmas court of 1157 was held at Lincoln. Afterwards, Henry returned north to ensure that castles taken from the Scots were properly garrisoned. Then, in the middle of January, he moved south through Yorkshire into Nottinghamshire, where he and Eleanor stayed at the royal manor of Blyth and the royal castle at Nottingham. They then crossed through Oxfordshire into Wiltshire, arriving in Worcestershire by Easter. After the Easter mass held in Worcester Cathedral, the King and Queen took part in a curious ceremony in which they renounced their crowns, taking them off and laying them upon the shrine of St Wulfstan, solemnly vowing never to wear them again.[22] Then it was on to Shropshire, Gloucestershire and Somerset, before pressing north to Carlisle in June.

Early in 1158, Constance of Castile had borne Louis VII a daughter, Marguerite, prompting her husband to complain about 'the frightening superfluity of his daughters.'[23] During his progress, Henry conceived the idea of marrying Marguerite to the Lord Henry. Should Louis die without a male heir, Marguerite would be his co-heiress with her sisters, and although the Salic law forbade succession to the throne by or through a woman, there is little doubt that Henry was confident of his ability to overcome this difficulty – by force if necessary – and annex the kingdom of France to his empire. Even if Louis did have a son, the marriage would bring peace between the two kingdoms and, Henry intended, a settlement advantageous to himself.

Clearly, the best person to broach the delicate matter of this betrothal was Becket, who had a flair for diplomacy, and in the summer of 1158, Henry sent him to France to negotiate with Louis. By design, Becket travelled with a magnificent escort, twenty-four changes of raiment and a heavily laden baggage train, all of which drew astonished comment from the French,[24] whom it was of course meant to impress. Becket's purpose was to overwhelm Louis with this outward display of England's wealth, then persuade him to marry his daughter to the son of his rival. To sweeten the French, he brought with him rich gifts, including chests full of gold and barrels of ale. 'Marvellous is the King of the English whose chancellor goes thus and so grandly,' observed the Parisians. The ploy worked: Louis received Becket like a visiting prince, and when Becket left France, with his baggage train much lighter, he had secured Louis' agreement to the betrothal.

At the end of July, the long royal progress came to an end when the King and Queen reached Winchester. On 14 August, having received news of his brother Geoffrey's death, Henry crossed to France, leaving Eleanor, nearly eight months pregnant, as co-regent with Richard de Lucy.

Henry went first to meet King Louis beside the River Epte near Gisors on the Norman border, where the final terms of the marriage alliance were agreed upon: Marguerite was to have the Norman Vexin and the castle of Gisors as her dowry,[25] although they were not to be formally handed over until 1164, unless the marriage had been solemnised earlier with the consent of the Church. In the meantime, they would remain in Louis' possession but in the custody of the Knights Templar. As a pledge of Louis' good intentions, Marguerite was to be handed over to King Henry immediately. Should the Lord Henry die before the marriage could take place, she would marry one of his brothers. This contract must have afforded Henry considerable satisfaction, since it restored to him the Norman lands and rights ceded by his father to Louis in 1151. As for Louis, he was gratified that his daughter would one day be a queen, and comforted himself for the prospective loss of the Vexin with the knowledge that the betrothed pair would not be married for a long time yet; anything might happen in the meantime.

Louis and Henry also discussed the future of Brittany, with Louis agreeing to support Henry's claim to be his brother's heir and recognising him as the overlord of Brittany, to the detriment of the rival heirs of Conan III. He then invited Henry to Paris to receive the Princess Marguerite.

After the meeting, Henry rode straight to Brittany and took possession of Nantes, its capital,[26] where the citizens, weary of civil war, afforded him a rapturous welcome as Geoffrey's rightful heir. His plan was to conquer the whole of Brittany, but as he had other priorities and claims on his resources at present, he was obliged to content himself with leaving his new vassal, Conan IV, grandson of Conan III, in charge at Nantes, confident that one day the whole of Brittany would be his.

In September, attended by only a small retinue, Henry was warmly welcomed by Louis and the French nobility in Paris, where he refused much of the lavish hospitality on offer. The Parisians were surprised at the contrast between the soberly dressed English King and the magnificent Becket. During the visit, Queen Constance relinquished the six-month-old Princess Marguerite into Henry's custody. As a condition of the betrothal, Louis had stipulated that under no circumstances was his daughter to be brought up by Queen Eleanor; Henry therefore placed Marguerite in the care of the trustworthy Robert of Neubourg, chief justice of Normandy, whose castle stood near the French border.

On 23 September 1158, Eleanor presented Henry with a fourth son, who was named Geoffrey[27] after the King's late father and brother. The Pipe Rolls show that, after her confinement, she heard a great many cases in her own assize court, travelling through Hampshire, Kent, Bedfordshire, Berkshire, Wiltshire and Devon. In Salisbury, on 29 November, she issued a judgement in favour of Matilda, Dowager Countess of Chester, and a certificate confirming a quit-claim. All of this business Eleanor carried out 'by writ of the King from over seas'.

That November, with their new-found friendship cemented by the marriage alliance of their children, Henry escorted Louis through Normandy on a pilgrimage to the abbey of Mont-Saint-Michel, where the chronicler Robert of Torigni was Abbot. On their arrival, both kings heard mass together and dined with the monks in their refectory. Having visited Marguerite on the way home and approved the arrangements made for her care, Louis returned to Paris with rich gifts from Henry and was heard to declare that there was no one he esteemed so highly as the King of England. 'Wonders never cease,' observed Robert of Torigni drily.

Towards the end of the year, Eleanor joined Henry at Cherbourg in Normandy for Christmas, leaving Robert de Beaumont in charge in England. Early in 1159, the royal couple were in Normandy, staying at Rouen and Argentan, although it was not long before they set out on another tour of Aquitaine. It was at around this time that Henry conceived a plan to reassert Eleanor's ancestral rights to the county of Toulouse. It is hard to believe that he was not influenced to do so by Eleanor, although he would have realised for himself, as Louis had eighteen years earlier, that there were considerable advantages to be gained from the acquisition of a wealthy domain that encompassed the key trade routes to the Mediterranean.[28]

In April, at Blaye north of Bordeaux, the King and Queen met Raymond Berenger V, Count of Barcelona, who was at war with Raymond V, Count of Toulouse; Henry formed an alliance with Raymond Berenger,[29] who agreed to support his claim to Toulouse and offered his daughter Berengaria as a bride for the Lord Richard, a plan that came to nothing. However, when King Louis heard of Henry's intentions, he begged him to desist, for the sake of their alliance, since Raymond of Toulouse was not only his vassal but also his ally and brother-in-law, being married to his sister Constance, whose son was the heir to Toulouse: Louis did not want to see his nephew dispossessed.[30]

Nevertheless, Henry persisted, demanding of Raymond V that he relinquish Toulouse to Eleanor. Raymond naturally refused and in May, Henry, by exacting punitive taxes, began raising a large army, summoning the lords of England, Normandy, Anjou and Aquitaine, and even the King of Scots, to meet him at Poitiers in June. Becket was given command of 700 knights. Louis was still protesting, yet when Henry pointed out to him that he himself had pressed Eleanor's claim to Toulouse and was therefore in no position to complain about Henry doing the same, he refused to abandon Raymond.

At Poitiers, where his formidable force had gathered, and where

Eleanor was probably to remain throughout the campaign, Henry was joined by the Count of Barcelona and disaffected vassals of the Count of Toulouse. On 24 June, the army marched south through the Périgord and took Quercy, a fief of Toulouse, with its fine city of Cahors. Early in July, Henry's forces laid siege to the city of Toulouse itself. Shortly afterwards, Louis himself arrived and took charge of the city's defences.

Henry was in a difficult position. He wanted Toulouse, and was confident of his ability to take it, but he was equally reluctant to break his oath of allegiance and make war on his overlord – not so much out of loyalty to Louis, but because it would set a dangerous precedent for his own vassals.[31] Ignoring the advice of Becket, who urged him to carry on with the siege,[32] he withdrew from Toulouse and deployed his men in harrying the surrounding area, in the hope of driving Raymond to surrender. He also sent a force north to raid the royal demesne, hoping to lure Louis away. But the French King, who was determined to protect the birthright of his sister's sons, would not leave Toulouse.[33]

By the time autumn came, Henry's army had been decimated by dysentery due to insanitary conditions, and at the end of September he was obliged to abandon the campaign; afterwards, he arranged a truce until the following May. From Toulouse, Henry rode north to Limoges and thence to Beauvais in Normandy to deal with a threatened invasion by Robert of Dreux. There is no record of him visiting Eleanor in Poitiers en route, and he was probably in too much of a hurry. Husband and wife were, however, reunited in time for Christmas, which they celebrated at Falaise in Normandy. It was one of the bitterest winters of the century.

Henry had now been out of England for seventeen months, but since his presence was still needed on the continent – he would be based mainly in Normandy for the next three years – he arranged for Eleanor to cross the Channel, not only to keep an eye on the affairs of his kingdom, but also to arrange for the immediate transfer of funds from his treasury, which he needed urgently. On 29 December 1159, in the face of a violent tempest, the Queen sailed from Normandy with young Henry and Matilda in the royal ship *Esnecca* (*The Snake*). Having docked safely at Southampton, she rode to Winchester to collect the royal gold. She then escorted it back to Southampton and herself accompanied it on its voyage on the *Esnecca* to Barfleur. After it had been handed over there to Henry's trusted officials, Eleanor returned to England.

The records indicate that for the next nine months the Queen was very busy with her duties as regent, doubtless exercising an authority that would never have been hers, had Becket not remained in France with Henry. Despite the severe weather, Eleanor embarked on an extensive tour of the country, which suggests that she wished to see for herself that it was being administered properly: the Pipe Rolls record her presence in London, Middlesex, Southampton, Berkshire, Surrey, Cambridge, Winchester and Dorset. It is unlikely she would have undertaken such a tour for private reasons.

Whilst she was in residence in Winchester Castle, she paid £22 13s 2d 'for the repair of the chapel, the houses, the walls and the garden of the Queen, and for the transport of the Queen's robes, her wine, her incense and the chests of her chapel, and for the boys' shields, and for the Queen's chamber, chimney and cellar'.[34] During her stay, she authorised thirteen writs for Exchequer payments amounting to £226 for her own expenditure and £56 for that of the Lord Henry. In London, she had the royal cups regilded at a cost of two silver marks.[35] During this period many writs were issued in her name.

In May, the truce with Louis and Raymond V expired, but Henry had come to terms with the fact that he had no realistic prospects of conquering Toulouse. Although Louis confirmed Henry in all his lands save Toulouse, and their alliance was salvaged, the two kings were essentially enemies once more;[36] as William of Newburgh observed, the confrontation at Toulouse marked the beginning of forty years of intermittent warfare between England and France.

During the summer Archbishop Theobald pleaded with the King to return to England, reminding him that it was a long time since he had seen his children: 'Even the most hard-hearted father could hardly bear to have them out of his sight for long,' he wrote. His appeal fell on deaf ears; Henry had his hands full on the continent, and although, in September 1160, he commanded Eleanor to join him in Rouen, bringing with her the Lord Henry and the Lady Matilda,[37] his motive was political rather than personal. The Queen of France was about to bear a child, and if it were a son, Henry hoped to arrange for his betrothal to Matilda. Eleanor must have travelled in some comfort, for the cost of her voyage in the *Esnecca* amounted to £7.[38]

Henry then took the Lord Henry to the border to meet Louis and present the boy as his heir to Normandy. The child went on his knees before the French King and did homage for the duchy, with his father looking on.

On 4 October, after a difficult confinement, Queen Constance bore a second daughter, Alys, 'and passed from this world'.[39] Desperate for a male heir, King Louis, now forty, immediately arranged to marry Adela of Champagne, the sister of his future sons-in-law, Count Henry of

Champagne and Count Theobald of Blois, both of whom were hostile to Henry II.

News of Louis' betrothal dashed Henry's hopes of ever absorbing France into his empire. Even if Adela failed to bear Louis a son, the powerful House of Blois would conspire to subvert his schemes. It occurred to him that Counts Henry and Theobald might even persuade Louis to abandon his alliance with Henry, in which case he would lose all hope of recovering the Norman Vexin.

There was no time to lose, therefore. The marriage of Henry's son and Louis' daughter must take place without delay. Louis' consent was implicit in the marriage contract, so there was no need to consult him beforehand. All the King needed was the Church's special dispensation for the marriage of two minors. It so happened that, following a schism in 1159, rival popes had laid claim to the triple crown of St Peter, and at that very moment two cardinal legates, emissaries from Pope Alexander III, were at Henry's court, seeking his support for their master. It was therefore easy for Henry to procure a dispensation.[40]

At the King's command, Marguerite was brought by her guardian from Neubourg (Eure) to Rouen, and there married to the Lord Henry in the presence of the two legates, one of whom, Henry of Pisa, officiated at the nuptials. The bridegroom was five, the bride not yet three – 'as yet little children crying in the cradles'.[41] After the wedding, Henry took Marguerite into his own household as a hostage against any reprisals by her father;[42] this naturally meant that she would be brought up in the care of Queen Eleanor, against Louis' express wishes. Henry also demanded that the Knights Templar surrender the Vexin to him immediately, which they did willingly. The King at once proceeded to fortify Gisors and other border strongholds.[43]

On 13 November, Louis married Adela of Champagne. When he found out how Henry had tricked him, he was furious. He protested that, since his daughter's wedding had taken place earlier than he had intended – he insisted, with some exaggeration, that he had not expected it to happen for another ten years – he was not obliged to surrender her dowry. But it was too late, and he had to content himself with expelling the Templars from Paris[44] and encouraging Theobald of Blois to take to arms against Henry. Fearing that Touraine was under threat, Henry hastened south and took Theobald's castle of Chaumont on the Loire as a warning. At that point the arrival of winter put an end to the fighting season.

Honour satisfied, Henry withdrew to Le Mans with Eleanor and their children, and there kept court in great state throughout Advent and Christmas.

On 18 April 1161, Archbishop Theobald, who had been such a true friend to Henry, died, leaving the King faced with the problem of finding another such to replace him. Immediately, he thought of Becket, but the Empress Matilda and the respected Gilbert Foliot, Bishop of Hereford (Bishop of London from 1163), warned him that the chancellor was too worldly a man for high ecclesiastical office.

There the matter rested, for in the spring of 1161 Henry was busy preparing for war against Louis, strengthening his castles on the Norman border and in Anjou, Maine and Touraine. At the same time, he was building a new royal residence outside Rouen. Trouble in Aquitaine, however, took him south in the summer. 'Amongst other vigorous deeds, he laid siege to Castillon-sur-Agen, and took it within a week, to the wonder and terror of the Gascons.'[45] The sparse surviving evidence suggests that he was also pursuing a policy of installing Norman administrators in the duchy, in an attempt to enforce centralised government upon its unruly barons. Unlike Eleanor, he did not repose much confidence in the ability of her uncle, Raoul de Faye, to act as her deputy.

His interference was widely resented. 'The Poitevins withdrew from their allegiance to the King of the English because of his pruning of their liberties.'[46] They even tried to have his marriage to their duchess dissolved, sending a deputation to the cardinal legates with a genealogical table showing that Henry and Eleanor were within the forbidden degrees of consanguinity. But the legates were, of course, in no position to dare offend Henry by even suggesting such a thing. They were still busy ingratiating themselves on Pope Alexander's behalf. Thus Henry was able that year to secure the canonisation of the Saxon king, Edward the Confessor, and so enhance the prestige of the English monarchy.

Whilst he was in Poitiers, Henry inspected the work being done on the choir of the new cathedral and gave orders for the building of another new church, as well as new city walls, bridges, a market and shops, setting new standards in town planning. He also arranged to have the great hall of the ducal palace refurbished with arcaded walls and bigger windows.

Eleanor had remained in Normandy. She was pregnant again, and at Domfront Castle in September 1161,[47] gave birth to her second daughter by Henry, who was named Eleanor in her honour and baptised by Cardinal Henry of Pisa; Robert of Torigni was her godfather. Three years had elapsed since Eleanor's previous child had been born, and historians have conjectured why, after bearing four children in as many years, there was such a gap. It may have occurred because, having presented Henry with three healthy sons in quick succession, Eleanor felt she deserved a rest from childbearing. She may simply not have conceived. Or, as several writers have suggested, she may have had a child whose birth and early death were not recorded by the chroniclers.

John Speed, the English antiquarian whose *History of Great Britain* was published in 1611, had access to sources now lost to us, and he records that Henry and Eleanor had a son named Philip, who was born between 1158 and 1162, but died young. Yet Francis Sandford, a genealogist who at the end of the seventeenth century made a detailed study of the royal line, does not mention him. It is possible that he existed: mediaeval chroniclers did not always mention royal infants who died young. Although William, Count of Poitiers, died at the age of three, he was his father's first-born heir and therefore worthy of note, but a fifth son who died young might have been considered relatively unimportant. However, the dates of birth of all Eleanor's other children by Henry are recorded – even the birth of her last child, John, who is usually accounted her fifth son. Moreover, the name Philip was an unusual choice, favoured by the French royal line, but never having been used by the forebears of Henry and Eleanor. Neither, however, had the name John been used. The name Philip could, of course, have been chosen as a compliment to Louis, but surely his own name would have been more appropriate. Since the evidence for this prince's existence is found only in much later sources and the circumstantial evidence is inconclusive, none of it should be relied upon.

During this year of 1161, concern was expressed in several quarters that the Lord Henry, now six years old, was still living with his mother and had not begun his formal education. Reflecting this concern, the Archbishop of Rouen ventured to write tactfully to the King on the matter:

> Although other kings are of a rude and uncultivated character, yours, which was formed by literature, is prudent in the administration of great affairs, subtle in judgement and circumspect in counsel. Wherefore all your bishops unanimously agree that Henry, your son and heir, should apply himself to letters, so that he whom we regard as your heir may be the successor to your wisdom as well as your kingdom.[48]

Henry took the point. It was customary for princes and the sons of the nobility to be sent away to other aristocratic households to be nurtured and educated. Thomas Becket had already accepted into his household a number of noble boys, and the King now arranged for his own son to join them. From this time onwards, Becket would refer to the Lord Henry as his adopted son.

Armed conflict between Henry and Louis had seemed inevitable,[49] but Louis had by now realised that opposing Henry over the matter of the Vexin was a hopeless cause, and in October the two kings met at Fréteval and made peace.

Henry and Eleanor kept Christmas at Bayeux that year. The King was still considering who should fill the vacant archbishopric of Canterbury, and by the time he and the Queen held their Easter court at Falaise, he had made up his mind that he wanted Becket. Becket was a loyal friend to him and would, Henry felt sure, support the radical plans he was formulating for reforming abuses within the Church, which in Henry's opinion had become too powerful. With a king's man as Archbishop of Canterbury, he would have no trouble in implementing them.

Summoning the Chancellor before him, the King commanded him to take the Lord Henry to England and have the barons swear fealty to him once more as their future king. When Becket brought the prince to say farewell to his parents, Henry took Becket aside.

'You do not yet fully comprehend your mission,' he said. 'It is my intention that you should become Archbishop of Canterbury.'[50]

Becket was horrified. He was aware of Henry's intentions towards the Church and realised that, as archbishop, he would be honour bound to oppose them. He was also aware that his enemies would be happy to use this as a means of driving a wedge between himself and Henry. He therefore begged the King to reconsider, warning him that, if he persisted in this appointment, their friendship would turn to bitter hatred. Besides, he was not even a priest, and had never celebrated a mass.[51]

Henry ignored his protests. Once his mind was made up, he would not be diverted from his chosen course. With a heavy heart, Becket departed for England. His last act as chancellor was to arrange the ceremony, which took place in Winchester at Whitsun, at which the barons paid homage to the Lord Henry. He also paid £38 6s 'for gold for preparing a crown and regalia for the King's son',[52] an indication that the King had plans to have his heir crowned in his own lifetime, as was the custom in France.

In London, in May 1162, in the presence of the Lord Henry and all the King's judges, the unwilling Becket was formally nominated archbishop; on 2 June he was ordained a priest, and the next day he was consecrated in Canterbury Cathedral, with tears of emotion streaming down his face; he was a man who wept easily.[53] On that day, it seemed to contemporaries that a miraculous transformation took place. 'As he put on those robes, reserved at God's command to the highest of His clergy, he changed not only his apparel, but the cast of his mind.'[54]

Overnight, it seemed, the proud and worldly courtier, statesman and soldier had become an ascetic priest committed to his spiritual duties. He had changed, he declared, 'from a patron of play actors and a follower of hounds to a shepherd of souls'.[55] Becket had never done things by halves, and he now threw himself wholeheartedly into his new role. 'He handled the Holy Sacraments with the utmost reverence and . . . so utterly abandoned the world that all men marvelled thereat.'[56]

Instead of his elegant raiment, he now wore a monk's habit, and beneath it, to remind himself of the weakness of the flesh, he wore 'a hair shirt of the roughest kind, which reached to his knees and swarmed with vermin; he mortified his flesh with the sparest diet, and his accustomed drink was water used for the cooking of hay'.[57] He performed extravagant acts of charity and humility,[58] such as washing the feet of thirteen beggars every day, dispensing alms to them and exposing his bare back frequently to the discipline of flagellation by his monks. His nights were spent in vigil. 'The King has wrought a miracle,' observed the sceptical Gilbert Foliot wryly. 'Out of a soldier and a courtier he has made an archbishop.' Foliot had been the only bishop to oppose Becket's election; a vigorous churchman and scholar, he would become one of the new Archbishop's greatest enemies.

As soon as he became archbishop, Becket shocked Henry by returning the great seal of England and resigning the chancellorship, making plain his intention to devote his life exclusively to the Church. When told that the burdens of two offices were too much for the Archbishop, the King voiced a suspicion that Becket no longer cared to be in his service.

Henry and Eleanor remained in Normandy for the rest of the year. They had intended to return to England in late autumn, but were prevented from doing so by storms in the Channel and were obliged to hold their Christmas court at Cherbourg. On 25 January 1163, they sailed to England. It was the first time Henry had set foot in his kingdom since August 1158.

10

'Conjectures which Grow Day by Day'

When the King and Queen landed at Southampton with their daughters Matilda and Eleanor, they were met by a large deputation of nobles and clergy, headed by Archbishop Becket. He came forward holding the hand of the Lord Henry, who emerged from the shelter of his guardian's cloak to greet his parents with fond embraces as the onlookers cried '*Vivat rex!*'.[1] Henry and Becket saluted each other and exchanged the kiss of peace; while William of Canterbury describes the King's manner as 'blithe', Herbert of Bosham claims that he gave Becket a dark look. The following day, however, they rode side by side to Westminster, deep in amicable conversation.

Henry would spend the next three years in England, implementing his plans for enforcing law and order in his realm. His return would mark the end of Eleanor's intermittent spells as regent of England; the last English writ in her name was issued in 1163. This does not mean to say that Henry had lost confidence in her ability to rule in his absence, for he would in future delegate his authority to her on the continent. For the present, however, she remained in England. During February, the Pipe Rolls record items purchased by her for the festivities arranged for the Lord Henry's eighth birthday.

Henry spent the spring of 1163 crushing a rising in south Wales. Although he did not subdue the Welsh entirely, every one of their princes paid homage to him at Woodstock that summer, acknowledging him as their overlord.

One of Henry's chief concerns at this time was the increase in crimes committed by the clergy, and he resolved to put an end to the legal process that made this possible. Lay persons who had committed felonies were dealt with in the King's courts, where they were punished with due severity, but anyone in holy orders – even the lowliest clerk – could claim benefit of clergy and be tried in the Church courts, which were not allowed to punish offenders by the shedding of blood and imposed only the lightest penalties. This dual system of justice was, in the King's view, scandalous, unfair and intolerable – it was said that over 100 murders had been committed by clerks and had gone largely unpunished since his accession – and he was determined to ensure that all offenders were tried in the royal courts. He was aware, however, that the enforcement of such a measure would be seen by many as an attack on the Church and its power, and would therefore meet with resistance. Nevertheless, he was determined to have his way.

The first sign of trouble between Henry and Becket manifested itself at a council of clergy held at Woodstock on 1 July, when the Archbishop condemned the King's plan to divert the larger part of his sheriffs' profits into the royal treasury. It appears that Becket seized on this reasonable proposal as an issue upon which to assert his authority as primate, and, surprisingly, he got his way.

The real showdown came on 1 October, when, at a meeting of the Great Council at Westminster, the King proposed that the Church should degrade and disown those 'criminous clerks' who had been found guilty in the ecclesiasatical courts and should 'hand them over to my court for corporal punishment';[2] this, he declared – rather stretching the truth – would be no innovation but merely a return to the customs of Henry I.

Like many people, Becket was aware of the abuses in the system, but as archbishop he found he could not sanction any infringement of the authority and liberties of the Church, which was fiercely protective of its immunity from secular interference. He therefore opposed the reform, and was supported, after some persuasion, by every one of his bishops.[3]

An exasperated Henry reacted by demanding that his bishops swear obedience to the ancient customs of the realm. Sensing that they might be outmanoeuvred, they all took the oath, but, at the insistence of the Archbishop, with the qualifying rider 'saving our order'. The King was not pleased.

'By the eyes of God!' he thundered. 'Let me hear no word of your order! I demand absolute and express agreement to my customs.' When both Becket and his bishops proved obdurate, Henry stormed out of the hall.[4] The following day, before he left Westminster at dawn, he confiscated Becket's manors of Eye and Berkhamsted, which he had bestowed upon him when chancellor,[5] and removed the Lord Henry from his household; the boy was not returned to his mother's care, but was given an establishment and servants of his own. Thus began one of the most famous rifts in history.

On 13 October, both king and archbishop were present in Westminster Abbey when the body of St Edward the Confessor was translated to a new shrine. It is likely that Eleanor and her children were also present at this ceremony. The Archbishop conducted the service and, on the surface, it seemed that all was well, but this was just an illusion.

Soon, it seemed to Henry that Becket was deliberately trying to provoke him at every turn. When the King decided to marry his brother William to the heiress Isabella de Warenne, widow of King Stephen's younger son (also called William), the Archbishop forbade it on the flimsiest of grounds, and when William of Anjou died soon afterwards – some said of a broken heart – Henry blamed Becket. Without consulting the King, as was customary, Becket then excommunicated a tenant-in-chief, William of Eynsford, as a result of a petty dispute; worst of all, he defied the King by going out of his way to ensure that crimes committed by clerks – including theft, manslaughter, rape and murder – went unpunished or earned only the lightest sentences.

In all these measures Becket was supported by a majority of the bishops. William of Newburgh later concluded that they were the ones responsible for the rupture within the kingdom, 'since they were more intent upon defending the liberties and rights of the clergy than on correcting and restraining their vices'.

Counselled by his mother, the Empress, who would over the next four years give him sensible advice as to how to deal with Becket, Henry took steps to win over public opinion to his side. He had Becket's enemy, Gilbert Foliot, transferred to the See of London to advise him and lead the opposition to the Archbishop. Foliot was a strong advocate, sufficiently acquainted with both canon and civil law to be convinced that Becket was wrong. A few other bishops, perturbed by the Archbishop's aggressive stance, began to distance themselves from him, and Pope Alexander III, who had reason to be grateful to Henry, urged Becket to submit to his master, warning him that he could 'expect no help from the curia in anything that might offend the King'.

By December, fearful of the Pope's displeasure, most of the bishops had deserted Becket, and public opinion popularly supported the King's stand against what was widely regarded as an abuse. At Woodstock, at Pope Alexander's behest, the Archbishop acknowledged defeat and finally gave the King his unqualified promise to observe the ancient customs of England.

At Christmas, the King and Queen were together at Becket's former castle at Berkhamsted. Thomas had spent large sums transforming the keep into a luxurious residence, and it was one of the more comfortable of Henry's houses. Royal plate was brought here from the treasury at Winchester in honour of the festival.[6]

The year 1164 saw the marriages of Eleanor's daughters by Louis: Marie married Henry, Count of Champagne, while Alix married his brother, Theobald, Count of Blois. There is no record of Eleanor having any contact with her daughters during the years after the dissolution of her marriage to their father, and she did not attend either wedding.

Henry was not content with Becket's private promise: he wanted to make him publicly submit to royal authority. At a council held at Clarendon on 25 January 1164,[7] he demanded that the clergy endorse a new code of sixteen laws, which became known as the Constitutions of Clarendon, and which Henry claimed enshrined the customs of his ancestors. The third article, which was one of those that did not, laid down that criminous clerks should be handed over to the royal courts for sentencing, and it prompted Becket to a further protest. However, Henry had wisely taken counsel of both canon and civil lawyers and knew that the Archbishop had no grounds for opposition.

The bishops, however, were unhappy at the King's demand, for they knew very well that a few of the Constitutions encompassed his own reforms, rather than the customs of his ancestors. Disregarding the King's anger — his howls were 'like the roaring of a lion'[8] — and his threats to resort to the sword in order to compel them to submit, they backed Becket, only to see him inexplicably capitulate and agree to 'perjure himself'.[9] He still refused to set his seal to the Constitutions,[10] but gave his consent 'in good faith', bidding the bishops do likewise. When the Pope saw a copy of the Constitutions, he agreed with Becket that the liberties of the Church were under threat, and condemned nearly every clause.

Fortified by papal support, Becket soon regretted his moment of weakness and imposed severe penances on himself in self-retribution. He also tried twice to escape to France, but was frustrated by adverse winds, untrustworthy mariners and the King's officers. His change of heart infuriated Henry, who was now determined to oust Becket from his archbishopric, a move that was supported by the bishops, who mostly shared Henry's view that Becket was too unstable for high ecclesiastical office.

In October, Henry had Becket arraigned at a council at Northampton on a charge of contempt of court.[11] Although Becket maintained that, as archbishop, he was not subject to the jurisdiction of the King, it was pointed out to him that he had been charged as a tenant-in-chief and not as archbishop, and as such he would be judged. When Henry also called him to account for the disposition of moneys that had passed through his hands as chancellor, it became clear to Becket that the King was out to ruin him. When he asked his fellow prelates for advice and help, he was dismayed to find that few of them were willing to support him.

At the end of a gruelling week, the Archbishop made a dramatic entrance into the court, carrying his episcopal cross himself, rather than having it borne before him by his cross-bearer, to signify that he claimed the protection of the Church against the ill will of the King.[12] 'He was always a fool and always will be,' observed Bishop Foliot.[13]

Having reminded an irate Henry that he had been released from all his liabilities as chancellor, Becket forbade the bishops to sit in judgement on him. They in turn, at Henry's behest, resolved to inform the Pope that Becket had breached the oath he had sworn upholding the Constitutions of Clarendon, and to request his deposition. The King then called for sentence to be passed on him, but Becket refused to wait to hear it, and stalked out of the room to shouts of 'Traitor!'[14]

That night, disguised as a monk, the Archbishop escaped from Northampton and fled to Flanders.[15] His departure excited little stir in England, and few missed him, although the King was struck speechless with anger on hearing of his flight and hissed, 'We have not finished with him yet!'[16] On the continent, Becket continued to make trouble for Henry: visiting the Pope at Sens, he portrayed himself so convincingly as a victim of the English King's deliberate attempt to limit the Church's power that he won Alexander's sympathy, and thereafter it would require the deployment of all Henry's skills in diplomacy to avoid an open breach with the Pope.

Becket also wrote numerous letters trying to enlist the sympathy of other European rulers, several of whom attempted to exploit the quarrel to their own advantage. Before long, orthodox churchmen all over Europe believed that Henry was hell-bent on persecuting the Church. Becket even wrote repeatedly to the Empress Matilda, but received little satisfaction from that quarter. A sympathetic Louis VII took the exiled Archbishop under his own protection and offered him refuge at the Cistercian abbey of Pontigny in Burgundy (in 1166, Becket moved to the abbey of Sainte-Colombe at Sens), but he also tried to heal the rift: between 1165 and 1170 he arranged no fewer than twelve interviews between Henry and Becket; of the ten that took place, all ended in failure. For the next six years, neither king nor archbishop would agree to compromise. What had begun as a dispute over a legal principle had turned into a battle of wills over whose was the greater authority.

Henry and Eleanor spent the winter of 1164–5 in the south of England,[17] keeping Christmas at Marlborough. On 24 December, when Henry received the envoys he had sent to enlist Louis' support against Becket and forestall Becket's appeal to the Pope, he was appalled to hear that Louis had taken Becket's part and expressed the hope that the Pope would receive the Archbishop with kindness 'and not heed any unjust accusations against him';[18] Henry was also informed that Becket had got to the Pope first and complained of harassment, and that Alexander had threatened Henry with excommunication.

'The King, burning with his customary fury, threw the cap from his head, undid his belt, threw far from him the cloak and robes in which he was dressed, with his own hands tore the silken coverlet off the bed, and, sitting down as though on a dung-heap, began to chew the straw of the mattress.'[19] He remained in a foul mood throughout Christmas Day, and on the 26th, 'giving way to unbridled passion more than became a king, he took an unbecoming and pitiful kind of revenge by banishing all the Archbishop's relatives out of England'.[20] Four hundred people were affected by this decree; all were stripped of their possessions and deported to Flanders, where they were reduced to begging for food.[21]

In February 1165, Henry crossed to Normandy. At Rouen, as a means of putting pressure on the Pope to abandon Becket, he opened negotiations for an alliance with the German Emperor Frederick Barbarossa, which would be certain to upset King Louis, the Pope – whose rival Frederick had supported – and, above all, Becket. The alliance was to be cemented by two marriages: that of Henry's eldest daughter Matilda to Henry the Lion, Duke of Saxony and Bavaria, the Emperor's cousin, foremost vassal and powerful ally; and that of Matilda's three-year-old sister Eleanor to the Emperor's infant son Frederick. Frederick Barbarossa had sent the imperial chancellor, Reinald of Dassel, Archbishop of Cologne, to Rouen to arrange the terms of the treaty.

Whilst Henry negotiated in Rouen, Eleanor remained at Winchester,[22] although not as regent. The Pipe Rolls reveal that at around this time she and her children visited Sherborne Castle in Dorset and the Isle of Wight before moving to Westminster. After concluding the marriage treaty, the Archbishop of Cologne crossed the Channel to pay his respects to the Queen and be introduced to her daughters; on Henry's orders, she had summoned a council to Westminster to confirm the new alliance.

On 1 May, pregnant once more, Eleanor left her other children in England and took Richard and Matilda to join Henry in Normandy[23] for a fortnight before he returned to his kingdom to undertake a new campaign against the Welsh. After his departure, Eleanor took up residence in Angers, having been entrusted with the government of Anjou and Maine in his absence. In this task, she seems to have been advised by her uncle, Raoul de Faye, who appears to have exercised considerable influence over her.

It was at around this time that Becket contemplated appealing to Eleanor to intervene on his behalf in his quarrel with the King. Both his friend John of Salisbury, who had voluntarily undertaken to share his exile, and John de Bellesmains, Bishop of Poitiers, warned Becket that he could hope for neither aid nor counsel from the Queen, 'especially since she puts all her trust in Raoul de Faye, who is no less hostile toward you than usual'. This is in fact the only surviving evidence of Eleanor's attitude towards Becket. What is unusual is that she appears to have been influenced more by her uncle than by her husband, which is perhaps the first indication that she and Henry had grown apart.

What is clear from this and the absence of other evidence is that, although Eleanor was hostile to Becket, she never became actively involved in his quarrel with Henry. Although Henry regularly consulted his mother on the matter, there is no record of him consulting Eleanor, although the very fact that Becket thought it worth while to appeal to her suggests that she wielded some influence over the King.

In his letter to Becket, the Bishop of Poitiers also added mysteriously that the relationship between Eleanor and her uncle was subject to 'conjectures which grow day by day, and which seem to deserve credence'.[24] He did not elaborate, but certainly whatever he was referring to was of a highly sensitive nature. He may have meant simply that Raoul de Faye was an undesirable political influence, yet it may also be inferred from the same remark that there was a degree of attraction between them. In the past, Eleanor had not scrupled to become too closely involved with one of her uncles; she was now forty-three, still fertile, and her marriage to Henry may have gone stale. It would have been all too easy for her to turn to the supportive Raoul for comfort; however, she was four months pregnant with her ninth child at this time, and we hear no more of the rumours about her relationship with Raoul de Faye, so it would be unwise to infer any sexual innuendo from the Bishop's letter.

Although Eleanor disappears from the records during the period from May to the end of July, it would appear that she remained in Angers, and she was certainly there at the end of August when momentous news arrived from France.

On 22 August 1165, King Louis' hopes were at long last fulfilled when Adela of Champagne bore him a healthy son at Gonesse near Paris. The infant was baptised Philip and immediately nicknamed 'Dieudonné', which means God-given, and 'Augustus', after the month of his birth. There were joyous celebrations in Paris, but Henry II cannot have shared Louis' joy, for the birth of an heir to the French throne put paid to his scheme to claim the crown of France for the Lord Henry in the right of his wife Marguerite. Two comets that appeared in the sky over England at this time were widely regarded as portending the death of a king or the ruin of a nation. Later, their appearance was linked to Philip's birth.[25]

Meanwhile, in Angers, Eleanor was having trouble enforcing her authority over Henry's vassals in Maine and on the Breton border, who were plotting rebellion against their overlord.[26] At the Queen's command, the Constable of Normandy raised a force against them, but was unable to overcome them, largely, it appears, because Eleanor's orders were treated with contempt by his men. Nor could the King come to her aid because he was heavily beset in Wales.[27]

It was perhaps during the summer of 1165 that Henry began his notorious affair with Rosamund de Clifford, although it is impossible to date this event with any certainty. During the Welsh campaign, Rosamund's father, Sir Walter de Clifford, a knight of Norman extraction, had performed his feudal service for the King, and it is possible that at some stage Henry received hospitality at Sir Walter's border stronghold at Bredelais, where he is thought by several historians to have made Rosamund's acquaintance.

According to Giraldus Cambrensis, Rosamund was very young when her affair with the King began, and he confirms that it lasted for some years, at least until 1174, when it was publicly acknowledged, and probably until shortly before Rosamund's death in 1176. The fact that the liaison was kept secret until 1174 would appear to substantiate William of Newburgh's assertion that Henry did not begin to be unfaithful to Queen Eleanor until she was past childbearing age.

It has been suggested that during their affair Rosamund was much neglected by the King, who was only in England for three and a half years during the course of it, yet it is possible that she travelled discreetly with him, especially since for much of this time he was not living with Eleanor. Rosamund is not thought to have borne the King any children: it was not until the sixteenth century that it was asserted that she was the mother of his natural sons Geoffrey and William Longsword, and no contemporary source ascribes any bastards to her.

In fact, there is very little information in contemporary sources about Henry's affair with Rosamund. It is through later legends, which have evolved over eight centuries, that it has become famous; indeed, no other mistress of an English king has ever inspired so many romantic tales. Unfortunately, even in the twentieth century many of these stories have been accepted as fact by historians.

The legends surrounding Rosamund de Clifford are of two types: legends about her death, which will be examined later, and legends about her affair with the King.[28] Early in the fourteenth century, a monk of Chester, Ranulf Higden, in his *Polychronicon* (*Universal History*), which was based on the works of Giraldus Cambrensis and many other, often less reliable sources, asserted that Henry II 'was privily a spouse breaker' and was not ashamed 'to misuse the wench Rosamund. To this fair wench the King made at Woodstock a chamber of wonder craft, wonderly made by Daedalus' work, lest the Queen should find and take Rosamund'.[29] This is the first reference to Henry building a bower and labyrinth for Rosamund at Woodstock. It is not mentioned again in any work until the late fifteenth century, when the London chronicler Robert Fabyan, drawing on Higden, described 'the house of wonder working or Daedalus' work, which is a house wrought like unto a knot in a garden called a maze'.

In fact, there is no contemporary evidence linking Rosamund de Clifford with the hunting lodge at Woodstock, nor is there any proof that a bower or labyrinth ever existed there. Henry did construct a cloistered garden by the spring at nearby Everswell, in 1166, with pools and benches, the remains of which were described by the diarist John Evelyn in the seventeenth century, but there is no evidence to link it with Rosamund.

During the sixteenth century, the Rosamund legends evolved into a literary tradition, and became the subject of much inventive Elizabethan verse. Michael Drayton wrote of the tower and labyrinth at Woodstock, while 'The Ballad of Fair Rosamund', composed by Thomas Delaney, portrayed its heroine as beautiful and virtuous, seduced in extreme youth by the King. By then, the bower had become a strong building of stone and timber, with 150 doors and a maze 'so cunningly contrived with turnings round about, that none but with a clue of thread could enter in or out'. In the morality tale 'The Complaint of Rosamund' by Samuel Daniel (1592), Rosamund is kept a captive of the King's jealousy at Woodstock, and realises too late that she should never have succumbed to his sinful advances.

During the centuries that followed, and particularly during the era of Romantic literature, many famous writers and playwrights – among them Joseph Addison, Agnes Strickland, Algernon Swinburne, Alfred, Lord Tennyson and even Winston Churchill – made little attempt to distinguish history from legend. Even today, some of Eleanor's biographers draw conclusions about Rosamund from the legends. The real truth is that we know very little about her.

In September 1165, Henry returned to England, having failed to subdue the Welsh. In savage retribution, he ordered the mutilation of the hostages he had taken, then took himself off to Woodstock, shelving the problems in Brittany and Aquitaine until the start of the next campaigning season in the spring.

In October, Eleanor gave birth to another daughter, Joanna, at Angers.[30] Henry, however, remained in England. The Pipe Rolls and other records show that between September 1165 and March 1166 he was based mainly at Woodstock, leaving only to make brief trips to Winchester and Clarendon. Nor, for the first time since their marriage, did he join Eleanor, who was at Angers, for Christmas, but held his court alone at Oxford. Some writers have inferred from this that he was indulging his passion for Rosamund at Woodstock, but this is pure supposition.

Henry was in fact hard at work on his programme of law reform. At an assize held at Clarendon early in 1166, he confirmed the Constitutions of Clarendon. It was his intention that from now on his justice would be enforced in every part of his realm, and, amongst other reforms, he authorised his sheriffs and judges to hunt down criminals beyond the county boundaries and impose more severe punishments.

At the beginning of March, the King prepared to sail to Normandy, but at the last minute changed his mind and returned to Woodstock,[31] with the intention, some writers fancifully suggest, of saying a final farewell to Rosamund. On 16 March, he was back at Southampton, whence he crossed to Falaise; he would not return to his kingdom for another four years. He marched immediately on Maine, there to teach the barons who had rebelled against him, as well as those who had slighted Eleanor, a lesson they would not forget, destroying their castles and crushing their resistance.[32] At Easter, he joined Eleanor at Angers and held court there. Around this time, she conceived her last child.

Late in May, Henry went to Chinon, an imposing fortress above the River Vienne in Anjou, which was one of his favourite residences. Whilst he was here, it was given out that he was laid low by illness, and he did not emerge until July. Although John of Salisbury believed it to be genuine, the illness may have been a tactical ploy designed to avert Becket's repeated threats of excommunication, since the Church's ban could not be imposed on someone who was sick. Despite the efforts of King Louis and others, Henry and Becket were no nearer reconciliation than they had been two years before.

At Pentecost, Becket went to Vézelay, where he preached a sermon and excommunicated all those who had been the authors of the Constitutions of Clarendon; he did not carry out his threat to excommunicate the King because of Henry's illness.[33] Henry wept tears of rage when he received at Chinon news of the excommunications,[34] and at his urgent request – and that of his ally the Emperor Frederick Barbarossa, whose support Alexander III so desired – the Pope agreed to annul the sentences and forbid Becket to molest Henry further. An angry Empress Matilda wrote in brisk terms to Becket, castigating him for showing the King such gross ingratitude for all the favours he had showered upon him, and warning him that his only hope of regaining royal favour lay in humbling himself and moderating his behaviour. Becket did not trouble to reply.

In July, the King finally turned his attention to Brittany, where his vassal, Count Conan IV, had failed to keep order during Henry's absence. The King deposed him, secured control of the whole of the county and – betrothing his own son Geoffrey, aged eight, to Constance, Conan's five-year-old daughter and heiress – rode to Rennes. There, in the name of Geoffrey, Henry formally took possession of what he was now pleased to call the duchy of Brittany. In the autumn, the lords of Brittany reluctantly paid homage to him at Thouars, but it would be two years before their resistance to his rule was crushed.

By October, Henry was in residence at Caen in Normandy, ready to deal with the Aquitanian rebels. Summoning them to meet him at Chinon on 20 November, he declared his intention of honouring them by holding his Christmas court at Poitiers, where he would present to them their future overlord. The Poitevins were unimpressed and went home to resume their plotting.

Henry had decided against Eleanor accompanying him to Poitiers. This may have been because he knew that she was opposed to his choice of the Lord Henry, rather than the Lord Richard, as her heir to the duchy of Aquitaine. Henry was already designated the heir to England, Anjou and Normandy, while Geoffrey had Brittany. If Henry received Aquitaine as well, Richard would have no inheritance at all. If, as seems highly likely, Richard was Eleanor's favourite son, then such an arrangement could not have won her approval. During the autumn, therefore, Henry sent her and their daughter Matilda back to England.

At the end of the year, having arranged for the Lord Henry to cross the Channel at a cost of £100,[35] the Queen spent some time travelling in Oxfordshire before retiring to the King's House (Beaumont Palace) in Oxford for her confinement.

It has been suggested by some of her biographers that during her travels she visited Woodstock with the intention of having her child there, only to find Rosamund de Clifford installed, which prompted her to withdraw in anger to Oxford. This is another example of the unsupported fictions that have attached themselves to Rosamund's name, and it is more likely that Eleanor had intended all along to be confined in Oxford, where she had borne her third son, Richard. On Christmas Eve 1166 (not 1167,[36] the date erroneously given in many history books), she gave birth to her last child, a son, whom she called John,[37] in honour of the saint on whose feast day he was born.

Henry again presided alone over his Christmas court, which was held that year at Poitiers. As he had promised, he presented the Lord Henry to the Poitevins as their future duke.[38]

Early in the new year of 1166, Henry quelled a rebellion by William Taillefer, one of Eleanor's uncles, in Aquitaine, then after Easter marched against the Count of Auvergne, who was intriguing with King Louis against Henry.

Eleanor seems to have remained in England. The Pipe Rolls record visits with her children to Carisbrooke Castle and payments to their governess, who was called Agatha.

She was also busy preparing for the Lady Matilda's wedding to Henry of Saxony. In July, the Emperor's envoys arrived in England to escort the eleven-year-old princess to Germany. Her parents had provided her with a magnificent trousseau, which included clothing worth £63, 'two large silken cloths and two tapestries, and one cloth of samite and twelve sable skins', as well as twenty pairs of saddlebags, twenty chests, seven saddles gilded and covered with scarlet, and thirty-four packhorses. The total cost amounted to £4,500, which was equal to almost one-quarter of England's entire annual revenue, and was raised by the imposition of various taxes, authorised by the King.[39]

During the summer Henry met Louis in the Vexin in an attempt to pacify the French King's growing hostility; he was not entirely successful, but in August, at the behest of the Empress Matilda, the two kings did agree on a truce of sorts.

This did not prevent Louis from supporting an insurrection in

Brittany, which kept Henry occupied during August and September. No sooner had he suppressed it than he received news that his mother, the Empress Matilda, whose health had for some time been failing, was seriously ill in Rouen with a fever. Henry hastened from Brittany to be with her, but she died on 10 September before he could reach her. Some sources state that she was veiled as a nun of Fontevrault on her deathbed. She was buried initially in the convent of Bonnes at Nouvelles and soon afterwards translated to Bec Abbey,[40] where her epitaph read: 'Here lies Henry's daughter, wife and mother: great by birth, greater by marriage, but greatest by motherhood.'

Later that month, Eleanor and the Earls of Arundel and Pembroke, with a large retinue, accompanied the younger Matilda to Dover,[41] where she embarked on the German ship that was to take her to her new life in Germany. One account claims that Eleanor sailed with her to Normandy, but if she did, she must have returned to England immediately.[42] For the next few weeks she was resident at Winchester, where she seems to have gathered her movable goods for shipment to the continent, for in December she required seven ships to transport her possessions to Normandy.[43]

The reason for this was almost certainly political. During the autumn, after having once again been obliged to make a progress through Aquitaine to quieten its rebellious lords,[44] it seems to have occurred to Henry that Eleanor's presence in the duchy, and the reassertion of her authority as duchess, might help to calm the opposition to his rule. Apparently, he had therefore decided that she should be based in Poitiers for the foreseeable future, and it was probably at his order that she arranged the removal of her effects to the continent. This was not, as some historians have speculated, a marital separation as such, since throughout their marriage Henry and Eleanor had, for political reasons, spent long periods apart, often in different countries. However, internal evidence suggests that it was not an entirely unwelcome change for Eleanor.

Once the King had imposed a superficial peace upon Aquitaine, he returned north to Normandy, where he remained until Christmas, when he and Eleanor presided together over a court held at Argentan.

On 1 February 1168, the Lady Matilda was married to the Duke of Saxony at Brunswick in Germany. Although twenty-four years her senior, Henry the Lion was a brave, cultivated and enlightened man who was a notable patron of the arts and the Church. The marriage proved happy and fruitful and led to the expansion of trade between England and the Empire.

Before the King could implement his plan to install Eleanor in Poitiers, the ill feeling in Aquitaine finally erupted into serious revolt. The powerful Lusignan family – 'who yielded to no yoke or ever kept faith with any overlord' – and the Count of Angoulême and other lords of Aquitaine rose up again in violent rebellion against Angevin rule, threatening to offer their allegiance directly to King Louis.[45] Henry hurried south to deal with them, taking Eleanor with him – perhaps in order to remind her vassals to whom they owed allegiance – and leaving her in the vicinity of Lusignan[46] in the care of Earl Patrick of Salisbury, Henry's deputy and military governor in Aquitaine, with a small force of soldiers.

It was perhaps on the way south that Eleanor left young John at Fontevrault, where for the next five years he would be reared as an oblate;[47] his parents had apparently decided to dedicate him to the Church, a common practice in an age when families were large and it was difficult to make adequate provision for every child. It is also possible that the Ladies Eleanor and Joanna were brought up at Fontevrault, although neither was destined for the Church, being valuable marriage pawns for Henry's foreign alliances.

The King, meanwhile, had begun methodically and ruthlessly to crush the rebel lords. Marching on the reputedly impregnable castle of Lusignan, which stood on the road between Poitiers and Niort, he razed it to the ground and ravaged the surrounding lands,[48] forcing the dispossessed Lusignans, along with other rebels, to seek aid and asylum from King Louis.

By Easter the rising had been crushed, and Henry rode north to meet Louis for a peace conference at Pacy on the Norman border, to avert the very real prospect of a war between them. But the Lusignans had not yet finished with him.

On 27 March, Eleanor, accompanied by Earl Patrick and a small escort, was travelling along a road near Lusignan. Her party was probably enjoying a hawking expedition, since the men wore no armour. Without warning, they were ambushed by Guy de Lusignan and his brother Geoffrey[49] at the head of an armed force. Their intention was to take the Queen hostage and ransom her for generous concessions from Henry. Hastily, the Earl bade the Queen mount his fastest horse and gallop to the relative safety of the ruined castle nearby, whilst he dealt with their attackers. During the ensuing skirmish, he was stabbed in the back as he hurriedly donned his hauberk, and it was left to his courageous nephew, Sir William the Marshal, to hold off the enemy, which he did with consummate skill before being wounded and captured.[50]

William the Marshal had recently been knighted; his surname was actually derived from the office of Marshal of England, which he would inherit from his brother in 1199, but for the purposes of clarity it will be used henceforth. Now aged about twenty-two, he was the fourth son of an obscure Wiltshire baron. With no inheritance to look forward to, he had sought to make a living as a soldier of fortune. He had gained a reputation as a champion at tournaments and won many rich prizes; the Queen herself had once watched his performance in the mêlée, and had been deeply impressed.

William was a tall man of dignified bearing with brown hair. He was devoted to the Angevin family, and in time many of its members would come to recognise the loyalty, courage and integrity for which Eleanor now had cause to be grateful.

The Queen, who subsequently gave money to the abbey of Sainte-Hilaire in Poitiers for annual masses for Earl Patrick's soul, was impressed by William's valour and ransomed him from the Lusignans, who had cruelly refused to dress his wounds. When he presented himself before her in Poitiers, she rewarded him and thereafter took a special interest in his career: 'valiant and courteous lady that she was, she bestowed upon him horses, arms, gold and rich garments, and more than all opened her palace gates and fostered his ambition, who had fought like a wild boar against dogs'.[51] She also, with the King's approval, appointed him guardian, tutor and master in chivalry to the Lord Henry, and before long the two became inseparable companions. Thus was the Marshal – whom Stephen Langton, Archbishop of Canterbury would later refer to as 'the best knight who ever lived' – launched on a spectacular career that would see him loyally befriending five English kings and would culminate, fifty years later, in his ruling England as regent for the young Henry III.

Henry and Louis had meanwhile negotiated rather complicated peace terms. It was Louis who urged that, rather than leave the whole of his empire to the Lord Henry, Henry should divide his lands between all his sons except John, who was destined for the Church. Henry agreed to this, failing to perceive Louis' real motives, for the French King greatly feared the might of the Angevins and knew well that a house divided against itself might ultimately lay itself open to conquest.

The peace terms were as follows: the Lord Henry was to pay homage to the French King for Anjou and Maine and also for Brittany, which his younger brother Geoffrey would hold as his vassal, while the Lord Richard was to pay homage to Louis for Aquitaine.

No sooner had this peace been concluded than word reached Henry of the latest outrage perpetrated by the Lusignans. However, before he could return to Poitou, he was informed that Eudes de Porhoët, the father of Conan IV of Brittany, had risen against him, determined to avenge Henry's seduction of his daughter Alice, whom the King had taken as a hostage for her family's good behaviour. There is reason to believe that this accusation was true, since in 1168 Alice bore Henry a bastard child whose sex and fate are unknown.[52] Henry, however, would not tolerate rebellion on any grounds and rode with a vengeance into Brittany, where, in July, he forced Eudes to surrender. By then, his shaky alliance with Louis was already crumbling; the French King had allied himself with Henry's other enemy, William the Lyon, King of Scots, thus forging the first in a long tradition of Franco-Scottish alliances. For the rest of the year Henry was kept occupied by inconclusive skirmishes with the French in the area around Argentan.

Throughout 1168, Eleanor seems to have remained in Poitiers, governing her own lands with Henry's approval and under his supervision. There were sound political as well as personal reasons for this arrangement, for her return to her own domains and the re-establishment of a ducal court did much to heal the wounds caused by thirty years of rule by alien overlords. Indeed, Eleanor did everything in her power to recover the loyalty of her vassals: she went on a progress throughout Poitou and Aquitaine, and received the homage of local lords at Niort, Limoges and Bayonne; she dismissed some of Henry's unpopular seneschals, encouraged exiled barons to return home and be restored to their lands, revived old fairs and customs, and renewed the ancient privileges of towns and abbeys.

According to Richard of Devizes, she had also decided to live apart from Henry and remain permanently in her own domains with her heir Richard, a decision that 'troubled' the King 'like that of Oedipus', although he did not oppose it. That it was Eleanor who initiated their separation is confirmed in a letter written by Rotrou of Warwick, Archbishop of Rouen, in 1173.[53] We do not know when she reached this decision, but it must have been after Henry's concord with Louis in June, because prior to that date the Lord Henry had been the designated heir to Aquitaine.

Historians have endlessly speculated as to the reasons for the separation. Some have suggested that Henry's love for Rosamund de Clifford was a major factor, yet the evidence suggests that Eleanor had turned a blind eye to his frequent infidelities almost from the time of their marriage – she cannot have failed to notice how his barons kept their wives and daughters out of the way of the King's lust[54] – and we know that she had tolerated the presence of his bastard son Geoffrey in her household. She was, after all, a woman of the world, and had, as we have seen, almost certainly indulged in affairs of her own. No contemporary chronicler asserts that she was jealous of Rosamund.

It has been claimed that Eleanor was hurt because Henry was in love with Rosamund, whilst his other affairs had been purely of a physical nature, yet Henry had in fact been emotionally involved with another woman before: prior to 1162, 'the King had at one time passionately loved' Rohese de Clare.[55] It is unlikely therefore that Henry's love for Rosamund was the chief cause of the breakdown. Nor was Eleanor humiliated by his public flaunting of his mistress, as some writers allege, since he kept his affair with Rosamund secret until 1174.[56]

Age may have had a bearing on Eleanor's decision. She was now forty-six, by mediaeval standards an old woman, while Henry, at thirty-five, was a vigorous man in his prime. She had borne him eight children and may well have felt that, having done her duty, she had no need to remain in a marriage that had gone stale. It has been suggested that Henry and Eleanor did not have sexual relations after John's birth in 1166, but this may not have been the case. It is true that Eleanor bore no children after John, but it would have been at least two years before she ceased to be fertile. It is perhaps significant therefore that it was in 1168, when she was perhaps undergoing the menopause, that Eleanor decided to separate from Henry.

She may also have decided that she preferred living in her native land with a relative degree of autonomy as its duchess than as Henry's wife and queen, relegated to a subordinate role. As we have seen, it suited Henry, and was in everyone's interests, for her to do this. Both Eleanor and Henry seem to have felt that, in view of the volatile nature of Aquitanian politics, she should be resident in the duchy with her heir to safeguard his inheritance, and they probably intended that in time he would become associated with her in the government of her lands and would ultimately relieve her of that responsibility. It has also been suggested – and with good reason, given what we know of the nature of her future relationship with him – that Eleanor found in the love of her son Richard the emotional fulfilment that was lacking in her relationship with Henry. It is clear that mother and son had a special affection for each other.

We may also speculate that, as in many marriage breakdowns, both partners had become incompatible. The King, as Giraldus pointed out, was a difficult man to live with, and both he and Eleanor were strong characters determined to have their own way. William FitzStephen makes it clear that Henry was not above venting his wrath on Eleanor, and implies that, out of fear and respect, she would resort to subterfuge and massaging the truth, in order to avoid the lash of his harsh tongue. Moreover, he lived a chaotic, often squalid existence, which Eleanor may well have contrasted unfavourably with the relaxed, civilised lifestyle she could enjoy in Aquitaine.

Despite her separation from the King, Eleanor retained an interest in events in other parts of the Angevin empire, maintaining a working relationship with her estranged husband in the interests of their children, fulfilling her ceremonial role as queen when necessary, and occasionally acting as the King's deputy in Normandy and Anjou.

Eleanor set up her court at Poitiers, taking up residence in the Maubergeonne Tower, where the recently refurbished private apartments were unusually spacious and luxurious. She continued to wear rich clothes and jewellery, as her grants to Poitevin merchants in the early 1170s confirm. Henry allowed her to have her children with her, and she also received into her household, which at times included as many as sixty ladies,[57] her daughter-in-law Marguerite of France and the affianced wives of her younger sons.

Raoul de Faye, as Seneschal of Poitou, remained one of her most trusted advisers, and in 1170 and 1173 his talents would also be deployed by Henry, in helping to negotiate the marriages of two of the royal children, Eleanor and John respectively.

It has been claimed by every one of her biographers that Eleanor's court at Poitiers was modelled on that of her Aquitanian forebears, and that it became a centre of chivalry, patronage and troubadour culture, a place where the art of courtly love flourished. Until recently, it was believed by serious historians – and is still believed by a few writers – that, in association with her daughter, Marie, Countess of Champagne, Eleanor presided at Poitiers over the now legendary Courts of Love.

It is true that the southern troubadours continued to sing the praises of their ageing Duchess in their songs and verses; Riguad de Barbezieux praises her as being 'more than a lady', while the notorious Bertran de Born, a troubadour and robber baron who was to become the close friend of the Lord Henry, dedicated many of his *chansons* to 'noble Eleanora'. It is also probably true, although there is little evidence for it, that Eleanor encouraged troubadours and poets to come to her court and receive the benefits of her patronage.

The Courts of Love, however, were almost certainly no more than a literary conceit invented between 1174 and 1196 by Andreas Capellanus, a chaplain at the court of Marie of Champagne at Troyes, for the purposes of his treatise on *courtoisie*, called *Tractatus de amore et de amoris remedio*. In this work, which was inspired by Ovid and written after Eleanor's court at Poitiers had been dismantled, Andreas describes Eleanor, her daughter Marie, her niece Isabella, Countess of Flanders, Emma of Anjou (Henry's bastard sister) and Ermengarde, Countess of Narbonne presiding over a tribunal at which young gallants sought judgement in intellectual disputes on the subject of courtly love. Those who had acted correctly towards their chosen ladies were awarded the palm of amorous courtesy.

The *Tractatus* claims that the judgements of the tribunal were made according to a 'code of love' comprising thirty-one articles. Eleanor's appearance in this work owes far more to her reputation than to her actual deeds. She is recorded as giving three undated judgements, whilst Marie of Champagne is alleged to have pronounced in 1174 – the only date given in the book – that true love cannot exist between husband and wife (a sentiment that Eleanor would perhaps have echoed).

Eleanor's first 'judgement' was against a woman who refused to take back a lover who, having obtained her permission to transfer his affections elsewhere, then returned to her, insisting that he had remained faithful. The second case was that of a woman who had to choose between a mature knight of great integrity and a young man devoid of worth. The Queen is portrayed as declaring that the woman would be wiser to choose the worthier man. Her third 'judgement' condemned consanguinous marriages. Since the *Tractatus* was written at the court of the Count of Champagne, who was hostile to Henry II, these last two judgements may be perceived to be a satirical comment on Eleanor's own marital history, for not only had she made two consanguinous marriages, but she had also left a reputedly saintly king for a younger man of dubious reputation.

Had these Courts of Love ever existed, they would undoubtedly have attracted publicity, for the doctrines expounded in them were still regarded as subversive in certain circles. Yet, apart from the *Tractatus*, there is no evidence in any contemporary source for their existence. Nor is there evidence that either of Eleanor's daughters by Louis ever visited her at Poitiers; nor that she visited them or was ever in contact with them. It must therefore be concluded that the Courts of Love were nothing more than a literary fiction.

11

'The Holy Martyr'

Henry spent the Christmas of 1168 at Argentan, while Eleanor held her own Yuletide court at Poitiers. On 6 January 1169, Henry, accompanied by his two eldest sons, both splendidly accoutred, and a fine retinue of knights and barons, met King Louis at the castle of Montmirail in Maine,[1] to enshrine their peace agreement in a treaty designed to secure a lasting peace between the two kings.

The Treaty of Montmirail provided that, after Henry's death, his dominions were to be divided between his three eldest sons: the Lord Henry was to receive England, Normandy and Anjou; the Lord Richard was to receive Aquitaine, and hold it – as his mother did – as a vassal of the French crown; and the Lord Geoffrey was to retain Brittany, holding it as a vassal of his eldest brother and in right of his future wife Constance. Finally, the betrothal of Richard to Alys of France was to take place forthwith, and she was to have as her dowry the county of Berry, which lay between the borders of Touraine and Aquitaine, and which Henry had long coveted.

On 7 January, after the treaty had been concluded, King Henry renewed his allegiance to Louis for his continental fiefs, and the Lord Henry did homage to his father-in-law for the duchy of Brittany, being afterwards appointed Seneschal of France;[2] he and his brother Richard also paid homage as heirs to the lands they were destined to inherit on their father's death.[3] It was agreed that Geoffrey would swear fealty to Louis in person at a later date; meanwhile, Louis formally approved his betrothal to Constance of Brittany.[4] Richard and Alys were betrothed, and she was formally handed over into Henry's wardship.[5]

Most chroniclers were puzzled at Henry II's decision to partition his empire,[6] and most modern historians have evolved theories as to why he made it, but the reason is probably not far to seek. Henry not only had sons to provide for, but he had also discovered how difficult it was to govern such an unwieldy collection of territories, while his later behaviour suggests that he had no confidence in any of his sons to maintain authority and control as effectively as he did. Dividing the empire between them would therefore ensure more effective government after his death and also keep these domains under Angevin rule.

Amy Kelly, one of Eleanor's biographers, has asserted that the Treaty of Montmirail exposed to the world the rift between Henry and Eleanor. In fact, it would appear that Henry had taken Eleanor's opinions into account, for rather than designating their eldest son as heir to all his dominions except Brittany, which he had every legal right to do, he ensured that her favourite son Richard was made heir to Aquitaine. Without the treaty, Richard could well have ended up with nothing.

At Montmirail, in return for Henry's promise to restore the lands and castles he had seized from the rebel barons of Aquitaine, Louis also undertook to try to reconcile these hostile vassals to their overlord. He also acted, once again, as mediator between Henry and Becket. Henry was now eager to see Becket restored to the see of Canterbury, for he wanted him to crown young Henry within his own lifetime, and offered to reinstate Becket if he would retract his denunciation of the Constitutions of Clarendon as 'heretical depravities'. On 7 January, at the earnest plea of King Louis, a reluctant Becket agreed and, coming face to face with Henry for the first time in over four years, prostrated himself before him and begged for mercy. Then he ruined it all, not only by offering to submit to the King's pleasure in all things 'saving the honour of God', but also by declaring defiantly that it did not become a priest to submit to the will of a layman.[7] Henry erupted in fury and abuse and stalked out, leaving the meeting to break up in uproar, with everyone, including Louis, castigating the Archbishop for his obduracy.[8]

In March 1169, Henry was busy restoring order in Poitou and Gascony and bringing the counts of Angoulême and La Marche to submission. Two months later, on his orders but in his absence, ten-year-old Geoffrey was enthroned in Rennes Cathedral and invested with the ducal crown of Brittany, receiving afterwards the homage of his Breton vassals.[9]

Sometime in August, Henry left Eleanor's domains, having established a peace of sorts. For the next few years, although he retained overall control, Henry would delegate much of his authority in Poitou and Aquitaine to Eleanor, intervening only when necessary. The slender evidence that survives suggests that she ruled wisely and well over her turbulent people, continuing to follow a policy of conciliation. During this period, she not only travelled extensively in Poitou and Aquitaine, but is also recorded as having visited Falaise, Chinon and other places in Normandy and Anjou, usually as a response to the needs of her children. As her heir, Richard was frequently at her side, learning about his future fiefs and how to administer them, and becoming increasingly associated with his mother in the running of the duchy.

In August, Henry went to Rouen, pausing on the way to hunt with his eldest son at Angers and meet at Bayeux with the Pope's legates, come to try to effect a peace between him and Becket. Predictably, the conference ended in failure.

Around this time, Henry opened negotiations for the marriage of his daughter Joanna to William II, King of Sicily, which he hoped would further cement the ancient ties of friendship between the dukes of Normandy and the Norman kingdom of Sicily.[10] In November, Henry met Louis at Montmartre outside Paris. They discussed the future disposition of the Angevin empire, and Louis agreed to cede the suzerainty of Toulouse to Richard when the latter inherited Aquitaine.

Becket was also at Montmartre, and on 18 November 1169, Henry met him again in another attempt to resolve their quarrel. But the Archbishop still would not agree to anything that was inconsistent with what he termed the honour of God, and the meeting ended with the King absolutely refusing to give him the kiss of peace.[11]

At Christmas, Henry held court with Geoffrey and Constance at Nantes in Brittany. There is no record of Eleanor being present. Chrétien de Troyes is said to have used this court as the model for his Arthurian romance Érec and Énide (c.1170), which is set in Brittany and depicts King Arthur sitting upon a throne emblazoned with a leopard, an emblem that was inextricably linked to the Angevins.

In January 1170, Eleanor was at Caen in Normandy with her eldest son. By now, Henry was set in his resolve to have the Lord Henry crowned. The coronation of the heir during his father's lifetime was a French custom, instituted by the Emperor Charlemagne, which the King, backed by his barons, wanted to see adopted in England in order to safeguard the succession. From the first he seems to have taken Eleanor into his confidence and relied on her co-operation in helping him carry his scheme to fruition.

There was only one obstacle in the way, and that was Becket. Traditionally, it was the prerogative of the Archbishop of Canterbury to crown the sovereign, but Becket was, of course, in exile, so Henry made plans for Roger de Pont l'Évêque, Archbishop of York, to carry out the rite instead, which constituted a gross insult to Becket and greatly offended traditionalists. Learning of this, the Archbishop forbade both the King and the Archbishop of York to proceed with the coronation, on pain of excommunication. The Pope also prohibited the ceremony, and instructed Bishop Roger of Worcester, first cousin of the King[12] and a strong supporter of Becket, to carry his orders to England. Becket further commanded the Bishop to excommunicate all those clergy who took part in the coronation. In ignorance of the fact that the Bishop was in league with his enemies, Henry ordered him to attend the coronation.

Henry was determined to proceed with his plans regardless of any opposition. On 3 March 1170, braving violent storms,[13] he crossed from Barfleur to Portsmouth, leaving Eleanor in charge of Normandy. With the assistance of Richard of Le Hommet, Justiciar of Normandy, the Queen took steps to ensure that all the Channel ports remained closed, in order to prevent Becket or his supporters from crossing to England and carrying out his threat to excommunicate the King. The Bishop of Worcester, on his way with the papal prohibition, was, to his chagrin, forcibly detained in Dieppe on Eleanor's orders.[14]

Having bullied his bishops into agreeing to crown his son in defiance of Becket, the King summoned the Lord Henry to England; the prince left Caen on 5 June, escorted by the Bishops of Sées and Bayonne.[15] On his arrival in England, his father knighted him in the presence of a great assembly of lords and prelates.

Despite the fact that splendid coronation robes had already been made for her in London,[16] Marguerite of France was obliged to remain behind with the Queen at Caen.[17] Henry had decided not to have her crowned with her husband at this stage because he believed that to do so in the face of archiepiscopal prohibition might offend Louis more than if she were not crowned at all.[18] Almost certainly Henry hoped to have his son crowned a second time, with Marguerite, and with Becket officiating.

On Sunday, 14 June,[19] the Lord Henry was crowned king of England in Westminster Abbey by Archbishop Roger of York with six bishops assisting. From now on he would be distinguished from his father by the title 'the Young King',[20] although Henry regarded this as no more than an honorary dignity and had no intention of relinquishing any degree of sovereign power to him.

The Young King was already exhibiting an alarming contempt for his father, which first became apparent at the coronation banquet in Westminster Hall, when the King insisted on acting as servitor to his son in order to underline the importance of his new status. Carrying a boar's head on a platter to the high table where young Henry sat with the

Archbishop of York, he jested, 'It is surely unusual to see a king wait upon table!'

'Not every prince can be served at table by a king,' agreed the Archbishop.

The Young King was deadly serious.

'Certainly, it can be no condescension for the son of a count to serve the son of a king,' he replied insultingly.[21] Henry's response is not recorded.

Many people were offended and angered by the coronation ceremony, not least the Pope and Becket, whose prohibitions Henry had defied: the latter referred to the crowning as 'this last outrage'. Some feared that Henry had laid England open to an imminent interdict, or even war, since King Louis was mortally offended that his daughter had not been crowned, and soon began making threats. Henry placated him by promising to have young Henry and Marguerite crowned together at some future date.

After his coronation the Young King was assigned his own household in England, under the control of his guardian, William the Marshal, but remained for a time under the governance of tutors and legal advisers.

At fifteen – an age at which people were considered adult in mediaeval times – young Henry was already displaying the characteristics that would manifest themselves more vividly as he matured. Most chroniclers agree that he was a youth blessed with extraordinary good looks, even going so far as to call him 'the most handsome prince in all the world'.[22] In this respect he took after either his mother Eleanor, whose beauty was legendary, or Geoffrey of Anjou, his debonair grandfather. Walter Map describes the Young King as 'lovable, eloquent, handsome, gallant, every way attractive, a little lower than the angels'. Map also claims that he was 'beautiful above all others in both form and face'. There is no hint of these good looks in the surviving representations of the Young King: not in his stylised tomb effigy in Rouen Cathedral, nor in photographs of a contemporary mural painting, depicting him with King Stephen, Henry II, Richard I and King John, which once adorned the Temple Church in London, but was destroyed in the Blitz of 1940: but then neither of these representations was intended to be a portrait.

The Young King was not only good-looking but 'most blessed in courtesy, most happy in the love of men and in their grace and favour'.[23] This popularity was due not only to his charm but also to his fast-growing reputation as a 'fountain of largesse', which drew to his side a great following of young aristocrats, eager for adventure and advancement. He kept a splendid court, dispensed generous and lavish hospitality[24] and enjoyed an extravagant lifestyle, living well beyond his means.

Thanks to the training of the Marshal and others, young Henry displayed 'unprecedented skill in arms'.[25] Jousting was a passion with him, which he indulged with great ardour as often as he could.[26] He was brave, could be energetic when he chose and was hailed by many as a chivalrous knight. He could also be merciful, and was praised by Giraldus for being 'the shield of the wrongdoer'.

However, in the years to come this youth who had been so blessed would 'turn all these gifts to the wrong side'[27] and become 'a prodigy of unfaith and a lovely palace of sin'.[28] What caused this was undoubtedly his deep dissatisfaction with his father's refusal to allow him any political power. It angered him that his younger brothers already had the freedom of their own domains, whilst he, the eldest, had nothing but meaningless titles. Yet despite his repeated requests to be allowed to govern England or, failing that, Normandy or Anjou, Henry would not permit the Young King to take possession of any part of his inheritance. Nor would the King allow him to rule England as regent during his absence abroad, but delegated this responsibility to his justiciar.

To add to the Young King's resentment and humiliation, Henry assigned him what both he and William the Marshal felt to be a shamefully meagre allowance – his famed largesse came either from the royal treasury or, when that ran out, from the profits of jousting[29] – and even insisted on choosing the members of his household. Henry also, with the approval of the Pope, banned tournaments in England on the grounds that too many young knights were being killed,[30] a move that must have caused anguish to the Young King.

It was as well that Henry did impose such constraints upon the boy. Although he was indeed reluctant to cede power to any of his sons, being incapable of regarding them as anything other than children and expecting them to be satisfied with empty titles, he must have realised that the eldest, who was also his favourite, was a weak, vain, idle, untrustworthy and irresponsible spendthrift,[31] who knew all too well how to manipulate others with a shallow charm that blinded them to his less endearing traits. Among these was a violent temper[32] and a talent for being laceratingly cruel and insensitive. He was also susceptible to the subversive influence of those eager to exploit his grievances with his father. In all, 'he was a restless youth, born for many men's undoing'[33] and 'inconstant as wax'.[34]

Despite all this, the King, no less than Eleanor, had high hopes of his children and was confident that he could mould young Henry into another ruler such as himself. The boy had had the best tutors and, like his brothers, mastered the skills of reading and writing. Since childhood he had attended the ceremonial court gatherings at Christmas, Whitsun and Easter, and had sat with his father in the assize courts, accompanied him on progress, inspected garrisons and been taught about the English legal and taxation systems. None of it seems to have made much impression on him.

Unfortunately, Henry was a fond parent: 'on his legitimate children, he lavished in their childhood more than a father's affection'.[35] Often absent, he took it for granted that his love was returned. He found it hard to find fault with his sons, and forgave them all too readily, even after they had caused him almost irreparable injury and pain. According to Walter Map, the Young King could usually allay his father's wrath simply by bursting into tears. Matters were only made worse by the fact that both parents seem to have competed for their children's affection. By all accounts, Eleanor was an indulgent mother who, for various reasons (both political and personal) would from now on be only too willing to take sides with her sons against their father.

The end result of all this was that their sons grew up spoilt and headstrong, determined to get their own way, regardless of whether or not they wrecked the King's careful policies in the process. In fact, their deeds reveal that they had little affection or respect for their father, an attitude Eleanor may well have encouraged, for as they grew older, she seems to have been more in touch with their developing minds than Henry was – she was certainly more sympathetic – and consequently exerted greater influence over them; some writers have gone so far as to suggest that she dominated them. She was certainly not above using them to achieve her own political ends, as time would prove.

Henry seems to have sensed the growing alienation of his sons, and as they matured 'he looked askance at them, after the manner of a stepfather'.[36] He may have recalled what Eleanor had told him of the curse laid by a hermit on William IX of Aquitaine, that his descendants would never know happiness in their children; it was a tale he was fond of repeating to Bishop Hugh of Lincoln.[37] Not only would there soon be serious discord between his sons and himself, but there was already much jealousy between them, which would on many future occasions erupt into open and vicious conflict. In later life, Richard I was fond of recalling another family legend and observing, with black humour, 'What wonder if we lack the natural affections of mankind? We are from the Devil, and must needs go back to the Devil!'

Eleanor was not present at the Young King's coronation. She had travelled south to Poitiers for the investiture of twelve-year-old Richard as Count of Poitou. The ceremony took place on 31 May in the abbey of Saint-Hilaire, where the young Count received from the Bishop of Poitiers and the Archbishop of Bordeaux the holy lance and standard of St Hilaire, the city's patron saint.[38] Afterwards, at Niort, he was presented to the lords of Poitou as their future overlord, and they paid homage to him as such.[39] After celebratory banquets and jousts to mark the occasion, the Queen visited Fontevrault, where she put her seal to a gift made to the chapter by Manasse, one of the King's stewards. Then she returned to Falaise, where she was soon afterwards joined by Henry, who had returned from England around 24 June.[40]

In the course of his journey he had met the Bishop of Worcester. Unaware that the Queen had prevented the Bishop from going to England, or that he had acted as a courier for the Pope, the King angrily denounced him as a traitor for boycotting the coronation, and an undignified row ensued. In the course of it, the Bishop revealed that it was Eleanor and the justiciar who were responsible for his absence, but the King refused to believe him.

'What? The Queen is in the castle of Falaise and Richard of Le Hommet is probably there also,' he said. 'Are you naming them as the instigators of this? You cannot mean that either of them intercepted you in contravention of my summons!'

Bishop Roger's reply was masterful, focusing on the Queen's role in the affair, rather than his own. 'I do not cite the Queen, for either her respect or fear of you will make her conceal the truth, so that your anger at me will be increased; or if she confessed the truth, your indignation will fall upon that noble lady. Better that I should lose a leg than that she should hear one harsh word from you.'[41]

The outcome of this episode is unrecorded, but there is no mention of the King publicly censuring Eleanor for her intervention. Doubtless she acquainted him with the real reason for it, in which case he would have had cause to thank her.

The Pope was now insisting that Becket and Henry make up their quarrel, thus enabling the Archbishop to put right the wrongs that had been done. Henry responded by declaring that he was ready to make peace, and, through the good offices of King Louis and Rotrou of Warwick, Archbishop of Rouen, the King and Becket met at Fréteval on 22 July. Throwing his arms around his erstwhile friend, Henry cried, 'My lord Archbishop, let us go back to our old love for each other, and let us each do all the good he can to the other, and forget utterly the

William IX,
Duke of Aquitaine,
Eleanor's grandfather.
Intelligent and
outrageously sensual,
he is regarded by
historians as the
first troubadour.

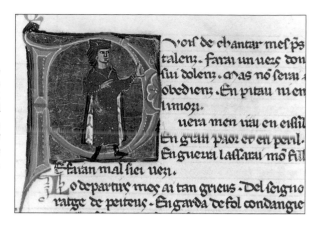

Eleanor's palace at Poitiers with the Maubergeonne Tower to the right

Louis VII, King of France, with his third wife, Adela of Champagne. He had loved his first wife, Eleanor of Aquitaine, 'almost beyond reason'.

Rock-crystal vase given by Eleanor to Louis, probably to commemorate their marriage in 1137. It is the only surviving artefact connected with her.

St Bernard of Clairvaux, one of the most influential and admired figures of the age. His attitude towards Eleanor was one of stiff disapproval.

Geoffrey Plantagenet, Count of Anjou, father of Henry II. 'Tall, handsome and red-headed', he was said to have 'carnally known Queen Eleanor' whilst she was married to Louis VII.

Eleanor's seal, dating from the time of her marriage to Henry of Anjou (the future Henry II of England) in 1152, shows her as Duchess of Aquitaine and Normandy.

Engaged capital said to represent Henry and Eleanor; this is one of several pairs of heads thought to have been carved to commemorate their nuptial progress through Aquitaine in 1152.

Henry, the Young King, eldest surviving son of Henry and Eleanor; he was 'beautiful above all others', but 'a prodigy of unfaith'.

(*Left*) Matilda, eldest daughter of Henry and Eleanor, and her husband, Henry the Lion, Duke of Saxony.

(*Opposite page, below left*) Richard I, King of England. Violent and rapacious, he was one of the greatest generals of the age and his mother Eleanor's favourite child.

(*Opposite, below right*) Berengaria of Navarre, queen of Richard I. Eleanor was too powerful to be relegated to the sidelines by her son's gentle and self-effacing bride.

Henry II, King of England. 'An excellent and beneficial ruler', but a restless and
impatient soul with a vigorous sexual appetite.

King John, Eleanor's youngest child. He was self-indulgent, promiscuous, indolent and greedy, and had no qualms about committing murder when it was expedient to do so.

Isabella of Angoulême, queen of King John. It was said that the King seemed chained to his bed, so hotly did he lust after her.

The controversial mural, dating from the last decade of the twelfth century, in the Chapel of Sainte-Radegonde at Chinon. From right to left, the figures probably represent Richard I, his sister Joanna, Countess of Toulouse (or, less probably, Queen Berengaria), Eleanor of Aquitaine and her grandsons Otto of Brunswick and Arthur, Duke of Brittany.

Eleanor of Aquitaine: a controversial figure during her own lifetime and the eight centuries that have elapsed since her death. One contemporary asserted that 'she surpassed all the queens of the world', while a more hostile chronicler claimed that, 'by reason of her excessive beauty, she destroyed or injured nations'.

The tombs of the Plantagenets in Fontevrault Abbey; from left to right, Henry II, Eleanor of Aquitaine, Richard I and Isabella of Angoulême. Originally in the crypt, they were vandalised during the French Revolution and their contents scattered. They have since been restored and moved into their present position in the abbey church.

hatred that has gone before.'[42] He admitted that he had wronged the Church over the matter of the coronation, and when he asked Becket to return in peace to Canterbury and re-crown the Young King, this time with Marguerite, the Archbishop accepted. The Constitutions of Clarendon were not mentioned, and king and primate retired in a spirit of reconciliation, although Henry had still not given Becket the kiss of peace. That, he promised, would be given to him after he had returned to England.

The King was unable to put in hand immediate arrangements for the Archbishop's return because, around 10 August, he fell seriously ill at Domfront with a tertian fever.[43] His life was despaired of – in France, it was at one time rumoured that he was already dead – and he dictated a will confirming the dispositions made under the Treaty of Montmirail. It was the end of September before he was fully recovered, and in thanksgiving he went on a pilgrimage with Eleanor to the shrine of Rocamadour in Quercy.[44] On returning through Aquitaine, he spent time attending to administrative business that had fallen into abeyance during Eleanor's long absence, and dealing with local disputes: at the request of the townsfolk of Souterraine, he sent in troops to deal with an unpopular provost.[45] Clearly, he was still in overall control of the duchy.

During this year 1170, relations between Henry and Frederick Barbarossa cooled, and a match between the King's daughter, Eleanor, and the Emperor's son no longer seemed desirable. Instead Henry sought to extend his influence across the Pyrenees and prevent a Franco-Castilian alliance by betrothing Eleanor to the twelve-year-old King Alfonso VIII of Castile;[46] she was to receive Gascony as her dowry, but only on the death of her mother.

In October, Henry at last issued Becket a formal safe-conduct to return to Canterbury and resume his episcopal duties, and wrote to the Young King, then in England, confirming that the Archbishop's return had his approval:

> Henry, King of England, to his son, Henry, King of England, greeting. May you know that Thomas, Archbishop of Canterbury, has made peace with me in accordance with my wishes. Therefore I order that you see to it that he and his followers should have their possessions in peace and with honour. Witness Archbishop Rotrou of Rouen, at Chinon.[47]

Soon afterwards Henry and Becket met for the last time at Chaumont near Amboise and reaffirmed their agreement.

'My lord,' said Thomas, 'my mind tells me that I will never again see you in this life.'

Henry took offence, thinking Becket believed that his intentions were treacherous.

'Do you think I am a traitor?' he frowned.

'God forbid, my lord,' was the answer.[48]

Becket was girding his loins for another battle. His anger against those bishops who had connived with the King over the coronation was still simmering, and on 30 November he sent a messenger to England to deliver letters excommunicating them.

On 1 December, Becket disembarked at Sandwich and rode to Canterbury, where he was accorded a warm welcome by both the clergy and the common people.[49] But several royal officers made it clear to him that they resented his return, and the Young King, whom he had once called his adopted son, refused to receive him at his court at Woodstock.[50]

On Christmas Day, from his pulpit in Canterbury Cathedral, the Archbishop publicly denounced the renegade bishops and published his sentence of excommunication on them.

What followed was not only the most cataclysmic disaster of the reign, but also an event that shook Christian Europe to its very foundations.

The evidence suggests that Eleanor spent Christmas with Henry at his hunting lodge at Bures in northern Normandy,[51] near Bayeux. Their children Richard, Geoffrey, Joanna and John were certainly present, and Richard's presence makes it likely that Eleanor was there too. The Young King was for the first time holding his own Christmas court at Winchester.

On Christmas Day, three of the excommunicate bishops – London, York and Salisbury – arrived at court and complained to Henry of Becket's high-handed conduct.[52] Henry and his barons listened to their catalogue of Becket's misdemeanours with mounting indignation.

'My lord, while Thomas lives, you will not have peace or quiet or see good days,' declared one lord.[53] The King 'waxed furious and indignant beyond measure, and, keeping too little restraint upon his fiery and ungovernable temper, poured forth wild words from a distracted mind'.[54]

'Who will rid me of this turbulent priest?' he is supposed to have cried, although no contemporary source quotes these words. Edward Grim, a monk of Canterbury, says that Henry railed at the cowardice of his vassals, snarling, 'A curse! A curse on all the false varlets and traitors I have nursed and promoted in my household, who let their lord be mocked with such shameful contempt by a low-born priest!'[55]

This was too much for four knights of his household, Reginald FitzUrse, William de Tracy (Becket's former chancellor), Hugh de Morville – who had served the King in the north as an itinerant justice since his accession – and Richard de Brito; without confiding their intentions to anyone, they quietly slipped away from Bures and made haste to England.[56] When Henry discovered they had gone, he realised in alarm what they had in mind and sent messengers to summon them back, but it was too late.[57]

On the afternoon of 29 December, the four knights confronted Becket in his study at Canterbury, making all kinds of wild accusations against him and threatening him with dire punishment if he did not leave England.[58]

'Stop your threats and stop your brawling,' commanded Becket. 'I have not come back to flee again.'[59] The knights withdrew into the courtyard, muttering insults, and began putting on their armour.[60]

Edward Grim has left an eye-witness account of what happened next. That evening, when the monks went in procession into Canterbury Cathedral for Vespers, 'the four knights followed them with rapid strides. When the holy Archbishop entered the church, the monks stopped Vespers and ran to him, glorifying God that they saw their father.' Then, fearful of the four knights who were advancing menacingly, the monks 'hastened, by bolting the doors to the church, to protect their shepherd from the slaughter'. But Becket 'ordered the church doors to be thrown open, saying, "It is not meet to make a fortress of the house of prayer, the church of Christ." And straightway [the knights] entered the house of prayer with swords sacrilegiously drawn, causing horror to the beholders with their very looks and the clanging of their arms.'

Everyone watching was 'in tumult and fright' except Becket, who retained his composure. He must have guessed the knights' purpose, and his behaviour suggests that he welcomed the chance of martyrdom.

'Where is Thomas Becket, traitor to the King and realm?' cried the knights.

'I am here, no traitor to the King but a priest,' replied Becket. 'Why do you seek me? I am ready to suffer in His name, who redeemed me by His blood.' So saying, he turned away and began praying. The knights closed in on him.

'Absolve and restore to communion those whom you have excommunicated!' they demanded.

Becket refused.

'Then you shall die!' was the reply.

Becket remained calm.

'I am ready to die for my Lord, that in my blood the Church may find liberty and peace,' he declared.

'Then they laid sacrilegious hands on him, pulling and dragging him that they might kill him outside the church.'

' "Touch me not, Reginald!" ' Becket thundered at FitzUrse. 'You and your accomplices act like madmen.'

FitzUrse, possessed by bloodlust, raised his sword. Becket immediately assumed an attitude of prayer, lifted his hands, and commended his cause and that of the Church to God, St Mary and the blessed martyr St Denis. At that, FitzUrse leaped at him and sliced the skin off the top of his head with his sword. As it descended, Edward Grim sprang to the Archbishop's defence, but the blade nearly severed his arm. His brother monks fled, but Grim remained by Becket's side, his uninjured arm supporting him. Seeing the Archbishop still on his feet, clinging to a pillar, the knights struck again, but a second blow on the head failed to prostrate him. At the third blow, Becket fell forward onto his knees and elbows, muttering, 'For the name of Jesus and the protection of the Church, I am ready to embrace death.'

As he lay there on the ground, 'the third knight [Richard de Brito[61]] inflicted a terrible wound, by which the sword was broken against the pavement and the crown was separated from the head, so that the blood white with brain and the brain red with blood dyed the surface of the Virgin Mother Church'.

The fourth knight, Hugh de Morville, had prevented the monks from returning 'so that the others might freely perpetrate the murder'. Their accomplice, a treacherous subdeacon called Hugh Mauclerc, who had accompanied them, now came forward, 'put his foot on the neck of the holy martyr'[62] and 'extracted the blood and brains from the hollow of the severed crown with the point of his sword',[63] scattering them all over the pavement and 'calling out to the others, "Let us away, knights; he will rise no more." '[64]

12

'The Cubs Shall Awake'

News of the murder of the primate of England sent the whole of Europe into shock. Some declared it was the worst atrocity since the crucifixion of Christ. William, Archbishop of Sens, averred that it surpassed the wickedness of Nero, the cruelty of Herod, the perfidy of Julian and even the sacrilegious treachery of Judas,[1] while King Louis wrote to the Pope: 'Such unprecedented cruelty demands unprecedented retribution. Let the sword of St Peter be unleashed to avenge the matryr of Canterbury.'[2] 'Almost everyone laid the death of the blessed martyr at the King's door',[3] and Henry was reviled throughout Christendom. It would be safe to say that his reputation never fully recovered.

Soon it became apparent that Becket dead was infinitely more powerful than Becket alive. No sooner had he fallen than he was being revered as a martyr – the people of Canterbury came hurrying to smear themselves with his blood, take it away in bottles or snip off pieces of his vestments[4] – and the cult of 'God's doughty champion'[5] soon spread with remarkable speed throughout Christendom. By Easter 1171 it was being claimed that miracles were taking place at his tomb.

The King had suffered two days of unbearable tension at Bures, waiting for news of the knights. Then, abandoning the Christmas festivities, he dismissed his vassals and retired to Argentan. It was there, on 31 December or 1 January 1171, that he was informed of Becket's murder.

Henry was almost paralysed with horror and remorse. Arnulf, Bishop of Lisieux, an eye-witness, informed the Pope:

The King burst into loud lamentations and exchanged his royal robes for sackcloth and ashes, behaving more like a friend than the sovereign of the dead man. At times he fell into a stupor, after which he would again utter groans and cries louder and more bitter than before. For three whole days he remained shut up in his chamber and would neither take food nor admit anyone to comfort him, until it seemed from the excess of his grief that he had determined to contrive his own death. So in consequence we began to despair of the life of the King, and so by the death of the one we feared in our misery that we might lose both.[6]

For six weeks Henry remained in seclusion, refusing to attend to business, take any exercise or indulge in recreational activities. In vain did the Archbishop of Rouen, summoned for the purpose, offer him spiritual comfort. In his misery, the King called upon God to witness, 'for the sake of his soul, that the evil deed had not been committed by his will, nor with his knowledge, nor by his plan. He directly submitted himself to the judgement of the Church and, with humility, promised to undertake whatever it should decide'.[7]

He sent envoys to protest to the Pope that he had never desired Becket's death, but Alexander refused to speak to them for a week.[8] However, having placed Henry's continental domains under an interdict, which was soon afterwards lifted, the Pontiff behaved towards him with commendable moderation. For many months he deliberated as to whether or not he should excommunicate Henry, as most people expected him to do, or extend the interdict to England. In the meantime, he simply forbade the King to venture onto consecrated ground until he had been absolved of his guilt.

At Winchester, the Young King professed himself relieved that none of his liegemen had been involved in the murder.[9]

On Easter Day, the Pope excommunicated the four knights, those 'satellites of Satan'[10] who had carried out the murder. For a year, they remained holed up in Knaresborough Castle in Yorkshire. Henry's ill-judged failure to punish them convinced many that they had acted on his orders. Later, Hugh de Morville made a penitential pilgrimage to the Holy Land, where he received absolution; he was afterwards restored to royal favour, dying in 1204. William de Tracy granted his manor in Devon to the cathedral chapter of Canterbury to expiate his sin, and in 1173 also went on pilgrimage, but died before he could reach Jerusalem.

Was it the murder of Becket that turned Eleanor against Henry? Certainly, between the Christmas of 1170 and that of 1172, something occurred to turn her feelings for her estranged husband into revulsion. Prior to Becket's murder, there is nothing to suggest that their separation was anything but amicable; indeed, Eleanor had spent most of the year supporting Henry's policies.

Although there is no record of Eleanor's reaction to Becket's murder, the fact remains that this event had the effect of turning most of Europe against the King. Eleanor seems to have supported Henry throughout his quarrel with Becket, but while quarrelling was one thing, the brutal murder of an archbishop was quite another – an outrage that inspired extreme revulsion in most God-fearing people. There were certainly other contributory factors, but it might not be too fanciful to conjecture that the murder went some way towards alienating Eleanor from Henry.

The Queen was certainly not on hand to console her husband in his anguish. Either she could not bring herself to do so, or (which is more likely), she had already returned to Poitiers. Details of her movements at this time are virtually non-existent.

In 1171, the Lord John was approaching five years old, and the King changed his mind about dedicating him to the Church. He had received an envoy, Benedict, Abbot of Chiusa, from Count Humbert of Maurienne (later Savoy and Piedmont), who ruled over a wide domain between Italy and Germany. Humbert was, however, by no means wealthy, and had no son to succeed him. Desirous of gaining a powerful ally, he now offered the hand of his eldest daughter, Alice, to the Lord John, who was the only one of Henry II's sons as yet unbetrothed. As Alice was Humbert's heiress, John would in time inherit the Count's domains and the Angevins would gain the desirable strategic advantage of controlling the western Alpine passes.

Henry was happy to enter into negotiations with Humbert, but for various reasons the matter dragged on for many months. It is not known whether or not John remained at Fontevrault during this period.

In the summer of 1171, the Pope sent two cardinal legates into Normandy to hear Henry's case and discuss with him the terms under which he might receive absolution for the murder of Becket, but the King, fearing excommunication, did not wait to meet with them. On 6 August, he returned to England,[11] having decided that this would be a good time to embark upon the conquest of Ireland, which had been granted to him by Pope Adrian IV in 1155. On 16 October, he set sail with an imposing army from Milford Haven, landing the next day at Waterford and riding north to Dublin, where he established his winter headquarters. He was to remain there, isolated by foul weather, until the next spring. This tactical withdrawal from the continental political arena allowed hostile tempers to cool, so that when the subject of Becket's murder was next raised, it would be approached in a more rational manner.

The Irish were not so amenable. They were resentful of Henry's distribution of land around Dublin to his followers, and remained in a constant state of rebellion against him. Nevertheless, the King managed to impose his authority over a substantial area and, in an astute bid to regain the Pope's favour, instituted reforms of the Church in Ireland, bringing it more into line with that of Rome.

On 17 April 1172, Henry returned from Ireland to learn that the papal legates were prepared to negotiate a reasonable settlement, and on 12 May he returned to Normandy with the Young King and Marguerite of France. Ten days later, in Avranches Cathedral, having declared on oath that he had neither wished for nor ordered Becket's death, but that he had, unwittingly and in anger, uttered words that had prompted the four knights 'to avenge him',[12] Henry was formally absolved by the Archbishop of Rouen of any complicity in the murder of Becket and was reconciled with the Church.[13] Afterwards, stripped of his outer garments and clad – to the astonishment of onlookers – in a hair shirt, the King knelt on the pavement outside the cathedral and was flogged by monks, as the Young King and the cardinal legates watched, the latter weeping with emotion.[14]

Henry then began making reparation. Amongst other things, the conditions of absolution required him to restore to the See of Canterbury the possessions he had confiscated, to make restitution to those who had suffered as a result of their support of Becket, and to take the Cross for a period of three years with the intention of leading a crusade against the Infidel. However, the Pope excused him from this last obligation in return for his promise to found three religious houses. Henry kept this promise: he established a Carthusian house at Witham, Somerset: refounded Amesbury Abbey as a cell of Fontevrault, and refounded and greatly enlarged Waltham Abbey in Essex.

The King was also required to do penance at some future date, and renounce any laws he had introduced that were detrimental to the Church; subsequently, he revoked the two most contentious articles of the Constitutions of Clarendon. Yet although it seemed that Becket, in the end, had won the moral victory, Henry did reserve to the crown the right to protect its interests if threatened by the processes of the Church, and this liberty eventually became enshrined in English law.

Richard was now nearly fifteen, and considered by his parents to be old enough to exercise power in Aquitaine. This did not mean that Eleanor intended to relinquish all her authority to her son, but that she wished to formalise his position and intended to rule her duchy in association with him.

On 11 June 1172,[15] in the abbey of Saint-Martial at Limoges, Richard, wearing a silk tunic and gold coronet, was invested with the ring of St Valerie, a Roman martyr and the city's patron saint, and publicly proclaimed Duke of Aquitaine. It seems probable that this ceremony was revived by Eleanor not only to emphasise the continuity of the ducal line, but also to make reparation to the people of Limoges for Henry's oppressive rule, under which they had suffered more than most.[16] After the investiture, there was a banquet such as had not been seen in the city for many years.

Richard, Duke of Aquitaine, was made of sterner stuff than the Young King. 'Henry was a shield, but Richard was a hammer,' observed Giraldus Cambrensis.

Eleanor's second surviving son was 'tall in stature' – his height has been estimated as six feet five inches – 'graceful in figure; his hair between red and auburn, his limbs were straight and flexible, his arms rather long, and not to be matched for wielding the sword, and his long legs suited the rest of his frame, while his appearance was commanding and his manners and habits suitable'.[17] He had inherited his father's piercing blue eyes. The realistic tomb effigies of him at Fontevrault and Rouen, although by different sculptors, show a remarkable similarity and may be attempts at a likeness.

He was essentially a child of the south. The *langue d'oc* was his native tongue, and he had spent most of his formative years in his mother's domains. He had received a very good education, not only in knightly and military skills, but also in the schoolroom, where he learned to read and write and mastered Latin. The troubadour culture of the south was an inspiration to him, leading him to compose competent verses and songs in both French and Provençal. He loved music, and would sing with and conduct the choir in his private chapel.[18] He was also a patron of artists and poets such as Bertran de Born, who became friends with Richard after years of enmity had existed between them.

It was Bertran who bestowed on his patron the nickname 'Oc e No' ('Yea-and-Nay'), which reflected Richard's single-mindedness and his determination never to break his word. The name stuck throughout Richard's life; the epithet 'Coeur-de-Lion' or 'the Lionheart' is not recorded until a decade after his death, and is thought to have been first used by the troubadour chronicler Peyrols, although Richard of Devizes had called Richard 'that fearful lion' during his lifetime.

He was undoubtedly his mother's favourite child.[19] She idolised him, referring to him as 'the great one', while he, she knew, 'reposed all his trust in her, next to God'.[20] Ralph of Diceto states that Richard 'strove in all things to bring glory to his mother's name'. This special relationship is reflected in official documents, where Eleanor calls John her 'dear' son ('*dilectum*') and Richard her 'very dear son' ('*carissimum*').

Richard was a person of consummate ability, gifted in many ways. A man of immense courage and daring, he would in time become renowned as one of the greatest generals and strategists of the age, who was greatly feared and respected by his enemies. Ralph of Diceto called him 'a man dedicated to the work of Mars'. Like the Young King, he was a master of the generous gesture, but less extravagant, less accessible and also notoriously avaricious. Unlike the Young King, he was not interested in tournaments, preferring to gain military experience in real warfare, but he loved hunting. He was a natural leader, and inspired many to follow him, either through fear or admiration. 'Why need we expend labour extolling so great a man?' asked one chronicler. 'He needs no superfluous commendation. He was superior to all others.'[21]

Like all the Angevins, Richard was of a volatile disposition and had a savage temper, although he was far more violent and cruel than his father. He was ruthless, unscrupulous and predatory. The author of the *Gesta Henrici Secundi* thought him 'bad to all, worse to his friends, and worst of all to himself'. He was proud, reckless, quarrelsome and obsessive, often to his own detriment. 'Impatient of injury, he was impelled irresistibly to vindicate his rights.'[22] Nevertheless, he could sometimes be forgiving towards those who had defied him.

The evidence that survives suggests that, as Richard grew older, he gained a reputation for promiscuity. He did not scruple to resort to rape: 'he carried off the wives, daughters and kinswomen of his freemen by force, and made them his concubines, and when he had sated his lust on them, he handed them over to his knights for whoring'. He was once accused by a preacher, Fulk of Neuilly, of begetting three shameless daughters: Pride, Avarice and Sensuality – to which he cynically retorted, 'I give my daughter Pride to the Knights Templar, my daughter Avarice to the Cistercians, and my daughter Sensuality to the princes of the Church.'[23] Unlike his father, he had only one acknowledged bastard, Philip, born of an unknown mistress before 1189, who perhaps married Amèlie, heiress of Cognac, and became Lord of Cognac. It has been suggested by later writers that a noblewoman, Jeanne de St Pol, bore Richard a son called Fulk, but there is no contemporary evidence for this.

Richard was ambitious, but he was not interested in usurping his elder brother's role. He 'cared not an egg' for England: all his ambition was focused upon Poitou and Aquitaine. Here, he was well known and popular, winning the affection of the common folk by acts of condescension and generosity.[24]

Whilst in Limoges, Eleanor joined Richard in laying the foundation stone of the abbey of St Augustine. The Queen's movements between June and December 1172 are not recorded, but she probably remained in Poitou and Aquitaine with Richard.

Henry was now becoming obsessed with bringing the Young King to heel. Determined to keep an eye on him, he dragged him from Avranches to the Auvergne to meet Count Humbert of Maurienne, who had come to finalise his daughter's betrothal to John. When the Count inquired as to the Lord John's inheritance, Henry told him that on his death John would receive three continental castles – Chinon, Loudun and Mirebeau – and some estates in the English midlands, all of which had hitherto been assigned to the Young King. Despite his fury, young Henry was forced to witness the marriage treaty.[25]

On 27 August, the Young King was crowned a second time at Winchester with Marguerite of France. The Bishop of Evreux officiated, since the See of Canterbury was still vacant and the Archbishop of York and the Bishops of London and Salisbury had been forbidden by the Pope to attend.[26] The King was not present at this second crowning, having gone to Brittany, but his hopes that it would go some way towards appeasing Louis were fulfilled,[27] and it was probably soon afterwards that the Young King and Queen began living together as man and wife.

Henry returned to Normandy in September, where, on the 27th, the Pope having approved the terms agreed at Avranches, he again received absolution.

During November, King Louis invited his daughter and son-in-law to Paris, ostensibly for a family reunion, but in reality in the hope of driving a wedge between the Young King and his father and exploiting this to his own advantage. He was well aware of the growing rift between Henry and his son, and Henry virtually played into his hands because, when the young couple visited him in Normandy before departing for Paris, and the Young King again demanded his inheritance, the King once again adamantly refused, even reproaching his son for his temerity, which only provoked further bitterness. Between the Young King and the old 'a deadly hatred sprang up'; the father had not only 'taken away [the son's] will', but had also 'filched something of his lordship'.[28]

In Paris, Louis listened sympathetically to the Young King's grievances and strongly advised him to demand a share of his father's dominions. But their plotting was abruptly curtailed because Henry, perhaps suspecting that Louis was up to something, summoned the Young King back to Normandy for Christmas. Burning with resentment, the young man obeyed, but he did not join his parents. Instead, in a typically extravagant gesture, he ordered his heralds to summon all the knights in Normandy called William to feast with him: 110 of them turned up.[29]

By this time, the Young King had become friendly with the troubadour Bertran de Born, who was twice his age. An intelligent but violent man of many talents, Bertran had become lord of Hautfort Castle in the Dordogne after driving his elder brother from their family estate. He had two passions in life: writing poetry and making war, and there were many who believed he exerted a sinister influence over the Young King. He was perhaps one of the people who 'whispered in his ear that he ought now by rights to reign alone, for at his coronation, his father's reign had, as it were, ceased'.[30]

Henry and Eleanor spent the festival at Chinon with Richard and Geoffrey. It is almost certain that Eleanor had taken the Young King's part, and that it was this issue that caused the final falling out between her and Henry, for by 1173 it is clear that her sympathies lay wholeheartedly with her sons and that, like a lioness fighting to protect her cubs, she was prepared to resort to drastic measures to ensure that they received their just desserts. Her estrangement from Henry was now virtually complete.

Henry's heavy-handed imposition of his authority and his loss of international prestige following the murder of Becket had by now led to the disaffection of a large number of his vassals throughout the empire, particularly in Poitou and Aquitaine. Their enmity and resentment appear to have been systematically exploited by the Queen and her three eldest sons and, combined with the support of King Louis, who feared that the dispositions of Montmirail were at risk through Henry's obduracy, a formidable coalition was formed.

The stage was now set for the most dangerous rebellion ever to confront the King. The origins of the conspiracy are unknown, but it is clear that different people had different objectives. The Young King and his brothers wanted autonomous power in the lands assigned to them, even if it meant the overthrow of their father; Eleanor wanted justice for her sons and, consequently, more power and influence for herself. This, she must have known, could only be achieved through the removal of her husband from the political scene. Undoubtedly she was prepared to countenance this, which is surely proof that whatever feelings she had had for him had long since died. Henry's vassals wanted an end to his dictatorial government, and were therefore prepared to support anyone who could offer an alternative; and King Louis was ready to seize any chance to undermine the might of the Angevins, even to the extent of allying himself with his former wife.

That there was contact between Eleanor and Louis is certain – he was her overlord and she had every right to ask him for aid against her enemies – but it was made so secretly that no details survive. The chroniclers are vague as to her role in the rebellion, but almost all of them imply that she was a prime mover in it, so it may therefore have been she who approached Louis. Gervase of Canterbury and William of Newburgh claim that the whole uprising had been devised and executed by her, while Richard FitzNigel asserts that, while the King's sons 'were yet young and, by reason of their age, easily swayed by any emotion, certain little foxes corrupted them with bad advice, so that at last his own bowels [i.e. his wife] turned against him and told her sons to persecute their father'. Ralph of Diceto accuses Eleanor of corrupting the minds of her sons with folly and sedition.

Others were not so sure: the anonymous *Gesta Henrici Secundi* states: 'the authors of this heinous treachery were Louis, King of France, and, as some say, Eleanor, Queen of England, and Raoul de Faye'. Roger of Hoveden also suspected Raoul de Faye of acting as Eleanor's evil genius. If all this is true, then the rift between Eleanor and Henry went very deep, so deep that Eleanor was prepared to resort to treason and the betrayal of her marriage bond to have her revenge.

The seer Merlin had foretold: 'The cubs shall awake and shall roar loud, and, leaving the woods, shall seek their prey within the walls of the cities. Among those who shall be in their way they shall make great carnage, and shall tear out the tongues of bulls. The necks of them as they roar aloud they shall load with chains, and shall thus renew the times of their forefathers.'[31] The cubs were widely believed to be the sons of Henry II, and in such a mood did they prepare to rise against their father.

13

'Beware of Your Wife and Sons'

On 21 February 1173, in response to overwhelming popular demand, Becket was canonised by Pope Alexander III. His cult had by now spread so widely that, soon afterwards, an order of Knights of St Thomas of Acre was established in the Holy Land. Many miracles were attributed to the new saint, numerous churches were dedicated to him, as well as a famous hospital in London, and his image appeared everywhere. The shrine erected to him at Canterbury grew rich and remained the most popular place of pilgrimage in Christendom until the Reformation, when Henry VIII dismantled it, appropriated its jewels for the royal treasury and had Becket's bones exhumed, tried, condemned and burned for having dared to oppose his king.

Between 21 and 28 February 1173, Henry and Eleanor and their two eldest sons hosted a week of lavish banquets and festivities at Limoges in honour of Alfonso II, King of Aragon, Sancho VI, King of Navarre, Count Humbert of Maurienne and Count Raymond V of Toulouse. During this assembly, the betrothal of the Lord John to Alice of Maurienne was finalised, and four-year-old Alice was committed to the care of Henry, who placed her in Eleanor's household. Count Humbert designated John his heir and gave the King four well-fortified castles.[1]

Raymond of Toulouse, having finally conceded Eleanor's ancestral claim to Toulouse, was at Limoges to pay homage to Henry and his sons and acknowledge them as his overlords. He had decided to throw in his lot with the Angevins because he had fallen out with the French King, the rift having occurred when Raymond repudiated Constance of France, Louis' sister. After that, Louis was no longer inclined to support Raymond's claim to Toulouse.

Some Poitevin nobles were angry that Raymond had paid homage to

Henry and the Young King, rather than just to Richard, whose right to Toulouse had been agreed by King Louis; it is likely that Eleanor was angry too, and that her anger strengthened her resolve to fight for her sons' rights.

It was during this week that the Young King spoke out publicly against his father's refusal to delegate power to him and his brothers, and against Henry's decision to assign to his brother John the castles and lands that were rightly his. He insisted that he had no wish to give John these properties, and that the King had no right to dispose of them without his consent. He also complained of not having been assigned any lands from which he could draw an income suitable to his royal estate.

When Henry refused to accede to his demands, the Young King pointed out that it was King Louis' wish, and that of the barons of England and Normandy, that he do so. At that moment, Henry realised that there were more forces at work against him than he had suspected, and guessed that Louis and others were actively working to drive a wedge between him and his heir. It does not seem to have occurred to him that Eleanor might be foremost among them.

There was much intriguing going on behind the scenes. Raymond of Toulouse is said to have encouraged Eleanor and her sons in their plotting,[2] but either his conscience or respect for his feudal oath, or simply a desire to stir up trouble, prompted him to take the King aside and warn him, 'I advise you, King, to beware of your wife and sons.'[3] But Henry obviously did not believe that Eleanor would stoop to such perfidy: in that age, it was unthinkable that a wife would so forget her marriage vows.

He nevertheless heeded the substance of Raymond's warning. In the belief that it was they who were sowing the seeds of sedition, he summarily banished many knights from the Young King's household, a measure that only served to fuel his son's hatred.[4] Then, early in March, as he rode north through Aquitaine, the King set the affairs of the duchy in order, placed his garrisons on war alert and left Eleanor in charge at Poitiers with Richard and Geoffrey, something he would certainly not have done had he suspected Eleanor of fomenting trouble against him. As far as he was concerned, it was the Young King who was causing all the trouble, and Henry was determined not to let him out of his sight.

Henry pressed on towards Normandy, dragging the Young King with him.[5] On 5 March, they stayed at Chinon, Henry insisting that they sleep in the same room, but during the night the Young King, 'following wicked advice',[6] prevailed upon the castle guards to lower the drawbridge and allow him to escape, and in the morning Henry woke to find his son gone. He immediately sent messengers after him, who returned with news that the Young King had crossed the Loire and headed north in the direction of Normandy. Henry gave chase, racing through Le Mans, Alençon and Argentan, but he was too late: his son had abruptly swung east, crossed the French border on 8 March and fled to Paris.[7]

It was clear that his escape had been planned, since fresh horses had awaited him along the route. It has been suggested that Eleanor had devised it, but it is unlikely she could have done so without the assistance and approval of King Louis. His son's escape confirmed Henry's worst fears.

In Paris, the Young King and King Louis pledged themselves to aid each other against their common enemy. Isolated at the French border, Henry sent a deputation of bishops to Paris to ask Louis to return his son.[8]

'Who is it that sends this message to me?' Louis asked.

'The King of England,' was the bishops' puzzled reply.

'That is not so,' retorted Louis. 'The King of England is here. But if you still call king his father, who was formerly king of England, know that he is no longer king. Although he may still act as king, all the world knows that he resigned his kingdom to his son.'[9]

Returning to Henry, the bishops warned him, 'Look to the safety of your castles and the security of your person.'[10] Henry correctly interpreted Louis' words as an open declaration of war. Soon afterwards, many of his vassals on both sides of the Channel openly declared their support for the Young King.[11] William the Marshal stood by him, and so did Bertran de Born, who is thought to have been one of those who strongly influenced the young man. The poet Dante, in his *Inferno*, pictures de Born burning in Hell for this:

> Bertran dal Bornio, be it known, am I,
> Who urged the Young King to rebel.
> Father and son at enmity I set.

'Soon after,' according to William of Newburgh, 'the younger Henry, devising evil against his father from every side by the advice of the French King, went secretly into Aquitaine where his two youthful brothers, Richard and Geoffrey, were living with their mother, and with her connivance, so it is said, he incited them to join him.'

Eleanor's involvement is also attested to by Ralph of Diceto, who says that Richard and Geoffrey 'chose to follow their brother rather than their father – in this, they say, following the advice of their mother

Eleanor'. Roger of Hoveden does not mention the Young King visiting Aquitaine, but says that the Queen sent her younger sons to France 'to join with him against their father the King'.

Geoffrey, Duke of Brittany, Eleanor's fourth son, was now nearly fifteen. Unlike his elder brothers, he was dark-haired, short of stature and neither good-looking nor of gracious bearing, although he could be charming and persuasive when he wanted. Nevertheless, despite being energetic, daring and skilled at the knightly arts, he possessed little of his brothers' talent for inspiring love, loyalty or confidence. The fact was that Geoffrey was dangerous, slippery, treacherous and grasping. He had joined the rebels not so much to support the Young King, but with a determination to rule Brittany without interference from his father.

He was perhaps the most intelligent of the Angevin brood, but he used his talents for evil purposes. Giraldus Cambrensis called him

> one of the wisest of men, had he not been so ready to deceive others. His real nature had more of bitter aloes in it than honey; outwardly he had a ready flow of words, smoother than oil, and, possessed by his syrupy and persuasive eloquence, was able to corrupt two kingdoms with his tongue. He was of tireless endeavour, but a hypocrite in everything, who could never be trusted and who had a marvellous gift for pretence and dissimulation.

Roger of Hoveden called Geoffrey 'that son of iniquity and perdition'.

Geoffrey's life would be that of an ambitious and opportunistic robber baron. Ruthless in warfare, he plundered at will, not hesitating to sack abbeys and shrines. He had few scruples, and confronted his critics with devious and shameless excuses. For instance, when someone asked him why he could not be at peace with his family, he complacently replied, 'Do you not know that it is our proper nature, planted in us by inheritance from our ancestors, that none of us should love the other, but that always, brother against brother and son against father, we try our utmost to injure one another?'[12]

Once her sons had left for Paris, Eleanor and Raoul de Faye encouraged the lords of the south to rise up in their support; there was jubilation in some quarters at the prospect of ending the rule of the autocratic Angevin, which the troubadour Richard le Poitevin echoed in a verse composed around this time:

> Rejoice, O Aquitaine!
> Be jubilant, O Poitou!
> For the sceptre of the King of the North Wind
> Is drawing away from you.

Soon afterwards, Raoul de Faye went to Paris, where he may have acted as Eleanor's envoy.

Henry had now begun to have suspicions about Eleanor's loyalty. There is some evidence to suggest that he had spies at her court, who would certainly have reported the visit of the Young King. Knowing that Eleanor wielded great influence over her boys, and perhaps feeling that their disaffection was rooted in the rift between himself and their mother, he commanded Rotrou of Warwick, Archbishop of Rouen, to write to Eleanor reminding her of her duty towards her husband, asking her to use her influence to bring their sons to submission, and threatening her with excommunication if she refused to co-operate:

> Pious Queen, most illustrious Queen, we all of us deplore, and are united in our sorrow, that you, a prudent wife if ever there was one, should have parted from your husband. Once separated from the head, the limb no longer serves it. Still more terrible is the fact that you should have made the fruits of your union with our Lord King rise up against their father. For we know that, unless you return to your husband, you will be the cause of general ruin. Return then, O illustrious Queen, to your husband and our lord. Before events carry us to a dire conclusion, return with your sons to the husband whom you must obey and with whom it is your duty to live. Return, lest he mistrust you or your sons. Most surely we know that he will in every way possible show you his love and grant you the assurance of perfect safety. Bid your sons, we beg you, to be obedient and devoted to their father, who for their sakes has undergone so many difficulties, run so many dangers, undertaken so many labours. Either you will return to your husband, or else, by canon law, we shall be compelled and forced to bring the censure of the Church to bear on you. We say this with great reluctance, and shall do it with grief and tears, unless you return to your senses.[13]

Eleanor had no intention of returning to Henry or of abandoning her sons' cause, and there is no record of her replying to the Archbishop's letter. It may well have convinced her that she would be safer at the court of her former husband, for sometime between the end of March and the beginning of May, she left Poitiers to follow her sons to Paris, accompanied by a small escort. Discovering that she was being pursued, she 'changed from her woman's clothes' and continued her journey disguised as a man, riding astride her mount. Soon afterwards, however, at an unspecified location, she was 'apprehended' by men in Henry's pay, 'detained in strict custody' and sent to the King in Rouen.[14] Historians have speculated as to whether she was betrayed by Poitevin spies working for Henry, since four Poitevins – William Mangot, Portedie de Mauzé, Foulques de Matha and Herve le Panetier – received valuable grants from him soon afterwards.[15]

For the King, this was perhaps the bitterest betrayal of his life, and his vengeance would be thorough. He made no public announcement of the Queen's arrest, not wanting her disaffection advertised, but had her immediately confined in one of his fortresses, although no chronicler specifies which; Rouen would seem to have been the most obvious choice, since it was in the midst of territory friendly to Henry. It has been suggested that it was Chinon, but that was in an area infected by rebellion. It could also have been Falaise, where other rebels were later held, but Eleanor was no ordinary prisoner. Indeed, Henry may have had her moved several times. The fact is that, for the next year, her whereabouts are unknown, which is what the King probably intended.

The chroniclers are unanimous in condemning Eleanor's treachery, which offended every contemporary concept of the duties and loyalty of a wife. Ralph of Diceto, looking into old chronicles, found more than thirty examples of sons rebelling against their fathers, but none of a queen rebelling against her husband. Giraldus Cambrensis was not surprised, however, and believed that Eleanor's conduct was inspired by God to punish the King for having entered into an incestuous marriage.

On the advice of King Louis, the Young King and his brothers had promised lands and income to anyone willing to ally with them. Philip of Alsace, Count of Flanders, offered his services in return for the promise of the earldom of Kent, the castles of Rochester and Dover, and £1,000 per annum in revenues.[16] His brother Matthew, Count of Boulogne, was promised the county of Mortain, and the Count of Blois great estates in Touraine. King Louis had a seal made specially for the Young King – he had left his own in Rouen – so that he could formalise these grants to his followers.

During the spring, Louis held a great court in Paris, which was attended by the Angevin princes. Here, the lords of France solemnly vowed to fight for the Young King, who in turn, with his brothers, undertook not to make peace with 'the former King of the English' without the consent of King Louis and his chief vassals.[17] Afterwards, Louis knighted Richard.

By late spring, the rebel coalition included not only Henry's sons and the King of France, but also the formidable might of the Counts of Flanders, Boulogne, Champagne and Blois, several lords of Anjou, Maine, Poitou and Brittany, a number of English magnates and even the King of Scots. Of all Henry's legitimate sons, 'John alone, who was a little boy, remained with his father',[18] having been withdrawn from the abbey of Fontevrault. Henry's bastard Geoffrey, recently elected Bishop of Lincoln, also remained staunchly supportive. But of Henry's domains, only Normandy stayed substantially loyal, and it was the duchy that consequently bore the full force of the first enemy onslaughts.

Hostilities broke out in May when the Young King, Duke Richard and the Count of Flanders attacked Pacy in Normandy, and King Louis, assisted by Geoffrey of Brittany, bore down on the Vexin; on 29 June, the castle of Aumale fell to them, followed soon afterwards by that of Driencourt. As Louis invested Arques, with Rouen as his ultimate goal, Philip of Flanders laid siege to Henry's massive border fortress of Verneuil, withdrawing at the end of July only when his brother, the Count of Boulogne, died of wounds inflicted by a mercenary's crossbow bolt.[19] In order to secure his succession in Flanders, Philip was obliged to retire from the conflict. Louis attempted to take Verneuil in his stead, but, hearing that Henry was advancing vengefully upon him 'like a bear whose cubs have been stolen, decided that the best course of action was flight. Mounting a swift horse, he retreated with all speed into France.'[20]

During the course of the rebellion there was little open warfare, although many castles were besieged and numerous villages and towns plundered and burned. 'Everywhere there was plotting, plundering and burning',[21] with Henry's sons 'laying waste their father's lands on every side, with fire, sword and rapine'. This scorched-earth policy was endorsed by most of the leaders, including the Count of Flanders, who declared, 'First destroy the land, and then one's foe.'

Although Normandy was the main theatre of revolt, there were risings in other parts of the Angevin empire. In Anjou and Maine, Henry's vassals openly renounced their loyalty to him. In September, Count William of Angoulême, the brothers Guy and Geoffrey de Lusignan and some of the lords of Poitou and the Angoumois – among them Geoffrey de Rançon – erupted in indignation at the King's high-handed oppression and his treatment of their duchess, and expelled his officials. Henry responded by invading Poitou with a large army of Brabantine mercenaries, who destroyed or captured castles in the region between Tours and Poitiers, burned vineyards and uprooted crops.[22] To the east, the rebellion in Brittany was speedily put down by Henry's Brabantines. Having capitulated, the Breton rebels were imprisoned in the castle of Dol.

Throughout the summer of 1173, the King fought hard to suppress the rebels. He enlisted the support of the Church by filling vacant sees with his own supporters, and despite the Young King's appeals to a sympathetic Pope for redress against his father's policies, the Church remained loyal to Henry, as did the justiciar, Richard de Lucy, the judiciary, the departments of state and the merchant classes who had prospered under his rule. Most people in England were on his side and, according to Ralph of Diceto, were so fearful of the rising spreading or the risk of invasion, that they dispatched everything except the Tower of London across the Channel to implore the King to come to the rescue of his kingdom. Thanks to all this support, he achieved significant success.

The Young King was too inexperienced to co-ordinate the various opposing armies, so it was King Louis who took command. Yet he too proved inept at organising the rebels into a cohesive force; nor was he able to prevent the divisions that arose between them. Nevertheless, Henry was hard pressed to vanquish his enemies: as soon as one group of rebels was overcome, his attention was at once diverted to another. Only by skill, swiftness – in July he marched 140 miles from Rouen to Dol in a day[23] – and a cool strategic appraisal of each situation did the King retain control.

Seeing Henry emerging victorious, his enemies began suing for peace. On 25 September, he met his sons and King Louis for a parley at Gisors, underneath the branches of an ancient elm tree, a traditional meeting place of the kings of England and France. Henry offered his sons castles and allowances – Richard was promised half the revenues of Aquitaine – but made no mention of delegating any authority to them. On the advice of Louis, who was still set upon crushing Henry's power, the princes rejected his terms.[24]

Meanwhile, England had been invaded from the north by the opportunist William the Lyon, King of Scots, who was not only sympathetic towards the Young King but also desirous of regaining Northumbria, which Henry had taken from him in 1157 and which the Young King had promised to return to him. The Scottish forces proceeded to lay waste the north of England, 'setting fire to barns, taking plunder and women, and tearing children half alive from their mothers' wombs'.[25] An army commanded by English lords marched north and, having driven the Scots back across the border, devastated the whole of Lothian with fire and sword. In the end, King William was forced to sue for a truce until January 1174.

A simultaneous invasion of England was launched from Flanders, on Michaelmas Day 1173, by the treacherous Robert de Beaumont, Earl of Leicester, the son of Henry's loyal justiciar, who had died in 1168. Earl Robert came at the head of a Flemish army;[26] having landed at Walton in Suffolk, he marched for Leicester, but in October, at Farnham, just north of Bury St Edmunds, his force was mercilessly annihilated by a peasant host wielding scythes and clubs, commanded by Humphrey de Bohun, the constable of England, and the justiciar, Richard de Lucy. Earl Robert and his formidable wife Petronilla were taken prisoner, deprived of their estates and sent to Falaise Castle, where other rebels were being held. The Earl's ally, Hugh Bigod, Earl of Norfolk, who was now seventy-eight and had spent his life switching his allegiance to serve his own interests, sued for peace, which brought the rising in East Anglia to an end. That left only pockets of rebellion in the north and the midlands.

The month of November found Henry and his Brabantine mercenaries south of Chinon, bearing down on Raoul de Faye's castle at Faye-le-Vineuse, which they took after a short siege. Raoul, however, evaded Henry, being still in Paris. At the same time, Duke Richard made an unsuccessful attack on the port of La Rochelle in Poitou.

The onset of winter forced both sides to negotiate a truce, but in the spring of 1174 the fighting broke out again on all fronts, and for a time Henry was busy subduing Anjou and Poitou. With the rebels in these domains virtually quiescent, he prepared to depart for Normandy, but on 12 May, Whit Sunday, he first visited Poitiers where he dismissed Eleanor's servants and dismantled her court.[27] When he left, he took with him his daughter Joanna, Marguerite and Alys of France, Emma of Anjou, Constance of Brittany and Alice of Maurienne, as well as valuables from the ducal palace.[28]

Back in Normandy, in June, Henry received alarming news from England. The King of Scots had crossed the border again and was laying siege to Carlisle, the north and midlands were seething with revolt, the castle of Nottingham had fallen, and the Young King and Philip of Flanders were planning another invasion from the continent. They had already sent a force under Ralph de la Haie to join Hugh Bigod, Earl of Norfolk, who, on 18 June, took the city of Norwich. The justiciar and other royal officials began once more bombarding the King with appeals for help.

A superstitious man, Henry saw these new misfortunes as divine punishment for his failure to do proper penance for the murder of

Becket,[29] and decided that this must be his priority before he attempted to deal with the insurgents.

At midday on 8 July 1174, Henry took ship for England from Barfleur. With him were the Lord John, the Lady Joanna, Marguerite and Alys of France, Constance of Brittany, Emma of Anjou, Alice of Maurienne and Eleanor: this is the first reference to the Queen by the chroniclers for over a year.[30] Many other ladies were in the party, probably to wait upon this host of royal females.

'A considerable number of ships had been assembled against the King's arrival',[31] and it required forty of them to transport the royal family and their personal servants, the King's household and court, and his army of Brabantine mercenaries to England. Nor was it an easy voyage:

> As they put out to sea, the waves started to look rough. The wind rose and fell hourly and made the sailors hesitant about the crossing. They put on subdued expressions in front of the King, their faces betraying signs of doubt. When the King learned that the wind was blowing directly against them, and that the strong gusts were steadily growing worse, he lifted his eyes to the sky and said, in front of everyone, 'If the Lord of the Heavens has ordained that peace will be restored when I arrive, then in His mercy may He grant me a safe landing. But if He is hostile to me, if He has decided to visit the kingdom with a rod, may it never be my fortune to reach the shores of my country.'[32]

God was indeed merciful, but Henry less so. As soon as they had all disembarked at dusk at Southampton and 'eaten a simple meal of bread and water',[33] Eleanor was taken away under guard, either to Winchester Castle or to Sarum Castle near Salisbury,[34] and there confined.

Queen Marguerite was sent, with her sister Alys and Constance of Brittany, to the castle of Devizes and there kept securely until such time as her husband could be brought to heel. Alice of Maurienne may have been with them, but she died soon after arriving in England. Emma of Anjou was given that year in marriage to Dafydd ap Owen, prince of eastern Gwynedd, who had offered loyal service to the King.[35]

Having disposed of his womenfolk and 'postponed dealing with every matter of state', Henry rode on to Canterbury 'with a penitent heart' to perform his long-awaited penance for his part in the murder of St Thomas.[36] Dismounting near the city on Saturday, 12 June, he laid aside the insignia of kingship and, 'clad in a woollen smock' as befitted a pilgrim, walked barefoot to the cathedral.[37] Prostrating himself before Becket's tomb, he remained long in prayer, while Bishop Foliot explained, in a sermon delivered to the watching crowds, that the King 'had neither commanded, nor wished, nor by any device contrived the death of the blessed martyr, which had been perpetrated in consequence of his murderers having misinterpreted the words which the King had hastily pronounced'.[38] Henry then 'requested absolution from the bishops present and, baring his back, received from three to five lashes from every one of the numerous body of ecclesiastics who were assembled'.[39] It is estimated that at least seventy monks participated in the flogging.

Afterwards, Henry remained lying before the tomb, 'constant in prayer, all that day and night. He neither took food nor went out to relieve nature, and would not permit a rug or anything of that kind to be provided for him.' At dawn on Sunday, he heard mass, drank water from a well dedicated to St Thomas and was given a phial of blood, perhaps that of the martyr. 'So he departed from Canterbury rejoicing, reaching London on the Sunday.'[40]

That night, sore and exhausted from flagellation and fasting, Henry summoned his physician for a bloodletting, then fell into a much-needed sleep, with his head resting on his elbow and a servant rubbing his feet,[41] which had been badly cut by hard stones on the walk to Canterbury.[42] Suddenly, there was a banging on the door.

'Who's there?' cried the keeper. 'Begone! Come in the morning, the King is asleep.'

But Henry was awake.

'Open the door!' he shouted, and in came a messenger, one Abraham, with marvellous news: an army led by Geoffrey, the King's bastard son, and the stoutly loyal Ranulf Glanville, Sheriff of Yorkshire, had achieved a decisive victory at Alnwick, and the King of Scots had been captured and was being held at Richmond Castle. Henry was so jubilant that he immediately rewarded Abraham with an estate in Norfolk, then raced off to tell his barons the good news and order all the bells in London to be rung. He had not expected to receive such a signal sign of divine forgiveness so soon.

'God be thanked for it, and St Thomas the Martyr!' he said fervently.[43] Others also saw the hand of a forgiving God at work on Henry's behalf, and believed the victory had come about through the intercession of the martyred Becket; in a devout age, it was felt that, with such allies on the King's side, his enemies must surely fail.

The taking of William the Lyon was indeed catastrophic for the English rebels, and, led by Hugh Bigod, they sued for peace. On 26

July, Bigod was reconciled to the King and renewed his allegiance.[44] With Henry's permission, Ralph de la Haie's army quietly left the country.

Learning that the rebellion in England had collapsed, Louis ordered the Young King and the Count of Flanders to call off their invasion, and joined with them in an attack on Rouen, which was from the first doomed to failure. The truth was that Henry's enemies had lost their confidence and knew they were fighting a losing cause.

By the end of July, England was finally at peace, and on 8 August, Henry returned to Barfleur with his Brabantine mercenaries and some Welsh troops. When this formidable force advanced on Rouen, Louis 'was reduced to a state of utter bewilderment' and on 14 August scuttled back to Paris with the Young King. He and the Angevin princes were now forced to concede defeat and accept the bitter truth that Henry was once more lord of all their destinies. His masterful victory against such overwhelming odds had also served to restore his reputation, which had been so shamefully tarnished by Becket's death.

Now the King seemed more invincible than ever. He was received in Rouen with such a ringing of bells as had never been heard there before.[45] In Falaise, William the Lyon was forced to sign a treaty surrendering Scotland to Henry as an absolute fief, paying homage to him as his overlord and promising that the lords of Scotland would follow suit. He was also obliged to surrender to the King the castles of Edinburgh, Stirling, Roxburgh, Jedburgh and Berwick.[46]

'Looking out for their own peace and quiet', Louis and Philip of Flanders 'did all they could to heal the breach between the King of England and his sons'.[47] The Young King and his brothers had no choice but to sue for peace, offering to submit to their father. Henry realised 'that the unusual humility' of his former enemies 'and their desire to make peace proceeded only from their inability to resist him', but he was willing to negotiate a peace, 'foreseeing the possibility of recalling his sons, whom almost everyone thought had gone seriously astray, to the fruits of a better life – his sons whom he loved so much, whom he had unceasingly tried to raise to the heights of honour'.[48]

Duke Richard did not cease campaigning against his father until the bitter end, yet when he came face to face with him at Montlouis near Tours on 29 September, he threw himself weeping at Henry's feet and begged his forgiveness. The King gently raised him and gave him the kiss of peace.

On 30 September, a compromise was reached at Montlouis, Henry assigning the Young King an income of £3,750 per annum[49] and two castles in Normandy, Duke Richard half the revenues of Poitou and two castles, and Geoffrey half the revenues of Brittany, with the rest to follow on his marriage to Constance.[50] The King had, in the circumstances, been more than generous, but he had not delegated one iota of his power and had forced the Young King to accept the original settlement of his former estates and castles on John, whose inheritance was now substantially increased by the addition of properties in England, Normandy, Anjou, Touraine and Maine. 'Thus the mighty learned that it was no easy task to wrest Hercules' club from his hand,' commented Richard FitzNigel.

Young Henry, Richard and Geoffrey 'gave assurance that they would never demand anything more of the Lord King their father beyond the determined settlement' and would 'withdraw neither themselves nor their service from their father'.[51] Yet although Henry generously excused their treason on the grounds of their 'tender age', and chose to believe that they had been led astray by troublemakers such as their mother and the King of France,[52] his relationship with his three eldest sons was naturally strained and would perhaps never recover from such devastating disloyalty. From now on, Henry's love for them would be marred by bitterness and distrust, and he would look to his other sons for true affection, making it clear that, of his legitimate sons, John was now his favourite. But John was not yet eight, and it was with his natural son Geoffrey that Henry enjoyed the most satisfying fatherly bond. Geoffrey had fought for him in the north of England throughout the campaigns of 1173–4, and after the victory at Alnwick, Henry had told him, 'You alone have proved yourself my lawful and true son. My other sons are really the bastards.'[53] From now on, Geoffrey would be one of the King's most valued counsellors.

There was to be no savage retribution, nor any executions. Once the Treaty of Montlouis had been concluded, the King, having given orders for the razing of all rebel strongholds and the release of all hostages, proclaimed a general amnesty for all who had risen against him – save his wife.

14

'Poor Prisoner'

'When the war was over and the fighting had stopped,' wrote Giraldus Cambrensis, 'the King, attributing his success not to divine mercy but to his own strength, hardened his heart and returned incorrigibly to his usual abyss of vice. He imprisoned Queen Eleanor his wife as a punishment for the destruction of their marriage.'

For the rest of Henry's life, Eleanor was to remain under restraint. Never again would he trust her, nor – for his own security – did he allow her much contact with her children, especially during the early years when she was a virtual prisoner: for the best part of a decade he had her kept in strict custody in the most strongly fortified towns.[1]

Because the King dealt so discreetly with Eleanor, the chroniclers have very little to say about her life during this period, and details of her imprisonment – which most of them found 'mysterious' – are fragmentary. During those years, according to the Pipe Rolls, Eleanor was confined mainly at Winchester and sometimes at Sarum, although she did occasionally stay elsewhere, since an allowance for her keep was also sent to Ludgershall Castle in Buckinghamshire and to houses in Berkshire and Nottinghamshire. Her custodians were men whom the King knew he could trust: Ranulf Glanville, a lawyer and diplomat who had served him as Sheriff of Yorkshire and in that capacity captured King William the Lyon; and Ralph FitzStephen, one of the royal chamberlains.

The twelfth-century town of Sarum occupied a windswept hilltop site, which was once an Iron Age fort and later a Roman town called Sorviodunum. It is now known as Old Sarum, and the newer town of Salisbury, founded in 1217, is situated nearby. In those days, the town was dominated by its Norman keep and cathedral and surrounded by a deep ditch. Today, only the cruciform foundations of the cathedral and the grassy circular mound on which the tower stood remain. In Eleanor's day Sarum was a bleak, inhospitable place. Water was scarce, the city was overcrowded and the wind so terrible that the clerks in the cathedral could hardly hear one another sing. They also suffered from chronic rheumatism, while the cathedral itself was repeatedly damaged by severe gales. There is no evidence that Eleanor, who was fifty-two at the onset of her confinement, suffered any lasting impairment to her health as a result of her stays here, for in old age she was to display as much energy and vigour as in her youth.

If the Pipe Rolls constitute a complete record, then Eleanor's allowance during these early years was a mere pittance. Her household was small and she was permitted only one personal maid, Amaria. After 1180, she seems to have lived in greater state, with chamberlains in her household – the names of two are recorded, Fulcold and William of Flanders.[2]

Unlike other prisoners, she lived in luxurious surroundings: Roger of Hoveden records that her prison was no worse than her palace at Winchester. There is no evidence to suggest that she was treated in any way but courteously, yet she was completely cut off from the outside world and therefore deprived of any means of plotting her escape or conspiring against her husband. Henry had had proof of how dangerous she could be, and he was taking no chances.

In Poitou and Aquitaine, the imprisonment of the Duchess provoked grief and anger,[3] yet, at the end of the day, most of her vassals were content to transfer their allegiance to her son Richard, who was not only a man but had also recently proved himself a doughty warrior. It was left to the poets to mourn the loss of Eleanor, and it must have been at this time that the chronicler Richard le Poitevin wrote this poignant lament, in which he envisages her suffering and weeping in her prison:

Daughter of Aquitaine, fair, fruitful vine! Tell me, Eagle with two heads, tell me: where were you when your eaglets, flying from their nest, dared to raise their talons against the King of the North Wind? It was you, we learned, who urged them to rise against their father. That is why you have been ravished from your own country and carried away to a strange land. Your barons have cheated you by their conciliatory words. Your harp has changed into the voice of mourning, your flute sounds the note of affliction, and your songs are turned into sounds of lamentation.

Reared with abundance of all delights, you had a taste for luxury and refinement and enjoyed a royal liberty. You lived richly in your own inheritance, you took pleasure in the pastimes of your women, you delighted in the melodies of the flute and drum, your young companions sang their sweet songs to the accompaniment of tambourine and cithara. You abounded in riches of every kind.

Now, Queen with two crowns, you consume yourself with sorrow, you ravage your heart with tears. I beg of you, Queen with two crowns, end your continual self-affliction. Why consume yourself with sorrow, why ravage your heart with tears each day? Return, O captive, return to your own lands if you can, poor prisoner. If you cannot, may your plaint be that of the King of Jerusalem: 'Alas, my exile has been a long one! I have lived with a crude, ignorant tribe.'

Where is your court, where are your guards, your royal escort, where are the members of your family? Where are your handmaidens? Where are the young men of your household? Where are your councillors of state? Some, dragged far from their own soil, have suffered a shameful death, others have been deprived of their sight, and still others are banished and wandering in divers places and are counted fugitives.

Eagle of the broken alliance, you cry out unanswered, because it is the King of the North Wind who holds you in captivity. But cry out and cease not to cry; do not weary, raise your voice like a trumpet, so that it may reach the ears of your sons. For the day is approaching when they shall deliver you and then shall you come again to dwell in your native land.

Like other commentators of the period, Richard le Poitevin saw Eleanor as the Eagle of Merlin's prophecies, as recounted by Geoffrey of Monmouth. Elsewhere, when referring to the rebellion, he calls her 'Queen Eleanor, described by Merlin as the Eagle of the Broken Covenant'. Similarly, another Poitevin writer, Guernes of Pont-Saint-Maxence, refers to Eleanor as 'the Eagless'. Nor was there any doubt in the mind of Richard le Poitevin that Henry was Merlin's King of the North Wind. Yet this writer's expectations were totally unrealistic. Eleanor would not be free to return to her native land for many years; nor were her sons, sympathetic though they were to her plight, in any position to rise in her favour.

With Eleanor disgraced and in prison, Henry began living openly with his mistress, Rosamund de Clifford. Giraldus Cambrensis noted disapprovingly: 'The King, who had long been a secret adulterer, now blatantly flaunted his paramour for all to see, not a rose of the world [*rosa mundi*], as some vain and foolish people called her, but a rose of unchastity [*rosa immundi*]. And since the world copies a king, he offended not only by his behaviour but even more by his bad example.' In that year, 1174, the King bestowed a manor on Sir Walter de Clifford 'for the love of Rosamund, his daughter'.

There is no evidence that Rosamund presided over the court in Eleanor's place; in fact, considering Giraldus' claim that Henry blatantly flaunted her, other chroniclers hardly mention her, and it was possibly the young Queen Marguerite who, on ceremonial occasions, stood in for her mother-in-law; the Pipe Rolls show that her allowance was increased at this time to a level far exceeding Eleanor's. Yet since Marguerite was often with her husband on the continent or in Paris, there must have been many occasions when Henry presided alone over his court.

After concluding the Treaty of Montlouis, Henry remained in Normandy with the Young King and his bastard son Geoffrey until the following spring; the King was now putting pressure on the Pope to confirm Geoffrey's election as Bishop of Lincoln, which he finally obtained in 1176.

Duke Richard and Duke Geoffrey had been sent off to administer their domains: Geoffrey went to Brittany, while Richard returned south to subdue the angry vassals of Poitou and Aquitaine – 'that hitherto untamed land'[4] – who had erupted in fury at the news of Eleanor's imprisonment.[5] Efficiently and savagely he ravaged the countryside and systematically reduced castle after castle, exacting a terrible vengeance on those who opposed him, who had their eyes gouged out, their hands cut off and their women raped by the Duke and his men. With his terrible reputation going before him, the land was soon quietened.[6] From now on Richard would spend his life engaged in a ceaseless succession of campaigns against his turbulent vassals, whose independence would be ruthlessly curbed by his iron hand and violent reprisals.

In October, Henry made peace with King Louis, and at Christmas he held court at Argentan with his four sons, feasting on 'the meat of four score deer' sent over from England.[7]

In the new year of 1175, because they wanted 'to return to their old familiarity', the princes 'decided to remove all suspicion by doing homage and allegiance to their father'. The younger sons, Richard and Geoffrey, swore fealty first at Le Mans, and the Young King on 1 April at Bures.[8] On that occasion, Henry raised his prostrate and weeping son, assured him of his love and assigned to him a generous allowance from the treasury.

On 9 May 1175, 'the two kings of England, whom the previous year the kingdom had not been big enough to contain, came together and crossed to England in a single boat'.[9] Relations between them were much improved: 'they ate together at the same table and rested their limbs in the same bedroom'.[10] Henry, 'turning his fatherly gaze to the needs of his son', even 'paid the Young King's onerous debts'.[11] On 28 May, they went on pilgrimage together to the shrine of St Thomas at Canterbury, where the King 'stayed up on all-night vigils, with prayer, fasting and scourging lasting into the third day'.[12]

With his empire at peace and stronger than it had ever been, Henry could now afford to devote more time to the affairs of his kingdom. Thanks to his wise and firm government, England was prosperous, peaceful and enjoyed great prestige in Europe. Foreign rulers sought to ally themselves with her, and even the native Irish kings paid homage to the English King.

After leaving Canterbury, the King and his son went on a progress through England so that the Young King could learn how to govern his future realm.[13] Yet, resentful of the fact that his brothers were permitted to rule their fiefs and not he, he chafed under his father's tutelage, although for many months he kept his resentment to himself.

According to Gervase of Canterbury, it was during 1175 that Henry first took steps to have his marriage to Eleanor annulled. Giraldus Cambrensis claimed that his purpose was to marry Alys of France, his son Richard's allianced bride, who was now fifteen, presumably with a view to bringing about closer relations between England and France.

Henry's friend, Hugh of Avalon, had always held that the King's marriage to Eleanor was adulterous and therefore invalid, and had warned that no good issue would come of it.[14] There were indeed good grounds for an annulment: Henry and Eleanor were more closely related that she and Louis had been, and their marriage could even be said to be incestuous, given that she had enjoyed sexual relations with Henry's father. It is more likely, however, that Henry pleaded consanguinity, not only to avoid further scandal, but because he could always claim that the marriage had been entered into by both partners in ignorance, in which case the heirs would be accepted by the Church as legitimate. Geoffrey of Anjou had warned him, before he married Eleanor, that he had known her carnally, so he could not therefore claim that he had married her in good faith, and in such a case their children would almost certainly be declared illegitimate.

However, in repudiating Eleanor, the King risked losing her vast inheritance. Should the Pope annul their union, her lands would revert to her and, on her death, pass to her sons. Furthermore, since she would no longer be Henry's subject, he had no grounds for keeping her a prisoner, but would have to send her back to Aquitaine, where she would be free to make mischief with her sons, her vassals and King Louis. She might also remarry and install a hostile neighbour on Henry's borders. Thus the King sought a way of setting her aside without any loss to himself.

It was probably during the summer of 1175 that Henry asked Pope Alexander III to send a legate to England to hear his case against Eleanor. However, since annulling their marriage was so serious a step and would have far-reaching political consequences, the matter had to be handled with absolute discretion. Therefore when the legate, Cardinal Uguccione Pierlone of Sant' Angelo, arrived, it was on the pretext of resolving the quarrel between the sees of York and Canterbury. Most chroniclers guessed, however, what was really on the agenda.

On 1 November, the feast of All Saints, Henry met Cardinal Pierlone at Winchester, where the matter of an annulment was almost certainly discussed. Gervase of Canterbury learned that the King – who was not noted for his generosity – had given the legate a large amount of silver, and understood that it was a bribe. But the legate refused even to listen to Henry's pleas for an annulment and, having apparently warned him of the risks involved in repudiating Eleanor, left England soon afterwards.

Famine followed hard upon the heels of plague,[15] and that winter was one of the coldest in living memory. Christmas found Henry and the Young King at Windsor. The land was covered in snow and ice, and a thaw did not set in until Candlemas in February 1176.

According to Giraldus, in the new year, Henry offered Eleanor the chance to take the veil at the abbey of Fontevrault and be appointed to the prestigious office of abbess in return for her consent to an annulment; if she agreed, he would not have to surrender her lands. In Fontevrault, moreover, she would be in Angevin territory and could be kept under supervision.

But Eleanor had no intention of retiring from the world or of giving up her crown or her inheritance, nor did she have any vocation, and at Easter 1176 she appealed to the Archbishop of Rouen against being forced to become a nun. When he refused to consent to her being committed to Fontevrault against her will, the King was obliged to appeal directly to the Pope for licence to have the marriage dissolved.

Duke Richard and Duke Geoffrey visited England at Easter 1176, joining their father and the Young King at Winchester for the Easter court. Historians have speculated that the annulment of the royal marriage was discussed and that the princes lent their support to their mother, but there is no evidence for this. What is certain is that, over Easter, the Young King voiced his dissatisfaction with being kept in England whilst his brothers were allowed their independence, and his suspicion that the King – who had allowed Richard and Geoffrey to pay homage to him before he permitted the Young King to do so – intended to exclude him from the succession.[16] Paranoid in his conviction that there was a sinister conspiracy against him, he accused his father of keeping him a captive in his palaces, of limiting his allowance and of preventing him from contacting his friends.

When he asked leave to visit the shrine of St James of Compostela in Spain, Henry saw this as the ruse it was, and suspected that the Young King's real intention was to join those dubious friends who had supported him during the rebellion. Nor had it escaped his notice that it would shortly be the start of the tournament season on the continent.[17] With grave misgivings, the King refused his son permission to go to Compostela, but allowed him instead to visit King Louis in Paris with Queen Marguerite, on condition that the Young King would afterwards travel south to Poitou to assist Richard against the rebels.[18] In order to prevent his son from using inducements to gain support against his father, Henry gave him a strictly limited allowance.

After the briefest of visits to Paris, the Young King hastened to Flanders where he unburdened his grievances to a sympathetic Count Philip.[19] What troubled him most was his inability to support his knights during the tournament season, so Philip provided him with horses and arms and subsidised him at great cost to himself. For the next few weeks, the Young King and William the Marshal excelled themselves in the lists.[20] When the season ended on St John's Day, the prince reluctantly rode south to Aquitaine to fulfil his promise to his father, although he did not stay long. Returning to Poitiers, he met up with some of his mother's barons who had risen against Henry in 1173–4 and, having lost everything, were now plotting the ruin of their overlord, Duke Richard. To them, the Young King was a hero, and he basked in their flattery and admiration.

The King had sent his vice-chancellor, Adam Chirchedune, to keep an eye on his son. Chirchedune, no fool, soon guessed what was going on, and wrote to Henry, warning him that the Young King was plotting treason. But the latter's spies caught him with the letter in his possession and he was dragged before their master with demands that he be flayed alive. The Bishop of Poitiers interceded for him, but the Young King was out for blood and ordered Chirchedune to be stripped naked and flogged in the public square of Poitiers.[21] When Chirchedune returned to England and reported what had happened to the King, Henry's rage knew no bounds.

The discovery of his scheming had, however, given the Young King a jolt, and, abandoning his fellow conspirators, he 'spent [the next] three years in tournaments and profuse expenditure. Laying aside his royal dignity and assuming the character of a knight, he devoted himself to equestrian exercises and carrying the victory in various encounters, spreading his fame on all sides around him.'[22]

In the early summer of 1176, the King concluded negotiations for the marriage of his eleven-year-old daughter Joanna to William II, King of Sicily, and preparations were put in hand for her departure. The princess was staying in Winchester at this time, and the Pipe Rolls suggest that in August Eleanor travelled there under guard from Sarum to say farewell to this daughter whom she might never see again.[23] Whether she also accompanied Joanna to Southampton is pure speculation, but it seems unlikely.

On 27 August, the princess took ship for France on the first stage of her journey to Palermo. She was escorted by John of Oxford, Bishop of Norwich, who had acted as Henry's envoy to the Sicilian court. The bridal party travelled south through France, then in the grip of a devastating famine, and took ship 'in dangerous weather conditions' across the Mediterranean and Tyrrhenian Seas to Sicily, whence, having safely delivered Joanna to King William and witnessed their formal betrothal, the Bishop returned to England.[24]

Eleanor was still at Winchester at Michaelmas.[25] After Joanna's departure, the Pipe Rolls record a payment of £28 13s 7d (£28.68) 'by the King's writ' for 'two cloaks of scarlet and two capes of scarlet and two grey furs and one embroidered coverlet for the use of the Queen and her servant girl'. It has been suggested that Joanna, seeing her mother in penury, pleaded with her father to ameliorate the terms of her imprisonment, yet all that this entry in the Pipe Rolls tells us is that the new clothes provided for the Queen were no better than those provided for her maid Amaria – even though scarlet was an expensive cloth – while the provision of one coverlet suggests that Eleanor and Amaria were obliged to share a bed.

On 28 September, the Lord John was betrothed to his cousin Hawise,[26] daughter and heiress of William, Earl of Gloucester, one of the most powerful English magnates and son of the Earl Robert, who had so staunchly supported the Empress Matilda; on his marriage, John would acquire widespread estates in England.

Between 1174 and 1176, Rosamund de Clifford retired to the nunnery at Godstow, near Oxford. It is not known whether she repented of her affair with the King and became a nun, or was ill and in need of nursing. It was probably the latter, because she died in 1176 (or possibly in 1177). The King had a beautifully decorated tomb erected to her memory before the high altar in the abbey church and, together with her father, Sir Walter de Clifford, and her brother-in-law, Osbert FitzHugh, gave generous gifts in her memory to the convent.

Rosamund's death would in time give rise to many legends, none of which have any truth in them. In the fourteenth century, the French *Chronicle of London* was the first source to assert that Queen Eleanor murdered Rosamund, giving a lurid account of how she stripped her of her gown, roasted her naked between two fires and, with venomous toads on her breasts, let her bleed to death in a hot bath at Woodstock. However, the Queen's name is given as Eleanor of Provence (who was the wife of Henry III and died in 1291) and the date of the murder as 1262! Also in the fourteenth century, the chronicler Ranulf Higden claimed that Rosamund was 'poisoned by Queen Eleanor', who discovered her hiding place at Woodstock when she found 'a clue of thread or silk' from Rosamund's sewing casket, learned the secret of the labyrinth 'and so dealt with her that she lived not long after'.

In the sixteenth century, the legends were further embroidered in popular ballads, in which Eleanor finds her way through the labyrinth and offers Rosamund the choice between a dagger or a bowl of poison, or even tears out her eyes. A late seventeenth-century ballad, 'Queen Eleanor's Confession', has Eleanor confessing the murder to Henry and William the Marshal on her deathbed, notwithstanding the fact that Henry predeceased her.[27] By the eighteenth century, the legends were accepted as fact, and it was not until the nineteenth century that writers began to question their veracity.

Of course, Eleanor could not possibly have murdered Rosamund, since she was securely held in custody at the time of her death. Nor could she have sent assassins to do the deed for her, because any contact with the outside world was strictly forbidden. The tales of the murder and her jealousy of Rosamund belong to later legend and are not substantiated by contemporary sources. Yet despite this, there remains to this day a persistent belief that there is no smoke without fire.

In 1191, Bishop Hugh of Lincoln visited Godstow and noticed in the choir a fine tomb, covered with silken cloths, surrounded by candles and lovingly tended by the nuns. 'He was told that this was the tomb of Rosamund, and that for love of her Henry, King of England, had shown many favours to the church.'

Shocked, the Bishop replied, 'Take her away from here, for she was a harlot, and bury her outside of the church with the rest, that the Christian religion may not grow into contempt and that other women, warned by her example, may abstain from illicit and adulterous intercourse.'[28] The body of Rosamund was thereupon re-interred in the nuns' chapter house, and the tomb inscribed with lines that were probably inspired by the exhumation of the corpse:

Hic jacet in tumba rosa mundi, non rosa munda;
Non redolet, sed olet, quae redolere solet.

Here lies the rose of the world, not a clean rose;
She no longer smells rosy, so hold your nose.[29]

In the fourteenth century Ranulf Higden stated that Rosamund's 'little coffin, scarcely of two foot long' and carved with realistic giants and animals, was still to be seen at Godstow. In the sixteenth century, the antiquary John Leland described how the tomb was destroyed during the Dissolution of the Monasteries: 'Rosamund's tomb at Godstow nunnery was taken up [of] late; it is a stone with this inscription, "Tomba Rosamundae". Her bones were closed in lead, and within that in leather. When it was opened, a very sweet smell came out of it.' The stone tomb was broken up, but at the end of the sixteenth century, another antiquarian, John Stow, claimed that the image of a cup had been engraved upon it, which seemed to give credence to the legend that Eleanor had poisoned her rival.

Giraldus Cambrensis states that, after Rosamund had retired to Godstow – and therefore before her death – the King consorted openly and shamelessly with Alys of France, his son's betrothed. Confident that he would be granted an annulment, he meant to make her Queen of England. That Alys was Henry's mistress is borne out by Ralph Niger, Roger of Hoveden, the *Chronicle of Meaux* and, later, by Ranulf Higden, although all these chroniclers are very discreet in their handling of the matter.

This new liaison of the King's was far more scandalous than that with Rosamund, since Alys was a royal princess and precontracted to her lover's son, and it only served to fuel the multiplying rumours about a royal annulment; Giraldus says that Henry intended to disinherit his sons by Eleanor and raise with Alys a new progeny, who would inherit his empire. It was also said that Henry intended naming John, the only one of Eleanor's sons who had not had his mind poisoned by her, as his heir

– a theory lent credence by the enrichment of John through his betrothal.[30]

On Christmas Eve, Henry was at Nottingham Castle, where he received the Bishop of Norwich, lately returned from Sicily. Joanna's wedding to William II took place on 13 February 1177 at Palermo Cathedral; it was a magnificent occasion, attended by a host of dignitaries. The city looked 'resplendent' and the bride wore a dress that had cost her father £114. After the ceremony, Joanna was crowned Queen of Sicily.[31] Thereafter she lived in almost oriental seclusion, her husband having adopted many of the customs of his Turkish subjects, including that of maintaining a harem.

By now, Henry's affair with Alys of France was becoming notorious. King Louis had almost certainly heard rumours – and perhaps the truth, from his daughter Marguerite and the Young King – for he suddenly demanded that Alys' marriage to Duke Richard be celebrated without delay. To ensure that Henry complied, he appealed to Pope Alexander to enforce the marriage or else lay all Henry's domains under an interdict.[32]

On 19 June, Marguerite of France bore the Young King a son, William, in Paris,[33] but joy at the birth of a direct heir to the Angevin empire was short-lived, for the infant died three days later. Henry received the 'unwelcome tidings' from his son whilst he was at Woodstock.[34]

He was still there when he learned soon afterwards that the papal curia had rejected his plea for an annulment of his marriage to Eleanor. The news might not have come as a shock, since he was well aware that putting Eleanor aside could have serious repercussions. But Henry was also informed that a papal legate was on his way to England to lay an interdict on all the King's lands if he did not at once marry Alys to his son.[35]

The King went to France on 18 August, resolved to straighten the matter out with Louis, face to face. They met at Ivry on the Norman border on 21 September,[36] and Henry managed to placate Louis with a vague promise that Alys would be married to Richard as soon as the legal formalities concerning the transfer of her dowry were completed. Good relations were restored and the two kings undertook to go together on a new crusade,[37] whereupon Henry hastened down to Berry to make it secure and thence to Aquitaine, to inspect Richard's conquests.

Richard had stayed aloof from the dispute, although his father's affair with his betrothed must have angered him. He certainly had no wish to marry her now, nor could he legitimately do so, since her relationship with Henry would render her union with his son incestuous. But Richard had other, more pressing matters on his mind. Having, with the aid of the Young King, subdued Poitou and the north of Aquitaine, he was now enforcing his authority in the south.

After Ivry, Henry took care to ensure that his affair with Alys was kept private, although his family certainly knew what was going on. During the next few years she would bear him a son[38] and a daughter, 'who did not survive',[39] and whose births were kept secret.

In 1177, Henry assigned Ireland to John. Since the new Lord of Ireland was only ten years old, his sovereign duties were carried out by a Viceroy, Hugh de Lacy. In September, the King's daughter Eleanor was sent to Castile for her marriage to King Alfonso VIII, which was solemnised in Burgos Cathedral. The modern biographer, Amy Kelly, claims that Queen Eleanor escorted the princess as far as Bordeaux, but this is highly unlikely and no contemporary source mentions it; in fact, Eleanor is not referred to by the chroniclers during this year. The younger Eleanor's marriage would prove fruitful and she would be responsible for introducing Poitevin culture into Castile.

Henry and his three eldest sons kept the Christmas of 1177 in such splendour at Angers that it would long be remembered as one of the most magnificent Christmas courts of the reign.[40]

Henry returned to England on 15 July 1178, and on 6 August, at Woodstock, knighted Duke Geoffrey.[41] Outwardly, relations between the King and his sons were peaceful at this time. The Young King was still 'rushing around all over France' attending tournaments and 'carrying off victory in various meetings. His popularity made him famous. The old King was happier counting up and admiring his victories and restored in full his possessions which had been taken away.' On 26 February 1179, the Young King returned to England 'and was received with due honour by the King his father'.[42]

Duke Richard was still heavily engaged in Aquitaine. 'Having suffered many attacks, he at length decided to conquer the proud Geoffrey de Rançon', who had refused to do him homage. 'He collected a force and on 1st May besieged the castle of Taillebourg. It was a most desperate venture and something which none of his predecessors had dared to attempt.' After only nine days, the great stronghold, which had been considered virtually impregnable, surrendered, and the local people watched aghast as it was razed to the ground on Richard's orders. This was a great triumph for him and established his reputation as one of the great generals of the age — news of it provoking alarm among the remaining southern rebels. 'Other castles in the area submitted to defeat within one month. Thus, with everything completed as he wished, Duke Richard crossed to England and was received with great honour by his father.'[43]

On 22 August 1179, King Louis, now fifty-eight and in poor health, began a five-day visit to England to make a pilgrimage to Becket's shrine. He was 'graciously received' by Henry at Dover, and the next day they travelled together in a solemn procession to the newly rebuilt cathedral at Canterbury; the choir of the previous church had burned down in 1174. Louis gave rich gifts to the shrine, including a great ruby known as the 'Régale of France', and spent three days in fasting, vigils and prayer.

On 26 August, Louis returned to France to prepare for the coronation of his fourteen-year-old son Philip, but soon afterwards he suffered a major stroke, which left him totally paralysed down his right side and effectively ended his reign.[44] When Philip was crowned on 1 November at Rheims, Louis was unable to be present.[45] The Young King attended, as Seneschal of France and the husband of Philip's sister, and preceded Philip, carrying the crown, into the cathedral. Richard and Geoffrey were also present and swore fealty to the new King for their domains, but Henry stayed away in order to avoid having to pay homage.[46] After the coronation there was a grand tournament at Lagny near Paris, at which the Young King and his knights were victorious over all their opponents.

Philip of France was a young man with a burning ambition, which was to break up the Angevin empire and incorporate Henry's continental domains into the kingdom of France.[47] This imperative was to govern all his future policies and make him a very dangerous adversary indeed.

Short of stature, stocky, with a red face, unkempt hair and primitive notions of personal hygiene, Philip was a plain man lacking in humour, grace and intellectual inclinations, yet he had real ability as a ruler, being tough on policy, clever, calculating and far more astute than his father. A political realist and pragmatist, he proved a crafty and greedy opportunist. Lacking the charm of the Angevins, he was over-cautious, timid and even neurotic: he would only ride docile horses and, ever suspicious, imagined there was an assassin hiding behind every tree. He had limited military skill but achieved his victories through cunning and persistence. His successes earned him a reputation as one of France's greatest kings.

Early in 1180, Henry appointed Eleanor's custodian, Ranulf Glanville, justiciar in place of Richard de Lucy, who had served the King loyally for a quarter of a century. Although Glanville retained responsibility for all the King's prisoners, he appears largely to have delegated to Ralph FitzStephen his custodianship of Eleanor, who seems to have resided mainly at Winchester from now on.

At the beginning of April 1180, the Young King returned to England to warn Henry that Philip was not such a king as his father had been, whereupon Henry decided that they should go together to meet Philip in the hope of maintaining the friendship between England and France. However, wary of Philip's influence and knowing the Young King to be susceptible, Henry first took his son to the tomb of his great-grandfather Henry I in Reading Abbey and made him swear 'in the presence of holy relics that he would follow his father's instructions in all things. After this, the elder King crossed the Channel from Portsmouth, the younger from Dover. On arriving in France, the elder King at once celebrated Easter at Le Mans.'[48] In June, he met Philip at Gisors and renewed the peace made with Louis at Ivry in 1177.

In Paris, on 18 September, Louis VII, who during the last months of his life had given all his wealth to the poor,[49] 'laid aside the burden of the flesh'[50] and his son succeeded as Philip II. The late King, his body clad in a monk's habit, lay in state at Notre-Dame before being buried in the Cistercian abbey of Barbieux in a fine tomb commissioned by his widow, Adela of Champagne, who would one day share it with him.

In July 1181, Geoffrey was at last married to Constance of Brittany. After the wedding, Henry returned to England and appointed the other Geoffrey, his bastard son, chancellor of England. Geoffrey had not yet been consecrated bishop of Lincoln, and the Pope was now insisting that he be consecrated immediately or resign the see. Declaring that he preferred horses and dogs to books and priests, he chose the latter. His father thereupon made him Archdeacon of Rouen and treasurer of York Minster, and gave him two castles in Anjou. Meanwhile, the Young King, Duke Richard and Duke Geoffrey had successfully supported King Philip in a war against Philip of Flanders.

Towards the end of 1181, news filtered through to England of Henry's daughters. Joanna had borne a son, Bohemond, who had died soon after birth, while Matilda's husband, Henry the Lion, Duke of Saxony, had quarrelled with the Emperor Frederick Barbarossa, having been unjustly held responsible for the failure of a campaign in Italy. The Emperor, jealous of the Duke's power – he owned sixty-seven castles and forty towns in Germany – had confiscated his estates, given them to his own supporters and declared him an outlaw. In November, the

Duke submitted to Frederick, but was exiled for seven years.[51] He and his wife and children fled from Germany with the intention of seeking refuge in France, Denmark or England.

On 4 March, Henry returned to Normandy to keep a watchful eye on affairs in the south, where there had been alarming developments. Duke Richard's harsh rule had earned him the bitter hatred of his vassals, and the turbulent lords of Aquitaine were again plotting revolt, hoping to overthrow him and offer their allegiance to the Young King instead. The evil genius behind this conspiracy was Bertran de Born, who had seduced the Young King into joining the rebels, taunting him with the derisory title 'lord of little land'. Jealous of his brother, and resentful because he had still not received what he thought was his due, young Henry had been easy to persuade.[52] Bertran had then gone on to inflame public opinion in the Limousin and the Dordogne against Richard by the clever deployment of propagandist *sirventes*, or satirical songs. He also boasted he could put a thousand of his own men in the field.

Foreseeing rich pickings for himself, Duke Geoffrey joined the Young King and, with an army of mercenaries and fortune-seekers, they invaded Poitou, which was suddenly plunged into a bloody civil war. In the summer, Henry intervened, riding south in an attempt to restore peace between his sons, but they were not prepared to listen. In fact, according to Giraldus, Henry was content for the time being to let the strife between his sons run its course, so long as it kept them from uniting against him.

He had to go back to Normandy to deal with a family crisis, for in the autumn, having failed to obtain asylum elsewhere, Duke Henry the Lion and the Duchess Matilda sought refuge at his court at Rouen.[53] Henry welcomed them with 'sumptuous hospitality',[54] took them under his protection and then proceeded, through diplomatic channels, to negotiate with the Emperor for their peaceful return to Germany. He also took a special interest in their children, the first grandchildren to delight his declining years. There were three boys – Otto, nine, Henry, eight, and the baby Lothaire – and three (possibly four) girls: Richenza, the eldest, who in England changed her name to Matilda, Gertrude, Ingibiorg and perhaps another called Eleanor after her grandmother. Henry treated these children as Angevin princes, especially Otto, who was to spend most of his youth at the English court and would adapt the Plantagenet leopards for his own coat-of-arms when he became the German Emperor Otto IV in 1209.

Once the campaigning season was over, Henry, hoping to divert the Young King from his ambitions in the south, summoned him to Rouen to greet his sister and her husband. He came unwillingly, seizing this opportunity to demand once more that his father cede Normandy or Anjou to him, saying that he wanted a capital seat where he and his queen could hold court without let or hindrance. When Henry prevaricated, the Young King stormed off in a temper to Paris, where King Philip lent a sympathetic and calculating ear to his grievances.

In bullish mood, the Young King returned to Rouen, where he declared dramatically that he would prefer to be banished or to take the Cross rather than ever again accept the subordinate role his father had decreed for him. When this fell on deaf ears, he threatened suicide, a mortal sin in those days.[55] At length, Henry appeased him by offering him a generous allowance, apartments in Argentan Castle, where Matilda was staying with her children (her husband having gone on pilgrimage to Compostela) and a year's pay for his soldiers. Somewhat mollified, the Young King accepted, and in return swore on oath to remain in the King's allegiance and to make no further demands.[56]

Henry had intended to go to England for Christmas, but concern over the Young King and the grave situation in Aquitaine kept him on the continent, and he held Christmas that year in the new castle of the Norman Exchequer at Caen.[57] It was a glittering gathering, designed to rival Philip's first full court in Paris, and in the hope of restoring peace, the King commanded all his sons to be present. He also summoned his lords and prelates to renew their allegiance before a vast throng of over a thousand knights and other guests.[58] The Young Queen presided over the court with Henry, and there was much festive cheer.

Only the Young King's behaviour struck a discordant note. He arrived in a foul mood, without William the Marshal, who had hitherto been his constant companion and was the master of his household, and he would not speak to his wife. Not surprisingly, a rumour soon spread that the Marshal had dared to look amorously upon Queen Marguerite. Hearing what was being said about him, William hastened to Caen and demanded that the King allow him to prove his innocence in an ordeal of combat, challenging those who had spread such calumnies to be his opponents in a three-day tournament. If he won, he declared, he asked no reward but the vindication of his honour; if he lost, he would be hanged for his crime. But no one dared take up his challenge, and he left the court in great distress. Soon afterwards, he departed on a pilgrimage to the shrine of the Magi at Cologne.[59]

Bertran de Born took advantage of the Young King's mood to drive further the wedge between him and Richard, calling him 'the prince of cravens' and suggesting that, if Geoffrey had been made Duke of Normandy, he would have known how to enforce his rights. He also reminded him that Richard had built the strongly fortified castle of Clairvaux on the Young King's side of the border between Anjou and Poitou.

Stung into action, the Young King erupted in a furious outburst against his father, threatening to renounce his titles and take the Cross if Henry did not allow him more autonomy or order Richard to dismantle his castle. Henry, moved by his son's tears and fearful that Philip would exploit any rift between them, decided to placate him by making Richard and Geoffrey do homage to their brother as their overlord. Geoffrey complied, but Richard refused outright, on the grounds that he owed allegiance only to King Philip for his domains;[60] he had had them, not from his father, he pointed out, but as a gift from his mother. Mention of Eleanor also prompted him publicly to castigate Henry for keeping her a prisoner. As for the Young King, Richard flared, if he wanted land, let him go and fight for it, as he, Richard, had had to do.[61]

After that, Richard would not sit at the same table as the Young King. Angrily, Henry broke up his Christmas court and withdrew to Le Mans with his feuding offspring. There, 'anxious to make peace between his sons', he attempted to patch up the quarrel, asking the Young King to concede that Aquitaine belonged to Richard and his heirs in perpetuity. The Young King was crafty in his response. 'So as not to incur his father's displeasure, he solemnly swore to do what he asked, as long as Richard would swear fealty to him on sacred relics. At this, Richard exploded in anger'[62] and stalked out, 'uttering nothing but threats and defiance'.[63]

After that, it was only a matter of time before the vassals of the Young King and Duke Richard took up cudgels on their lords' behalf and the fighting began again. 'The Young King gathered a numerous army and, leaving his father, he ordered all his allies to join battle against Richard'.[64] Geoffrey again sided with the Young King and Richard's rebellious barons,[65] and when Raymond of Toulouse and Duke Philip of Burgundy offered their support, and the rebels began looking to England for aid, it appeared to an alarmed Henry as if there might be another revolt against his empire itself.[66] He thereupon summoned his feudal levies, sent orders that all suspected English dissidents be imprisoned, and marched south to subdue the rebels.

When Henry arrived before Limoges,[67] the Young King's soldiers shot at him, and although his son protested that it had been an accident, the same thing happened again shortly afterwards. On both occasions, the King narrowly escaped being killed.[68] Again the Young King apologised, but 'war was in his heart' and it was obvious that he secretly lusted for his father's death.[69] In vain did Henry's secretary, Peter of

Blois, write a letter castigating him for his behaviour: 'Where is your filial affection, your reverence, the law of Nature? Where is your fear of God?'[70]

When Henry stopped his allowance, the Young King ran out of funds with which to pay his army and, with William the Marshal – now restored to favour – and a mercenary band, joined his brother Geoffrey in sacking and plundering monasteries and shrines and terrorising rural communities.[71] He had become, wrote Peter of Blois, 'a leader of freebooters who consorted with outlaws and excommunicates'. Early in June 1183, he and his men brazenly looted the very altar treasure and the famous sword of the hero Roland from the lofty shrine of Rocamadour as horrified pilgrims looked on.[72]

'Then the Young King's life was cut short, as if by a weaver, and with it the hopes of many fighting for him and hoping to rule with him after his father's death.'[73]

The weather had been stiflingly hot, and after leaving Rocamadour, the Young King fell violently ill with dysentery and fever. With a few followers, he tried to reach Limoges, but at the village of Martel in Quercy he was forced to take lodgings in a house belonging to a burgher, Étienne Fabri,[74] which still stands today. The Bishop of Agen came to see him and he made a fervent confession of his sins. As his condition worsened, his case seemed hopeless and the Bishop was sent to fetch the King.

Henry's advisers, however, suspected a trap, and instead of hastening to his son's bedside, which he would have preferred to do, the King sent his physician, some money and, as a token of his forgiveness, a sapphire ring that had belonged to Henry I.[75] He also sent a message expressing his hope that, after his son had recovered, they would be reconciled.

On Saturday, 11 June, the Young King realised he was dying and, overcome with remorse for his sins, asked to be garbed in a hair shirt and a crusader's cloak and laid on a bed of ashes on the floor, with a noose round his neck and bare stones at his head and feet, as befitted a penitent.[76] His conscience was troubling him because he had once sworn to go on pilgrimage to the Holy Land and had never fulfilled that vow, but William the Marshal set his mind at rest by promising to fulfil it for him.

When Henry's ring was brought to him, he begged that his father would show grace and mercy to the Queen his mother, held now for so long in captivity, and that all his companions would plead with Henry to set her at liberty.[77] He also asked the King to provide for the needs of the Young Queen and ordered that all his possessions, save the ring, be given to the poor. A monk who had been summoned to hear his last confession asked why he did not give away the ring also.

'Because I wish my Judge to know that my father sent it me as a token of forgiveness,' he replied.[78] He died late in the evening, 'young in years' – he was only twenty-eight – 'but full of time when measured by the experiences of his life'.[79] After his death, it proved impossible to remove the ring from his finger.

Not one of his companions dared face the King with the news, so Bernard Rossot, a monk of Grandmont, was sent to break it to him. He found Henry at Mas near Limoges, sheltering from the afternoon heat in a peasant's hovel.

'I am not a bearer of good news,' said the monk.[80] Henry guessed what he had come to tell him and, having dismissed his entourage, sought to find out every detail of the Young King's death, then 'threw himself upon the ground and greatly bewailed his son'.[81] He was so distraught that Peter of Blois was moved to reprove him for his 'excess of grief'.

At the Young King's request, his eyes, brain and entrails were buried beside the grave-site chosen by his father in the monastery of Grandmont, which was among those he had recently sacked. He had asked for his body to be buried in Rouen Cathedral, but as his funeral cortège passed through Le Mans on its way north, the citizens seized the body, which was garbed in the Young King's linen coronation garments,[82] and buried it in their own cathedral. The indignant people of Rouen threatened to burn Le Mans to the ground if the corpse was not surrendered to them, but the King intervened in their favour, commanding that his son be buried in the place he had chosen, 'on the north side of the high altar',[83] where his tomb effigy may be seen today.

The King sent Thomas Agnell, Archdeacon of Wells, to break the news of her son's death to Eleanor at Sarum. Agnell found her calm and, surprisingly, prepared. She had had a dream, she told him, that foretold her loss. She had seen her son lying on a couch with his hands together as if in prayer, and it had struck her that he looked like a tomb effigy. On his finger could be seen a great sapphire ring – the one his father had, unknown to Eleanor, sent him – and above his white face there hovered two crowns. The first was the one he had worn at his coronation, but the second was a circlet of pure dazzling light that shone with the incomparable brightness of the Holy Grail.

The Queen asked Agnell, 'What other meaning than eternal bliss can be ascribed to a crown with no beginning and no end? And what can such brightness signify, so pure and so resplendent, if not the wonder of everlasting joy? This second crown was more beautiful than anything which can manifest itself to our senses here on Earth. As the Gospel says, "Eye hath not seen, nor ear heard, neither have entered into the heart of Man, the things which God hath prepared for them that love Him.'"

After she had dismissed him, Agnell praised her composure and the way in which she had 'fathomed the mystery of the dream and had, in consequence, borne the news of her son's death with great discernment, strength and equanimity'.[84] Yet her grief went very deep: a decade later, in 1193, she told Pope Celestine III that she was tortured by the memory of the Young King.[85]

The Young King's death removed one of the most dangerous threats to Henry's security and left Richard the undisputed heir to England, Normandy, Anjou, Poitou and Aquitaine. The rebel coalition immediately collapsed, but the Duke's retribution was vicious: some rebels were drowned, some run through with swords and others blinded, as an example to future would-be conspirators.

The widowed Marguerite of France was allowed to retain some of her dower properties in Normandy and Anjou, although Henry kept a tight grip on others and on the Vexin, despite Philip's demands that he return them. In 1186, however, Philip agreed that the Vexin should be assigned to the dowry of his sister Alys,[86] on condition that Henry paid Marguerite a large allowance. That same year she returned to Paris[87] prior to marrying Bela III, King of Hungary; she died on a pilgrimage at Acre in the Holy Land in 1197.

Bertran de Born wrote a poignant lament for the Young King: 'Youth stands sorrowful, no man rejoices in these bitter days. For cruel Death, that mortal warrior, has harshly taken from us the best of knights.' Moved by his eloquence, Henry restored to him his castle of Hautfort, which had been confiscated during the revolt.[88] As for William the Marshal, who had been the Young King's guardian, mentor and friend, he kept his promise and, taking the Young King's cross, departed immediately on a pilgrimage to the Holy Land, grieving for his lost master.

The chroniclers, however, drew a moral lesson from the Young King's death, which left 'for the approval of the wise the opinion that sons who rise up against fathers to whom they owe everything are worthy only of being disinherited'.[89]

15

'Shame, Shame on a Conquered King!'

In 1183, Henry was fifty and, thanks to his ceaseless exertions, aged beyond his years.[1] His hair was grey, his stocky body had become corpulent, and years of sitting in the saddle had made him bow-legged. Thanks to a well-aimed kick from a horse, he was lame in one leg. His health had deteriorated and he was often troubled by chronic illnesses of an unspecified nature.

Eleanor had now been his prisoner for a decade. She was sixty-one, and it appears, from her interview with Thomas Agnell, that years of confinement had wrought their effect and taught her wisdom, patience and true piety. The death of their son and the Young King's dying request, together with the pleas of their daughter Matilda, may well have prompted a change in Henry's attitude towards her, but it was in fact for political reasons that he summoned her to Normandy in the late summer of 1183.

Philip of France was insisting that certain properties in the duchy belonged to the Young Queen in right of her late husband, but Henry was adamant that they had in fact once belonged to Eleanor and that she had assigned them to her son for his lifetime, after which they would revert to her. To underline this, Henry determined that Eleanor should visit those lands to reassert her right to them.[2] Geoffrey of Vigeois says that Eleanor stayed in Normandy for six months. This marked the beginning of a period in which she would be allowed greater freedom, albeit under supervision. Gervase of Canterbury asserts that Eleanor was released in 1185 at the instance of Archbishop Baldwin of Canterbury, but this is at variance with other sources, which confirm that she was set at liberty in 1183.

Once again, she was to assume her place as Queen, even occasionally appearing in public at Henry's side,[3] although she did not normally reside with him and there is no suggestion that their personal estrangement had ended. Yet there may have been some vestiges of affection between them: according to Giraldus, those whom Henry had once hated he rarely came to love, yet those 'whom he had once loved, he rarely regarded with hatred'. What he and Eleanor now achieved was a working, mutually beneficial relationship designed to pre-empt any resentment against the King on the part of their sons for the way in which he had treated their mother. Nevertheless, as events would show, Henry remained suspicious of Eleanor.

Henry was at this time keeping Alys under guard at Winchester.[4] Philip was insisting that he honour the agreements made at Ivry and Gisors and marry her to Richard forthwith,[5] but again Henry stalled. Personal considerations apart, the last thing he wanted to see was Richard allied by marriage to the French King, whom he suspected would use this alliance to turn Richard against him. In any case, Henry was more preoccupied with making peace between his sons and an equitable settlement for them.

Since the dispositions of the Treaty of Montmirail could no longer apply, Henry sought, late in 1183, to make a fairer division of his empire between Richard and John: it seemed unfair that Richard should receive England, Normandy, Anjou, Poitou and Aquitaine and John only Ireland and some estates in England and on the continent. This state of affairs prompted Henry to nickname John 'Lackland', an epithet that, in the light of future events, was curiously prophetic.

John was undoubtedly Henry's favourite legitimate son. Now sixteen, he was about five feet six inches tall[6] and favoured his brother Geoffrey in looks, having thick, dark red, curly hair and a strongly built body, which, as he grew older, became portly as a result of over-indulgence in good food and wine. We do not know what John really looked like: his effigy in Worcester Cathedral is a stylised representation that was sculpted some years after his death and cannot be termed a portrait in any sense of the word.

John had been well educated, firstly at Fontevrault, then in the household of the Young King, and latterly in that of the justiciar, Ranulf Glanville; since Glanville was also Eleanor's custodian, it is possible he sometimes brought the boy to visit his mother. Giraldus thought that, of all the Angevin brood, John and Geoffrey were the most alike, and that John was at least as bright as his clever brother, having a sharp, inquiring mind and being able to read. In later life he acquired many theological manuscripts from Reading Abbey, and also works by Pliny and French historians, all of which would form the nucleus of the future royal library. Although he showed no interest in the songs and culture of the troubadours, he loved music. Yet for all his education, he was 'light minded',[7] preferring the superficial to the substantial.

John was self-indulgent and greedy, and had a relaxed approach to life. He loved hunting, hawking, carousing, gambling and playing backgammon with amusing companions. He was a genial host who dispensed lavish hospitality, and his wit, conversational skills and very accessibility brought him popularity of a sort. He lived in luxury, spending extravagantly on fine clothes and gold ornaments for himself, and accumulated a large collection of jewellery. He was also, by the standards of his day, fastidious.

Like his father, he was rampantly promiscuous, and even noblewomen were not safe from being abducted and raped by him. 'Not a woman was spared if he was seized by the desire to defile her in the heat of his lust.'[8] When, as a young man, he tried to seduce the wife of Sir Eustace de Vesci, Eustace smuggled a whore into John's bed in her place. The next day, when John boasted to Eustace about how good his wife had been in bed, Eustace could not resist telling him the truth, thereby provoking so angry a reaction that he was obliged to flee the court.[9]

John had at least seven bastards, probably more. The mother of his daughter Joan, who married Llywelyn ap Iorwerth, Prince of Wales, was Clementia, wife of Henry Pinel. The names of other mistresses appear in the records, but none seems to have enjoyed John's attentions for long, although he was generous to them while they were in favour. The evidence suggests, however, that he was emotionally shallow.

Usually lethargic and indolent, John could, when he wished to, display as much energy and vigour as Henry II and Duke Richard. Although he disliked war and had no time for tournaments, he displayed on occasion talent and even brilliance as a military commander, but was all too often fatally dilatory, a failing that later earned him the nickname John Softsword. He was intelligent and able, but also ruthless, tenacious, restless and impatient like his father, and temperamentally incapable of keeping faith with anyone, having a notorious reputation for being untrustworthy, cunning, crafty and suspicious of all around him.

William of Newburgh called John 'Nature's enemy': although the tales of his cruelty have undoubtedly been exaggerated, he was certainly capable of being cruel,[10] and had no qualms about committing murder when it was expedient to do so. Having inherited the notorious Angevin temper, he would, when in a rage, bite and gnaw his fingers, or even set fire to the houses of those who had offended him.

John was by no means a good man, yet later chroniclers, looking back on his reign, would paint a much blacker picture of him than those writing in his youth or his early years as king. 'Foul as it is, Hell itself is defiled by the very presence of John,' wrote Matthew Paris in the thirteenth century. Roger of Wendover called him a cruel tyrant who had failed as a king. Many of these later chroniclers in fact embellished and exaggerated the scandalous tales and rumours that abounded during John's reign and after his death.

John's bad press in the monastic chronicles may be attributed to his failures as a king and his cynical contempt for religion; he quarrelled with the Church during his reign and was excommunicated. It may be that his early years in Fontevrault had had a detrimental and lasting effect on him, although his critics would claim that it was his immorality that led him astray from the teachings of the Church. He 'led such a dissipated life that he ceased to believe in the resurrection of the dead and other articles of the Christian faith [and] made blasphemous and ribald remarks',[11] his favourite oaths being 'By God's teeth!' or 'By God's feet!'[12] He took a gleeful pleasure in shocking churchmen, rarely observed feast or fast days, and once, seeing a buck slaughtered at the end of a hunt, remarked, 'You happy beast, never forced to patter prayers nor dragged to Holy Mass.'[13] His scepticism was alarming in that age of faith.

It has been suggested that John was conceived at a time when his parents' marriage was soured by his father's infidelities and born at the height of Henry's affair with Rosamund; that consequently his mother did not love him and abandoned him to the nuns of Fontevrault, and that it was this that accounted for his flawed character. There is, however, no evidence that Eleanor did not love her son: on the contrary, it was she who made tremendous efforts to secure his peaceful succession to the throne, and there is ample evidence of a supportive bond between them.

Eleanor may have been a distant mother – she was a prisoner for much of John's childhood – but Henry spoiled John. The boy had inherited the charm that characterised his family, but it blinded others, especially his indulgent father, to his faults, which seem to have gone largely unchecked in youth. After removing John from Fontevrault, Henry kept him frequently with him and did his best to provide this son with a great inheritance, sometimes, as we have seen, with disastrous results. He was about to make another blunder now.

Summoning Richard, Geoffrey and John to Angers,[14] Henry commanded them to make peace with each other and with him, as their father and their liege lord. He demanded that Richard cede Poitou and

Aquitaine to John, so that John could swear fealty to him as their new ruler. An appalled Richard – who regarded himself first and foremost as a southerner, who had been brought up from infancy as his mother's heir and had spent years fighting to impose his authority on his unruly subjects – could not bring himself to give the King an answer, and stole away from Angers, burning with resentment. Arriving back in Poitou, he sent Henry a message declaring that under no circumstances would he yield a furrow of his land to anyone.[15]

Soon, Richard had further cause for grievance. The repeated postponement of his marriage to Alys of France had led Philip to believe that Henry still intended to repudiate Eleanor and dispossess his sons, so that he could marry Alys himself and start a new family.[16] Richard himself was suspicious of Henry's intentions, and now realised that his own marriage to Alys was politically to his advantage, for it would gain him a powerful ally in the French King and thereby help to protect and consolidate his position as Henry's heir, since Henry would not risk alienating Philip by disinheriting his sister's husband. Setting aside any scruples he may have had, Richard appealed to the Church to support him, while Philip asked Henry for a parley to discuss the matter.

The two kings met on 6 December 1183 at Gisors. Henry declared that he could not assign the Young King's lands in Normandy and Anjou to his widow because they belonged to Eleanor, and he could prove this. Geoffrey of Vigeois asserts that it was at this time that Henry summoned Eleanor from England to make her six-month progress through these lands, but that cannot have been so, since Eleanor was at Berkhamsted the following Easter, and it is more likely that she had begun her tour in the late summer and was still in Normandy at the time of the conference.

When Philip asked what was to become of Alys, Henry promised that if she were not immediately married to Richard, she would soon be married to John. Hearing this, both Philip and later Richard were alarmed, for it seemed to confirm their suspicions that Henry really did mean to make John his heir, which may well have been the case, although the evidence to support such a theory is inconclusive.

Their business concluded, Henry did homage to Philip for his continental domains, ominously revoking into his own hands all the territories he had assigned to his sons,[17] thus making them completely dependent on him.

Henry had desired peace with his sons, but it became clear that this was only on his own terms, and their resentment would cause such discord during the remaining years of his life that 'he could find no abiding state of happiness or enjoyment of security'.[18]

Eleanor returned to England probably early in 1184. She kept Easter at Becket's former castle at Berkhamsted, where she was visited by her daughter Matilda, then seven months pregnant. Although she was from now on allowed more freedom of movement, the Queen was still in the custody of Ralph FitzStephen, who at Easter received payment of £32. 14s for her allowance for the period 1 April to 24 June. After Easter, Eleanor moved to Woodstock, where she seems to have stayed until June.[19]

On 10 June, Henry himself returned to his kingdom, where 'all his subjects were enjoying the delights of peace'.[20] 'Within a few days, at Winchester, the Duchess [Matilda of Saxony] bore a son, called William',[21] who would be brought up in England. Eleanor was present for the confinement. During this year her name begins to appear more frequently in the Pipe Rolls, which indicate that her household had perhaps been enlarged and record gifts from the King, at a cost of over £28, of a scarlet gown lined with grey miniver, a saddle worked with gold and trimmed with fur, some embroidered cushions, and various items for the Queen's maid Amaria.

Alys of France was still being held at Winchester, but there is no record of her meeting Eleanor. Later events would show that the Queen had no love for this girl with whom Henry had tried to supplant her. It is likely that Henry's affair with Alys was still ongoing, although the Pipe Rolls hint that he in fact had another mistress at this time. There is an intriguing payment of £55 17s 'for clothes and hoods and cloaks, and for the trimming for two capes of samite and for the clothes of the Queen and of Bellebelle, for the King's use'. Since the clothes and trimmings were hardly for the King's use, we must assume that Bellebelle was.

In July, Eleanor and the Duke and Duchess of Saxony, with their children, moved to Berkhamsted, where they stayed for the rest of the summer.[22]

The dispute between Henry and Richard over the assignment of Poitou and Aquitaine to John had still not been resolved. In the autumn of 1184, Geoffrey allied himself with John and together they raided Poitou; in retaliation, Richard plundered Brittany.[23]

In November, the King ordered his warring sons to lay down their arms and come to England, where he intended to force them to a settlement. On the 30th, St Andrew's Day, Eleanor was at long last reunited with them when, at Henry's command, she joined him and their children at a court convened at Westminster to bring about a concord between the royal princes[24] and elect a new Archbishop of Canterbury.

Henry had invited Eleanor for a purpose. Ostensibly she was there to witness the reconciliation of her sons, but he also wanted her support for his future plans regarding their inheritances. Summoned to the council chamber, she was seated in the place of honour and watched as Richard, Geoffrey and John were called forward to make peace publicly with one another and give the kiss of peace.[25] The King then asked Eleanor, as Duchess of Aquitaine, to approve the assignment of Poitou and Aquitaine to John, on the grounds that it constituted a fairer distribution of his empire, but the Queen, supported by Richard, the newly elected Archbishop Baldwin of Canterbury and some lords of the council, refused to co-operate. Realising that King Philip, as her overlord, would undoubtedly also support her, if only to drive a wedge through the Angevin family, Henry backed down.

Before Christmas, the King sent Geoffrey to Normandy to take charge of the duchy in his absence, a move that astonished observers and led to rumours that Henry was contemplating naming Geoffrey as his heir. Geoffrey's duchess, Constance, had recently given birth to her first child, a daughter, who was baptised Eleanor in honour of the Queen;[26] during the following year, 1185, Constance bore another daughter, Matilda or Mary, who died young.

At Christmas, the remaining members of the family were together again at Windsor.[27] The chroniclers record frustratingly few details of these royal gatherings, yet entries in the Pipe Rolls confirm that they were occasions of some splendour, payments being made for wines, spices, wax for candles, cattle, furs and 'entertaining trifles suitable for feasts'. After Christmas, Richard returned to Poitiers, while Eleanor remained in England; early in 1185 she was at Winchester, probably in the company of Matilda and her family.

Around this time, when it became clear that King Baldwin IV was dying of leprosy, Heraclius, the Patriarch of Jerusalem, led an embassy to England to offer Henry the throne of Jerusalem for his son John. The prospect of a crown had John on his knees begging his father to accept it on his behalf, but for various reasons Henry refused.[28] Instead, he decreed, John should go to Ireland and govern it on his behalf. On 31 March, he knighted his son at Windsor, and arranged for him to depart for Ireland on 25 April. It seemed that John would have a kingdom after all: the Pope sent him a golden crown adorned with peacocks' feathers, hoping that his father would see fit to have him crowned King of Ireland.

Henry and Eleanor were still in England when, in April, 'a mighty earthquake was heard throughout nearly the whole of [the realm], such as had not been heard in that land since the beginning of the world'.[29] Lincoln Cathedral collapsed[30] and many houses were left in ruins.

On 16 April, the day after the quake, Henry left England for Normandy. He was still determined to bring Richard to heel, and to this end, in late April, summoned Eleanor and the Duke and Duchess of Saxony to join him.

> When they arrived, he sent instructions to his son Richard that he should without delay surrender the whole of Poitou with its appurtenances to his mother Queen Eleanor, because it was her heritage; and he added that, if Richard in any way delayed to fulfil his command, he was to know for certain that the Queen his mother would make it her business to ravage the land with a great host. And Richard surrendered all Poitou to his mother.[31]

How far Eleanor concurred in this scheme is not known. She had herself ceded her lands to her son once he was old enough to rule them, and had not been afraid to speak out against Henry's scheme to give them to John. She would surely have spoken out against this new arrangement if it had not found favour with her, yet perhaps her new-found liberty was as yet too precarious for her to risk defying Henry again: and the prospect of regaining Poitou may well have been tempting, although she must have known that Henry was only doing this to show Richard who was master and that he would never again allow her to set up her court in Poitiers. Nor is it likely that she personally had any intention of laying waste Poitou; it was more probably Henry who was determined to assert her right to it, and thereby his own.

Richard now 'heeded the wise advice of his friends' – and perhaps his mother – 'and, laying aside the weapons of wickedness, returned with all meekness to his father', having surrendered not only Poitou but 'the whole of Aquitaine to his mother'.[32] He returned to Henry's court in Normandy 'and remained with his father like a tamed son'.[33]

Eleanor was with them; she travelled around the continent with Henry until April 1186. From now on, although Henry was in overall control of the government of Aquitaine, he would at various times share it with Eleanor and Richard; on some occasions, charters to the same beneficiaries would be issued by all three. Roger of Hoveden asserts that at one time Eleanor was exercising sovereign power in Bordeaux, yet within the next two years she would resign her authority to her son, and Richard would again be the virtual ruler of the duchy.[34]

One charter issued by Eleanor around this time was addressed to 'the Archbishop of Bordeaux and all her officers of Aquitaine. With the assent and at the wish of her lord Henry, King of England, and of Richard, Geoffrey and John, her sons', she gave to the abbey of Fontevrault 'and the nuns there serving God' a rent of £100 and the proceeds of a wine tax 'for the weal of the soul of her lord the King and of her own and of her son Richard and her other sons and her daughters and her predecessors'. This charter was confirmed by similar charters issued by Henry and Richard.

Henry, it was clear, had plans for the future disposition of his empire, but was not prepared to divulge them. This only caused bad feeling between him and his sons, a situation that King Philip was determined to exploit. Duke Geoffrey was staying with him in Paris at this time, as close as a blood brother, it was said.[35] Being dissatisfied with his duchy of Brittany, he wanted Anjou also, and 'while engaged in active service with the King of France, he made great efforts to annoy his father'.[36] Philip, naturally, abetted him in this.

Meanwhile, John had arrived in Ireland and attempted to establish his authority there. During the eight months of his stay, however, he succeeded in alienating both the native Irish kings and the Anglo-Norman colonists. When the kings came to pay homage, John and his entourage of irresponsible young lords insulted them by contemptuously pulling at their long beards and laughing and sneering at them. John displayed no ability as an administrator or military leader, and, arbitrarily seizing lands granted to Anglo-Norman settlers, gave them indiscriminately to his favourites. At length, unable to bear any more, the Irish kings set aside their differences and united against him.

By the end of the year, the King realised that this situation could not be allowed to continue. Appointing a viceroy, John de Courcy, he recalled John, and for much of the rest of the reign would keep him with him. The Pope's crown would never be used.

In 1185, the Duke and Duchess of Saxony were at last able to return in safety to Germany, although Henry the Lion would not be restored to favour until 1190, when he made peace with the new Emperor, Henry VI. Some of the ducal children – Otto, William and Matilda – were left with their grandparents in Normandy to be brought up at Henry's court.

In the early spring of 1186, Henry and Eleanor held court together in Normandy. In March, Philip again raised the matter of his sister Alys and forced Henry to sign a treaty providing for her to be married to Richard, with the Vexin as her dowry. Around the same time, Henry installed his own custodians in the strongest of Richard's former castles in Aquitaine and ordered his son to deal with a hostile Raymond of Toulouse. Richard 'was very offended, but he made no complaints to his father'.[37]

On 27 April, with 'all his European lands at peace', Henry sailed with Eleanor from Barfleur to Southampton in the same ship.[38] The King went straight to Marwell to visit the Bishop of Winchester, then spent the night at Winchester itself,[39] where he and Eleanor would remain for at least part of the summer. A second custodian, Henry of Berneval, was appointed at around this time, and some modern historians have inferred that this was because Eleanor had once again begun plotting against Henry, yet there is no evidence for this, and Berneval was probably a relief for Ralph FitzStephen.

Duke Geoffrey remained in Paris throughout the summer, occupied with various nefarious schemes, but these never came to fruition because on 18 or 19 August 1186 he died. Roger of Hoveden says he succumbed to a fever, yet other sources state that he took part in a tournament but was unsaddled in the mêlée and trampled to death.[40] He was buried in the choir of Notre Dame[41] 'with but few regrets from his father, to whom he had been an unfaithful son, but with sore grief to the French'.[42] Philip was so mad with grief at the loss of his friend that he had to be forcibly restrained from throwing himself upon the coffin in the open tomb.[43] Geoffrey's half-sister, Marie, Countess of Champagne, was present at his funeral, and gave money for masses for his soul. He left Constance, his widow, pregnant with their third child.

After learning of Geoffrey's death, Henry sent for John, who stayed with him until Christmas, which they celebrated at Guildford Castle in Surrey. There is no mention of Eleanor being present.

Although John was his favourite of his sons by the Queen, Henry knew better than to trust him. Some years earlier, he had commissioned murals for what became known as the Painted Chamber in Winchester Castle, but had asked for one panel to be left blank. Sometime prior to the Young King's death in 1183, he had had it filled in:

> There was an eagle painted, and four young ones of the eagle perched upon it, one on each wing and a third upon its back, tearing at the parent with talons and beaks, and the fourth, no smaller than the others, sitting upon its neck and awaiting the moment to peck out its parent's eyes. When some of the King's close friends asked him the meaning of the picture, he said, 'The four eaglets are my four sons, who cease not to persecute me even unto death. And the youngest, whom I now embrace with such

tender affection, will some day afflict me more grievously and perilously than all the others.'[44]

'A man's enemies are the men of his own House,' observed Giraldus.

Henry returned to Normandy on 17 February 1187. Eleanor did not accompany him, and during 1187 seems to have resided mainly at Winchester.[45] On 29 March, at Nantes, Duke Geoffrey's widow, Constance, bore him a posthumous son, Henry wanted him named after himself,[46] but 'the Bretons called their new duke Arthur',[47] in memory of the legendary king of that name who had once ruled Brittany, and as a defiant gesture of independence from Angevin rule. King Philip, as Arthur's overlord, immediately claimed his wardship, but Henry – fearing that once Philip got a foothold in Brittany there would be no getting him out – refused. It was left to Constance of Brittany to act as regent for her son, although Henry did not trust her and in 1188 married her to a loyal vassal whom he could depend on, Ranulf de Blundeville, Earl of Chester. Later evidence strongly suggests that Eleanor did not like or trust Constance either.

The mounting rivalry and tension between Henry and Philip seemed set to erupt into war. The French King was growing more and more angry and frustrated about Henry's continuing deferment of Alys' marriage to Richard, and demanded that both she and her dowry of Berry and the Vexin be immediately returned to him. But when Henry tried to put him off by suggesting that she be married instead to John, whom he would make Duke of Aquitaine, Philip marched at the head of an army into Berry and took Châteauroux, the first episode in a war that would drag on intermittently for twenty-seven years. When Henry and Richard joined forces to resist him, Philip requested a parley, and on 23 June, 'rather than submit to the doubtful judgement of Mars', the two kings concluded a truce at Châteauroux.[48]

Immediately afterwards, Richard, whose resentment had festered for many months now, deserted his father and rode to Paris to ally himself with Philip. The two young men became very close friends: 'Philip so honoured him that every day they ate at the same table, shared the same dish, and at night the bed did not separate them.'[49] Some modern writers have inferred from this that Richard and Philip had a homosexual relationship, yet the chroniclers do not hint at it – which they would certainly have done, had there been any cause for scandal – and it was quite customary for people of rank to share beds in an age when most household retainers were obliged to sleep on pallets on the floor. However, 'there grew up so great an affection' between Richard and

Philip 'that King Henry was much alarmed and, afraid of what the future might hold in store, he decided to postpone his return to England until he knew what lay behind this great friendship'.[50] His alarm was justified, for Philip, who foresaw that by sowing discord amongst Henry and his sons he would weaken their power, confided to Richard Henry's plans to marry Alys to John and make John Duke of Aquitaine; stung by his father's perfidy, Richard offered to assist Philip in his war against Henry when their truce expired.

War of another kind was looming on the horizon. On 4 July, at the Horns of Hattin, near the Sea of Galilee, the army of the King of Jerusalem was utterly annihilated by Turkish forces led by their brilliant commander, Saladin. After that, the Turks swept all before them and, on 2 October, to the horror of Christendom, occupied Jerusalem – that most holy of cities and the destination of vast numbers of pilgrims – and massacred the Knights Templar and Hospitaller. All that now remained of the crusader kingdom were three seaports.

The duty of the leaders of the West was clear: they must unite to free the holy city from the Infidel. The Pope proclaimed a new crusade, and on the day after receiving the news of the fall of Jerusalem, Duke Richard took the Cross from the Archbishop of Tours,[51] fervently proclaiming himself the champion of Jerusalem and vowing that he would dedicate his life to liberating the Holy Sepulchre. He had not consulted his father's wishes beforehand,[52] and when Henry heard of his resolve, he took to his chamber in grief and stayed there, refusing to transact any business, for four days. Yet when Richard declared he would not commit himself to the venture until Henry assured him that his position as heir to the Angevin empire was secure, Henry – fearful for his own security – refused to do so, which left Richard all the more certain that his father meant to leave everything to John.

Henry is believed to have orchestrated the risings that broke out in Aquitaine and Toulouse just after Richard took the Cross, in order to divert him from plotting mischief with Philip.[53] On 22 January 1188, Henry and Philip met at Gisors, where they received the Archbishop of Tyre, who was touring Europe enlisting support for the crusade. Succumbing to his persuasive arguments, both kings, on impulse, took the Cross, and swore to maintain their truce whilst they were campaigning together in the Holy Land. Henry returned to England on 30 January 1188 to raise money for the crusade, imposing a punitive tax called the 'Saladin tithe'.

That spring, despite their truce, Henry and Philip again began quarrelling over Alys and her dowry, and in June, Philip attacked Henry's border strongholds in Berry, whereupon Henry, realising that he would have to meet force with force, decided 'to make an attack on France'.[54] He raised a large army of English and Welsh soldiers and, on 10 July, left England for the last time. Before his departure, he visited Sarum, perhaps to say farewell to Eleanor, whom he would never see again. He may also have seen to arrangements for her safe-keeping, since it appears that the Queen had once again been deprived of her liberty,[55] probably because Henry feared she would take Richard's part against him.

Richard, meanwhile, having quarrelled with Philip, had led a force from Aquitaine and driven the French out of Berry. On 16 August, Henry and Philip met at Gisors in a final attempt to resolve their differences. Philip spent three days hectoring Henry over Alys and her dowry, but Henry doggedly maintained that the Vexin was his, and both kings 'withdrew in discord',[56] with Philip ordering that the ancient elm of Gisors, the traditional meeting place of the kings of England and France, be cut down, a gesture that made his hostile intentions plain. When Henry saw the savaged stump, he was moved to declare war on his rival.

Yet he was in no fit state to go to war. Ageing and corpulent, he tried to ignore the many ailments that beset him (among them an anal fistula), and invaded France, making desultory assaults on castles near Mantes. There was fighting in Normandy and Anjou, and Henry succeeded in wooing away Philip's allies, the Counts of Blois and Flanders.

Just when it seemed that Henry, against all the odds, was winning, Richard succumbed to Philip's blandishments and again deserted his father. On 18 November, when the two kings met at Bonmoulins for a second peace conference, Richard accompanied Philip and, primed by him, demanded that Henry name him his heir, give him immediate possession of Anjou, Maine and Touraine, and allow his marriage to Alys to take place without further delay and prevarication. When Henry, predictably, refused all these demands, Richard shouted, 'Now at last I believe what heretofore has seemed incredible!'[57]

Despite his father's presence, he knelt before Philip and, defiantly proclaiming himself the heir to Henry's continental fiefs, paid homage to the French King as his liege lord for all those domains 'saving his father's lands while he lived and the loyalty which he owed his father'.[58] The French barons were so incensed at Henry's refusal to give Richard what they believed to be his due that they drew their swords and attacked the King and his entourage, forcing them to withdraw to the safety of a nearby castle.

When the campaigning season ended, a truce lasting until Easter was agreed by all parties, and Henry withdrew to Le Mans, ill and in low spirits. During the winter, the Pope's legate, John of Agnani, and several bishops used all their diplomatic skills to bring about a settlement, so that the crusade could go ahead, but with little success.

Henry kept his last Christmas at Saumur in Anjou. His health was declining, and when the truce expired at Easter 1189, he had to defer meeting Philip and Richard to discuss a settlement because he was too incapacitated to do so.

They finally did meet on 4 June at La Ferté Bernard, where Henry refused to reach a compromise and again proposed that Alys be married to John. As far as Richard was concerned, this was the clearest indication yet that his father meant to disinherit him in favour of John, and when Philip refused to consent to Henry's proposal, the three leaders 'withdrew on both sides as enemies'.[59] Philip and Richard then reopened hostilities by invading Henry's lands, taking one castle after another; and, one by one, the King's barons in Maine, Touraine and Anjou, tired of his autocratic and oppressive rule, deserted him. When Philip's army appeared before the walls of Le Mans, Henry's birthplace, the King – in an attempt to drive off the French – ordered that a suburb be fired, but the wind so fanned the flames that the city itself caught fire and Philip was able to breach its defences. As the French stormed into the city, Henry and his knights were forced to flee. Drawing rein on a hilltop overlooking Le Mans, the King's bitterness burst forth.

'Oh, God, Thou hast vilely taken away the city I loved best on Earth!' he cried. 'I will pay Thee back as best I can. I will rob Thee of the thing Thou lovest best in me, my soul!' Giraldus Cambrensis, who recounts these words, says that Henry uttered a lot more, which it was wiser not to repeat.

Aiming to strike north to Normandy, which had remained loyal, Henry ordered a force led by William the Marshal to guard his back. Soon afterwards, the Marshal confronted Richard, leading a French army, and levelled his lance in readiness for battle.

'By God's legs, Marshal, do not kill me!' shouted Richard. 'I wear no hauberk.'

'May the Devil kill you, for I will not!' cried William, and thrust his lance into Richard's horse, unseating him.[60] Then he cantered off to warn the King of Richard's approach, enabling Henry to evade a direct confrontation of arms with his son.

The weather was now unbearably hot and many of Henry's followers succumbed to dysentery or fatigue, dying by the wayside. The King's captains advised him he must nevertheless press on to Normandy, but his anal fistula was now badly abscessed, and he was unable to go further. Sending the remainder of his knights to Alençon to obtain reinforcements, and accompanied by his bastard son Geoffrey and William the Marshal, Henry, leaving Touraine open to occupation by Philip and Richard, retreated via the back roads to Chinon. When he arrived, he was clearly suffering from the effects of blood-poisoning and could barely walk; nor, thanks to his abscessed wound, could he stand or sit without discomfort. He was also worrying about what had become of his son John, who had mysteriously disappeared.

On 4 July, the day after Tours fell to the French, Henry dragged himself from his sickbed and rode to another meeting with his enemies at Colombières[61] (now Villandry), a village between Tours and Azay-le-Rideau. On the way, he was forced to rest at a house of the Knights Templar at Ballan, complaining, 'My whole body is on fire.'[62] When his knights rode ahead to tell Philip that Henry was ill, Richard insisted he was feigning it. On hearing this, Henry, sick and weak, had his men prop him up on his horse and rode on in a thunderstorm to Colombières. Seeing him looking so unwell, Philip, for pity, offered to have a cloak spread on the ground for him to sit on, but Henry retorted stiffly that he had not come to sit but to learn the price he must pay for peace. He remained on his horse, his men holding him upright as he wearily undertook to agree to whatever Philip should demand.[63]

Philip thereupon forced Henry to submit to the most humiliating of terms. He was to pay homage to Philip for all his continental domains, agree to leave all his lands, including England, to Richard, and order his barons on both sides of the Channel to swear fealty to Richard as his father's heir. He was to pardon all those who had fought for Richard and was to promise to go on crusade by Lent 1190. He was to surrender Alys into Philip's custody and arrange, without delay or excuse, for Richard to marry her after returning with him from Jerusalem; finally, he was to place himself wholly at Philip's will, pay an indemnity of 20,000 marks, and surrender three strongholds in Anjou or the Vexin as tokens of his good faith. Defeated, Henry accepted these terms without demur and turned to leave, but Philip insisted that he give Richard the kiss of peace. He reluctantly complied, but as he drew away from his son, his last words to him were, 'God grant that I may not die until I have had a fitting revenge on you.'[64]

He was then carried back to Chinon in a litter, calling down the wrath of Heaven upon Richard,[65] cursing his sons, himself and the day he was born, and uttering blasphemies. 'Why should I worship Christ?' he cried. 'Why should I deign to honour Him who takes my earthly honour and allows me to be ignominiously confounded by a mere boy?'[66] However, when he arrived at Chinon, at the behest of a very shocked Archbishop of Canterbury, he went to the chapel and made his peace with God, confessing his sins and receiving absolution and communion.

In June, Matilda of Saxony, the eldest daughter of Henry and Eleanor, died in Germany, aged thirty-four, and was buried in the cathedral church of St Blasius in Brunswick, of which she was co-foundress. Henry probably did not live long enough to hear of her death.

On 5 July, Henry's vice-chancellor, Roger Malchat, brought him a list of those vassals who had treacherously supported Richard and were to be spared punishment.

'May Jesus Christ help me, Sire!' exclaimed Malchat in distress. 'The first name here is Count John's, your son.'

This, for Henry, was the worst blow of all.

'Is it true that John, my heart, John, whom I loved more than all my sons, and for whose gain I have suffered all these evils, has forsaken me?' he lamented.[67]

From that moment he lost the will to live. He turned his face to the wall and dismissed Malchat, muttering, 'Say no more. Now let the rest go as it will. I care no more for myself, nor for aught in this world.'[68]

During the remaining hours of his life, he either slept or lapsed into delirium, moaning with grief and pain. His bastard son Geoffrey stayed with him, cradling his head, soothing him and warding off flies. In a moment of lucidity, Henry blessed him, declaring he was the only one of his sons who had remained true to him, and expressed the wish that he should be made Archbishop of York; he also gave Geoffrey his signet ring with the two leopards on it.[69] He then became delirious once more, crying again and again, 'Shame, shame on a conquered king!'[70] before falling into a coma.

On Thursday, 6 July 1189, he died at Chinon. Geoffrey, faithful to the end, was the only one of his sons to be present at his deathbed, but as soon as he had left the chamber, the scavengers descended: the dead King's attendants stole all his personal effects, even the clothes he wore, and it was left to a young knight, William de Trihan, to cover his nakedness with a short cloak of the type that had once earned Henry the nickname Curtmantle.[71]

Although the trappings of kingship had been pilfered, Geoffrey and William the Marshal proved resourceful in laying out their master's body for burial. A woman gave them a fillet of gold embroidery to use as a crown, and they managed to find a ring and a sceptre. 'On the morrow of his death, he was carried out for burial adorned with regal pomp: a golden crown on his head, gloves on his hands, a gold ring on his finger, holding a sceptre, wearing shoes of gold fabric with spurs on his feet, and girded with a sword. He lay with his face exposed.'[72]

When Duke Richard, now the undisputed heir to his father's possessions, was informed by William the Marshal of Henry's death, he hastened to Chinon. As he looked upon the body on the bier, 'one could not tell from his expression whether he felt joy or sorrow, grief, anger or satisfaction',[73] and it was noted with disapproval that he knelt to pray for 'scarcely longer than the space of a paternoster'.[74] But when he rose to his feet, everyone watched with horror as 'blood began to flow from the nostrils of the dead King, and ceased not to flow so long as his son remained there, as if his spirit were angered at Richard's approach. Then, weeping and lamenting, Richard accompanied the body of his father to Fontevrault, where [on 10 July] he had him buried'[75] in the nuns' choir,[76] deeming it more fitting a resting place than Grandmont, where Henry had asked to be buried. A tomb with a fine effigy was soon afterwards raised to his memory, and Ralph of Diceto transcribed the epitaph that was engraved upon it:

> I am Henry the King. To me
> Divers realms were subject.
> I was duke and count of many provinces.
> Eight feet of ground is now enough for me,
> Whom many kingdoms failed to satisfy.
> Who reads these lines, let him reflect
> Upon the narrowness of death,
> And in my case behold
> The image of our mortal lot.
> This scanty tomb doth now suffice
> For whom the Earth was not enough.

The judgements passed on Henry II by his contemporaries were harsh. Giraldus Cambrensis and Ralph Niger viciously condemned what they described as his oppression, injustice, immorality and perfidy. Gervase of Canterbury bristled with disapproval of him, whilst an anonymous monk of Evesham claimed that he had had a vision of the King suffering the worst torments of Hell for his sins. Only Ralph of Diceto wrote of his good qualities.

A decade later, William of Newburgh recalled how 'ungrateful men, and those bent on evil courses, talked incessantly of the wickedness of their monarch, and would not endure to hear good spoken of him.' Yet by then Henry's critics had had cause to revise their opinions. 'To such men in particular the hardships of the days that followed alone brought understanding. Indeed, the evils that we are now suffering have revived the memory of his good deeds, and the man who in his own time was hated by many is now declared everywhere to have been an excellent and beneficial ruler.'[77]

Today, despite his ignominious end, Henry II is remembered as one of the greatest of England's mediaeval kings and one of the most successful rulers of his time. His memory soon came to be revered by his successors as an example of a firm and wise prince, who brought peace and prosperity to a troubled realm and left his mark on every English institution.

16

'The Eagle Shall Rejoice in Her Third Nesting'

One of Richard I's first acts as king was to send William the Marshal to England with orders for the release of Queen Eleanor from captivity[1] and letters authorising her to act as ruler of England until he was ready to take possession of his royal inheritance. When he arrived in Winchester, William was surprised to find Eleanor 'already at liberty and happier than usual';[2] news of Henry's death had preceded him,[3] and the Queen's custodians, bearing in mind the love King Richard had for his mother, as well as his fearsome reputation, had not demurred when she demanded to be set free. Thus the Marshal found her, 'more the great lady than ever',[4] already presiding over a hastily assembled court, to which people were rushing to pay their respects.[5]

The Marshal informed Eleanor that she had been 'entrusted with the power of acting as regent by her son. Indeed, he issued instructions to the princes of the realm, almost in the style of a general edict, that the Queen's word should be law in all matters.'[6]

Eleanor now came into her own. At sixty-seven – a great age in those days – she emerged from captivity an infinitely wiser woman, yet she had not lost any of her energy or her dignity, and her new authority sat easily upon her. More powerful than ever before, she was eager to grasp the reins of government and exert her influence over her son, who would need all the help he could get to rule his vast empire. Such was the respect that she commanded that she would be the second power in the realm during the first half of the reign. In the circumstances, 'could any be so uncivil or so obdurate as not to bend to that lady's wishes?'[7] No one dared.

Having listened to Richard's instructions, the Queen devoted her energies to drumming up support for him in England; after spending most of his life in Aquitaine, he was a stranger to his new subjects.

Gathering her retinue, which included the justiciar, Ranulf Glanville, Eleanor rode to Westminster, where she decreed 'that every freeman in the whole realm must swear that he would bear fealty to the Lord Richard, lord of England, in life and limb and earthly honour as his liege lord, against all men and women, living or dead, and that they would be answerable to him and help him to keep his peace and justice in all things'.[8] Many lords and prelates flocked to Westminster, where, on behalf of the King, the Queen received their oaths of fealty in the presence of the Archbishop of Canterbury. At around this time, Eleanor restored to her former ally, Robert de Beaumont, Earl of Leicester, the estates King Henry had confiscated after the rebellion of 1173–4, in which he had supported Richard and the Young King.

After a few days in London, the Queen set off on a progress through the southern shires, 'moving her royal court from city to city and from castle to castle, just as she pleased'.[9] 'She arranged matters in the kingdom according to her own pleasure, and the nobles were instructed to obey her in every respect.'[10] Wherever she went, she received oaths of homage on Richard's behalf and dispensed justice in his name. She transacted the business of court and chancery, using her own seal on deeds and official documents,[11] and styling herself 'Eleanor, by the grace of God, Queen of England'. She also issued edicts decreeing that uniform weights and measures were to be used for corn, liquid commodities and cloth, and that a new standard coinage, valid anywhere in England,[12] was to be issued. In Surrey, she founded a hospital for the poor, the sick and the infirm.

As the King had directed, Eleanor sent messengers to every shire relaying his wishes that, 'for the good of King Henry's soul', all those who had been unjustly imprisoned were to be released, on condition that they promised to aid the new King in preserving the peace of the realm.[13] Although William of Newburgh spoke for many when he complained that, 'through the King's clemency, these pests who came forth from the prisons would perhaps become bolder thieves in the future', this amnesty held much personal appeal for the Queen since, she said, she had found 'by her own experience that prisons were distasteful to men, and that to be released therefrom was a most delightful refreshment to the spirits'.[14] It was generally a popular measure, and Eleanor introduced others designed to win the people's love for their new sovereign.

She gave orders for the relaxation of the harsh forest laws, and pardoned felons who had been outlawed for trespassing or poaching in the royal forests.[15] 'She contained the depredations of those sheriffs who were charged with the care of the forests, intimidating them with the threat of severe penalties.'[16] She married off wealthy heiresses formerly in the wardship of King Henry to powerful young men known to be loyal, or to those whose loyalty needed to be courted.[17] She revoked King Henry's order that relays of royal horses be stabled and groomed, at great expense, in religious houses, a move that was thankfully welcomed, especially by the poorer monasteries; furthermore 'Queen Eleanor distributed the horses as gifts' to the abbeys 'with pious liberality'.[18]

In her every act, she displayed 'remarkable sagacity',[19] demonstrating all the qualities of a wise, benevolent and statesmanlike ruler. Her contemporaries were impressed, and many now found it hard to credit the scandalous rumours about her conduct in her younger days. Looking back from the perspective of the thirteenth century to the periods when she was the ultimate authority in England during the frequent absences of King Richard, Matthew Paris pronounced that her rule had made her 'exceedingly respected and beloved'. It is indeed on her performance in these later years that her modern reputation chiefly rests.

Eleanor's mercy did not, however, extend to Alys of France, whom she had brought up as a daughter and of whom she now had custody. On her orders, the princess remained straitly confined at Winchester. Alys was now twenty-nine, and her future was still unsettled, but if Eleanor had her way, it was going to have nothing to do with Richard.

On 29 July 1189, having seized King Henry's treasure at Chinon, Richard was invested as Duke of Normandy in Rouen Cathedral and received the homage of his Norman vassals. On the 31st he reached a settlement with Philip at Gisors, assuring him that he intended to marry Alys immediately after returning from the Holy Land, and agreeing to depart on crusade with him the following spring. Richard also made peace with those vassals who had supported his father and, in a curious volte-face, prompted no doubt by guilt and a new consciousness of the loyalty due to a king, denounced as traitors those who had risen with him against Henry. William the Marshal was one of those who received a pardon, and Richard rewarded his faithfulness to the late King by awarding him the hand of the richest heiress in the gift of the crown, Isabella, the daughter of Richard de Clare, Earl of Pembroke and Striguil. The Marshal inherited these earldoms through his wife and became overnight one of the foremost of Richard's vassals.

On 13 August Richard sailed from Barfleur to Portsmouth, where, thanks to Eleanor's efforts, he was welcomed with enthusiasm. Two days later, again to popular acclaim, he 'was received with stately ceremony'[20] at Winchester, where he secured the royal treasure and was reunited with his proud mother. Aware that, through rebelling against his father, 'he had earned the disapproval of good and wise men', Richard now

> sought to make up for his past excesses by doing all he could to show honour to his mother. He hoped that his obedience to her would atone for his offence against his father. These events revealed the truth of a prophecy which had puzzled all by its obscurity, that the Eagle of the Broken Alliance should rejoice in her third nesting. They called the Queen the eagle because she stretched out her wings, as it were, over two kingdoms, France and England. She had been separated from her French relatives by divorce, while the King had separated from her marriage bed by confining her to prison. Richard, her third son, was her third nestling, and the one who would raise his mother's name to great glory.[21]

Summoning Ranulf Glanville into his presence, Richard formally pardoned him, for by releasing the Queen from captivity in contravention of the late King's orders, Richard also granted Eleanor the power to punish those who had been her gaolers, but she declined to do so. On 17 September, Richard, who had himself imposed a heavy fine on Glanville, dismissed him from his office,[22] appointing William de Mandeville, Earl of Essex, a loyal servant of Henry II, and Hugh de Puiset, Bishop of Durham, as co-justiciars in his place. Hugh de Puiset was an ambitious aristocrat whose mother, Agnes of Blois, had been King Stephen's sister. Consecrated Bishop of Durham in 1153, he had long exercised almost princely power in the north of England, and was connected to the strong Percy family. Now aged sixty-four, he was a cultivated man who had established a fine library at Durham Cathedral and acquired vast experience in the world of politics and diplomacy.

Shortly after Richard arrived in Winchester, John joined the court, then accompanied the King and Eleanor on a progress that took them via Salisbury and Marlborough to Windsor, where they were greeted by the chancellor, Richard's half-brother Geoffrey. It is clear that Richard did not trust Geoffrey; he even seems to have suspected him – with little cause – of having designs on the throne. Yet he could not afford to alienate him, since he dared not risk leaving an enemy to make mischief in his kingdom while he went on crusade.

Richard therefore honoured his father's dying wish, and nominated Geoffrey as Archbishop of York; he was duly elected by the canons of York on 10 August, and paid the King £3,000 for the privilege.

Eleanor, who distrusted Geoffrey,[23] was against the appointment – despite his talents and abilities, he was hot-headed, difficult and quarrelsome, and had no love for the half-brothers who had betrayed their father – but the King overrode her protests.[24] He did nevertheless insist that Geoffrey be ordained to the priesthood, which would preclude him from entertaining any illicit notions of kingship; he also heeded Eleanor when she urged him not to lead an army into Wales to subdue some border raiders until after his coronation.[25]

On his election to the see of York, Geoffrey, at Richard's request, resigned his office of chancellor, and the King appointed in his place a Norman, William Longchamp, the recently elected Bishop of Ely, who had been Richard's chancellor in Aquitaine. Of short stature, with a limp and a stammer (Giraldus Cambrensis likened him to a deformed and hairy ape), Longchamp – who was falsely rumoured to be the grandson of a runaway serf of Beauvais – was regarded by the barons as an upstart. He was indeed of humble origin, but had clawed his way to the top by pandering to the needs of his masters. An able and practical man, he was over-ambitious and over-confident, and used his newly won power to advance his own and his family's interests. Vastly unpopular, he made no secret of his loathing for all things English, and alienated many by his arrogance and blundering tactlessness. Yet for all his faults, he was unswervingly loyal to the King.

On 29 August, John married his cousin, the heiress Hawise of Gloucester, at Marlborough, and was thereafter styled Earl of Gloucester. Despite the fact that many churchmen were denouncing the marriage as uncanonical, Richard had given permission for it to take place, and John was so eager to gain control of Hawise's vast estates that he did not wait for Pope Clement III to reply to his request for the necessary papal dispensation. In the meantime, Archbishop Baldwin of Canterbury pronounced the marriage null and void and laid both parties' estates under an interdict. John appealed to the Pope,[26] yet although Clement saw fit to grant a dispensation and revoked the interdict, he forbade the couple to have sexual relations. His injunction may have come too late, yet it is perhaps significant that there is no record of the couple having any children.

At the time of the marriage, Richard gave John the county of Mortain in Normandy and six English counties: Nottinghamshire, Derbyshire, Dorset, Somerset, Devon and Cornwall, making him the wealthiest and most powerful English magnate. John was also given full responsibility for Ireland. Many believed this advancement betokened Richard's intention of naming John as his heir, even though Arthur of Brittany had a better claim.

Throughout these weeks preparations had been in hand for the new King's coronation. On 1 September, Richard and Eleanor rode in state through streets hung with tapestries and garlands and spread with fresh rushes[27] to St Paul's Cathedral in London, whence they were escorted by 'a ceremonious procession'[28] of nobles and prelates to Westminster Palace. On 3 September, Richard I was 'solemnly anointed King' in Westminster Abbey by Archbishop Baldwin of Canterbury.[29] It was the most magnificent coronation England had ever witnessed, and set many precedents for future such events.

'At his coronation were present his brother John and his mother Eleanor, counts and barons, and an immense crowd of men and soldiers.'[30] The robes provided for Eleanor and her attendants cost £7 0s 6d, which included £4 1s 7d for a cape made of five and a half ells of silk, trimmed with squirrel and sable; other items purchased for the Queen included ten ells of scarlet cloth, two sables, a piece of miniver, and linen.[31] According to Roger of Hoveden, all women were barred from Richard's coronation, but Diceto states that 'Queen Eleanor was invited at the request of the earls, barons and sheriffs'.

After the coronation, the King 'celebrated the occasion by a festival of three days, and entertained his guests in the royal palace of Westminster', where he 'gratified all by distributing money to all according to their ranks, thus manifesting his liberality and great excellence'.[32] The guests 'feasted so splendidly that the wine flowed along the pavement and walls of the palace'.[33]

Women, even Eleanor, were excluded from the coronation banquet in Westminster Hall because the King was as yet unmarried. Unfortunately, the occasion was marred by a very ugly incident. After Richard and his guests had feasted, 'the leaders of the Jews arrived, against the express decree of the King'.[34] The Jews were not popular in western Europe, not only because of their beliefs, but because it was rumoured that they sacrificed Christian children and, more pertinently, they were seen as usurers. Usury, or making a profit from money-dealing, was regarded as a sin by the Church, but a lot of Christians were not averse to borrowing large sums from the Jews, many of whom had grown wealthy through charging high rates of interest. This provoked jealousy, resentment and racial prejudice, which was further fuelled by enthusiasm for the coming crusade and a consequent deep distrust of all non-Christians, so that at the time of Richard's coronation hatred for the Jews was rampant in England.

Only the previous day, 'the King had forbidden by public notice that any Jew or Jewess could come to his coronation', so the arrival of their leaders sparked outrage. 'The courtiers laid hands on the Jews and stripped and flogged them, and threw them out of the King's court. Some they killed, others they left half dead.' Yet this was only the beginning. 'The people of London, following the courtiers' example, began killing and robbing and burning the Jews. Yet a few escaped that massacre, shutting themselves up in the Tower of London, or hiding in the houses of their friends.'[35]

Despite the measures taken by the King to halt it – the Jews were officially under his protection – this wave of anti-Semitism spread throughout his realm and marred the first months of his reign, and there were attacks on the Jews in Bishop's Lynn (now King's Lynn), Norwich, Lincoln and Stamford.

Despite his lion-hearted reputation, Richard I was to prove a failure as King of England. He would spend only ten months of his reign in his kingdom, and would bleed it dry for his crusade and continental wars. He spoke no English, and was in every respect a southerner. He lacked his father's skills as an administrator. Yet, despite his undoubted ferocity and severity, he captured the imagination of his subjects, who admired his chivalrous exploits and applauded his near-obsessive dedication to freeing the Holy Land from the Infidel. The verdict even of his enemies was that he was 'the most remarkable ruler of his times'.

As soon as he was crowned, Richard threw himself with near-superhuman energy into preparing for the project that had come to dominate his imagination and his life: the crusade. Henry II had left a handsome sum in the treasury,[36] but the King was in debt to King Philip, had overspent on his coronation and had substantially reduced his revenues, due to his generosity to his brother. He was consequently desperately in need of funds to finance his venture and milked his kingdom dry, imposing crippling taxes on his subjects and selling off lands and public offices at exorbitant prices. 'Everything was for sale: powers, lordships, earldoms, shrievalties, castles, towns, manors and suchlike.'[37] Even those who had taken the Cross could, with the Pope's blessing, buy themselves out of it at punitive cost. 'The King most obligingly unburdened all those whose money was a burden to them,' observed Richard of Devizes drily.

'If I could have found a buyer, I would have sold London itself,' Richard declared.[38] It was clear to everyone that he regarded his kingdom as no more than a bank from which to draw funds, and his popularity temporarily diminished. It was rumoured that he might never return to England, but would give it to John and either take the throne of Jerusalem or go back to Aquitaine after the crusade.

An example of the King's rapacity occurred when Abbot Samson of

Bury St Edmunds offered to buy the royal manor of Mildenhall for its assessed value of 500 marks; Richard told him this was an absurd amount, and demanded 1,000 marks. Eleanor was less grasping. When the Abbot paid this extortionate sum, she was due her 10 per cent in queen's gold, but when he offered her a gold cup worth 100 marks in lieu, she returned it to him 'on behalf of the soul of her lord, King Henry'.[39]

Richard arranged to join Philip at Vézelay on 1 April 1190 in order to travel together to Jerusalem. In November 1189, the King went on pilgrimage, leaving Eleanor in charge of the government of the realm during his absence. On 20 November, the papal legate, John of Agnani, arrived at Dover without a royal warrant to enter the kingdom or any form of safe-conduct, an act of gross diplomatic discourtesy that Eleanor was not prepared to tolerate. She therefore sent to command him either to stay in Dover or return forthwith to Rome.[40]

In December, Richard restored to Eleanor her dower, augmenting it with the dower rights enjoyed by the consorts of Henry I and King Stephen.[41] He then made arrangements for the government of his kingdom during his absence on crusade, appointing as custodians of the realm Hugh de Puiset, now sole justiciar after the death of William de Mandeville in November, and, because he did not entirely trust de Puiset, William Longchamp, the new chancellor. Hugh de Puiset was to rule England north of the River Humber, and William Longchamp the area south of it. This was by no means a comfortable arrangement, since the two men were rivals and Longchamp's prime objective was to oust de Puiset from power and rule alone.

Although Eleanor was not formally designated regent, it is clear that both de Puiset and Longchamp deferred to her authority, as the King seems to have expected them to do, in the hope that Eleanor would keep the peace between them. She also had an official role, for Richard temporarily resigned to her his powers as Count of Poitou and Duke of Aquitaine, although she delegated these to her grandson, Otto of Brunswick, who became her deputy in Aquitaine.

On 12 December, despite being ill with a fever, Richard left England in order to settle affairs in his continental domains before setting out on the crusade, sailing from Dover to Calais. One of his first acts on arriving in Normandy was to grant a charter to the Cathedral of Nôtre Dame at Rouen 'at the petition of his dear mother, Eleanor, Queen of the English, for the weal of his soul and those of his father and mother'. It would have been only natural for Eleanor to feel concern at the prospect of her favourite son leaving for his great venture into the Holy

Land, and the inclusion of her late husband in the charter perhaps indicates that time had mellowed her animosity towards Henry.

The Queen spent the autumn and winter of 1189 in the south, staying in turn at Winchester, Salisbury, Hampshire, Windsor and Canterbury. The records indicate that she remained active in public affairs.

Richard held his first Christmas court at Bures in Normandy with great solemnity, and at the end of December met Philip again, at Nonancourt, to discuss preparations for the crusade. Already his fleet of more than a hundred great ships was being assembled on the coast of England, and he was accumulating provisions and drawing up strict rules of conduct for his crusading army: bearing in mind how the presence of Eleanor and her ladies had hampered the progress of the Second Crusade, he decreed that no women were to accompany the army, a decision that was endorsed by a papal bull.

On 2 February 1190, at Richard's summons, Eleanor sailed to Normandy and joined him at Bures, taking John, Alys, Archbishop Geoffrey and a host of prelates with her. Soon afterwards, Alys seems to have been placed under guard in Rouen, where she remained a prisoner.

In March, Richard convened a family conclave at Nonancourt, attended by Eleanor, Count John and Archbishop Geoffrey. Significantly, John had not been given any share in the regency. In the months since John's advancement, Richard had perhaps come to regret giving him such a wide power base. He must have realised that John was patently untrustworthy and might well try to make mischief during his absence. Despite Eleanor's pleas, he now made John swear on oath that he would not set foot in England for three years. But their mother remained adamant that this was unjust, and soon afterwards persuaded Richard to release his brother from his promise and give him leave to return to the kingdom at will. It was a decision that both Richard and Eleanor would have cause to regret.

Since Richard did not trust Geoffrey either, he was also required to promise to stay out of England for three years. Eleanor did not attempt to mitigate his exile. Shortly afterwards, Richard met Philip at Dreux and arranged to postpone their departure until July.

During the absence of the royal family, there was trouble in England. In March, the tide of anti-Semitism swamped York, where 150 Jews who had sought refuge in Clifford's Tower were burned to death. Soon after Easter, when William Longchamp, in the King's name, went north to punish the perpetrators of this outrage, many of whom were friends of Hugh de Puiset, he did his best to undermine the Bishop's stranglehold on power in the north and even ordered his arrest. Despite buying his freedom with castles and hostages for his good behaviour, de Puiset was furious to find himself again cast into prison, this time by Longchamp's brother Osbert at Howden, Yorkshire.

This left Longchamp in sole charge of the government: not only was he chancellor, but also acting justiciar and, from June 1190, papal legate, at the King's behest. He was determined to make the most of his power. 'The laity found him more than a king, the clergy more than a pope, and both an intolerable tyrant.'[42] He was continually progressing around the realm like royalty, attended by a squad of henchmen; he strengthened all the fortresses in his control, including the Tower of London; he hired an army of mercenaries from abroad; and he exacted punitive taxes to finance not only the crusade but also his own extravagant lifestyle.

In the spring, Eleanor seems to have accompanied Richard to Anjou to help him set his affairs in order before he set off alone on a short progress through Poitou and Aquitaine.[43] Charters issued under the Queen's seal at this time[44] suggest that she stayed at Chinon, or possibly nearby, while he was away; one charter was to the abbey of Fontevrault, 'for the repose of Henry's soul', while the rest conferred endowments upon other religious houses and the Knights Hospitallers of the Priory of France, in return for prayers for a successful outcome to the crusade and the safe return of King Richard. Eleanor also witnessed a judgement given by Payne de Rupefort, Seneschal of Anjou, in favour of the Abbess of Fontevrault in a dispute with the Mayor of Saumur over 'local rights'.

Both Richard and Eleanor were deeply concerned at this time about the succession, since the King as yet had no direct heir to succeed him in the event of his being killed on crusade. There were three possible successors, none of them very desirable: Arthur of Brittany, the late Duke Geoffrey's son, who was just three years old and was being raised in a hostile court presided over by his mother Constance; the unreliable Count John; and Archbishop Geoffrey, whose bastardy was a barrier to his succession. It was imperative that the King marry as soon as possible and get himself a son.

The question was, whom should he marry? It seems that Richard, perhaps influenced by Eleanor, had changed his mind about wanting to espouse Alys. Alys' affair with Henry II would forever lie as an impediment between them, casting doubt on the legitimacy of any children they might have. Marriage with Alys was therefore out of the question, although Richard would have to pick his moment to broach the matter diplomatically with King Philip.

Richard favoured an alliance with Navarre, the little kingdom that straddled the Pyrenees. King Sancho VI was friendly – he had once asked King Henry to free Eleanor from captivity – and could be relied upon to protect the southern borders of his ally from the predatory French during his absence. Such an alliance would also promote trade between England and Navarre. Moreover, Sancho had an unmarried daughter, Berengaria. Richard had seen her during a visit to the Navarrese court at Pamplona in 1177, and had much admired her accomplishments and charms.[45] The contemporary writer Ambrose goes so far as to assert that Richard 'had loved her very much from the time when he was Count of Poitou and she had been his heart's desire'.

It may have been Eleanor who revived his interest in her now. William of Newburgh claims that she planned to provide her son with a worthy wife who would give him an incontestable heir. A Castilian chronicle of the Third Crusade, *La Gran Conquista de Ultramar*, which was written in the thirteenth century under the direction of King Alfonso X and is the first Spanish source to refer to Berengaria of Navarre, states:

> When Eleanor knew that her son was to marry the sister of the King of France when he returned, she was very sad, for she did not like the French lineage. She pondered as to how it might be possible to rescind this marriage, and inquired as to where she could find a wife for her son. She was told that the King of Navarre had two sisters [*sic*[46]] and that she could probably get one of these for her son. On hearing this, the Queen asked the King of Navarre to send one of his sisters to be married to the King of England. The King was happy when he heard this news and he prepared the elder sister, who was called Berengaria, as was fitting for this princess.[47]

Eleanor would have approved of Berengaria: she was a southerner from a court that had assimilated the troubadour culture of Aquitaine, and her reputation was unbesmirched. As far as Sancho and Berengaria were concerned, Richard was a splendid catch.

During his progress in the south, which took him to Bayonne near the Navarrese border, Richard almost certainly came to an understanding with Sancho, either through the good offices of Eleanor or by a direct approach, but it had to be kept secret for fear of offending Philip at this crucial time. To all intents and purposes, Richard was still betrothed to Alys and would marry her after the crusade had been successfully concluded. Richard was now resolved that his marriage to Berengaria should take place as soon as possible, and arranged that, after his departure, Eleanor should travel south to collect his bride and escort her to wherever he was at the time, so that the nuptials could take place immediately.

When Richard returned to Chinon, his affairs on the continent were finally in order and preparations for the crusade were almost completed. On 24 June, having issued stern ordinances governing discipline amongst his troops, Richard said a final farewell to Eleanor at Chinon before departing on his great venture.

At Tours, where he mustered his army, he received his pilgrim's scrip and staff, although when he leaned on the staff and broke it some saw it as a bad omen.[48] Richard was unconcerned, and travelled on to Vézelay where the crusader hosts were gathering. On 2 July, he joined Philip there and the two of them made their final arrangements, agreeing to share equally the spoils of the crusade. As Bertran de Born pointed out, the contrast between the two leaders could not have been more marked: 'Tell Sir Richard from me that he is a lion, and King Philip seems to me a lamb.'

For the present, however, the two kings had set aside their differences, and on 4 July, at long last, with banners flying, they set off together at the head of the vast army on their long journey to the Holy Land. It was an awe-inspiring sight. 'Had ye but seen the host when forth it came! The Earth trembled with its coming.'[49]

17

'The Admiration of Her Age'

After Richard's departure, Eleanor dispatched John to England – possibly to keep an eye on Longchamp – then, in the late summer or early autumn of 1190, herself left for Bordeaux on the first stage of her journey to collect Berengaria. Some modern writers suggest that the princess was brought to Eleanor at Bordeaux, but there are several contemporary accounts of Eleanor crossing the Pyrenees to Navarre, accompanied by a Poitevin retinue and 'with no thought for her age' or the dangers of escorting Berengaria through the Alps in winter.[1]

Richard of Devizes describes the Queen at this time as 'still indefatigable for every undertaking, although sufficiently advanced in years; her power was the admiration of her age'. How far her reputation had been rehabilitated may be perceived from his description of her as 'an incomparable woman, beautiful, gracious and chaste, powerful and modest, meek and eloquent, strong-willed yet kind, unassuming yet sagacious, qualities which are rarely to be met with in a woman'. She was 'even now unwearied by any task, and provoked wonder by her stamina'. Yet even this admiring chronicler could not resist a veiled reference to Eleanor's colourful past, rumours of which had been revived by memories of the previous crusade: 'Many know what I wish none of us had known. The same Queen, in the time of her former husband, went to Jerusalem. Let none speak thereof. I also know well. Be silent!'

King Sancho VI received Eleanor in Pamplona and hosted a magnificent banquet in the Olite Palace in her honour; his daughter's betrothal could not as yet be celebrated openly, because Richard was still precontracted to Alys of France.

Berengaria was then about twenty-five – rather old for a bride in those days. The historian Ambrose, who saw her in 1191 in Sicily, described her in conventional terms as 'a prudent maid, a gentle lady, virtuous and fair, neither false nor double-tongued. She was the wisest lady in all truth that might anywhere be found.' Her father was a great patron of Provençal literature, enjoyed the works of Virgil and Ovid, and could speak the *langue d'oc*; it is likely therefore that Berengaria had imbued a great deal of southern culture during her extended spinster-hood, and possible that she was able to read and also converse with her future husband in his native tongue.

The truth is that very little is known about Berengaria. There is a beautiful effigy on her tomb in Le Mans, but although it portrays a young woman, it was probably modelled after her death at the age of sixty-five or more.[2] It cannot therefore be considered a faithful representation. Nor are the chroniclers agreed as to whether Berengaria was good-looking: while William of Newburgh describes her as 'a damsel famed for her beauty and eloquence' and Roger of Hoveden calls her 'the beautiful Navarroise', Richard of Devizes states that she was 'more accomplished than beautiful'.[3]

What is clear is that from the first Berengaria played a passive role, not only with her future husband, but also with her mother-in-law, to whom she was dutifully subservient. Her marriage to Richard might in other circumstances have relegated Eleanor to the side-lines as queen dowager, but Eleanor was too powerful to be displaced thus, and it was Berengaria who became the subordinate, signing herself as 'the humble Queen of England' and remaining very much in the background.

It seems that Queen Eleanor was satisfied with Richard's choice, and soon afterwards she and her future daughter-in-law left Navarre, escorted by King Sancho's envoys and a large retinue.[4] The route they took to their rendezvous with Richard is not known for certain – the chroniclers' accounts vary – but probably took them north to Montpellier, then over the Alps and across the plains of Lombardy in northern Italy. By Advent, Richard had received news that they had safely traversed the Alps and were on their way south to meet up with him in Sicily.[5]

Richard and Philip had gone their separate ways to the Mediterranean. Philip, who was in a noticeably bad humour with his ally after Richard had refused to be pinned down over Alys, took the overland route, while Richard rode south to Marseilles where, since his fleet had not yet arrived, he was obliged to hire ships to take him to Sicily, leaving orders for his own vessels to follow him.

At the end of September he arrived at Messina on the north-eastern coast of Sicily, where he quickly became embroiled in local troubles. To begin with, the people of Messina were hostile to the crusaders: they closed the city gates to them and refused to give them any supplies. Richard was having none of that, and effortlessly stormed the city, then commandeered it as his headquarters. But his problems were far from over.

In November 1189, when his sister Joanna's husband, King William II of Sicily, had died childless, William's illegitimate nephew, the ape-like[6] Tancred of Lecce, had usurped the throne. By rights, the crown of Sicily should have passed to William II's aunt, Constance of Hauteville, wife of the new German Emperor Henry VI, but anti-German feeling was rife in Sicily, and Tancred was the obvious choice of the people. Fortunately for Tancred, the Emperor was preoccupied with establishing his own position in Germany, but the usurper needed money and wasted no time in seizing Queen Joanna's dowry, stealing many valuable treasures left her by her husband, and placing her under house arrest in a fortress in Palermo.

When Richard arrived in Sicily, he found Joanna a prisoner and a complacent Philip, happy to take sides against his Plantagenet rival, already installed in the palace of her gaoler. Richard immediately demanded Joanna's release,[7] and Tancred did not demur, sending her to her brother in Messina with her treasure, which Richard appropriated to help fund the crusade. Tancred refused, however, to surrender her dower and a legacy left by King William to Richard,[8] and the wrangling over this kept Richard in Sicily until the spring of 1191.

The King welcomed his sister with all honour, and it was not long before Philip of France was casting amorous glances in her direction. Roger of Hoveden states that people noticed how relations suddenly improved between Richard and Philip after her arrival, and that when Philip met Joanna his face 'glowed with a joyful expectation'. But Philip was a married man, and when Richard realised what he wanted, he appropriated the priory at La Bagnara on the coast of mainland Calabria and established Joanna there, out of the French King's reach.[9]

At Christmas, the King entertained Philip at Messina, and was afterwards heartened to hear a holy man, Abbot Joachim of Corrazzo, predict that he would be victorious over Saladin. In February, probably as a preparation for his coming marriage, or perhaps as an act of purification before setting off for the Holy Land, Richard, stripped to his breeches, and kneeling outside a church door in Messina, publicly confessed to 'sins against nature' and 'the foulness of his past life'. A bishop granted him absolution and thrashed his bared back with rods as a penance, and pious hopes were expressed that the King would return to his iniquity no more. 'Happy is he who after repentence has not slipped back into sin,' observed a chronicler.

Meanwhile, Eleanor and Berengaria, having made the hazardous journey through the winter-bound St Bernard Pass, were making their way across the plains of Lombardy;[10] food was scarce here because Philip's army had recently passed through and stripped the region of its crops and provender, leaving very little sustenance for the inhabitants. The Queen and her party were without safe-conducts and had to buy them from feuding Italian princes. They were also at risk from the predatory freebooters who roamed the ravaged land, waiting to ambush and rob unwary travellers,[11] but fortunately they passed unscathed.

Passing through Milan, the royal ladies and the Navarrese ambassadors travelled south-east to Lodi, where they had a brief meeting with the Emperor Henry VI, who was on his way to Rome to be crowned by the Pope. No details of the meeting survive, but Eleanor was one of the witnesses to a charter issued by the Emperor to Conrad, Bishop of Trent.[12]

After having failed to obtain a sea-passage from Pisa to Sicily, the Queen waited there for instructions from Richard.[13] He ordered her to proceed to Naples, where his galleys would be waiting to take her to Messina. Late in February, Eleanor and Berengaria duly embarked, escorted by Count Philip of Flanders, who was on his way to join the crusading host, but when their ships approached the coast of Messina, only Philip's was allowed to dock. Tancred's officials insisted that Eleanor and Berengaria had too great a retinue to be accommodated in Messina, and forced them to sail on round the south of Italy to Brindisi on the east coast.

Richard was furious, and on 3 March met Tancred at Catania to demand why his mother and the princess of Navarre had been so rudely treated. Tancred showed him letters which proved that Philip had been poisoning Tancred's mind by insinuating that Richard was plotting to deprive him of his kingdom.[14] It had not escaped Philip's notice that Queen Eleanor was on her way south with a bride for Richard, and he was desperate to prevent anything from blocking the latter's marriage to his own sister and all the political advantages it would bring him. He had therefore persuaded Tancred to forbid Eleanor and Berengaria to land and so give him the time he needed to retrieve the situation.

Over their five-day meeting, Tancred confessed to Richard that he had believed Philip's lies. He had heard that the Emperor was in Italy and might press his claim to the kingdom of Sicily. He had also heard that Eleanor had had a meeting with Henry, and was fearful that the

Angevins had formed a league with him, with a view to setting him up as king in Tancred's place. Richard was able to reassure Tancred that his fears were groundless, and the two kings reached a friendly agreement. Richard recognised Tancred as King of Sicily,[15] while Tancred finally capitulated over the matter of Joanna's dowry, paying the English King 40,000 gold bezants in full settlement, and it was agreed that his infant daughter should be betrothed to Arthur of Brittany, whom Richard now designated his heir in the event of his dying childless.[16] The two kings celebrated their agreement by exchanging gifts: Richard gave Tancred what was reputed to be King Arthur's sword Excalibur, said to have been dug up at Glastonbury when the supposed tomb of the hero-king was discovered there,[17] while Tancred gave Richard nineteen ships.

Richard now sent a large ship under the command of a Sicilian captain to convey Eleanor and Berengaria south from Brindisi to Reggio, on the toe-cap of the Italian boot. Here, on 30 March 1191, they were welcomed with great honour by Richard, who took them on board his own ship and sailed with them, and thirty wagons laden with provisions that they had brought him,[18] up the coast to the priory at La Bagnara, where Joanna was waiting to greet them. There is, unfortunately, no eye-witness account of the meeting between King Richard and his future bride or of the reunion between Eleanor and Joanna, who had not seen each other for fourteen years.

Leaving Berengaria in the care of Joanna at La Bagnara, Richard escorted his mother across the Straits of Messina to join the crusading host in Sicily. They had much to talk about.

In March, shortly before Eleanor's arrival, Richard had confronted Philip with the evidence of his perfidy, but the French King indignantly dismissed Tancred's letters as forgeries and accused Richard of fabricating excuses for not marrying Alys. Angrily, he demanded that the marriage take place without further delay.

'If you put her aside and marry another woman, I will be the enemy of you and yours so long as I live,' he threatened.[19] There is no doubt that Richard's rejection of his betrothal to a princess of France would bring shame and humiliation upon the French monarchy, and Philip was desperate to avert such disgrace.[20] Knowing he could evade the issue no longer, Richard was driven to divulge the real reason for his failure to go through with the marriage, revealing that 'the King of England, his own father, had been intimate with [Alys] and had a son by her'.[21] Philip was inclined to regard this shocking disclosure as no more than an insulting excuse – the evidence suggests that he could never bring himself to accept it as the truth – but when Richard produced witnesses to testify to the truth of it, Philip had no choice but to release him from their twenty-year-old agreement in the presence of a gathering of lords and prelates, although he did so only on payment of a quit-claim of 10,000 marks (which came out of Tancred's bounty) as compensation for Richard's breach of promise.[22] The two kings then signed a treaty, but this did little to allay the bitterness that Philip felt towards Richard for having so dishonourably repudiated Alys.

Richard arranged for Alys to be given back into Philip's custody as soon as they returned from the Holy Land and to return with her the Norman Vexin and the castle of Gisors, which had been her dowry.

Because it was Lent – a season during which the Church would not solemnise marriages – the nuptials of Richard and Berengaria had to be postponed. Humiliated by the exposure of his sister's shame, and irritated at the frustrating delays in Sicily, Philip insisted that Richard put off his wedding until they reached Acre, but Richard refused; he intended to marry his princess as soon as possible. Still angry, and barely on speaking terms with Richard, Philip left Messina for the Holy Land on the morning of Eleanor's arrival, not wishing to receive the bride who would supplant his sister as queen of England.

During her journey through Italy, the Queen had received letters containing disturbing news from England of William Longchamp's abuse of power. Concern had also been expressed over the ambition of Count John. John had exploited Longchamp's unpopularity, building up his own power base by courting the chancellor's opponents, and was now engaged in a duel with him for political supremacy.

Eleanor and her clerks wasted no time in acquainting Richard with their concerns, the Queen confessing she was dismayed at the rapidity and thoroughness with which Longchamp had ousted all his rivals for power.[23] On her advice, Richard issued a mandate to Walter of Coutances, Archbishop of Rouen, to go to England and take charge of the situation there. Coutances was a Cornishman born, a scholarly, devious and able politician who had loyally served the Angevins for fifteen years in chancery as Keeper of the Seal, and as treasurer of Rouen, Archdeacon of Oxford and (until 1184) Bishop of Lincoln. He was no friend to Longchamp, and had already secretly counselled John to raise baronial support against him. Eleanor, for her part, was to return immediately to Normandy, from where she would be able to monitor events.

Because of the urgency of the situation, the Queen spent only four days with her children in Sicily.[24] During her stay, she ordered wedding garments for the King, and finalised with him the arrangements for Berengaria's dower, ceding certain nominal interests in Poitou to the princess for her lifetime. Richard had decreed that only on Eleanor's death would his wife receive the full dower of the queens of England. Before she left, the Queen entrusted Berengaria to the custody of Queen Joanna; fortuitously, there had sprung up a warm friendship between the two women, who had now joined the King and his mother in his luxurious quarters just outside the walls of Messina. On 2 April, Richard bade farewell to Eleanor as she began her journey back to Normandy, escorted by Walter of Coutances, Sir Gilbert de Vascoeuil and several great lords.[25] With her, the Queen carried several royal mandates and letters patent, enabling her to exercise sovereign authority during the King's absence.

From Messina, Eleanor's party sailed to Salerno. On 14 April, Easter Sunday, they arrived in Rome in time for the consecration of the new Pope, Celestine III,[26] whom Eleanor had known during the early days of her first marriage, when the former Giacinto Bobone had visited the court of France, and later, when, as an archdeacon, he had supported Henry II in his quarrel with Becket and been generously rewarded.

At King Richard's request, she had an audience with the octogenarian Pontiff at the Castello Radulphi, during which she obtained his confirmation of Geoffrey's election as Archbishop of York,[27] putting paid to any dynastic threat from that quarter. She also revealed to the Pope her concern over the behaviour of his legate, William Longchamp, and secured the appointment of Walter of Coutances as super-legate, with powers overriding those of the chancellor.[28] Before leaving Rome, Eleanor borrowed 800 marks from money-lenders to cover her travelling expenses.[29] She then set off, via Acquapendente, on the long trek across the Alps.

On 10 April, Richard's fleet, 200-strong, sailed from Messina for Outremer. In order to comply with the ruling that no women accompany the crusading army, Berengaria and Joanna were sent on ahead in a large dromond of their own. The fleet was divided by severe storms in the Gulf of Adalia, and the King's ship was saved only by his expert seamanship.

Berengaria's ship foundered on the coast of Cyprus, where she was threatened by the island's tyrannical Greek ruler, Isaac Comnenus. The King came to her rescue, capturing Cyprus from the tyrant; having given his word not to put him in irons, Richard had him fettered in silver chains. It was on the island, on 12 May 1191, that Richard and Berengaria were married. The wedding took place in the chapel of St

George at Limassol,[30] the bride wearing a mantilla and the groom the outfit his mother had chosen – a rose-coloured belted tunic of samite with a mantle of striped silk tissue threaded with gold crescents and silver suns; a scarlet bonnet embroidered with gold beasts and birds; and buskins of cloth of gold with gilded spurs.[31] Immediately afterwards Berengaria was crowned Queen of England by John FitzLuke, Bishop of Evreux. The King 'was in genial mood'[32] and the nuptials were marked by three days of feasting.

'Presumably the bride was still a virgin,' remarked Richard of Devizes, implying that Richard had perhaps anticipated his wedding night. His voracious sexual appetite was by now notorious. The late-thirteenth-century chronicler Walter of Guisborough claimed that the King had married Berengaria 'as a salubrious remedy against the great perils of fornication'. Yet the marriage was not very old before he became embroiled in a rather more damaging scandal.

Richard had taken pity on the young daughter (whose name is not recorded) of Isaac Comnenus and had entrusted her to Berengaria's care. According to Geoffrey de Vinsauf, an eye-witness, she was a mere child, but several chroniclers allege that the King spent long hours in the girl's company and hint darkly that his interest in her was less than honourable. It was sufficient to arouse disapproval amongst the clergy who attended him, especially in view of his recent penance.

On 5 June, taking Berengaria and Joanna with him, Richard sailed east to the Holy Land, arriving three days later at the city of Acre, which had been under siege by the forces of Guy de Lusignan, King of Jerusalem, for two years now. Since the founding of the crusader kingdoms of Outremer, Acre had been the major port for Jerusalem; it was therefore of great commercial and strategic importance, and its recapture was the primary objective of the crusaders.

The arrival of King Richard and his army boosted the confidence of the exhausted, famished and demoralised besiegers. He took command at once and reorganised operations with his usual energy and efficiency, despite having contracted malarial fever. Saladin himself was so impressed by his enemy's fortitude that he sent him gifts of fruit and food. Richard chivalrously responded by presenting the Emir with a black slave. Although the two never met, they had a high regard for each other, despite being bitter foes.

On 12 July, thanks to Richard's strenuous efforts, Acre surrendered and the King moved with his wife and sister into the royal palace. He was annoyed to find that, alongside his own standard, another banner was flying from the roof – one that had no right to be there, since its owner, Duke Leopold of Austria, had played little part in the taking of the city. An enraged Richard ordered it to be torn down and flung into the filthy moat, and made disparaging remarks about Leopold,[33] insults the Duke never forgot, and which would one day have serious consequences for the English King. That night, Leopold withdrew with his men from the crusade, swearing vengeance.

The victory at Acre was also marred by Richard's savage retribution. He announced that, unless Saladin came to terms within a week, every Saracen prisoner would be taken outside the city and put to death in order to avenge the massacre of the Templars and Hospitallers in Jerusalem in 1187. Saladin refused to surrender; nor would he free Christian prisoners or deliver up the True Cross. Consequently, ignoring the pleas of his fellow crusaders, Richard gave the order for the mass beheading of between 2,700 and 3,000 Turkish men, women and children.[34] It was an atrocity that is remembered with horror to this day in the Middle East,[35] and for centuries afterwards Turkish mothers would discipline their children with threats of 'Malik Ric' ['evil Richard'].

Richard's triumph aroused only jealousy in the breast of his ally, Philip, who had also fallen a victim to malaria. On 22 July, he announced to a contemptuous Richard that he was too ill to go on with the crusade and was returning to France.[36] His real purpose, however, was to lay claim to Artois and Vermandois and then – which was far more important to his future plans – undermine the stability of Richard's continental domains during the absence of their ruler.

By 24 June, Eleanor had returned via Bourges to Rouen, where she took up residence, keeping a wise eye on events across the Channel. Walter of Coutances, meanwhile, had travelled on to England,[37] where to his dismay he found political chaos.

At the end of March, John had taken Walter of Coutances' advice and incited a revolt against the chancellor, seizing the royal castles of Tickhill and Nottingham. The chancellor suddenly found himself fighting on two fronts, for the marcher baron Roger Mortimer chose this moment to launch an insurrection on the Welsh border. Having reduced Wigmore Castle, Longchamp raced across the country to besiege Lincoln, which John had occupied. John, whose anger knew no bounds when he heard that Longchamp supported Richard's decision to name Arthur his heir, was now consumed with a deadly determination to bring down the chancellor.[38] This was the situation when Walter of Coutances took charge of affairs.

Careful not to offend either Longchamp or John and make enemies of them, the Archbishop acted as a conciliator. He went to great lengths to work with Longchamp on an equitable basis, not revealing his commission to supersede him should the need arise. The chancellor found Coutances sympathetic, for it was clear that, while Longchamp – however misguidedly – was acting in what he thought to be the King's best interests, John was intent only upon serving his own interests. Nevertheless, Richard of Devizes accuses Coutances of duplicity in his dealings with Longchamp.

Indeed, at that time, it seemed very likely that John might soon be king. Many believed – and John himself deliberately fostered this belief – that Richard would never return from the Holy Land[39] and it seemed unlikely that the English barons would accept Arthur of Brittany, a boy of four, as their ruler. John, whose popularity had benefited from his self-appointed role as leader of the opposition to the hated Longchamp, would almost certainly be their preferred choice.

By the end of July, thanks to Coutances' careful handling of the situation, a settlement was reached. John was made to surrender the castles he had taken, and Longchamp, realising that his power had been cleverly limited and eager to make concessions, now sought to ally himself to John by agreeing to support his claim to the succession over that of Arthur of Brittany, Richard's designated heir.[40] This, however, did not prevent John from continuing to intrigue against Longchamp, and at one point the latter warned Coutances that John was plotting to seize the crown itself.

On 22 August, leaving Berengaria and Joanna at Acre, King Richard began his march towards the greatest prize of all – Jerusalem itself. This was no easy venture, for his provisions were dwindling and the army was shadowed by the Saracens all the way, but by the end of August the King was at Ascalon, and on 7 September he won a brilliant victory over Saladin on the plains of Arsuf, fighting with terrifying ferocity; two days later, the crusaders took Jaffa (modern Tel Aviv).

So far, the crusade had been a resounding success, but now Richard succumbed again to the malaria and dysentery that plagued many crusaders, and was seriously ill for several weeks. Philip had gone home to France, and several of Richard's allies and friends had perished, among them Philip of Flanders and Archbishop Baldwin of Canterbury. Yet the King was determined to press on with the great enterprise as soon as he was able.

On 18 August, Geoffrey had been consecrated Archbishop of York at Tours. Ignoring his undertaking to Richard to remain out of England for three years, he prepared to cross the Channel to take up his episcopal duties.

William Longchamp was determined to keep him out of the kingdom. He asked Baldwin VIII, the new Count of Flanders, to prevent Geoffrey leaving the continent, and ordered the sheriff of Sussex to forbid him to disembark. On 14 September, however, Geoffrey landed at Dover, only to be confronted by Longchamp's sister Richent, wife of the castellan of Dover, and by a party of knights, who demanded that he take an oath of fealty to the King and the chancellor. Geoffrey refused, saying that he had already sworn fealty to the King and had no intention of doing so to a traitor, then prudently sought sanctuary in the Benedictine priory of St Martin at Dover. The next day, however, he found himself besieged by troops summoned by the irate Richent. Four days later, in violation of the rights of sanctuary, he was dragged by the arms and legs from the altar where he had been assisting at mass, and pulled through the mud to Dover Castle, where he was imprisoned in a dungeon.[41]

The people of England were outraged at such mistreatment of an archbishop and, recalling the fate of Becket, adopted Geoffrey as their hero of the hour, hailing him as another champion of the liberties of the Church. Longchamp was held responsible for his plight, and in vain did the chancellor protest that he had never ordered Geoffrey's arrest. No one believed him, and he hastened to order the Archbishop's release. But the damage had been done. Bishop Hugh of Lincoln excommunicated the castellan of Dover and his wife and those who had dared lay hands on the Archbishop, and Geoffrey was brought in triumphal procession through the streets of London, while Longchamp took refuge at Windsor.

Seeing Longchamp in such a precarious position, John pressed home his advantage, setting himself up as the champion of the righteous and oppressed. Rallying the chancellor's enemies – among them Geoffrey of York and Hugh de Puiset – at his own castle of Marlborough, he marched via Oxford to Reading, where he issued writs for the Great Council to assemble on 5 October. Longchamp was summoned to meet John at a bridge on the River Loddon, four miles from Reading, but dared not turn up. Deserted by all his supporters, he fled to the Tower of London and barricaded himself in.[42]

When the council met, Walter of Coutances listened to the complaints against the chancellor, heard John accuse him of breaching the limits of his authority and 'moving pompously along bearing a sneer in his nostrils',[43] then called for his deposition, to which all present were in agreement.

On 7 October, Count John came to London at the head of an army, which he ordered to occupy the city. Summoning the citizens to St Paul's Cathedral, he had Longchamp's misdemeanours proclaimed, and was gratified to hear their approval of the chancellor's deposition and banishment. In reward, John bestowed upon them the right to self-government under an elected mayor, a privilege that Londoners had long coveted. On the authority of the papal mandate obtained by Queen Eleanor, Walter of Coutances was thereupon appointed head of a council of regency, in which capacity he immediately sequestered all Longchamp's estates on behalf of the crown.

On 29 October, having surrendered his castles and given up his brothers as hostages, Longchamp was transferred from the Tower to Dover Castle, whence he escaped, disguised as a woman, aiming to flee the realm. John was much amused to hear, however, that he had been arrested after his disguise had been discovered by an amorous fisherman, and agreed that he be allowed to go into exile in France.

Freed of this encumbrance, John now devoted all his energy, charm and talent to consolidating his own position as the future king. Richard of Devizes states that he made a point of travelling far and wide throughout the realm, making himself known – as Richard had never made himself known – to all classes, and courting the favour of the commons. Drawing on his huge revenues, he showed himself liberal, affable, magnificent and lavishly hospitable. Not only did he preside over his own court, but he dispensed his own justice. He also spread rumours that Richard had named him as his heir and that the King would never return from the crusade. 'It lacked nothing but that he should be hailed as king,' observed Richard of Devizes. But the English barons remained impervious to his devious ploys: they had no intention of replacing Richard with his untrustworthy brother while there was a chance that the King might return to reproach them for it. Nevertheless, while there was still a strong likelihood that John might soon be king, most magnates showed themselves friendly towards him, fearful of his future vengeance if they did not.[44]

Longchamp, meanwhile, made his way to Rouen, demanding as chancellor of England – an office of which only King Richard could deprive him – and as papal legate to see the Queen and lay his grievances before her. This put Eleanor in a dilemma: she fully approved of his dismissal – Longchamp had been nothing but a troublemaker – and had nothing to say to him, yet she did not want him going to Paris to stir up trouble with the French. Nevertheless, that was what he did, bribing some citizens to afford him the welcome merited by his high office.[45]

In Paris, he met two cardinals from Rome, Jordan and Octavian, who had been sent by the Pope to heal the rift between Longchamp and Walter of Coutances[46] and who were prepared to lay Longchamp's grievances before Queen Eleanor at Rouen. The Queen, however, refused to see them, declaring herself satisfied that justice had been done. Secretly, she feared that the cardinals had come on Philip's behalf, since Alys was still a prisoner at Rouen,[47] and Eleanor had received no instructions from Richard for her release. When the cardinals tried to cross the Norman border at Gisors, the Seneschal of Normandy raised the drawbridge against them and informed them that they could not pass without the Queen's safe-conduct.[48]

The cardinals 'swelled with rage' on being denied entry, but Eleanor refused to be intimidated by their threats of excommunication, and in the end they were obliged to depart, muttering that it was 'meet for the servants of the Lord to suffer contumely for His adversaries'. As a parting shot, they excommunicated the Seneschal and placed Normandy under an interdict, although Eleanor was specifically excluded from the ban.[49]

It was the season of anathemas. Longchamp excommunicated every member of the regency council except John, and in retaliation the bishops excommunicated Longchamp and placed his diocese of Ely under an interdict. This brought great misery to the people living there, who spent the winter cut off from the comfort of the Church's sacraments.[50]

On 2 November, Geoffrey was solemnly enthroned as Archbishop in a magnificent ceremony in York Minster. A jealous Hugh de Puiset failed to attend, however, and when he ignored Geoffrey's summons to explain his absence, the Archbishop excommunicated him. This angered those canons of York who had voted against Geoffrey's election and would have preferred Bishop Hugh, and when the Archbishop high-handedly refused to heed their protests, a major row developed, which rapidly reached a stalemate.

By October, Richard had been joined in Jaffa by his wife and his sister, who remained in residence in the city after the King, having dragged himself from his sickbed, had pressed on towards Jerusalem. What he did not know was that, during his illness, his allies had concluded a truce with Saladin's brother Safadin, and that if any assault was to be made on the Holy City, it would be made by him alone.

Richard himself now tried to bargain with Saladin, offering his sister Joanna as a bride for the Emir's brother Safadin, with a view to them jointly ruling the Holy Land as King and Queen of Jerusalem, on condition that Christians be granted access to the holy places, but this plan was scuppered by an offended Joanna, who stoutly, and very publicly, refused to marry a Moslem.

In Normandy, around this time, the Queen appointed the talented Peter of Blois as her chancellor and Latin secretary. Now fifty-six this Breton aristocrat had been educated in the schools of Paris and had for a time been attached to the court of Sicily. Such was his reputation as a scholar that Henry II invited him to England and conferred upon him several court offices, including that of secretary to the King. Later, he had served Archbishop Baldwin in the same capacity. A brilliant writer, his letters are peppered with sharp, acerbic wit and perspicacious observation; Henry II had been so impressed by them that he had amassed a collection. Peter was, however, a difficult man to work with, being vain, pedantic and eternally dissatisfied with his position in life, complaining constantly that he never received the preferment his talents deserved. Nevertheless, he stayed with Eleanor for some years and served her well.

In the Holy Land, winter fell. In December, Richard reached Beit-Nuba, only twelve miles from Jerusalem, but severe seasonal rains precluded any assault on the Holy City. He spent Christmas at Latrun, west of Jerusalem, in the company of Berengaria, Joanna and King Guy of Jerusalem. When he discovered how he had been deserted by his allies, his rage was terrible indeed.

Eleanor spent the Christmas of 1191 holding court either at Bures or at Bonneville-sur-Touques (near modern Deauville) in Normandy. Whilst there, she learned of Philip's return to a hero's welcome in France, and that, in order to retrieve his own reputation, he was now imputing his sudden abandonment of the crusade to Richard's insolence, pride and treachery.[51] He was even uttering dark hints that he had been poisoned, although his symptoms were merely those of severe malaria and dysentery. Aware that Philip's accusations were all ploys to enable him to ignore the Truce of God and have his revenge on Richard for abandoning Alys,[52] and receiving the alarming intelligence that he was planning to invade Normandy,[53] Eleanor immediately realised that it would be up to her to maintain the peace in the Angevin domains, since the French King would be sure to take advantage of any disputes. Above all, John's ambition must be contained.

In the middle of the winter of 1191–2, determined to thwart Philip's treacherous designs, Eleanor commanded the seneschals of all castles guarding the Angevin borders to repair and strengthen their fortifications and ensure their garrisons were fully manned. When, in the third week of January, Philip launched an assault on Gisors, it failed.[54] That same month, the French King demanded the return of his sister Alys, but Eleanor, who had no mandate for this, refused. Then came news of John's perfidy.

Philip had wasted no time in wooing John with false promises. Early in 1192, after his own barons had refused to break the Truce of God and invade Normandy, he offered John all Richard's continental domains in return for John's undertaking to marry Alys and surrender Gisors to Philip. Notwithstanding the fact that he already had a wife, John eagerly agreed and prepared to cross the Channel with an army of mercenaries in order to pay homage to Philip for the promised lands and lay Normandy wide open to him.

Fortunately, warnings about his activities reached Eleanor in Normandy.[55] 'Fearing that the light-minded youth might be going to attempt something, by the counsels of the French, against his lord and brother',[56] and knowing that no one but herself had the power to restrain him, 'with an anxious mind'[57] she made haste to England. On 11 February she arrived in Portsmouth – just in time to prevent John from sailing from Southampton.[58]

With her usual energy, the Queen 'tried in every way' to make John abandon his treasonous schemes. 'Remembering the fate of her two elder sons, how both had died young before their time because of their many sins, her heart was sad and wounded. She was therefore determined, with every fibre of her being, to ensure that faith would be kept between her younger sons, so that their mother might die more happily than had their father.'[59]

She was also resolved to remind the lords of England of their vows of allegiance to the King, and summoned four meetings of the Great Council, which were held in turn at Windsor, Oxford, London and Winchester.[60] She publicly proclaimed her loyalty to the absent Richard and made every English magnate swear a new oath of fealty to him. Then, with the backing of those magnates, and the staunch support of Walter of Coutances, she threatened to confiscate all John's castles and estates if he defied her and crossed the Channel.[61] Eventually, 'through her own tears and the prayers of the nobles, she was with difficulty able to obtain a promise that John would not cross over for the time being'.[62] After this, John retired in dudgeon to Wallingford, another royal castle he had appropriated.

The neutralisation of John effectively put paid for the present to Philip's plans to invade Normandy. The French barons were still refusing to violate the Truce of God by attacking the lands of an absent crusader, so their King's hands were effectively tied. Nevertheless, the

Queen and the regency council were taking no chances. Even in England, castles and towns were manned against an invasion.[63]

During her visit to England, Eleanor claimed her share of queen-gold on the aid levied on the tenants-in-chief of the crown for the King's marriage. She granted her damsel, Amicia, sister of Hugh Pantulf, the manor of Wintreslewe (which cannot now be identified) as a reward for faithful service, whereupon, with Eleanor's blessing, Amicia donated half of the estate to the nuns of Amesbury Abbey, a cell of Fontevrault, 'for the weal of her lady, Eleanor, Queen of England'.[64]

The Queen made a tour of some of her properties, among them several manors in William Longchamp's diocese of Ely, which still lay under an interdict. The consequences of the Church's ban were brought vividly home to the Queen, who could see for herself how badly the people's lives had been affected by it:

> That matron, worthy of being mentioned so many times, Queen Eleanor, was visiting some cottages that were part of her dower. There came before her, from all the villages and hamlets, wherever she passed, men, women and children, not all of the lowest orders; a people weeping and pitiful, their feet bare, their clothes unwashed, their hair unshorn. They spoke by their tears, for their grief was so great that they could not speak.[65]

Patiently Eleanor listened as her suffering tenants told her of the miseries they had endured through being deprived of the sacraments. What appalled her most was that 'human bodies lay unburied here and there in the fields because their bishop had deprived them of burial. When she learned the cause of such suffering, the Queen took pity on the misery of the living because of the dead, for she was very merciful. Immediately dropping her own affairs and looking after the concerns of others, she went to London',[66] where she prevailed upon Walter of Coutances to revoke the interdict and allow Longchamp to return to England and resume his pastoral duties.

Longchamp had already been in touch with John and offered him a huge bribe if he would help him return to England. Now he found himself invited back, and in March he landed at Dover, armed with a renewed legateship.[67] His arrival was courteously announced to the Queen in council by two papal nuncios who had accompanied him, but it provoked deep concern amongst the magnates, and it was made clear to Longchamp – and to John – that he was only welcome in his capacity as bishop of Ely, and not as chancellor. In March, he turned up at a council meeting, but the magnates would have nothing to do with him. Only Eleanor spoke up for him, and although there was gossip that he had bribed her to do so, this was highly unlikely, since her prime concern was that he attend to the suffering souls in his diocese.

In London, Eleanor spoke with Hugh de Puiset, the excommunicated Bishop of Durham, and asked him to go to France to persuade the Roman cardinals to lift their interdict on Normandy. The Bishop refused to leave England, however, until the Archbishop of York had lifted the ban on himself.

Eleanor was thus prompted to effect a reconciliation between the two warring prelates, and summoned them to appear before her on 15 March in the round church of the Knights Templar in London to account for their conduct and submit to her mediation. They obeyed, but Geoffrey foolishly attempted to overawe Eleanor by having himself preceded into the church by a solemn procession of clergy, with his archiepiscopal cross borne ceremonially before him, which strictly speaking was only permitted him in his own diocese. He compounded his error by blatantly refusing to co-operate with the Queen in resolving his differences with de Puiset. When an irate Eleanor threatened the sequestration of all the estates of the See of York if he did not comply with her wishes, Geoffrey made a pretence of patching up the quarrel, but to little effect, since it dragged on until the King's return.

At Walter of Coutances' insistence, Hugh de Puiset now went to France on the Queen's behalf and requested the cardinals to remove their interdict on Normandy. They proved stubborn, yet it was eventually lifted after the Queen made a personal appeal to the Pope.[68]

Still determined to be rid of Longchamp, the councillors turned to John for support and waited on him at Wallingford. He agreed to help them, but only in return for a bribe equal to or exceeding that which Longchamp had offered him.[69]

'You see, I am in need of money,' he told them shamelessly. 'To the wise, a word is sufficient.'[70] In desperation, the lords agreed that it was 'expedient' to withdraw the required sum from the Treasury. Not only did they need John's help, but they dared not antagonise him.

For John had not lain quiescent for long. He had soon gone off again on his perambulations of the realm, exacting oaths of loyalty to himself from various barons and appropriating funds from the exchequer. In April, an alarmed Eleanor, not knowing what else she could do to curb John's ambition, sent an embassy headed by John of Alençon, Archdeacon of Lisieux, to Richard, informing him of Philip's attempt to lead John into treachery, warning him of John's subversive activities and urging him to come home.

Even Eleanor now realised that Longchamp's presence in England would only cause further problems. She, John and the barons all wrote to the chancellor, and 'all with one voice admonish him to bolt, and to cross the Channel without delay – unless he has a mind to take his meals under the custody of an armed guard'.[71] On 3 April, bowing to this intense pressure, Longchamp again fled the realm. His departure brought a kind of peace to the troubled kingdom. Even John gave no trouble, but remained on his estates, attending to private business.

Philip of France had, however, succeeded in undermining the loyalty of some of Richard's southern vassals, notably Count Élie of Périgord and the Viscount of Brosse, but Élie de la Celle, the King's faithful seneschal of Gascony, aided by Berengaria's brother Sancho, held firm and crushed the rebels. The empire was still safe for Richard.

Richard had now been in the Holy Land for a year, and was still no nearer to launching an assault on Jerusalem than he had been the previous December. He had fought and sweated with his men, looked diligently to their safety, worked as a stonemason and labourer when the need arose, and during a siege at Darum in May 1192 was seen helping to drag cumbersome catapults for a mile across the sand. During the spring he had suffered such a severe attack of fever that his life was despaired of.

In July, ascending the heights above Emmaus, he glimpsed the distant city of Jerusalem and shielded his eyes, that he might not behold the city God had not permitted him to deliver. He knew now that he had to relinquish his dream of reconquering it. The Christian allies had been divided by bitter quarrels, and what had begun as a holy enterprise had degenerated into a forum for insults and petty squabbles. The time for a united push against the Saracens had long gone.

Returning to the coast, Richard sailed north and was just in time to relieve Jaffa from an assault by Saladin. Leaping into the sea without waiting even to arm himself fully, he waded purposefully to shore in order to rally the defenders, and when he rode out in full view of the enemy host, challenging any of them to meet him in single combat, there were no takers.

Sadly, the fall of Jaffa would turn out to be the last engagement of the crusade. In August, Richard fell ill again – he had never fully recovered from his bout of malaria the previous year – and at his request Saladin sent him fruit and snow. Worn out by his ceaseless exertions, disease, disappointment in his allies, famine and the extremes of the eastern climate, which alone had killed thousands of crusaders,[72] Richard now began to think of going home. His mother's letters and other disturbing news from England had convinced him that he should return, and he began negotiating a long truce, which would enable him to do so.

News from Outremer was irregular and often frustratingly fragmentary. Eleanor learned that, on 29 September, the King had dispatched Berengaria, Joanna and the daughter of Isaac Comnenus homewards on a ship sailing towards Sicily.[73] Then she heard that Richard had concluded a three-year truce – the Peace of Ramla – with Saladin, which left the crusaders with a coastal strip of land incorporating Acre and Jaffa, which would from now on be ruled by the new nominal King of Jerusalem, Eleanor's grandson, Henry of Champagne; furthermore, the truce secured for all Christians the right to make pilgrimages to Jerusalem unmolested by the Turks, who would retain possession of the Holy City until the twentieth century.

After the truce, Saladin invited Richard to view the holy places, but he refused, declaring he was not worthy. 'Sweet Lord,' he wept, 'I entreat Thee, do not suffer me to see Thy holy city, since I am unable to deliver it from the hands of Thine enemies!'[74]

Eleanor knew that the King had left Acre on 9 October, intending to be back in England in time for Christmas. Reports asserted that his ship, the *Franche-Nef*, had been sighted near Brindisi or had stopped briefly at both Cyprus and Corfu, then sailed on in the direction of Marseilles; in Normandy, expecting his imminent return, his subjects gathered to welcome him.[75]

But, bewilderingly, there was no further news of him. As the autumn turned into winter, the crusaders began arriving home, boasting of the brave deeds of King Richard, but no one knew where he was. Fears were now voiced that some calamity had befallen him on the journey, and throughout England his subjects lit candles for him and offered up prayers for his safety. It was also suggested, behind closed doors, that Philip and John had colluded in a sinister plot to assassinate the King. The situation in Normandy was so tense that the Queen again gave orders for the strengthening of defences on the border. That year, she kept her Christmas court at Westminster. By then, Berengaria, Joanna and the Greek princess had reached Rome.[76]

Then came the blow. Early in January 1193, Walter of Coutances sent to the Queen a copy of a letter sent by the Emperor on 28 December to the King of France, informing him that, on 21 December, 'the enemy of our empire and the disturber of your kingdom, Richard, King of England' had been taken prisoner 'in a humble village household near Vienna' by 'our dearly-beloved cousin, Duke Leopold of Austria',[77] the former ally whom Richard had mortally offended after the fall of Acre.

18

'The Devil is Loosed!'

After leaving Acre in the company of his chaplain Anselm, a clerk, two noblemen and a party of Knights Templar, King Richard's ship had sailed west for Marseilles, stopping at Pisa for supplies on the way, but had then been driven back by fierce storms to the island of Corfu. Here the King managed to hire two Romanian pirate vessels to take him up the Adriatic to northern Italy, but after being driven ashore by tempests at Ragusa (modern Dubrovnik), where he transferred to another vessel, he found himself blown by strong winds past Pula and was finally shipwrecked on the coast of Istra, just south of Trieste.[1]

Richard decided to make his way homewards overland and struck north through the friendly domains of King Bela III of Hungary, but was then obliged to cross the border into the territory of his mortal enemy Duke Leopold of Austria. In order to preserve his safety, he disguised himself as a merchant called Hugo.

He was recognised, however, by the Duke's loyal vassal, Count Mainard of Gortz, who pursued him, took all his knights prisoner and informed Leopold of his presence in Austria. Richard and his three remaining attendants managed to evade Mainard, but soon found that all the roads were being watched. The King was now suffering from a recurrence of malarial fever, and, posing as a pilgrim, took refuge 'in a humble house in a village in the vicinity of Vienna',[2] where he was set to work turning chickens on a spit. Here he was found by the Duke's men, arrested and taken to the secure fortress of Dürnstein (now a ruin), high on a steep slope above the River Danube. Imprisoned there in solitary confinement, he was guarded day and night by soldiers with drawn swords.[3]

Leopold, meanwhile, had hastened to inform his cousin and overlord, the Emperor Henry VI, of Richard's capture. Henry was a ruthless young man who had already earned a notorious reputation for vicious cruelty, and was no friend to Richard, who had recognised his rival Tancred as king of Sicily and whose father had supported his greatest opponent, Henry the Lion, Duke of Saxony. In his letter announcing the capture of 'the disturber of your realm, Richard, King of the English' to the King of France, Henry wrote that he knew the news would 'afford most abundant joy to your own feelings'.[4] While the Emperor insisted that Richard was being held as a punishment for 'the treason, treachery and mischief of which he was guilty in the Promised Land',[5] both he and Philip were aware of just how valuable a prisoner he was, and each planned to gain the greatest advantage to himself from this novel situation. Anxious that Richard should not escape, Philip urged the Emperor to ensure that he was kept in the closest confinement.

No one troubled to inform the English government of the King's arrest and imprisonment, but Walter of Coutances had his spies in France and they were able to obtain for him a copy of the Emperor's letter, which he sent to Eleanor with a covering note of his own, exhorting her with many scriptural precepts to bear the news with fortitude. Nevertheless, knowing what it was to be a prisoner, her sorrow was great.[6] Her first thought was that she must go to Austria herself to see Richard and negotiate his release, but she knew she dared not leave the realm at such a time.[7]

There was general consternation in England when the King's fate was made public, not least because of the reputation of the Austrians. 'They are savages, who live more like wild beasts than men,' wrote Ralph of Diceto. No one knew where Richard was being held, so Eleanor sent the Abbots of Boxley and Pont-Robert (Robertsbridge) to Austria to find him.[8] She also dispatched Savaric FitzGeldewin, Bishop of Bath, to the court of the Emperor, whose cousin he was.[9]

Tormented by the conviction that her son's imprisonment was a punishment from God for her sins, and wasting away with anxiety,[10] the Queen sought solace in the prayers of the nuns of Fontevrault, which she solicited twice at this time, sending gifts from Winchester and Westminster.

Berengaria and Joanna were in Rome when they heard the news of Richard's capture, and decided to stay there, fearing that the Emperor would try to take them hostage also, if they ventured forth on a homeward journey that was hazardous at the best of times.

The Pope, shocked to learn that Leopold of Austria had violated the Truce of God by imprisoning the crusader king, summarily excommunicated him, and threatened Philip of France with an interdict if he trespassed on Richard's lands.[11]

A popular tale, first recounted by the Minstrel of Rheims in the mid-thirteenth century and typical of the legends that later attached to Richard the Lionheart, relates how Richard's French minstrel, Blondel le Nesle, learning of his captivity, went searching for him in Austria, loudly singing the verses of songs they had composed together outside castle after castle, hoping for a response. At Dürnstein, when a familiar voice issuing from an arrow-slit high above him echoed a chorus, he knew he had found the King. Most historians dismiss this tale as a myth, but it is not entirely implausible, and there is contemporary evidence that a troubadour called Blondel le Nesle actually existed.

Despite the fact that she had been assigned no official role, Eleanor set aside her personal sorrow and assumed control of the government of Richard's kingdom in his absence. In this task she was ably assisted by Walter of Coutances, Hugh de Puiset and other councillors. The Queen, who was now 'exceedingly respected and beloved', ruled England 'with great wisdom and popularity'.[12]

The government's priority was to keep Richard's kingdom secure until his return, but there were fears that King Philip would exploit the situation to his own advantage and seize Richard's continental possessions.[13] Eleanor was also concerned about John's intentions,[14] and with good reason, for 'when John heard that his brother was in prison, he was enticed by a great hope of becoming king. He won over many people all over the kingdom, promising much, and he quickly strengthened his castles'.[15] He then sped across the Channel to Normandy and proclaimed himself Richard's heir.[16] Receiving a lukewarm response from the Norman lords, he moved on to Paris, where, accorded a warm welcome, 'he made a pact with the King of France that his nephew Arthur, Duke of Brittany, should be excluded from the hopes the Bretons nourished for him'.[17]

John then paid homage to Philip for all the Angevin lands on the continent[18] – and, it was rumoured, for England as well, over which Philip had no feudal jurisdiction. Rumour also credited John with promising to marry Alys and hand over to Philip Gisors and the Norman Vexin.[19] But John's sights were set on England for the present, and with money given him by the French King, he proceeded to raise an army of Flemish mercenaries. He and Philip also agreed to do everything in their power to keep Richard in captivity.

Realising that the unity of the kingdom was essential at this time of crisis, the Queen exacted new oaths of allegiance to the King from the lords and clergy. 'Queen Eleanor, the King's mother, and Walter of Coutances and other barons did their utmost to conserve the peace of the kingdom, seeking to join together hearts which were permanently at loggerheads.'[20]

In February 1193, in return for the promise of part of the ransom Henry VI intended to demand, Leopold handed over his illustrious prisoner to the Emperor,[21] who had Richard moved from Dürnstein to the eleventh-century castle of Trifels, perched high above the little town of Annweiler in the forests on the Swabian border.[22] His journey took him via Ratisbon (Regensburg) and Würzburg, and it was just south of Würzburg, at Ochsenfurt, in the middle of March, that the Abbots of Boxley and Pont-Robert briefly met their king, whom they found in good spirits, determined to outwit the Emperor.[23]

Richard's brother-in-law and Henry VI's chief adversary, Henry the Lion, Duke of Saxony, and other German princes protested vehemently against Richard's continuing imprisonment, but the Emperor silenced their protests by threatening to have the King executed for his alleged crimes if they did not desist. This was a mere bluff, for he secretly intended to use his captive for more lucrative purposes.

On 23 March, Richard was brought before the imperial council, or Diet, at nearby Speyer on the Rhine[24] to answer certain charges, but spoke up so well for himself that the Emperor was moved to give him the kiss of peace.

Present at this ceremony was Richard's loyal servant Hubert Walter, Bishop of Salisbury, who had learned of his master's capture in Sicily, whilst travelling back to England from the Holy Land, and had immediately gone to Rome to seek the Pope's advice as to what he should do. Celestine told Hubert to go to Germany and seek out the King, then assist him as best he could. Hubert had hastened north, tracking down his master by trailing rumours from town to town.[25]

Richard had a high opinion of Hubert Walter. Tall, elegant and handsome, Hubert hailed from East Anglia and was the nephew of the former justiciar Ranulf Glanville. An expert lawyer and administrator, he had served the Angevins well, first as chaplain to Henry II, then as a royal judge, a baron of the exchequer, Dean of York and latterly as Bishop of Salisbury. During the crusade he had worked tirelessly to assist injured and dying soldiers, and Richard had entrusted him with the task of leading his army home. When Hubert arrived at Speyer, the King decided that he was the obvious candidate to replace Archbishop Baldwin of Canterbury, and sent him back to England with letters authorising the Queen to secure his appointment as primate.

During March, the two abbots returned from Germany and reported to

Eleanor that they had seen the King. They also warned her that the Emperor was likely to demand a large ransom in return for Richard's release.

Eleanor was alarmed to learn that her beloved son was now a prisoner of the Emperor, for she had heard something of Henry's reputation, and it was probably this that prompted her to write the first of three extraordinary letters to Pope Celestine III. After his initial censures, the Pontiff had promised three times to send a legate to intercede with Richard's captors, but had failed to do so. Eleanor felt that he should be doing a lot more to alleviate the situation, and now angrily castigated him for his tardiness in aiding a crusader who was supposed to be under the Church's protection.

Copies of the letters she sent were preserved amongst the papers of her secretary, Peter of Blois, who almost certainly had a hand in their composition, since his style is evident in parts, and it is unlikely – although not impossible – that Eleanor was sufficiently erudite to include so many citations from scripture. Some modern historians believe that Peter composed the letters himself as an exercise in Latin rhetoric. There is no record of their dispatch, nor of their receipt in Rome. Yet this does not mean to say that the Pope never received them, since most letters of the period are lost. It is true that these remarkable letters were not attributed to Eleanor until the seventeenth century, yet why the connection was not made earlier remains a mystery, given the salutations, the authenticity of the detail and the passionate sentiments expressed, which are in keeping with what we know from other sources of the period of Eleanor's feelings, actions and character. Moreover there is some evidence of a papal response to the second letter. The conclusion must be, therefore, that Eleanor not only initiated this correspondence but was also its co-author.

Because so few of Eleanor's letters survive, this one has been quoted at length, since it gives us such a graphic and intimate view of the Queen's personal feelings, and in particular the anguish and anger she felt at this time, and her fears for her son – rare in a mediaeval royal letter:[26]

> To the reverend Father and Lord Celestine, by the grace of God, the Supreme Pontiff, Eleanor, the miserable and – would I could add – the commiserated Queen of England, Duchess of Normandy, Countess of Anjou, entreats him to show himself to be a father of mercy to a pitiful mother.
>
> O holiest Pope, a cursed distance between us prevents me from addressing you in person, but I must give vent to my grief a little,

and who shall assist me to write my words? I am all anxiety, both within and without, whence my very words are full of suffering. Without are fears, within contentions, and I cannot take one breath free from the persecution of my troubles and the grief caused by my afflictions, which beyond measure have found me out.

I am all defiled with torment, my flesh is wasted away, and my bones cleave to my skin. My years pass away full of groans, and I wish they were altogether passed away. O that the whole blood of my body would now die, that the brain in my head and the marrow of my bones were so dissolved into tears that I might melt away in weeping. My very bowels are torn away from me. I have lost the staff of my old age, the light of my eyes, and would God accede to my prayers He would condemn my ill-fated eyes to perpetual blindness that they no longer saw the woes of my people.

Who may allow me to die for you, my son? Mother of mercy, look upon a mother so wretched, or else, if your Son, an unexhausted source of mercy, requires from my son the sins of the mother, then let Him exact complete vengeance on me, for I am the only one to offend, and let Him punish me, for I am the irreverent one. Do not let Him smile over the punishment of an innocent person. Let He who now bruises me take up His hand and slay me. Let this be my consolation – that in burdening me with grief, He does not spare me.

O wretched me, yet pitied by no one. Why have I, the Lady of two kingdoms, the mother of two kings, reached the ignominy of this abominable old age? My bowels are torn away, my very race is destroyed and passing away from me. The Young King and the Count [*sic*] of Brittany sleep in the dust, and their most unhappy mother is compelled to live that without cure she may be ever tortured with the memory of the dead.

Two sons yet survive to my comfort, who now live only to distress me, a miserable and condemned creature. King Richard is detained in bonds, and his brother John depopulates the captive's kingdom with the sword and lays it waste with fire. In all things the Lord has become cruel towards me, turning His heavy hand against me. His anger is so against me that even my sons fight against each other, if indeed it can be called a fight in which one languishes in bonds and the other, adding grief upon grief, tries by cruel tyranny to usurp the exile's kingdom.

O good Jesus, who will grant me Your protection and hide me in Hell itself until Your fury passes away, until Your arrows, which are in me, by whose very vehemence my spirit is drunk up, shall cease? I long for death, I am weary of life, and though I thus die constantly, I yet desire to die more fully. I am reluctantly compelled to live, that my life may be the food of death and a means of torture. Blessed are those who pass away by a fortunate abortion and never know the capriciousness of this life, who do not know the waywardness of this life and the unpredictable events in our inconstant fate!

What do I do? Why do I yet live? Why do I, a wretched creature, delay? Why do I not go, that I may see him whom my soul loves, bound in beggary and irons? At such a time as this, how could a mother forget the son of her womb? Affection for their young appeases tigers, nay, even the fiercer witches.

Yet I fluctuate in doubt, for if I go away, I desert my son's kingdom, which is laid waste on all sides with fierce hostility, and in my absence it will be destitute of all counsel and solace. Again, if I stay, I shall not see the face of my son, that face which I so long for, and there will be no one who will study to procure the liberation of my son. But what I fear still more is that this most fastidious of young men will be tortured for an impossible sum of money, and, impatient of so much affliction, will be easily brought to the agonies of death.

O impious, cruel, and dreadful tyrant [i.e. the Emperor], who has not feared to lay sacrilegious hands on the Lord's Anointed; nor has the royal unction, nor the reverence due to a holy life, nor the fear of God, restrained you from such inhumanity.

Yet the Prince of the Apostles still rules and reigns in the Apostolic See, and his judicial rigour is set up as a means of resort. It rests with you, Father, to draw the sword of Peter against these evildoers, which for this purpose is set above peoples and kingdoms. The Cross of Christ excels the eagles of Caesar, the sword of Peter is a higher authority than the sword of Constantine, and the Apostolic See higher than the imperial power.

Is your power derived from God or from men? Did not the God of Gods speak to you through His apostle Peter, that whatsoever you bind on Earth shall be bound also in Heaven, and whatsoever you loose on Earth shall be loosed also in Heaven? Why then do you so long negligently, nay cruelly, delay to free my son, or is it rather that you do not dare? Perhaps you will say that this power is given to you over souls, not bodies: so be it, I will certainly be satisfied if you bind the souls of those who keep my son bound in prison.

It is your province to release my son, unless the fear of God has yielded to a human fear. Restore my son to me, then, O man of God, if indeed you are a man of God and not a man of mere blood. For know that if you are slow in releasing my son, from your hand will the Most High require his blood.

Alas, alas for us, when the chief shepherd has become a mercenary, when he flies from the face of the wolf, when he abandons in the jaws of a bloodthirsty beast the lamb put in his care, or even the chosen ram, the leader of the Lord's flock. The good shepherd instructs and informs other shepherds not to fly when they see a wolf approaching, but rather to lay down their lives for their sheep. Save, therefore, I entreat you, your own soul, whilst, by urgent embassies, salutary advice, by the thunders of excommunication, general interdicts and terrible sentences, you endeavour to procure the liberation, I will not say of your sheep, but of your son. Though late, you ought to give your life for him, for whom as yet you have refused to say or write one word. My son is tormented in bonds, yet you do not go to him, nor send anyone, nor are moved by the sorrow which moved Joseph. Christ sees this and is silent, but at the last judgement there shall be a fearful retribution for those who are negligent in doing God's work.

Three times you have promised us to send legates, yet they have not been sent. If my son were in prosperity, we should have seen them run in answer to his lightest call, expecting plentiful rewards from his munificent generosity and the public profit of his kingdom. But what profit could they consider more glorious than the freeing of a captive king and the restoring of peace to the people, quiet to the religious, and joy to all? But while the wolf comes upon its prey, the dogs are mute: either they cannot, or they will not, bark.

Is this the promise you made me at the Castello Radulphi,[27] with such protestations of love and good faith? What benefit did you gain from giving my simple nature mere words, from mocking the faith of the innocent with a hollow trust? Alas, I know now that your cardinals' promises are but empty words. You alone, who were my hope after God and the trust of my people, force me to despair. Cursed be he who trusts in man!

Where is my refuge now? You, O Lord my God. The eyes of Your handmaiden are lifted up to You, O Lord, for You recognise my distress. You, O King of Kings, Lord of Lords, grant sovereignty to Your Son, and save the son of Your handmaiden.

Do not visit upon him the crimes of his father or the wickedness of his mother.

We know from a certified public report that, after the death of the Bishop of Liège, whom the Emperor is said to have killed with a fatal blow from his sword, though wielded by a distant hand, he miserably imprisoned the Bishop of Ostia, four of his provincial bishops, and even the archbishops of Salerno and Trèves. And the apostolic authority ought in no way to deny that unlawfully and tyrannically he has also taken possession of Sicily. The Emperor's fury is not satisfied with all these gains, but his hand is still stretched out. Fearful things he has already done, but worse are still certainly to be expected.

Where is the promise the Lord made to His Church: 'I shall make thee the pride of ages, a joy from generation to generation'? Once the Church trod upon the necks of the proud with its own strength, and the laws of emperors obeyed the sacred canons. But now things have changed not only canons, but the makers of canons are restrained by base laws and profane customs. No one dare murmur about the detestable crimes of the powerful, which are tolerated, and canonical rigour falls on the sins of the poor alone.

The kings and princes of the Earth have conspired against my son, the Lord's Anointed. One tortures him in chains, another ravages his lands with a cruel enmity. The Supreme Pontiff sees all this, yet keeps the sword of Peter sheathed, and thus gives the sinner added boldness, his silence being presumed to indicate consent.

But I declare to you that the time of dissension foretold by the Apostle is at hand, when the son of eternal damnation shall be revealed. The fateful moment is at hand when the seamless tunic of Christ shall be rent again, when the net of Peter shall be broken, and the solid unity of the Catholic Church dissolved. These are the beginnings of sorrows. We feel bad things, we fear worse.

I am no prophetess, but my grief suggests many things about the troubles to come. Yet it also steals away the very words which it suggests. A sob stops my breath, my sadness saps the strength of my soul, and absorbing grief shuts up by its anxieties the vocal passages of my soul. Farewell.[28]

It appears that the Queen received no response to this letter. At eighty-seven, Celestine was of too timid a disposition to risk incurring the enmity of the Emperor, whose armies were even now invading papal territory and whose men had recently cut the throats of papal emissaries.[29] For decades, the papacy had been in conflict with the Empire, and all Celestine wanted was to preserve the peace so that he could target corruption within the Church. In any case, he was aware that, as a result of the recent schism, the standing of the papacy was poor, and any representions he might make on Richard's behalf to the Emperor would be treated with contempt.

In Lent, John returned to England ahead of his mercenary force, intent upon establishing himself as king. Having failed to enlist the support of William the Lyon, King of Scots, he was successful in hiring more mercenaries in Wales. He then went to London, where he demanded that the regency council surrender its powers to him. When the magnates refused, he did his best to convince them and the Queen that Richard would never return, repeating all kinds of alarmist rumours to that effect, which were then circulating in France. At one point, he even announced that Richard was dead, but no one believed him. The council's firm stand was supported by Geoffrey of York and William the Marshal, and it was boosted by Eleanor's refusal to be intimidated by her son, as well as by Richard's widespread popularity.

Making his intentions even clearer, John began stirring up rebellion, urging the magnates to join him and seizing several royal strongholds. He himself garrisoned Windsor Castle, to which Walter of Coutances and other magnates immediately laid siege. At the same time, Hugh de Puiset invested John's castle at Tickhill.

Meanwhile, Philip had invaded Normandy. On 12 April he took Gisors, then overran the Vexin, laying wide open the rest of the duchy to conquest. Having seized Neaufles, he marched on the capital Rouen, where he set up his siege engines and demanded that the citizens surrender to him and deliver up his sister Alys.[30] Robert de Beaumont, Earl of Leicester, the seneschal of Rouen, whose lands had been restored to him by Eleanor in 1189, refused to comply, although he declared, with an air of menace, that he would be pleased to offer Philip the hospitality due to his master's overlord, and would also conduct him to visit his sister, provided he entered the castle alone and unarmed. Philip, ever suspicious, suspected a trap to take him prisoner and exchange him for Richard, and angrily demurred. In his fury at being thwarted, he had his own siege engines destroyed and ordered that every cask of wine from his stores be emptied into the Seine. Then he marched back to Paris, vowing that he would revisit Rouen with a rod of iron.[31]

Expecting John's army of Flemish mercenaries to arrive in England at any time, the Queen and council took urgent measures for the defence of the realm. 'By order of Queen Eleanor, who then ruled England, at Passiontide and Easter and thereafter, nobles and common people, knights and peasants, flew to arms and guarded the sea coast that looks towards Flanders',[32] while fresh oaths of fealty to Richard were again exacted from the magnates. When the first mercenaries arrived, they were either killed or imprisoned in chains. Those following prudently turned their ships about and sailed back to Flanders.

This was the situation when Hubert Walter returned to England. Not optimistic about Richard's chances of an early release, he urged the Queen and the regency council to adopt a conciliatory policy towards John. If Richard never returned, John would become king and might well exact vengeance on those who had opposed or offended him. Furthermore, John's co-operation in raising ransom money from his tenants might be needed. Eleanor and the magnates took Hubert's advice, and a truce was arrived at. Under its terms, John agreed to surrender Windsor and his castles of Wallingford and the Peak to his mother, who would hold them for a certain time; if Richard had not been released by then, she would return them to John.

Not having heard from the Pope, Eleanor had for a time held her peace, yet mounting anger and despair soon prompted her to send Celestine a second letter[33] berating him for his failure to help Richard and urging him to take some action:

> To the reverend Father and Lord Celestine, by the grace of God, the Supreme Pontiff, Eleanor, by the wrath of God, Queen of England, Duchess of Normandy, Countess of Anjou, begs him to show himself to be a father to a pitiable mother.
>
> I had decided to remain quiet in case a fullness of heart and a passionate grief might elicit some word against the chief of priests which was certainly less than cautious, and I was therefore accused of insolence and arrogance. Certainly grief is not that different from insanity while it is inflamed with its own force. It does not recognise a master, is afraid of no ally, it has no regard for anyone, and it does not spare them – not even you.
>
> So no one should be surprised if the modesty of my words is sharpened by the strength of my grief. I am mourning a loss that is not private, but my personal grief cannot be comforted – it is set deep in the heart of my spirit.
>
> Please listen to the cry of the afflicted, for our troubles have multiplied beyond number. You, the father of orphans, the judge of widows, the comforter of those who mourn and those who

grieve, a city of refuge for everyone, and because of this, in a time of so much misery, you are expected to provide the sole relief for everyone from the authority of your power.

Our king is in a difficult position and he is overwhelmed by troubles from every direction. Look at the sorry state of his kingdom, the evil of the times, the cruelty of the tyrant who does not stop making an unjust war against the King because of his greed, and that tyrant who keeps him bound in prison-chains and kills him with fear.

If the Church of Rome keeps quiet about the great injuries to the Lord's Anointed, may God rise up and judge our plea. Where is the passion of John against Herod, the passion of Pope Alexander III, who solemnly and terribly excommunicated Frederick, father of this current prince, with the full authority of the Apostolic See? [The Emperor] has no due regard for the Apostolic keys, and he reckons the law of God merely as words.

All the more reason why you ought to seize the sword of the spirit, which is the Word of God, much more firmly. May the Word of the Lord not have been stuck in your throat, may the mortal fear in you as a man not destroy the spirit of freedom. It is easier to suffer at the hands of men than to forsake the law of God. The enemies of Christ Crucified trust in their own strength – their end is ruin, their glory will be in chaos.

But the time is nearly upon us when the hand of God will exact a timely vengeance upon them. For if they escape judgement during their human life, a more terrible divine judgement is hanging over them. Their present joy is a passing moment, for in truth their eternal punishment will be fire and worms.

Please, I beg you, do not let a worldly eminence deter you. What afflicts the Church and sets the people murmuring, and considerably diminishes their esteem for you, is that in such a crisis, in spite of the tears and lamentations of entire provinces, you have not sent to those princes a single nuncio from those around you. Often your cardinals, with sovereign powers, execute an embassy for matters of little importance to pagan regions. Yet for a cause so desperate and deplorable as this, you have not even sent even the humblest sub-deacon, not even one acolyte. For nowadays papal legates are sent for a profit, not in respect of Christ, not for the honour of the Church, nor for the peace of kingdoms, or for the safety of a people. But in freeing a king, what profit or result could be more glorious for you than to exalt the honour of the Sovereign Pontiff?

You would not have injured the Apostolic See too much if you had gone to Germany in person for the release of such a great prince. For the man to whom one used to pay honour so courteously in prosperous times one ought not to desert so casually in harsh times. Why do you not weigh in the scales the advantages of justice which Henry, of good repute and the father of King Richard, displayed to you, as we saw, at the critical point of your greatest suffering? He exercised the tyranny of Frederick, which was to the advantage of you, for when Frederick, the author and promoter of the great schism, had sworn against Pope Alexander III, who, as you know, was rightly elected, and gave his allegiance to that apostate Octavian, and when the Church generally was in difficulties all over the world because of the confusion resulting from the schism, King Henry, saddened at the tunic of Christ being torn for so long, was first to give allegiance to Alexander, then with prudent counsels brought the King of France over to the Apostolic side.[34] He then fortified that side and strengthened it with support, so bringing the ship of Peter, threatened with certain shipwreck from the quarrel, to a safe harbour.

Without doubt our anticipation has grown quite strong with an unfailing hope and a firm faith. God will look upon the prayers of the humble and He will not despise them. So it is good for the King to wait in silence for the salvation of the Lord. Blessed is the man who trusts in the Lord. Indeed, just as now the sorrows of the people and the tears of all hang over him, so he will be freed by prayers at the right time, to the joy of the whole world. O Lord, in Your virtue will the King be exalted, and the Roman Church, which must now take too much of the blame for delaying his release, will feel ashamed, since it did not recognise how much difficulty so great a son as mine was in.[35]

On 19 April, Richard wrote to 'his dearest mother, Eleanor, Queen of England' and the regency council, thanking them for taking good care of his realm, and informing them that he had just concluded with the Emperor 'a mutual and indissoluble treaty of love'.

Philip of France had offered Henry VI a large bribe to keep Richard in prison, but Henry, a near-megalomaniac who cherished dreams of reigning supreme over the princes of Europe, had no intention of furthering Philip's territorial ambitions. Instead, he resolved to obtain every last advantage to himself from Richard's release, and had agreed to grant him his freedom upon payment of the extortionate sum of 100,000 silver marks[36] (the equivalent of twice England's annual revenue and worth several million pounds today) and the delivery of a number of noble hostages, to be chosen from the sons of the English and Norman baronage.[37] In addition, Richard was to promise to help the Emperor overthrow Tancred of Sicily, whose kingdom he had already invaded. Richard had no choice but to agree reluctantly.

The King urged that his subjects do everything in their power to raise the ransom and asked that the money collected be entrusted 'to my mother, and by her to whomsoever she shall appoint'.

The King also informed the council that, following Hubert Walter's departure, William Longchamp, hearing of his master's plight, had come winging his way from Paris to Germany and had used his diplomatic skills to help negotiate the treaty with the Emperor and have Richard released from solitary confinement. 'After an audience with the Emperor [wrote the King], he secured our removal from the castle of Trifels, where we were formerly imprisoned, to Hagenau, where we were received with honour by the Emperor and his court.'[38]

After this, Richard was treated not so much as a prisoner as an honoured guest.[39] He was permitted to hold court at Speyer or Worms, and to attend to the business of his kingdom, which was facilitated by his being in constant correspondence with his 'much beloved mother'[40] and his councillors. He received a constant stream of visitors from England and many other lands, much to the amazement of the Germans, and cultivated the friendship of many German princes, who would be useful allies to him in the future. In better health now, he went hunting and hawking, and enjoyed challenging his warders to wrestling matches, exchanging crude jokes with them or getting them drunk with the Rhenish wines provided for his table.[41]

When informed of the treachery of John, the King appeared unconcerned. 'My brother John is not the man to conquer a country if there is anyone to offer the feeblest resistance,' he remarked disparagingly.[42] 'Always cheerful', he was confident that he would soon be returning home to deal with his enemies.[43]

Richard sent Longchamp back to England with his letter and the ransom demand, with instructions to collect both money and hostages and escort them to the imperial court, but the regency council did not trust the former chancellor and it was made very clear to him that he was regarded as nothing more than a messenger. The bishops refused to revoke his excommunication and London closed its gates to him.

With her customary vigour, Eleanor immediately set to work to raise the King's ransom from a land and a people that had already been bled dry to finance the crusade.[44] The government imposed a harsh levy on every one of Richard's English subjects: every freeman was to give one-quarter of his annual income; those clergy living on tithes were to give one-tenth; whilst poorer folk had to give what they could. 'No subject, rich or poor, was overlooked. No one could say, "Pray let me be excluded."'[45] The churches and abbeys were stripped of their wealth: 'the greater churches came up with treasures hoarded from the distant past, and the parishes with their silver chalices'. The Cistercian monks, who had no treasures, donated the profits from one year's wool-yield from their flocks, as did the Order of Gilbertines.[46]

On 1 June, at a council held at St Albans, the Queen appointed five officers to oversee the raising of the ransom: Hubert Walter, who had been elected Archbishop of Canterbury in May; Richard FitzNigel, Bishop of London; William d'Albini, Earl of Arundel; Hamelin of Anjou, Earl of Surrey, a bastard brother of Henry II; and Henry FitzAilwin, London's first mayor. As the money came in, it was stored in large chests in the crypt of St Paul's Cathedral, under the seals of the Queen and Walter of Coutances.

Richard's continental subjects were also made to contribute. The Queen sent her officers into Anjou and Aquitaine to collect ransom money, and herself exacted 100 marks from the abbey of St Martial at Limoges, where Richard had been invested as Duke of Aquitaine.[47] A considerable percentage of the ransom was raised abroad — more money was raised in Caen than in London — but the greater share came from England, which had a more efficient system of tax collection.

Probably in response to Eleanor's letters, the Pope at last bestirred himself and threatened to lay England under an interdict if Richard's subjects failed to raise his ransom.[48] Obviously regretting her scathing attacks upon him in her earlier letters, the Queen responded with humility: 'I beseech you, O Father, let your benignity bear with that which is the effusion of grief rather than of deliberation. I have sinned and used the words of Job; I have said that which I would I had not said. But henceforth I place my finger on my lips and say no more. Farewell.'[49] The existence of this third letter is good evidence for the authenticity of this correspondence: if Eleanor's first two letters had been merely literary exercises, why would she need to have composed a letter of apology?

Because of the King's great reputation, many of his subjects gave willingly. John, however, who had agreed to assist in raising the ransom, ruthlessly milked his tenants, then forged the great seal in order to appropriate for himself the money collected, to fund his treasonable activities.

In council at Ely, the Queen set about choosing which noble boys

should go to Germany as hostages,[50] a task that caused great grief to
many families.[51] Richard had directed that those selected be taken to
Germany by William Longchamp, but several barons, alarmed by
rumours of Longchamp's alleged homosexuality, declared they would
rather entrust their daughters to him than their sons. This enabled
Eleanor to veto a suggestion that her grandsons of Saxony be among the
chosen.

We know very little about how the hostages were finally selected, or
about the outcome of appeals lodged by their distraught relatives. Soon
afterwards, Richard, possibly at Eleanor's request, summoned Longchamp to join him in Germany, whereupon the Queen was able to
make other, more acceptable, arrangements for the transfer of the
hostages.

Berengaria was also active in raising the ransom. Learning of her
distress at her husband's imprisonment, Pope Celestine was moved to
provide an escort of cardinals to see her, Joanna and the princess of
Cyprus safely north via Pisa to Genoa, where she took ship for
Marseilles. Here she was met by Alfonso II, King of Aragon, who gave
her a safe-conduct through his territories, then arranged for Raymond,
Count of St Gilles, heir to the Count of Toulouse, to conduct her to
Poitou. Here Berengaria settled for a time and applied herself with great
dispatch to the business of collecting ransom money.

At Worms in June, Richard and the Emperor reached a new agreement.
Instead of aiding Henry against Tancred, Richard undertook to increase
his ransom by 50,000 marks and the number of hostages to 200. He also
agreed to the betrothal of his niece Eleanor of Brittany to the son of
Leopold of Austria and the surrender of Isaac Comnenus – still a
prisoner in his silver chains – and his daughter to the Emperor.[52]

News of this agreement drove Philip to seek a truce with Richard,
who in July, through his representatives, agreed that Philip might keep
those lands he had conquered in Normandy. Anticipating that Richard
would soon be free, Philip sent John a warning: 'Look to yourself. The
Devil is loosed!' John immediately abandoned his plans to usurp the
English throne and fled to Paris.[53]

Soon afterwards, he agreed to surrender parts of Normandy and
Touraine to Philip in return for the French king's promise to help him
take possession of the rest of Richard's continental domains. When John
wrote to England, canvassing the support of the barons, Eleanor
persuaded the regency council to confiscate all his estates. The lords of
Normandy also resisted John's ambitions, and the Pope carried out his
threat and pronounced both him and Philip excommunicate.

In England, the government struggled to meet the increased ransom demand. Despite the measures taken, not nearly enough money had been raised to begin with. A substantial number of people had either evaded payment or flatly refused to contribute; some tax collecters had even made off with the money.[54] The council was forced to impose a second, then a third levy, while those who had rebelled with John were heavily fined.

The delay affected Richard badly. Despite the freedoms he was permitted, he was experiencing the frustration and desolation common to many captives. He had taken to composing poems and songs to express his feelings, the most famous of which is '*J'a nuns hons pris*' – 'I have many friends but their gifts are few . . .' In it, he refers bitterly to Philip, 'my overlord, who keeps my land in torment' in contravention of his feudal oath. He also complains that everyone has forsaken him. This song, one of only two of Richard's compositions to survive, was written in Provençal with a musical score, and was dedicated to his half-sister, Marie, Countess of Champagne.

In October, envoys from the Emperor arrived in London to see how the collection of the ransom was progressing, and were royally entertained. When they left, they took with them 100,000 marks weighing thirty-five tons – two-thirds of the ransom money. The balance was to be delivered as soon as it had been collected.

Shortly afterwards, Richard wrote to Eleanor, commanding her and Walter of Coutances to bring to Speyer in person the ransom money and the hostages, along with his royal regalia and an impressive retinue. It had been agreed by the Emperor that, subject to the receipt of both money and hostages, the King would be released on 17 January 1194.[55]

Eleanor immediately began assembling a fleet in the east-coast ports of Dunwich, Ipswich and Orford. In December 1193, with the King's approval, she appointed Hubert Walter justiciar and, leaving him in charge in England, left for Germany. With her she took an impressive retinue,[56] which included Walter of Coutances and some of her southern vassals, notably the ageing Saldebreuil of Sanzay, Aimery, Viscount of Thouars and Hugh IX de Lusignan, as well as her ten-year-old granddaughter Eleanor of Brittany, who was to marry Duke Leopold's son, and the princess of Cyprus. Finally there were earls, bishops, chaplains, clerks, the forlorn group of hostages and a strongly armed force to guard the great chests containing the ransom money.

Although it was deepest winter, the Queen's ships had a smooth crossing over the North Sea. After disembarking, she and her entourage made their way overland to the Rhine, and travelled down it by boat towards Speyer.

On 6 January 1194, Eleanor arrived in Cologne in time to celebrate the Feast of Epiphany, and was welcomed by the Archbishop, Adolf of Altena. By 17 January, the date set for Richard's release, the Queen had arrived in Speyer, only to learn that the release date had been unaccountably postponed.[57] The reason for this was that Philip and John had offered the Emperor a sum greatly exceeding the English ransom if he would either deliver up Richard to them or keep him in custody until Michaelmas 1194, by which time they hoped to have overrun his territories.[58] Henry was making a pretence of considering their offer in order to wring new concessions from Richard.

At Candlemas, on 2 February, a suspicious Eleanor was received by the Emperor at his court at Mainz in the presence of King Richard and a host of German princes. The Queen was overjoyed to be reunited with her son after an absence of nearly three years, and was therefore utterly dismayed when the Emperor announced that Philip and John had outbid her for his captive.[59]

With the Archbishops of Cologne and Mainz acting as go-betweens, both Eleanor and Walter of Coutances made strong representations to Henry, while Richard's cultivation of the German princes now bore fruit, for they protested violently against the Emperor's failure to honour his word. At length, after forty-eight hours of fraught negotiations – the details of which are not fully known – Henry, who had had no intention of aiding his rival Philip, agreed to release King Richard in return for his acknowledgement of the Emperor as his overlord for England and the surrender of Walter of Coutances as a hostage for the King's good faith.[60]

These were humiliating terms, and the Queen, Walter of Coutances, the Bishop of Bath 'and many other nobles approached the King in person, briefly telling him the unhappy news'.[61] 'By the advice of his mother Eleanor',[62] who had 'with great difficulty' helped to bring about this mitigated settlement[63] – Henry had originally demanded that Richard recognise him as the suzerain of all his lands – the King reluctantly accepted the Emperor's conditions and delivered up his kingdom to his captor. Then, after paying homage to Henry, he received it back as a fief of the Empire.[64]

Henry VI believed that he had secured a valuable ally against the pretensions of the King of France,[65] and as Richard's overlord would, in the years to come, encourage him in his wars against Philip. He also used the ransom money to finance his campaign against Tancred of Sicily, and on Tancred's death in 1194 assumed the crown of Sicily.

Richard's alliance with the Emperor also brought about a reconciliation between the latter and Henry the Lion. As for Leopold of Austria, he received what Ralph of Diceto believed was divine punishment for his treatment of Richard, for in December 1194 he was involved in a riding accident and had to have his foot amputated.

At nine o'clock[66] on the morning of 4 February, after the ransom and hostages had been handed over, Richard was formally released and 'restored to his mother and freedom'.[67] Eleanor was so overcome with emotion that she broke down in tears, as did many of those looking on.[68]

That same day Richard and Eleanor began their journey back to England, travelling northwards along the Rhine. On the way they spent three days enjoying the 'rich luxuries and splendid feasts' provided for them by Archbishop Adolf at Cologne. On the last day, they attended a mass of thanksgiving in the cathedral, where the Archbishop took as his introit the text, 'Now I know truly that the Lord has sent His angel and has rescued me from the hand of Herod'[69] – a gracious compliment to Eleanor.

The royal travellers received similar ovations in other towns, notably Louvain, Brussels and Antwerp, where the Duke of Louvain held a special reception in their honour in his castle. Wherever he went, Richard had Eleanor sit in the place of honour at his right hand. He also took this opportunity to forge alliances with German and Flemish princes against France, their common enemy.

On 4 March, the King and Queen, with their train, boarded an English ship, the *Trenchemer*, in the Scheldt estuary. Richard's trusty admiral, Stephen de Turnham, assisted by experienced local pilots, navigated the vessel through the islets in the estuary by day, but that night, for greater protection from predatory French ships, the royal party slept on board a great galley sent over from Rye, one of the Cinque Ports.[70] The next morning they again boarded the *Trenchemer*, and put out to sea from the port of Shouwen,[71] escorted by the galley. The voyage took several days because of the need to evade French ships in the North Sea and the Channel.

At nine o'clock[72] on the morning of 12 March,[73] the little convoy docked at Sandwich, and the King set foot in his realm for the first time since December 1189. The sun shone exceptionally brightly, and many later claimed they had recognised it as an omen of the crusader's return.

As soon as they landed, Richard and Eleanor rode to Canterbury, where they gave thanks for the King's safe return at the shrine of Becket.[74] The following day they pressed on to Rochester, where Hubert Walter and a vast crowd were waiting to greet them.

'The news of the coming of the King, so long and so desperately awaited, flew faster than the north wind',[75] virtually extinguishing the last vestiges of support for John. One of his supporters, the castellan of St Michael's Mount in Cornwall, dropped dead with fright on learning that the King had returned.[76]

On 23 March, Richard, with Eleanor riding by his side, made a state entry into London, where, 'to the great acclaim of both clergy and people, he was received in procession through the decorated city into the church of St Paul's'[77] to give thanks for his restoration. Afterwards, as they rode to the Palace of Westminster, they were 'hailed with joy along the Strand'.[78] A few days later, the King and Queen visited both St Albans Abbey and the shrine of St Edmund at Bury St Edmund's in Suffolk, where they again gave thanks for his safe return to his realm.[79]

Richard was now obliged to interrupt the celebrations in order to root out John's few remaining supporters from Nottingham Castle and other strongholds. Nottingham surrendered at the King's approach, and other rebel fortresses followed suit.[80]

On 30 March, Richard presided over a meeting of the Great Council in Nottingham Castle. Eleanor was present, as were Geoffrey of York, Hugh de Puiset, William Longchamp and Bishop Hugh of Lincoln, and for four days they discussed the affairs of the kingdom. High on the agenda was the question of what to do with John; the council wanted to auction off his confiscated possessions, but the Queen pointed out that this might drive him further into the arms of Philip. In the end, the council summoned John to appear within forty days to account for his conduct, or else suffer banishment and forfeiture of all his honours, titles and estates. In gratitude for Longchamp's loyal service, Richard restored him to full authority as chancellor. He also ransomed Walter of Coutances, who returned to England in May, for 10,000 marks.

On 2 April, Richard and Eleanor rode to the royal hunting lodge at Clipstone (now a ruin known as King John's Palace) in Sherwood Forest.[81] The King had never visited Sherwood before, and it 'pleased him greatly'.[82] This is the context in which many later legends of Robin Hood were set, but the evidence for Robin Hood's identity is sparse and confusing: if he existed, he probably lived in the thirteenth or early fourteenth century. It was not until 1521, in the Scottish writer John Major's book, *The History of Greater Britain*, that the Robin Hood legends were set in the reign of Richard I.

The King and Queen celebrated Easter at Northampton,[83] where Eleanor witnessed a royal charter granting various honours to the King of Scots. It was at around this time, possibly in celebration of his restoration, that Richard added the third leopard to his coat of arms; the three leopards of England, used to this day as the royal heraldic device, first appeared on his seal, and that of Eleanor, in 1194.

In order to purge himself of the dishonour of imprisonment, Richard staged what appears to have been a second coronation, or formal crowning ceremony, on 17 April, when 'he received the crown of the kingdom from Hubert Walter, Archbishop of Canterbury' in Winchester Cathedral.[84] The wording of this passage suggests that the ceremony was more than a formal crown-wearing, which is what some modern historians believe it was; the triannaul ceremony of crown-wearing had in any case fallen into disuse for forty years. The Queen proudly watched the proceedings from a dais in the north transept, surrounded by a bevy of aristocratic beauties.[85] Berengaria was not present, having remained in Poitou.

The Pope had written urging Richard to take up the Cross again and return to the Holy Land, but the King was impatient to recover the lands Philip had seized in Normandy. Having raised an army, he travelled with Eleanor to Portsmouth around 23–5 April, and early in May set sail for the continent[86] with one hundred ships,[87] but rough winds carried them back to port, where they were delayed by bad weather for a fortnight and obliged to outlay £100 on lodgings.[88] At last, on 12 May, Richard and Eleanor set sail for Barfleur.[89] Neither of them would ever set foot in England again.

19

'The Staff of My Old Age'

Having arrived in Normandy, to great rejoicing,[1] Richard and Eleanor made a triumphal progress via Bayeux and Caen[2] to Lisieux, where they were welcomed by the Archdeacon, John of Alençon, and lodged in his house. The evidence strongly suggests that, determined to bring about a reconciliation between her sons, Eleanor had already summoned a destitute John, now abandoned by Philip, and given him advice as to how to approach the King to beg for forgiveness.[3]

Whilst Richard and Eleanor were at supper one night, John arrived 'in a state of abject penitence', and begged to speak to his mother, that he might beseech her good grace to intercede for him with the King. 'Through the mediation of Queen Eleanor', Richard agreed to see John and be reconciled with him.[4] 'Falling at his feet' and bursting into tears, John 'sought and obtained his clemency'.[5] Richard, who had never taken his little brother – who was now twenty-six – seriously, raised him up and gave him the kiss of peace, saying, 'Think no more of it, John. You are but a child, and were left to evil counsellors. Your advisers shall pay for this. Now come and have something to eat.'

So saying, he commanded that a gift of fresh salmon, meant for his own table, be cooked and served to John.[6]

For the next five years, John kept a low profile, serving his brother loyally, attending to the affairs of his estates, which Richard restored to him in 1195, and staying out of mischief.

This left Richard free to turn his attention to expelling Philip from Normandy and returning the whole duchy to its rightful suzerainty. For the rest of his reign he would be engaged in a bitter and unceasing struggle with the French King, defending his territories against the latter's aggressive ambition, and would never again have the chance to return to the Holy Land, which was still his chief desire. Now thirty-seven, he was putting on weight, but was still a magnificent and terrifying figure on a horse, and able to move 'more swiftly than the twisted thong of a Balearic Sling'.[7]

Walter of Coutances and William Longchamp had joined the King in Normandy, leaving England in the capable hands of Hubert Walter. Longchamp served Richard faithfully until his death in 1197, while Coutances helped him rule Normandy for the rest of the reign.

Philip was determined to seize Rouen, liberate Alys and march south to recover Berry. To this end he was busily besieging Verneuil, whilst his forces were attacking castles on the Loire with a view to driving a wedge between Anjou and Aquitaine. Richard drove off Philip, relieved his castles, and within a very short time had recovered those lands in Touraine that John had ceded to the French. In June 1194, he won a decisive victory over Philip at the Battle of Fréteval, driving the French army to an ignominious rout; Philip fled so fast that he left his treasure, archives and seal on the battlefield, and was forced to hide in a wayside chapel until Richard's pursuing soldiers had passed.

Richard then rode south, where he ferociously suppressed a rebellion incited by the French King in Aquitaine, taking prisoner 300 knights and 40,000 soldiers. On 23 July, through the mediation of the Church, he and Philip concluded a truce until November 1195, although neither had any intention of observing it. After that, determined to recover the rest of the lands ceded by John to Philip, Richard concentrated on consolidating his position and strengthening his defences. He had already lifted the ban on tournaments.

Eleanor, meanwhile, had withdrawn with a much-reduced household to the abbey of Fontevrault, the refuge of many high-born widows. At seventy-two, after ruling England for eighteen turbulent months, and having reconciled her sons, she doubtless felt entitled to a rest. She did not, however, take the veil, but lived at the abbey as a guest in her own apartments, making generous donations and in return being honoured and served as a queen. And there she seems to have remained for much of the rest of Richard's reign.

After 1194, references to Eleanor in contemporary sources are few, and are mainly connected with the payment of queen-gold and matters arising from her dower rights,[8] but there is enough evidence to show that, although she had partially retired from public life, she was still in touch with the affairs of the world and occasionally active in an administrative capacity. Powerful men still deferred to her wisdom, and Fontevrault was centrally placed between Anjou and Poitou, enabling

Eleanor to keep an eye on her own lands and her son's. Richard
sometimes stayed at nearby Chinon, and doubtless rode over to see her
whenever he did so.

Contemporary records give only occasional tantalising insights into
Eleanor's life during these years. She supported the monks of Reading
Abbey by asking the King to remit part of a fine payable by them to
Walter of Coutances.[9] In 1196, she granted to her butler, Engelram, her
manor of Eaton Bray near Dunstable, as a reward for good service, and
in April that year gave financial assistance to the Abbot of Bourgeuil,
who could not pay a tithe on wine.[10] At Saumur, she found in favour of
the nuns of Fontevrault in a dispute over a corn crop.

At the same time the old Queen looked to the salvation of her soul
and prepared for death. By contemporary standards she had been
granted an extraordinarily long span, and in the natural order of things
could not expect to live much longer. But Eleanor was no ordinary
woman, and her public life was by no means over.

Richard held his Christmas court at Rouen that year, but there is no
record of Eleanor's presence there, nor at any of his future Christmas
courts. It would appear that she now made a habit of keeping Christmas
at Fontevrault.

Since Richard's liberation, Queen Berengaria had apparently been living
on her dower properties in Maine.[11] She had not been summoned to
England to join in the celebrations for the King's return, and her
husband had made no attempt to see her after arriving in Normandy. In
fact, he had gone back to his former promiscuous ways.

The saintly Bishop Hugh of Lincoln had even visited him to reproach
him for his neglect, asking in what state his conscience was. Richard
replied it was 'very easy'.

'How can that be, my son, when you live apart from your virtuous
queen and are faithless to her? Are these light transgressions, my son?'
reproved the Bishop.[12] The King, unfortunately, took no notice, but his
behaviour was becoming a scandal.

During Lent, whilst hunting in a forest in Normandy, Richard met a
hermit. Recognising him, the holy man soundly castigated him for his
unlawful pleasures, and warned him to 'remember the destruction of
Sodom, and abstain from illicit acts, for if you do not, God will punish
you in fitting manner'. Richard ignored him, too.

At Easter 1195, however, he fell seriously ill. Believing himself on his
deathbed, he recalled the hermit's warning and 'was not ashamed to
confess the guiltiness of his life, and after receiving absolution, he took

back his wife, whom he had not known for a long time, and, putting aside illicit intercourse, he remained faithful to her, and they became one flesh, and the Lord gave them health of body and soul'.[13]

Just what were the sins that Richard I felt compelled to confess? Since 1948, when John Harvey first propounded the theory in his book *The Plantagenets*, historians have speculated as to whether or not the King was homosexual. In 1191, he had publicly repented of his 'sins against nature' and 'the foulness of his past life'. Now he had promised never again to indulge in 'illicit intercourse'.

'Illicit intercourse' and 'illicit acts' could both of course mean sex outside marriage, and there is no shortage of contemporary reference to Richard's promiscuity. He had at least one bastard. It was not unusual for monastic chroniclers to regard extra-marital sex as 'foulness' and even as a 'sin against nature'.

It is the hermit's reminder of the destruction of Sodom that has prompted twentieth-century historians to speculate that Richard was bisexual. Although every reference in the Bible to the wickedness of the cities of the plain is unspecific in detail, in the first century AD, the Jewish Greek philosopher and scholar Philo, in his work *De Abrahamo*, and early Christian writers such as the author of the Book of Jude in the Apocrypha, defined the sin of Sodom as intercourse with a member of the same sex. By the twelfth century, the association was well known, and in 1300 sodomy was being referred to in England as an 'unkindly sin that is not twix woman and man'.[14]

This is not to say, however, that Richard was a homosexual. It was also known that the destruction of Sodom was a punishment for many sins, and the hermit's allusion was probably not specifically to homosexuality but rather to general promiscuity, or even unnatural sexual intercourse with women, which was also regarded as sodomy. Nor, it must be said, was it ever suggested before 1948 that Richard was a homosexual, because his reputation was in fact that of a womaniser. William of Newburgh testifies to his pursuit of women, and in the thirteenth century, the chronicler Walter of Guisborough asserted that Richard's need for women had been so great that he had summoned them even to his deathbed, against his doctor's advice. Another legend circulating after Richard's death, recounted by a Dominican friar called Stephen of Bourbon, relates how the King lusted so intensely after a nun of Fontevrault that he threatened to burn down the abbey if he could not sleep with her; when told that it was her eyes that had enticed him, she cut them out with a knife and sent them to him. There is no contemporary evidence to corroborate these stories and others of a similar nature, but they were believable at the time because they were in keeping with what people knew of Richard's character.

Had Richard bedded men, it is unlikely it would have remained a secret – kings, after all, lived their lives on a very public stage – and the resultant scandal in an age when such practices were regarded as not only a mortal sin but also criminal would have drawn comment from the chroniclers, who did not hesitate to report how William Longchamp was suspected of fancying boys. Nor would the King's enemies have hesitated to make political capital out of it.

Whether the King and Queen really resumed sexual relations after their reunion is another matter. Around this time, it was rumoured that Richard was so certain he would never have a legitimate heir that he again resolved to name Arthur of Brittany as his successor. Although the King and Queen are described as living together conjugally at Poitiers later in the year, it is perhaps significant that they never had any children, although this cannot be taken as evidence that the King was homosexual. Berengaria may have been barren; Richard, after all, had one acknowledged bastard, Philip of Cognac. There was no question of the marriage being dissolved, since Berengaria's brother Sancho VII had staunchly defended Richard's territorial interests in the south against French aggression during the King's captivity in Germany, and was a valuable ally.

In August, Richard finally bowed to Philip's demands and delivered up Alys to him. Philip immediately married her off to his vassal, William III, Count of Ponthieu,[15] and she spent the rest of her life in peaceful obscurity. The date of her death is not recorded.

During the summer of 1195, learning that the Emperor was urging Richard to make war on him, Philip violated the truce and began raiding Normandy, attacking and looting castles. But both sides were short of funds, there was famine in Normandy, and by the end of the year the two kings were striving to achieve a more lasting settlement. The Treaty of Louviers formally ceded the Norman Vexin to Philip, but returned everything else he had wrested from Richard.[16]

At Christmas 1195, Richard and Berengaria held court together in Poitiers. Seeing the people suffering so much as a result of the famine, the Queen persuaded her husband to dispense generous relief to them.

Despite the continuing famine, Richard feared that Philip would soon launch another assault on Normandy, and in the spring of 1196 began building one of the greatest of all medieval castles, Château Gaillard (meaning Saucy Castle), on the rock of Les Andelys on the Norman frontier, where it commanded a wide bend of the Seine and was strategically placed for defending Rouen and facilitating the recovery of the Norman Vexin. The King himself personally supervised its design and construction, into which were incorporated the most advanced defences, and it became not only his headquarters but one of his favourite residences; he was fond of referring to it as his daughter.

The building of Château Gaillard was sufficient to provoke Philip into renewing hostilities. The new fortress was said to be impregnable. When a jealous Philip looked upon it for the first time, he declared, 'If its walls were made of solid iron, yet would I take them.' His words were repeated to Richard, who retorted, 'By God's throat, if its walls were made of butter, yet would I hold them!' It is said that, during hostilities, he personally threw three French prisoners over the ramparts to their deaths, and blinded fifteen others.

During the spring of 1196, Richard again named Arthur his heir and demanded that the Bretons surrender the boy, now nine, into his custody as his ward, and that his mother Constance bring him to Normandy to pay homage to his uncle. Constance duly left Nantes with Arthur and travelled towards Rouen. On the way, however, she was abducted and imprisoned by her second husband, Ranulf de Blundeville, whom the insular Bretons, resenting him styling himself Duke of Brittany, had sent into exile. Richard marched into Brittany at the head of an army, intent upon rescuing his nephew, only to discover, to his fury, that Arthur had been secretly taken by his tutor to the French court to be brought up with Philip's son Louis.

Eleanor had no wish to designate either Arthur or the unreliable John to succeed her in Poitou and Aquitaine. That spring, with Richard's consent, she named her grandson, Otto of Saxony, as her heir.

In October 1196, Richard married his sister Joanna to Count Raymond VI of Toulouse, the son of Raymond V – whom Eleanor had regarded as a usurper – by Constance of France. The marriage took place in Rouen in the presence of Queen Berengaria, Joanna's close friend, and finally put an end to the ancient dynastic feud between the counts of Toulouse and the ducal House of Aquitaine. Eleanor now happily ceded her claims to Toulouse to her daughter, whose son Raymond, born in 1197, would one day inherit the title. King Richard gave Joanna Agen and Quercy for her dower.

Unfortunately, the marriage was not happy. Count Raymond had been married three times already, and had at one time been excommunicated for marrying the enchanting Bourguigne de Lusignan whilst still wed to Beatrix of Béziers; in 1196, having tired of

Bourguigne, and eager to marry King Richard's sister, he had repudiated her and shut her up in a religious house run by austere Albigensian heretics. He also maintained a harem. Despite this, Richard regarded him as a valuable ally.

In the summer of 1964, a mural dating from the last decade of the twelfth century was uncovered in the chapel of Sainte-Radegonde at Chinon. It depicts five figures, all on horseback, as if on a hunting expedition. Their leader is a bearded man wearing a crown; he is followed by two women, one seemingly young with long auburn hair, the other also crowned and gesturing to the first of two smaller men bringing up the rear of the procession. He is leaning towards her with what appears to be a hawk or falcon – although only its feet survive, since the surface of the painting is somewhat damaged – on his extended wrist. Behind him is the smallest figure, a youth in a white cap.

The identification of these figures as members of the Angevin family rests on three factors: firstly, the location of the mural, in the heartland of the Plantagenet empire; secondly, the fact that two figures are wearing crowns; and thirdly, the similarity between the design on the cloak-linings of the two crowned figures and that on the tomb enamel representing Geoffrey of Anjou, father of Henry II, at Le Mans. The design on Geoffrey's tomb, however, is an inverted version of the design in the mural, and it may be that, like chevrons, this pattern was simply a popular motif in the twelfth century. It appears to have no heraldic significance.

It has long been thought that the two women are meant to be Eleanor of Aquitaine and her future daughter-in-law, Isabella of Angoulême, and this section of the mural has therefore been reproduced in several books about Eleanor. Surprisingly, the male figures have in every case been omitted, and it is only recently that the traditional identifications have been questioned. In an article published by the University of Poitiers in December 1998, an Israeli professor, Nurith Kenaan-Kedar, has suggested that the mural either depicts King John with Eleanor and Isabella of Angoulême, in which case it dates from c. 1200, or that it shows Eleanor being led into captivity by Henry II in 1173/4; the Queen is said to be accompanied by her daughter Joanna and two of her sons, one of whom is Richard. To him she has given a falcon, the symbol of the duchy of Aquitaine, which she has ceded to him.

There are several problems with these hypotheses. If the figures represent King John, Eleanor and Isabella of Angoulême, who then are the two young men at the rear? Is this merely a hunting expedition with attendants? If so, why is Eleanor gesturing meaningfully towards one of the youths? Although it is almost certain that John took his bride to meet Eleanor, who was then in retirement at Fontevrault, there is no reason why this unrecorded meeting should merit being portrayed in such an important painting.

Clearly, the mural is of some significance. Yet it is unlikely that it portrays an ignominious event that had taken place some twenty years before it was painted, namely Eleanor's departure for England and captivity, after inciting her sons to rebel against their father. Henry had dealt so discreetly with Eleanor after her capture that we do not even know where she was imprisoned during the year before her transfer to England. It is hardly likely that either he or his son Richard would commission a mural commemorating her disloyalty and disgrace. Nor was Eleanor allowed any contact with her sons for several years after her arrest.

Of course, the mural may be a symbolic rather than a literal representation. Even so, Eleanor had ceded the duchy of Aquitaine to Richard in 1172, a year before the rebellion, and it is unlikely that this event would have been recorded in a church outside her dominions. Furthermore, there is no record of a falcon or hawk (the two are indistinguishable in heraldry) being the emblem of Aquitaine. The arms of Aquitaine, which were probably adopted by Eleanor herself, were a gold lion on a red ground, as shown in MS. 4790 in the Bibliothèque de L'Arsenal in Paris. This is also the emblem of the city of Bordeaux, whilst the city of Poitiers likewise has a lion as its symbol.

It has been suggested by some authorities on heraldry that the falcon was an early Angevin device, a pun on the name Fulk, the name of five counts of Anjou, but this would not explain its use as the emblem of Aquitaine. In fact, the falcon device was not used by any royal personage until the fourteenth century, when Edward III adopted it as a badge. Nor is there any evidence to show that it was used at all as an emblem in twelfth-century England or France.[17]

This is not to say that the mural is without dynastic significance. Given the fact that it has been dated to the last decade of the century, the evidence strongly suggests that it was perhaps completed late in 1196 and reflects certain important events in that year. The King who leads the procession is almost certainly Richard I. He is bearded, as Richard's effigy at Fontevrault shows him bearded, whilst Henry II's is clean-shaven. Given the special relationship between Richard and his mother, it follows that the crowned woman is Eleanor herself. She is shown gesturing at a young man who may be her grandson, Otto of Brunswick, whom she had designated her heir in the spring of 1196.

The youth behind him may be either Arthur of Brittany, who Richard had that same spring named as his own heir, or – less probably – Count John.

The young woman riding with Eleanor may be Berengaria, whose marriage to Richard the Queen had arranged, and who had recently been reunited with him. Alternatively, this figure, who is uncrowned, could represent Joanna, who had married Raymond of Toulouse in 1196 and brought to an end the decades-old dispute over the suzerainty of Toulouse.

With Eleanor in permanent residence at nearby Fontevrault, it would have been natural for Richard to commission a mural, portraying her as central to Angevin policies, at Chinon, one of his foremost strongholds. It would also have been appropriate for him to make it very clear to both John and Arthur and their supporters how the Angevin empire was to be disposed of on his death.

The year 1197 found Richard and Philip again at war over Normandy. Philip took Aumale, but Richard – with the aid of a Brabantine mercenary force led by the redoubtable, and ruthless, captain, Mercadier, who was one of Eleanor's subjects from the Périgord – managed to recover some of the territory taken during his captivity by the French.

In May, fighting for his brother, John took captive Philip's cousin, Philip of Dreux, the martial Bishop of Beauvais, who was imprisoned in the custody of Hugh de Neville at Rouen.

Although Richard was driven back from Arras in August 1197, he was beginning to emerge as the victor in the struggle. Mercadier and his mercenaries had laid waste wide swathes of Philip's territories, plundering, burning, looting and killing; not even priests were spared. Many of Philip's vassals, including the Counts of Flanders and Boulogne, declared for Richard, whilst others chose to remain neutral. Again, Philip was forced to call for a truce.

During 1197, the Emperor Henry VI died; on his deathbed, he released King Richard from his feudal oath. He was succeeded as King of Sicily by his infant son Frederick, but clearly a young child could not wield power as Holy Roman Emperor. The German princes favoured Otto of Saxony, Richard's nephew, and in June 1198, at their request, the King put pressure on the electors and persuaded them to elect Otto as King of the Romans and future Emperor. Thus he secured Germany and Italy as friendly allies, while Otto relinquished his right to succeed his grandmother Eleanor in Aquitaine.

It was at around this time that Eleanor lost, within a few months of each other, her two daughters by Louis. The date of Alix's death is not known for certain – it is variously given as 1197 or 1198 – but Marie, whom the poet Rigaud de Barbezieux called 'the joyous and gay Countess, the light of Champagne', passed away on 11 March 1198; it was given out that she had died of sorrow on learning that her eldest son Henry, King of Jerusalem, had fallen to his death from a window of his palace in Acre. Richard had been attached to his half-sister, and it is possible that she had been reunited at some stage with her mother, although there is no documentary evidence of their ever meeting after Eleanor's marriage to Louis was annulled.

In September 1198, Richard overran the Vexin, reclaiming Gisors with such ferocity that Philip was nearly drowned in the frantic retreat of the French; in a letter to Hugh de Puiset, Richard gleefully related how 'the King of France drank river water on that day'. A record 100 French knights were also taken prisoner. It was at this point that the Church intervened to negotiate a peace between the two kings.

The Bishop of Beauvais was now being held by Richard in a dungeon at Château Gaillard, which many regarded as an outrage. The new Pope, the formidable Innocent III, who would emerge as one of the greatest pontiffs of the Middle Ages, was determined to have the Bishop freed, and sent a legate, Cardinal Peter of Capua, to order Richard to release him on the grounds that it was forbidden by canon law to imprison a bishop.

The King was in no mood to obey, and unleashed a flood of abuse upon the legate, shouting that the Holy See had never intervened on *his* behalf when he was being held captive – an attitude that echoes the sentiments expressed in Eleanor's letters to Celestine III – and accusing the Bishop of Beavais of being no better than a brigand and the Cardinal of being a traitor, liar, simoniac and suborner. Then Richard sent him from his presence, commanding him never to come before him again.

When Eleanor learned what had happened, she was much disturbed, having heard of Pope Innocent's ruthlessness. She therefore arranged for the Bishop to escape – probably by bribing or duping his gaolers – and offered him asylum in her own domains. Then she let it be known that Richard had freed him. In this way she averted the threat of excommunication falling upon her son and avoided making an enemy of Innocent and driving him over into Philip's camp. It was a brave thing to do, considering just how angry Richard could be when he was thwarted; yet there is no record of any recriminations, and it is likely that, once his wrath had cooled, Richard saw the wisdom of Eleanor's actions.

On 13 January 1199, Richard and Philip met on the River Seine – Richard in a boat, Philip on the bank – near Château Gaillard and concluded a five-year truce, during which they would each keep the territories they now held. Philip's chances of conquering Richard's domains now seemed remote, for the English King had an iron grip on his possessions, and powerful allies.

In March 1199, Richard stayed for a few days at Chinon, and may have visited Eleanor at Fontevrault. He was on his way south to seize by force some treasure that had been discovered at the village of Châlus, near Limoges in the Limousin, which he claimed was rightfully his. With him went Mercadier and his mercenaries.

The treasure – a pot of Roman coins – had been unearthed in a field by a ploughman, who surrendered it immediately to Achard, Lord of Châlus. It was then demanded of Achard by his overlord, Aimar, Count of Limoges. As word of the find spread, so the description of the treasure became embroidered, and the King was eventually informed that it was a golden statue, resembling an emperor and his family seated around a golden table. He immediately laid claim to it as supreme overlord of Châlus.

Richard was warned by those who knew better that such a treasure did not exist, but he insisted on going to Châlus, where on 4 March he laid siege to Lord Achard's castle, and set his engineers to tunnelling beneath its walls. Then he sat down to await the castle's surrender.

On the evening of 26 March, all was quiet, and the King did not bother to don his armour before he and Mercadier went 'reconnoitring the castle on all sides'. All he had with him was his helmet and a shield. Seeing him so vulnerable, 'a certain arbalister, Bertram de Gurdun,[18] aimed an arrow from the castle and struck the King on the arm, inflicting an incurable wound'. Angry and in pain

> the King rode to his quarters and issued orders to Mercadier and the army to make assaults on the castle without intermission, until it should be taken. After its capture, the King ordered that all the people were to be hanged, him alone excepted who had wounded him, whom he would have condemned to a more shocking death, as we supposed.[19]
>
> After this, the King gave himself into the hands of Mercadier, who, after attempting to extract the iron head [of the arrow], extracted the wood only, while the iron remained in the flesh. But after this butcher had carelessly mangled the King's arm in every part, he at last extracted the arrow.[20]

After suffering this torture, Richard, who had a splendid constitution, expected to recover, but within a day or so the wound grew inflamed and then putrid and he began to suffer the effects of gangrene and blood-poisoning. Soon, it became clear that his chances of survival were poor.

When he realised he was dying, Richard sent a messenger to Fontevrault, calling upon Eleanor to come to him without delay. He also 'ordered Bertram de Gurdun to come into his presence, and said to him, "What have I done to you, that you have killed me?"'

Bertram boldly replied, 'You slew my father and my two brothers with your own hand, and you had intended now to kill me. Therefore take any revenge on me that you may think fit, for I will readily endure the greatest torments that you can devise, so long as you have met with your end, having inflicted evils so many and so great upon the world.'

Richard was so moved and impressed with the archer's speech that 'he ordered him to be released, and said, "I forgive you my death. Live on, and by my bounty, behold the light of day." And then, after being released from his chains, he was allowed to depart, and the King ordered 100 shillings of English money to be given him. Mercadier, however, the King not knowing it, seized him and, after the King's death, first flayed him alive, then had him hanged'.[21] The *Annals of Winchester*[22] claim that this was at the behest of Richard's sister, Joanna, but this is not corroborated by any other source.

On receiving Richard's summons, Eleanor dispatched Matilda, Abbess of Fontevrault, to break the news to Berengaria and warn John, who was visiting Arthur in Brittany, to escape while he could and hasten to Chinon to secure Richard's treasure. She then travelled 'faster than the wind'[23] across the hundred miles that separated Fontevrault from Châlus, escorted by Abbot Luke of Turpenay,[24] and arrived at the King's bedside on 6 April.

On that day, his chaplain, Milo, Abbot of Le Pin, heard the King's last confession.[25] Richard asked to be buried at his father's feet in contrition for having rebelled against him. He ordered that messengers be sent to the constable of Château Gaillard, William the Marshal and the Archbishop of Canterbury, with instructions, given under his seal and Eleanor's, for the peaceful transference of power to his successor. Having done this, and set aside his hatred for King Philip, he received Holy Communion.[26]

In the late evening of 6 April, Richard I 'ended his earthly day'[27] at the age of forty-one, having changed his mind about bequeathing his kingdom and his continental possessions to Arthur, and left them instead to his brother John. This change of heart might have been brought about by Eleanor, who clearly had no time for her Breton grandson and his mother, and who must have realised that, with Arthur in thrall to Philip, the future of the Angevin empire would be in jeopardy. The Queen

> was present at the death of her very dear son, who reposed all his trust in her, next to God, that she would make provision for the weal of his soul, and she intends that his wishes shall be carried out. She will attend to those wishes with motherly concern and is especially counting on the help of her beloved Luke, Abbot of Turpenay, who was present at the deathbed and funeral of her very dear son and played a larger part in these events than anyone else.[28]

On the day of Richard's death, Châlus fell to his men, but there was no sign of the treasure, nor does history record what became of it.

When the Abbess Matilda broke the news about Richard to Berengaria at Beaufort Castle, just north of Saumur, the younger Queen was inconsolable. Pressing on to find John, the Abbess met up with Bishop Hugh of Lincoln, and told him of Berengaria's distress. He had heard that the King was dead, and was in fact on his way to Fontevrault for the funeral, but, breaking his journey, he went to Beaufort, comforted Berengaria with wise words of faith and celebrated a requiem mass. Then he escorted the Queen to Fontevrault for her husband's obsequies.[29]

On Palm Sunday, which fell on 11 April, the body of Richard I 'was most honourably buried with royal pomp'[30] in Fontevrault Abbey at the feet of his father,[31] as he had requested; his heart had been sent to Rouen for burial, and his brains and entrails to Charroux in Poitou.[32] Hugh of Lincoln officiated, and the two queens, Richard's mother and his wife, as chief mourners, led a congregation that included the Bishops of Poitiers and Angers and the abbots of Turpenay and Le Pin. The Pope sent Cardinal Peter of Capua to represent him, charging him to convey the Apostolic condolences to the Queen.

Eleanor was aware that Richard had many sins to answer for, and on the day of his funeral issued a charter granting to the community of Fontevrault her 'town of Jaunaium [probably Jaunay-Clan, just north of Poitiers] for their kitchen, for the weal of the soul of my very dear lord, King Richard, that he may sooner obtain the mercy of God', as well as £100 Angevin for new habits for the nuns, 'for the soul of her very dear lord King Richard'.

That year, Eleanor founded a chapel to St Lawrence, an early

Christian martyr, at Fontevrault, granting an annuity of £10 Poitevin on condition that 'Lord Roger, her chaplain, a brother of Fontevrault, who is to celebrate in her chapel of St Lawrence, shall receive the said £10 annually as long as she shall live'. Also in 1199, another of Eleanor's charters gave 'alms to the abbey of Fontevrault, for the religious maids of Christ there serving God, for the weal of the souls of the kings of England, the Lord Henry her husband, and the Lord Richard her son, and of her own beloved and faithful man, Peter Fulcher of La Rochelle, his heirs and his children for ever, freed from all accustomed services to the lord of Poitou, as granted of her own free will'.

In 1200, Eleanor granted several properties in England to Richard's cook, Adam, and Joan, his wife. There were further grants to others who had served Richard and Eleanor: Roger, another cook, Henry of Berneval, one of Eleanor's custodians during her imprisonment, Renaud of Martin, who received a bakehouse in Poitiers, and Agatha, former governess to the royal children, who was given a manor in Devonshire. All these grants were made for the late King, 'our son of blessed memory; may his soul be at peace for ever'.

Berengaria was left almost destitute by Richard's death; John withheld most of the estates left to her, and for many years she was constantly petitioning him for moneys due to her. On one occasion, the Knights Templar intervened on her behalf to obtain payment and save her from penury.

It has been claimed by many writers that Berengaria was the only English queen who never set foot in England, but in fact she was a frequent visitor to the court of King John, as is attested to by the numerous safe-conducts given to her and her servants, which specifically granted them exemption from all customs at the ports. In 1216, she toured England after the King had given her permission to travel wherever she pleased in the realm, and in 1220 she was amongst the vast throng gathered in Canterbury Cathedral to witness the translation of Becket's bones to a new shrine in the Trinity Chapel.

During her widowhood, Berengaria lived at Le Mans, one of her dower properties, and devoted the rest of her life to charitable and pious works, caring for beggars and abandoned children. In 1200, she founded the Cistercian monastery of l'Éspan near Le Mans; thirty years later, she became a nun there, under the name Juliana. The date of her death is not recorded, but she died beloved of the poor for her goodness and generosity, and was buried in the abbey in a fine tomb with a graceful effigy. In 1672, this was moved to Le Mans Cathedral, where it may be seen today.

Eleanor had lost her favourite son, the man whom she had called 'the staff of my old age, the light of my eyes'. It had been a terrible blow to her, possibly the worst of the many blows she had been called upon to endure, but there was little leisure for grieving. She knew that, once again, she had to come out of retirement and resume her public role, in order to help secure her youngest son's inheritance.

20

'The Most Reverend Eleanor'

John wisely heeded Eleanor's summons and left Brittany immediately. On 14 April 1199, having learned of Richard's death, he arrived at Chinon, determined to take possession of the royal treasure stored there. It is possible that Eleanor rode over from Fontevrault to assist him, since one chronicler claims that it was she who forcefully persuaded Robert of Thornham, seneschal of Anjou, to deliver up both the castle and its treasury to the new King.[1] John was also joined at Chinon by members of Richard's court, who offered their allegiance to him as the late King's heir, and by Aimery,[2] Viscount of Thouars, one of Eleanor's most powerful vassals, whom John appointed custodian of Chinon and seneschal of Anjou and Touraine in place of Robert of Thornham, who was compensated with the stewardship of Poitou and Aquitaine.

Later that day, John went on to Fontevrault. Despite the fact that the Abbess had forbidden visitors to enter the crypt or enclosures during her absence, he insisted on paying his respects at his brother's tomb, hammering on the abbey door until Bishop Hugh of Lincoln persuaded him to go away.[3] Later the Bishop obtained Abbess Matilda's permission to escort the new King to the tombs of his father and brother.[4] Hugh, however, had his doubts about John's accession: he was among those who regarded the marriage of Henry II and Eleanor as adulterous, and believed that nothing good would issue from the 'spurious brood' of such a union. It is also clear that he had a low opinion of Eleanor herself.[5] For these reasons, he later refused John's invitation to join the royal household.[6]

John was still at Fontevrault on Easter Sunday, but although he attended mass, he refused, as usual, to take Holy Communion and earned himself a stern rebuke from Bishop Hugh, who had also made him sit through a very long sermon, despite receiving three requests from John to hurry up and finish, as he was hungry. Afterwards, the Bishop showed the new King a sculpted relief of the Last Judgement and pointed to the souls of the righteous ascending into Heaven, but John indicated the damned being dragged by devils into Hell and retorted provocatively, 'Show me rather these, whose good example I mean to follow!' The Bishop despaired of him, and others were scandalised by John's behaviour.[7]

It was by no means certain that Richard's former domains would all accept John as their ruler. Arthur of Brittany had the better dynastic claim, but the law of primogeniture was by no means established at this time; moreover, Arthur was a mere boy and John a grown man, although to vassals desirous of gaining autonomy and throwing off the harsh yoke of Angevin rule, a child ruler could be a positive advantage. On hearing the news of King Richard's death, Philip, who knew that he could count on the support of many disaffected lords, immediately proclaimed twelve-year-old Arthur of Brittany as the rightful heir to the Angevin empire.

Around this time, Constance, who had escaped from the clutches of her second husband, Ranulph de Blundeville, and whose marriage to him had since been dissolved on the grounds of her desertion, married Guy of Thouars.[8] Guy was the younger brother of Eleanor's vassal, Count Aimery of Thouars, whose fief lay in northern Poitou, on the marches of Brittany. There were fears – largely unfounded, as it turned out – that the marriage would bring Count Aimery over to Arthur's side.

Apart from King Philip, Arthur's leading supporter at this time was the powerful and influential William des Roches, whom the young Duke now appointed seneschal of Anjou in defiance of John, who had preferred Aimery of Thouars to the post. Soon after Easter, William des Roches, with Arthur, his mother Constance and a Breton army, marched on Angers, which fell without a blow. This was the signal for the barons of Anjou, along with those of Maine and Touraine, to declare for Arthur. They had long desired independence, and saw this as their opportunity of achieving it. They did not appreciate that, if Philip had his way, they would merely be exchanging one overlord for another – himself.

Eleanor was outraged. She ordered that Anjou be laid waste as a punishment for its support of the usurper, then, accompanied by Aimery of Thouars and Mercadier and his mercenaries, she bore down on Angers, where Arthur was staying with his mother. At her approach, Constance fled with Arthur to join forces with Philip near Le Mans, whereupon Mercadier and his men sacked the city, which now fell to Eleanor, and took many prisoners.[9]

John rode to Le Mans, but the city garrison refused him entry. Warned that the forces of Arthur and Philip were approaching, he fled north to Normandy, enabling Philip and Arthur to make a triumphal entry into Le Mans, where Arthur swore fealty to Philip for Anjou, Maine and Touraine.

On 21 April, back at Fontevrault, the Queen, in gratitude to Abbot Luke for his support during the last terrible weeks, made a gift to the abbey of St Mary of Turpenay of the pool of Langeais, near Chinon, 'for the weal of the soul of her dearest son Richard' and in return for the community's 'annual celebration' of his anniversary. Berengaria, who had probably remained in seclusion at Fontevrault since Richard's burial, was a witness to this grant. It is sometimes claimed in modern biographies that Eleanor and Berengaria actually visited Turpenay, but a charter of Maurice, Bishop of Poitiers, confirms that 'this gift was made by the Queen at Fontevrault', where she 'invested, Luke, Abbot of Turpenay, with it, in the presence of Peter of Capua, cardinal, and many others'.[10]

England and Normandy had accepted John's succession without protest, and on 25 April 1199, John was invested as Duke of Normandy by Walter of Coutances in Rouen Cathedral.[11] It was not a dignified ceremony: the new Duke shocked the clergy by chatting with the young men in his retinue during the solemn rite and giggling so much that he dropped his ducal lance. Many regarded this as a bad omen.

Le Mans was still holding out for Arthur, so John raised an army in Normandy and marched south in the hope of wresting his troublesome nephew from Philip's custody, only to find that his prey had fled by night to join the French King in Tours. In his fury, John took revenge on the city, pulling down its walls and castle, burning and destroying houses and streets, taking many leading citizens prisoner and slaughtering the townsfolk. He then returned to Normandy to guard the duchy against invasion from France.

Philip now withdrew with Arthur to Paris, where the boy was lodged in the Cité Palace and resumed his education. The King had him taught with his own son, Louis, who was the same age. Both boys were provided with the best tutors, trained in knightly skills and groomed for kingship. Arthur was never allowed to forget that he was the rightful ruler of the Angevin empire, and was soon displaying the greed and ruthlessness of his race.

Eleanor was now satisfied that the situation in the Angevin heartlands had stabilised sufficiently to permit her, towards the end of April, to ride south to her own domains,[12] attended by a vast train of lords and prelates. She had decided, in view of the obvious hostility of Philip and Arthur, that it would be politic for her to make a comprehensive tour through Poitou and Aquitaine in order to secure assurances of military aid and the loyalty of her vassals, towns and clergy for John, whom she had decided to name as her heir.

On 29 April, Eleanor arrived in Loudun, where there came before her Raoul de Mauléon, the former lord of La Rochelle and the Talmont, once the favoured hunting lodge of Eleanor's father and grandfather. Raoul 'begged her to restore to him' those properties. It is not known on what pretext he had been deprived of them, but

> she, wishing to have his service, which she required for herself and her son John, restored to him the castle of Talmont, and has given him and his heirs forever whatever right she had there. For La Rochelle [for which Eleanor had other plans] she has given him in exchange the castle of Banaum, with all her rights there, saving the endowments she and her predecessors had bestowed there. And for this exchange, the said Raoul de Mauléon has quit-claimed to her and her heirs forever all his rights in La Rochelle. And on those terms, Raoul has done her liege-homage, swearing to defend her and her land, and all the honour pertaining to her.[13]

A charter issued by the Queen on 4 May to the newly rebuilt monastery of St John at Poitiers, confirming privileges granted by her forebears, states that she had returned to her capital 'within a month of the death of her dearest son King Richard'.[14] She also granted the city of Poitiers its right to self-government. The next day, she rode south-west to Niort.

Here, she was joined by her daughter Joanna, Countess of Toulouse, who was pregnant with her third child[15] and in a desperate state. Her husband Raymond had treated her unkindly and been unfaithful to her, but that was the least of her problems. Whilst he was away making war on one of his vassals in the Languedoc in the spring, some of the lords of Toulouse had risen against him and Joanna had courageously raised an army to suppress their revolt. She had laid siege to the rebel stronghold at Cassée, but some of the knights in her army had turned traitor. Having sent provisions into the castle, they had set fire to their own camp. Joanna, who had been burned in the fire, had barely escaped with her life, and had ridden north to seek help from her brother Richard but, on the way, had learned of his death and sought out her mother instead. Eleanor sent Joanna to be cared for by the nuns of Fontevrault, then continued on her way.

Indefatigable in her efforts, the Queen spent the early weeks of the summer touring her domains, attending to business, hearing petitions, dispensing justice, mediating in disputes, distributing largesse, issuing charters, making grants of lands and castles – she even gave away estates that had been assigned to Berengaria – and confirming and conferring privileges.[16] In return for the promise that they would look to their own defences, she granted charters conferring independence from feudal jurisdiction to at least four towns besides Poitiers, putting an end to the disputes that overshadowed relations between the lords and an increasingly vocal bourgeoisie, which were irksome to both sides. In fact, throughout her reign as duchess, and thanks to her enlightened policy and patronage, Aquitaine had witnessed the extraordinary growth and increased prosperity of many towns and cities. As Eleanor had foreseen, the new communes would help to impose law and order throughout her unruly domains. King Philip was so impressed by her far-sighted policy that he adopted it himself in France.

Through these measures, which brought the people flocking to her, Eleanor bought the loyalty of her vassals, even such troublesome lords as Hugh IX and Geoffrey de Lusignan, who, along with many others, now renewed their oaths of allegiance.

From Niort, the Queen rode west via Andilly to La Rochelle, where she issued a charter granting to the men of the port and their heirs 'a corporation, which shall enable them to defend and preserve their own rights more effectively; and we desire that their free customs shall be inviolably observed and that, in order that they may maintain them and defend their rights and ours, and those of our heirs, they shall exert and employ the strength and power of their commune, whenever necessary, against any man'.[17] Eleanor also attended the installation of the first mayor of La Rochelle, William of Montmirail.

South of La Rochelle lay the Île d'Oléron, to which Eleanor granted two charters, one conferring independence and the other, addressed 'to the beloved and faithful marines of Oléron', confirming 'the former grants of that venerable and illustrious man, our Lord Henry, King of England, on condition that the islanders of Oléron keep faith with our heirs'.[18] In 1200, King John issued his own charter to the island, 'confirming all that our dearest and most venerable mother has granted during her life'.[19] Whilst at Oléron, Eleanor is also said to have drawn up a code of laws governing maritime trade, which are regarded as the basis of all French sea laws.

From here, Eleanor progressed east, probably through Rochefort, to

Saint-Jean-d'Angély and thence south to Saintes, where she endowed an abbey.[20]

On 25 May 1199, confident that his continental possessions were secure for the moment, John crossed to England to claim his kingdom,[21] which had been held safely for him by Hubert Walter and William the Marshal.[22] Two days later, on Ascension Day, he was crowned in Westminster Abbey.[23]

As King of England, John has received a bad press, although recent studies of the official documents of his reign have shown that he was a gifted administrator who showed a concern for justice and ruled 'energetically enough'.[24] Unlike his brother Richard, he showed real concern for his kingdom, and travelled more widely within it than any of his Norman and Angevin predecessors, dispensing justice and overseeing public spending. During his reign, as a result of his personal intervention, the Exchequer, Chancery and law courts began to function more effectively. The records also suggest that the King took a more than ordinary interest in the welfare of his common subjects.

As the anonymous annalist of Barnwell stated, however, 'John was indeed a great prince but scarcely a happy one, and he experienced the ups and downs of fortune. He was munificent and liberal to outsiders, but a plunderer of his own people, trusting strangers rather than his subjects, wherefore he was eventually deserted by his own men and, in the end, little mourned.'

Many of John's troubles arose, as the chronicler said, from bad luck, but the worst failures of his reign were the result of his own indolence and stubbornness. He faced the impossible task of holding together an unwieldy empire in the face of unprecedented French aggression, yet he alienated many of those who could have aided him in this by his duplicity, suspicion and arbitrary acts. As a result, few of his vassals trusted him.

During his stay in England John appointed Hubert Walter chancellor and made William the Marshal Earl Marshal of England, or chief of staff. On 20 June, after visiting the shrine of Becket at Canterbury,[25] the King returned to Normandy, where on 24 June his barons rallied to him at Rouen, offering their support against Philip and Arthur. John, however, concluded an eight-week truce with Philip, buying himself valuable time in which to consolidate his position; as for Philip, he was in no position to sustain a prolonged struggle, since France was impoverished as a result of previous wars.

Sometime during the summer of 1199, certainly before 30 August, John had his childless – and controversial – marriage to Hawise of

Gloucester annulled in Normandy by the Bishops of Lisieux, Bayeux and Avranches, on a plea of consanguinity,[26] although he managed to keep hold of her lands. Hawise, who had not been crowned queen, did not contest the action, and she and John seem to have remained friendly, since he continued to send her presents. She remarried twice, and died without issue in 1217. She was buried in Canterbury Cathedral.

After his marriage was annulled, John looked around for an advantageous alliance, and by early 1200 had sent envoys to ask King Sancho I of Portugal for the hand of his daughter;[27] this was either Theresa, whose seven-year marriage to Alfonso IX of Léon had been annulled in 1198, or – which is more likely – Berengaria, who was unwed.

In the middle of June, Eleanor visited Philip at Tours and swore fealty to him for Poitou and Aquitaine, underlining the independence of these fiefs from the Angevin empire and shrewdly pre-empting any schemes the French King might have had for setting up Arthur as their ruler.[28] The chroniclers record few details of the meeting, although they do state that Philip gave Eleanor the kiss of peace. There is no record of Eleanor meeting her grandson Arthur.

The Queen resumed her progress, travelling south to Bordeaux, which she reached on 1 July. Three days later, 'she inspected the charters granted by her father and her dearest son Richard, King of England, in favour of Sainte-Croix of Bordeaux, which charters she now confirms'.[29] She also visited the nearby abbey of La Grande-Sauve, where she was shown a deed of privilege to which was attached the seal of Thomas Becket, as chancellor. Eleanor now granted a new charter renewing those privileges, recalling in it how

> the late King Henry, our very dear husband of gracious memory, and we ourselves long ago took the monastery of La Grand Sauve under our special protection. But that Henry, as well as our son Richard, having both since died, and God having left us still in the world, we have been obliged, in order to provide for the needs of our people and the welfare of our lands, to visit Gascony. We have been brought in the course of our journey to this monastery, and we have seen that it is a holy place. For this reason we have commended both ourselves and the souls of those kings to the prayers of this community; and that our visit may not have been unserviceable, we hereby confirm the ancient privileges of this foundation.[30]

Upon leaving Bordeaux, she followed the course of the Gironde north to Soulac before crossing the river to Royan. She may then have returned briefly to Fontevrault, pausing on the way to settle a dispute in favour of the nuns of nearby Montreuil. Sometime after the end of May, she issued a charter 'to the blessed Mary and the nuns of Fontevrault', granting an annuity of £100 'for the weal of her soul and of her worshipful husband of sacred memory, King Henry, of her son King Henry, of goodly memory, and of that mighty man King Richard, and of her other sons and daughters, with the consent of her dearest son John'.[31]

Having completed her grand progress, during which she is estimated to have travelled over 1,000 miles, Eleanor temporarily closed her chancellory at Vienne and went north to Rouen, where she met up with John on 30 July. Thanks to his mother's efforts, John's position was more secure than it might have been, and he acknowledged his debt to her, and his trust in her, in a decree proclaiming that the Queen was to retain Poitou and Aquitaine for the rest of her life; furthermore, 'we desire that she shall be lady not only of all those territories which are ours, but also of ourself and of all our lands and possessions'.

During August, John and Eleanor were joined at Rouen by Joanna, who was in the last months of pregnancy and clearly unwell. Count Raymond was refusing to pay his absent wife an allowance, so on 26 August, to save her from destitution, John gave 'his dearest sister Joanna 100 marks of rent, by the advice of his dearest mother and lady, Eleanor, Queen of the English'.[32] In view of Joanna's state of health, he also assigned her '3,000 marks for making her will, according to the disposition she shall make for distribution by the hands of the most reverend Eleanor their mother, to be paid at the four terms which the Queen and archbishops shall set'.[33] In her will, Joanna asked Eleanor to divide those 3,000 marks 'among religious houses and the poor';[34] she directed also that a donation be made in her name for the nuns' kitchen at Fontevrault.

Early in September, it became painfully apparent that Joanna was dying. Realising this, the anguished Countess begged to be veiled as a nun of Fontevrault, that she might set aside the vanities of her rank and end her life in poverty and humility. This was a very unusual and astonishing request, since she was a married woman and about to give birth, and it was also forbidden by canon law, but when Eleanor and others tried to dissuade her, the Countess insisted that it was what she wanted. It was customary in such unusual cases to consult the Abbess of Fontevrault, who had the power to commute the rules. Abbess Matilda was duly sent for, but Eleanor, fearing that Joanna might not live until she arrived, asked Hubert Walter, the Archbishop of Canterbury, who happened to be in Rouen at the time, to do the veiling. This was most irregular, and the Archbishop counselled the Queen to be patient and await the coming of the Abbess. He also visited Joanna and tried to divert her from her purpose, but she was adamant in her resolve.

Impressed by her fervour, and taking pity on her state and that of her anguished mother, Hubert Walter convened a committee of nuns and clergy, who all agreed that Joanna's vocation must be inspired by Heaven. On their advice, the Archbishop set aside protocol and his scruples and admitted Joanna to the Order of Fontevrault in the presence of Eleanor and many witnesses. Joanna was so weak that she could not stand to make her vows, and died shortly afterwards.[35] Her infant was born minutes later – possibly cut out of her lifeless body, since there is no mention in the sources of her being in labour, although it is possible that she did die in childbed – but survived only long enough to be baptised with the name of Richard.[36]

Eleanor arranged for Joanna and her son to be buried at Fontevrault, near Henry II and Richard I. Once again, she found herself mourning the loss of a child. Of the ten she had borne, only two yet lived: John, and Eleanor, who was in far-off Castile.

After Joanna's death, Eleanor informed her vassals in an open letter that she 'has gone to Gascony, taking with her the original of the testament of her dearest daughter, Queen Joanna, that the Count of St Gilles [sic] may see it'. The Queen begged her bishops 'to carry out its provisions, according to the transcript of it she sends them, in the presence of William, Prior of Fontevrault, as they love God and her'.[37]

On her return from Gascony, Eleanor formally ceded Poitou and Aquitaine to 'her very dear son John as her right heir', whilst retaining sovereignty and a life interest for herself, and commanded her vassals to receive him peacefully and do him homage.[38] It is likely that she had made up her mind to do this before paying homage to Philip in June, and there was nothing that Philip, having accepted that homage, could do about it, since she had every right to make her son her heir, and no one could deny that she was getting rather old to rule such wide and troublesome domains. But her gift meant that John, having inherited these domains, might prove as formidable an adversary as Richard had been, and a jealous Philip could now view his former ally only as a threat to his ambitions and therefore a potential enemy.

By this time, however, a rift had developed between Philip and Arthur. Philip had garrisoned many of the castles loyal to Arthur in

Anjou, Touraine and Maine, but there was mounting resentment against this on the part of Arthur and his friends, who feared that the French King meant to occupy those castles on a permanent basis. A disaffected William des Roches now switched his allegiance to John, and called upon Aimery of Thouars to act as mediator. With his help, and without Philip's knowledge, William, Arthur, Constance and Guy of Thouars stole away from Paris and made for Brittany.

Warned of their flight, and determined to lay his hands on Arthur, John lay in wait for them near the ruined city of Le Mans. Leaving Arthur and his mother in a safe place, the three barons attempted to parley with John, but finding that he was not prepared to negotiate, managed to warn the Duchess that an ambush was planned. Constance, Guy and Aimery fled back to Paris with Arthur,[39] and John immediately dismissed Aimery from his stewardship of Chinon for his 'treachery', an unwise step that alienated a powerful vassal who might otherwise have remained loyal. Only William des Roches was reconciled to the King – at Eleanor's persuasion, it is said. John forgave him and made him hereditary seneschal of Anjou, Maine and Touraine in place of Aimery. Based at Chinon, he had regular contact with Eleanor when she was at nearby Fontevrault, and witnessed at least one of her charters.

The loss of such a valuable ally was a blow to Philip, who was involved at this time in a bitter conflict with the papacy over his matrimonial tangles, which would lead to his excommunication. He sued for peace, and after Christmas concluded with John a five-year truce, whereby, in return for a payment of 30,000 silver marks,[40] payable upon confirmation of these terms by a treaty, Philip abandoned Arthur and, in his name, relinquished all his dynastic claims and recognised John as King Richard's heir. He also agreed that Arthur would do homage to John for Brittany. In return, John ceded the Vexin and the Norman county of Evreux to Philip. What Philip would not agree to do, however, was surrender the young Duke into the custody of his uncle. Nevertheless, the meeting ended with the two kings 'rushing into each other's arms'.[41]

The truce also provided, amongst other things, for the marriage of Philip's twelve-year-old heir Louis to one of John's Castilian nieces, a union that John hoped would check Philip's territorial ambitions. The princess would have as dowry lands taken by King Richard from Philip.[42] The English barons felt that John had made far too many concessions to Philip, and disparagingly bestowed upon him the nickname Softsword, which unfortunately stuck.[43]

It was decided that, because John had to go to England to raise the 30,000 marks, Eleanor should travel to Castile to select one of the princesses, and then convey her back to France.[44] This was a strenuous task for an old lady of seventy-seven, but Eleanor may have welcomed the opportunity of being reunited with her daughter and namesake, whom she had not seen for nearly thirty years.

After the truce was agreed,[45] the Queen set off from Poitiers, accompanied by Élie of Malemort, Archbishop of Bordeaux, and the mercenary captain Mercadier, on whom she obviously placed great reliance. Her journey was not without adventure, for just south of Poitiers she was ambushed and taken prisoner by her turbulent vassal, Hugh de Lusignan, who threatened to hold her captive until she had ceded to him the rich county of La Marche. This fief had long ago been sold by his forebears to Henry II, and had been retained by Richard I, who did not want subversive lords using it as a power base. Hugh had long desired to recover La Marche, but it was also claimed by Count Aymer of Angoulême, a powerful, independent-spirited and untrustworthy baron who had allied himself to King Philip against Richard. Realising that the Castilian marriage was of greater importance than a disputed fief, and deciding that Hugh – who had been one of Richard's friends and had distinguished himself during the crusade – was a more worthy claimant, Eleanor capitulated, and was set free to continue her journey south towards Bordeaux.

Once more the Queen crossed the Pyrenees, this time in the depths of winter, then travelled through Navarre and the kingdom of Castile to either the capital Toledo or the city of Burgos, arriving before the end of January in the year 1200.

Of their twelve children, King Alfonso VIII and Queen Eleanor had two[46] remaining unmarried daughters, Urraca and Blanche, who were both beautiful and dignified. Urraca, as the elder, was the obvious choice as a bride for the heir to France, but, according to the late Spanish chronicle of Pedro Niño, Eleanor rejected her, ostensibly on the grounds that the French would never accept a queen with such an outlandish name, and chose Blanche instead. It was a wise choice, for Blanche of Castile would prove almost as formidable a queen as her grandmother had been, and keep France stable during the minority of her son, the future saint, Louis IX. It is possible that Eleanor perceived that Blanche possessed extraordinary qualities, even at the tender age of sixteen.

There was no need to hurry back, since marriages were not solemnised during Lent, so Eleanor stayed for nearly two months at the sophisticated Castilian court, which – due to the influence of its queen – had embraced the culture and architecture of the south, yet offered

Moorish luxuries reminiscent of the courts of the East. In his verses, the troubadour Pierre Vidal refers to the younger Eleanor keeping her husband elegant company in his gracious court,[47] while another poet, Ramón Vidal, gives us a brief glimpse of 'Queen Leonore modestly clad in a mantle of rich stuff, red, with a silver border wrought with golden lions'.[48]

Late in March, Eleanor, accompanied by Blanche, journeyed through the pass of Roncesvalles into Gascony, and was back in Bordeaux by 9 April. Then something terrible happened. 'While she was staying at the city of Bordeaux on account of the solemnity of Easter, Mercadier came to her'; it was decided that he would escort the Queen and princess north through Poitou. But 'on the second day in Easter week, he was slain in the city by a man-at-arms in the service of Brandin',[49] a rival mercenary captain. This avoidable tragedy was too much for the elderly Queen, who was 'fatigued with old age and the labour of the length of her journey'. Unable to continue to Normandy, she rode in easy stages with Blanche to the valley of the Loire, where she entrusted her granddaughter to the care of the Archbishop of Bordeaux, who would escort her to King John. Her duty done, an exhausted Eleanor 'betook herself to the abbey of Fontevrault, and there remained'.[50]

21

'The Brood of the Wicked Shall Not Thrive'

It would seem that Eleanor now intended to live out her remaining days at Fontevrault. Here, she was attended by her chaplain, Roger, her secretary, Guy Diva, her clerks, Joscelin and Renoul, and 'her dear maid, Aliza, Prioress of Fontevrault', to whom in that year, 1200, she made a gift of £10 Poitevin.[1] Abbess Matilda had long been a good friend.

But the world kept intruding into the peace of the abbey.

On 22 May, John and Philip concluded the Treaty of Le Goulet, which enshrined the terms of the truce. Philip formally recognised John as Richard's heir, and John paid homage to him for his continental territories. It was also arranged that Arthur should hold Brittany of John as his vassal and that the young Duke should swear fealty to the uncle he hated.[2]

The following day, Blanche and Louis were married by the Archbishop of Bordeaux near the Norman border; their nuptials could not be solemnised in France because, as a consequence of Philip's irregular conjugal affairs, Pope Innocent had laid it under an interdict. Philip was barred from the ceremony, but provided lavishly for the celebrations that followed, during which young Arthur of Brittany distinguished himself in a tournament.[3] Arthur paid homage to John for Brittany, then returned to France with King Philip and the bridal pair.[4] The union of the future Louis VIII and Blanche of Castile, which produced twelve children, would ensure that Eleanor's descendants would one day sit on the throne of France.

In early summer, Eleanor fell ill with an unspecified complaint and John visited her at Fontevrault. She advised him 'to visit immediately his

Poitevin provinces and, for the sake of their peace and preservation, she desired him to form an amicable league with the Count of La Marche'.[5] John took her advice, and in July rode south. He was still in the midst of negotiations for a marriage alliance with Portugal, and that month sent another embassy to Sancho I.[6]

On 5 July, John arrived at Lusignan Castle, where he attended a ceremonial gathering hosted by Ralph de Lusignan, Count of Eu,[7] brother of Hugh le Brun, the new Count of La Marche, with whom John had come to make peace. The King also effected a general reconciliation between himself and the Counts of Angoulême and Limoges, who had rebelled against King Richard.[8]

Among the guests was the daughter and heiress of Count Aymer of Angoulême, a beautiful and precocious thirteen-year-old called Isabella.[9] She had been betrothed to Hugh de Lusignan some months earlier – the exact date is not known – to cement a reconciliation between their two rival houses. After her betrothal, Isabella had been sent to be trained in the skills of a feudal châtelaine in the household of her betrothed. Her marriage had been deferred because of her youth, but was due to take place soon.

John took one look at Isabella and was smitten.[10] 'It was as if she held him by sorcery or witchcraft,' observed a shocked Roger of Wendover. The thirty-three-year-old King made no secret of his burning desire for her, and her parents, aware that a union with the King would be a far more prestigious alliance than that with a mere count, encouraged his advances.

John immediately broke off negotiations with Portugal and informed Count Aymer that he meant to marry Isabella instead. The Count was only too pleased to give his consent. At that point, John sent an unsuspecting Hugh de Lusignan to England on official business, to get him out of the way.

John should have realised that marrying Isabella would be an ill-advised step – indeed, political suicide – since it would make enemies of the Lusignans, who were powerful and potentially troublesome vassals. Yet no one could have predicted just how disastrous the consequences would actually be.

The chroniclers imply that John was too much in thrall to Isabella's charms to care, yet although they deplore his headlong rush into a marriage based, as they believed, on love alone – almost unheard of in royal circles in those days – there were sound political advantages to be gained from such an alliance, of which John was doubtless aware. Not the least of these was securing the friendship of the influential, yet fickle Count Aymer and the loyalty of the hitherto unruly fief of Angoulême, which was strategically placed on the approaches to Gascony, and of the neighbouring fiefs allied to it, as well as the succession to Angoulême on Aymer's death.[11]

It would also seem that John had deliberately gone after Isabella with the intention of breaking her betrothal to Hugh de Lusignan, fearing that the union of two such powerful vassals might in the long run prove detrimental to himself and the stability of the Angevin empire. Yet there is no doubt that he was strongly attracted to her.

It was essential that the agreement between John and Aymer be kept secret from the Lusignans. Lying through his teeth, Isabella's father offered some pretext to summon her home to Angoulême. When told of the great marriage that had been arranged for her, the girl wept bitterly and protested loudly, but to no avail. On 23 August, John arrived at Angoulême with Élie, Archbishop of Bordeaux, and Isabella was informed that she must travel south to Bordeaux, where she would be married on the morrow – the date originally set for her marriage to Hugh de Lusignan.[12]

On 24 August, John and Isabella of Angoulême were married by the Archbishop in Bordeaux Cathedral.[13] King Philip, who may have anticipated that this union would cause divisions in the empire, willingly gave his consent to the marriage.[14]

The King was 'madly enamoured' with his bride: in her 'he believed he possessed everything he could desire'.[15] It was said that he seemed chained to his bed, so hotly did he lust after her. The new Queen was 'a splendid animal rather than a stateswoman',[16] but there is little evidence that she returned her husband's love. Within a few years, lust and endurance had degenerated into mutual hatred, and Isabella, who bore John five children, turned into an 'evil-minded, adulterous, dangerous woman, often found guilty of crimes, upon which King John seized her paramours and had them strangled with a rope on her bed'.[17] By then, the Poitevins, who had never forgiven her for jilting Hugh de Lusignan, were likening Isabella to Queen Jezebel.

When the Lusignans learned how Hugh had been robbed of his bride, they initially did nothing. Yet the insult rankled and festered, and would in a very short time lead to a deadly conflict that would have far-reaching and tragic repercussions. Hugh accepted the bride chosen for him by John, who was the King's ward Matilda, daughter of Count Vulgrin of Angoulême, Aymer's deceased elder brother, and she bore him a son, who became Hugh X,[18] but this was not considered adequate compensation for the loss of so valuable a matrimonial prize as Isabella.

Immediately after the wedding, the King and Queen rode north via Poitiers to Chinon, and it is almost certain that, while they were staying there, John took his bride to Fontevrault to meet her mother-in-law. It would appear that Eleanor was impressed: Isabella was a southerner, like herself, the daughter of one of her own vassals, and she had spirit. Soon afterwards, the old Queen dowered the girl with the cities of Niort and Saintes.

From Chinon, John escorted Isabella to Normandy, taking her on a progress through the duchy, then crossed with his bride to England early in October. Having been acknowledged as Queen of England by the magnates in council at Westminster, Isabella was crowned on 8 October by Hubert Walter in Westminster Abbey.[19]

Late that year Bishop Hugh of Lincoln died in Lincoln's Inn, London. On his deathbed, he prophesied the ruin of the Angevin dynasty, saying:

> The descendants of King Henry must bear the curse pronounced in Holy Scripture: 'The multiplied brood of the wicked shall not thrive; and bastard slips shall not take deep root nor any fast foundation', and again, 'The children of adulterers shall be rooted out'. The present King of France will avenge the memory of his virtuous father, King Louis, upon the children of the faithless wife who left him to unite with his enemy. And as the ox eats down the grass to the very roots, so shall Philip of France entirely destroy this race.[20]

These predictions were strangely accurate, foretelling not only the events of John's reign but also those occurring in 1483–5, when the Plantagenet dynasty came to an ignominious end.

During the winter and early spring, the King and Queen went on a progress through their realm, which took them to Lincoln, where John and William the Lyon acted as pall-bearers at the funeral of Bishop Hugh. John and Isabella kept their first Christmas court together at Guildford. In February 1201 they were at York, and at Easter they revived the ancient custom of crown-wearing at Canterbury.[21]

Eleanor was again unwell in the early months of 1201. Whether this was a recurrence of her former illness, or a different disease, is not known, but it did not prevent her from continuing to work behind the scenes in the interests of peace in Poitou, which was being threatened by the Lusignans. Hugh had finally made a formal protest to John about the theft of Isabella, and when John had ignored him, he and his kinsmen had risen in rebellion. In March, in retaliation, John confiscated La

Marche and sent in his officers, with an armed force, to take over its administration. Shortly afterwards he bestowed it upon his father-in-law, Count Aymer.

Eleanor knew there was one vassal upon whom she could count in this situation, and that was Count Aimery of Thouars, who came at once to Fontevrault at her summons. After talking with him about the situation, she felt a lot better in every way, and after he had gone, she wrote warmly of him to John, determined to effect a reconciliation between them:

> I have been very ill, but I want to tell you, my very dear son, that I summoned our well-beloved cousin, Aimery of Thouars, to visit me during my illness, and the pleasure which I derived from his visit did me good, for he alone of your Poitevin barons has wrought us no injury, nor seized unjustly any of your lands. I made him see how wrong and shameful it was for him to stand by and let other barons rend your heritage asunder, and he has promised to do everything he can to bring back to your obedience the lands and castles that some of his friends have seized. I was much comforted by his presence, and through God's grace am convalescent.[22]

The Queen ordered her secretary, Guy Diva, to write to the King in similar vein, and she also wrote to Aimery, urging him to protest his loyalty in writing to John.[23] Both King and Count heeded her advice, and soon afterwards made peace with each other. In this present crisis, John found Aimery a valuable ally.

He was to need many more such. When John ordered Guarine of Clapion, the seneschal of Normandy, to seize Driencourt, a castle owned by Hugh de Lusignan's brother, Ralph, Count of Eu, the Lusignans indignantly revoked their oaths of allegiance to John and appealed to King Philip, their ultimate overlord, for justice. Fearing armed French intervention, Eleanor summoned her grandson Arthur to visit her at Fontevrault, and wrung from him a promise that he would do everything in his power to preserve the peace in Poitou and Aquitaine. But Philip was in fact in a contrite mood: having recently submitted to the Pope and got the interdict on France lifted, he was reluctant to offend Innocent again by breaking his truce with John. He therefore appealed to the Lusignans to cease harrying their suzerain.

The Lusignans ignored him; they were now in open revolt, and Eleanor and Aimery both urged John to return from England to deal with them. Count Aymer of Angoulême, in gratitude for the gift of La

Marche, also offered his support. John sent orders to his officials to pester and plunder the Lusignans and 'do them all the harm they could'.[24] Every castle belonging to them in Poitou and Normandy was either besieged or seized.

On 31 May, John and Isabella crossed to Normandy and took up residence at Château Gaillard.[25] At the beginning of July, they visited Philip in Paris, where they were 'honourably entertained' and given gifts and champagne.[26] The French King was friendly and offered to act as mediator between John and the Lusignans. He agreed not to demand immediate redress for the Lusignans' grievances, on condition that John agreed that those grievances could be aired in a court presided over by Philip and the peers of France. John consented, and there the matter rested for a time.

Late in July, Philip's mistress, Agnes of Méran, who had been the cause of his conflict with the Pope, died, leaving him in a much stronger position. Free now of matrimonial tangles,[27] he was waiting only for Innocent to legitimise his children by Agnes; once that had been accomplished, he would not be so concerned about antagonising the papacy. Already, he had begun to devise how he might use John's quarrel with the Lusignans to bring about the fulfilment of his dream to break the power of the Angevins on the continent.

John and Isabella spent the remaining weeks of the summer of 1201 at Chinon with Berengaria, whilst the rumbles of discontent echoed from Poitou. Thanks to Aymer of Angoulême and Aimery of Thouars, however, Aquitaine lay peaceful. Eleanor remained at Fontevrault; contemporary sources do not record anything of her for the rest of the year.

During the first week of September, Constance of Brittany died in childbirth at Nantes.[28] Some sources claim that she had contracted leprosy. Sometime earlier she had made her peace with John and had since identified herself and her son with the Angevin interests, but after her death Arthur came increasingly under the influence of King Philip, and his attitude to King John grew ever more aggressive.

John's arbitrary measures had alienated many of those who might have supported him. By the autumn, several southern barons, among them Raymond of Toulouse and Aimar of Limoges, had defected from their allegiance and joined forces with the Lusignans.

Fearing that Philip would support this formidable coalition, John wished to avoid having the dispute with Hugh le Brun settled by the court of France. In October, he suddenly accused the Lusignans of treason and challenged them to a trial by combat, in which both sides would be represented by champions nominated by themselves. The Lusignans refused, and again appealed, most urgently, to King Philip and the lords of France for justice. This time, Philip was ready to exploit the situation. John was summoned with the Lusignans to appear before the French court in Paris, but although a date for the hearing was agreed upon, he spent the winter cancelling or postponing it.

By the end of the year, Arthur of Brittany, who had ambitions of his own, had allied himself to Philip and the Lusignans against John. John and Isabella spent Christmas at Caen.

In March, Philip was elated to learn that the Pope had legitimated his children by Agnes of Méran. Freed from the threat of papal censure, he now proceeded to deal with John. On 28 April 1202, Philip issued a final summons ordering John to present himself at the French court to answer the charges laid against him and submit to judgement by the peers of France.[29]

John responded by protesting that, as King of England and Duke of Normandy, he was not answerable to a French court. Philip retorted that he had been summoned as Duke of Aquitaine, Count of Poitou and Count of Anjou,[30] but John ignored him and pointedly failed yet again to appear on the appointed day. His continuing prevarication gave Philip the legal pretext he needed to declare the English King a contumacious traitor and confiscate all his continental territories except Normandy, which he was within his rights as overlord to do and which would lend validity to what he had in mind. Accordingly, 'the assembled barons of France adjudged the King of England to be deprived of his lands which he and his forefathers had hitherto held of the King of France'.[31]

Philip then declared the truce broken and launched an armed onslaught on Normandy's frontier defences, determined to conquer the duchy and make it part of the French royal demesne. It was Philip's intention that Brittany and John's other territories – Anjou, Maine, Touraine and Poitou – should be held by Arthur, as his own vassal. In July, at Gournay, Arthur, now fifteen, 'was knighted by King Philip and betrothed to his small daughter' Marie,[32] then did homage to Philip for the Angevin territories. The King gave Arthur 200 French knights and told him to take possession of his inheritance,[33] whereupon Arthur 'marched forth with pompous noise'[34] towards Poitou.[35]

John was now facing a war on two fronts, and he was by no means prepared for it. He could not count on the support of his brother-in-law and former ally, Alfonso VIII of Castile, since, through his daughter's marriage, that monarch had now identified himself with French interests. Yet providence was to grant John a stroke of extraordinary luck.

When war broke out between John and Philip, Eleanor, outraged at Arthur's temerity in attempting to wrest Poitou from its designated ruler, declared her support for John and, in the last week of July, set out from Fontevrault with a small military escort, intending to install herself in her capital, Poitiers, and deter Arthur from taking possession. Near the Angevin border, she lodged at the decaying castle of Mirebeau, once a mighty stronghold of Count Geoffrey of Anjou. This fortress dominated a small walled town, twenty miles north-east of Poitiers.

Unfortunately, Arthur, then at Tours, learned of her whereabouts. 'Following some evil and rash advice', he set out with Hugh de Lusignan, his uncle Geoffrey and 250 soldiers, 'to besiege the castle of Mirebeau',[36] intending to take the old Queen hostage and barter her for Queen Isabella, thereby enabling him to wrest huge concessions from John.[37] The castle was not adequately provisioned for a siege, nor were its defences very strong, but Eleanor, 'fearing capture' – for she was aware of her immense value as a potential hostage – instructed her men-at-arms and the garrison to defend the fortress. She also smuggled out two messengers, one with orders for 'her son John to bring her aid as soon as possible',[38] and the other to summon William des Roches, seneschal of Anjou, from Chinon.

Contemporary sources suggest that she then played for time by dragging out negotiations with her grandson:

> Arthur managed to speak with his grandmother, demanding that she evacuate the castle with all her possessions and then go peaceably wherever she wished, for he wanted to show nothing but honour to her person. The Queen replied that she would not leave it, but if he behaved as a courtly gentlemen, he would quit this place, for he would find plenty of castles to attack other than the one she was in. She was, moreover, amazed that he and the Poitevins, who should be her liegemen, would besiege a castle knowing her to be in it.[39]

She refused adamantly to submit to Philip's disposition of her domains in return for her freedom.

John was 'on the road to Chinon'[40] when, on 30 July, he heard of Eleanor's plight. 'The King immediately set out with part of his army'[41] and marched day and night to Mirebeau, covering a distance of over eighty miles in forty-eight hours. On the way he was joined by William des Roches, who offered to lead the attack on condition that the King agreed he would not execute Arthur or any other of the rebels, but would consult William as to their fate.[42] John gave his word.

On approaching the town in the early hours of 1 August,[43] the King was informed that his mother had been forced to lock herself into the keep, since the walls of Mirebeau and the outer defences of the castle had been breached by Arthur's men.[44]

'The rebels had entered the town and closed up with earth all the gates except one',[45] which they left open so that supplies could be brought to them. Soon after dawn on 1 August, an unsuspecting Arthur and Hugh de Lusignan were breakfasting on roast pigeons[46] while their men were dressing and arming themselves. Before they knew it, William des Roches and his troops had entered the gate and launched an assault on them, 'the armed upon the unarmed', throwing them into disarray. 'After heavy fighting, the King entered the city',[47] and the besiegers were easily overcome. Arthur was seized by William de Braose, Lord of Brecon, the siege was raised and Eleanor, unharmed, was escorted to safety.

Nearly every member of Arthur's company was captured or killed. But the greatest triumph for John lay in taking prisoner not only Arthur himself, who was the chief prize, but also Hugh and Geoffrey de Lusignan. More than 250 knights,[48] irrespective of their rank, were ignominiously chained together and bundled into ox-carts, then paraded as trophies along the roads leading to the Loire crossing, before being incarcerated in prisons in England and Normandy.[49] Hugh de Lusignan was imprisoned in chains in a tower at Caen.

It was a brilliant victory, the most significant in John's career, and testimony to his ability to achieve military greatness. It left him in a very strong position, with his arch-enemies in his own hands as hostages with which to bargain with Philip. Even Philip recognised that John now had the upper hand, and, 'upset by the misfortune', withdrew his forces from the Norman border, fired and plundered Tours in vengeance,[50] then returned to Paris, where he 'remained inactive for the rest of the year'.[51]

John himself wrote to his English barons:

> Know that, by the grace of God, we are safe and well, and God's mercy has worked wonderfully with us, for on Tuesday, the feast of St Peter ad Vincula, we heard that the Lady our mother was closely besieged at Mirebeau, and we hurried there as fast as we could. And there we captured our nephew Arthur and all our

other Poitevin enemies, and not one escaped. Therefore God be praised for our happy success.

But John, through his own stupidity, failed to consolidate his position and lost his advantage. He treated his prisoners appallingly. The Lusignans were quickly ransomed and released, after swearing fealty to John and surrendering their strongholds,[52] but most of the knightly prisoners – who could also have been ransomed to John's advantage – were manacled in irons in his dungeons. At Corfe Castle twenty-two of them starved to death. Arthur's sister, Eleanor, 'the pearl of Brittany', also taken at Mirebeau, was imprisoned at Bristol Castle (where she would remain, albeit generously treated, until her death forty years later in the reign of John's son, Henry III). As for Arthur himself, he was on 10 August shut up in a dungeon in Falaise Castle in Normandy[53] and was never seen in public again.

John's treatment of these captives provoked an outcry, even among his own supporters, many of whom – including Aimery of Thouars and William des Roches – deserted him. Aimery had been horrified to see some of his own kinsmen in chains, and William was angry because John had broken his promise. At this critical juncture, they transferred their allegiance to King Philip.

After leaving Mirebeau, Eleanor returned to Fontevrault. Before parting from John, she had charged him, on her malediction, not to harm Arthur.[54] Paulus Emilius, the biographer of Philip Augustus, claims that she interceded most forcefully on Arthur's behalf.

Eleanor was now eighty, and had experienced enough worldly strife to make her long for the cloister. The Annals of Fontevrault confirm that, on her return to the abbey, she took the veil and entered the community as a nun. Nevertheless, she seems to have maintained contact with her officers in her domains, and it is possible that she was permitted to leave the abbey to visit Poitiers on at least one occasion.

In the autumn of 1202, Aimery of Thouars and William des Roches seized the city of Angers and the surrounding territory. Then they and other lords demanded Arthur's release, some threatening to transfer their allegiance to Philip until the young Duke was set free. In November, despite their promises to John, the Lusignans joined the rebel coalition.[55]

John again spent Christmas at Caen, 'feasting with his queen and lying in bed until dinner time',[56] to the scandal of the court. By that time, rumours were circulating that Arthur was dead.[57]

22

'A Candle Goeth Out'

John would have had every justification for executing Arthur: the young Duke had broken his feudal oath and committed treason against his overlord, had been arrested whilst besieging his grandmother on his uncle's territory, and had made plain his intention of invading and conquering Poitou. Yet Arthur was John's nephew, his own flesh and blood, and Queen Eleanor had exhorted the King to spare her grandson's life. Undoubtedly, John shrank from the consequences of ordering Arthur to be publicly put to death, and the outcry that would inevitably follow.

Arthur had been imprisoned at Falaise in the custody of John's chamberlain, Hubert de Burgh,[1] and under the guardianship of his captor, William de Braose, who was one of John's most trusted advisers and councillors. In January 1203, John had Arthur brought before him at Falaise. 'The King addressed him kindly and promised him many honours, asking him to separate himself from the French King and to adhere to the side of his lord and uncle.' But Arthur

> ill-advisedly replied with indignation and threats, and demanded that the King give up to him his kingdom of England with all the territories which King Richard had possessed at his death, since all these possessions belonged to him by hereditary right. He swore that unless King John quickly restored [them] to him, he would never give him a moment's peace for the rest of his life. The King was much troubled at hearing his words.[2]

Ever suspicious, John now believed that some of his barons were secretly in league with Arthur, and went in constant dread of what might happen were Arthur to escape.

The King asked some of his magnates what he should do about Arthur. They told him that there would be no peace while his nephew lived. With brutal candour, they 'suggested that he should order the noble youth to be deprived of his eyes and genitals, so that he would thereafter be incapable of princely rule' and unable to beget any traitorous progeny. 'John ordered three servants to go to Falaise and perform this detestable act', but when Arthur, 'realising the dire sentence which his uncle had pronounced on him, burst into tears and pitiful complaints', two of them shrank from doing the deed. When the third insisted on carrying out his orders, Hubert de Burgh angrily sent them all away, at which 'Arthur, with a sad heart, took a little comfort'.[3]

Hubert had defied John to spare his king the consequences of an act of which he would repent when his anger had cooled — an act, moreover, that would surely alienate many of the barons. But he did not trust John, and in a ploy to forestall him from sending less scrupulous henchmen to do harm to Arthur, 'had it announced through the castle and the whole region that the sentence had been carried out and that Arthur had died from a broken heart and from the bitter pain of his wounds'. In Falaise and elsewhere, the bells tolled for his passing, and his clothes were distributed among the lepers.[4]

But Hubert had not reckoned upon the men of Brittany rising in rage against John for 'having performed such a detestable deed' on his nephew and causing his death, and he was forced to confess to John that the boy was in fact very much alive.[5]

Many, however, did not believe Hubert. It began to be bruited about that Arthur had in fact been murdered, and rumours to that effect rapidly gained currency in Paris, Brittany and even Poitiers during the weeks that followed.

In January 1201, Queen Isabella found herself cut off from John and besieged at Chinon by Aimery of Thouars, who hoped to ransom her for advantageous terms. Arriving at Le Mans, a frantic John[6] was informed that the roads were impassable. Fortunately, a mercenary force led by one Peter of Préaux rescued the Queen and escorted her to Le Mans two days later, to the King's immense relief. After that, John would not leave her side and lost interest in conquering his enemies.[7] Roger of Wendover described him as the most uxorious of men, and claimed that his obsession with his wife made him soft and incompetent.

In fact, John was preoccupied with the problem of his nephew of Brittany. He was most displeased with Hubert de Burgh, and in

February or March 'gave orders that Arthur should be sent to Rouen to be imprisoned in the new tower there, and kept closely guarded'.[8] On 8 March, Robert de Vieuxpoint was appointed seneschal of Rouen and the Duke was placed in his keeping.[9] At the end of March, John bought Vieuxpoint's loyalty – and probably his secrecy – by granting him two castles and their bailiwicks in Westmorland.[10]

'Not long after that, Arthur suddenly vanished.'[11]

On 2 April 1203, John left Rouen and, accompanied by William de' Braose and three justiciars, sailed down the Seine to his manor of Molineux, one of his favourite residences. Around this time – and possibly on this day – William de Braose declared to the King and his barons that he was now relinquishing his guardianship of Arthur and could take no further responsibility for what happened to him.[12] Possibly he knew that John was planning something and did not wish to become involved or implicated in it.

'I know not what fate awaits your nephew, whose faithful guardian I have been,' he told the King, then added pointedly, 'I return him to your hands in good health and sound in all his members. Put him, I pray you, in some other, happier custody. The burden of my own affairs bids me resign.'[13] John seems to have taken him literally at his word.

What really happened to Arthur is not known for certain, but a plausible account of what might have befallen him exists in the *Annals of Margam*, a chronicle written in the early thirteenth century by the monks of a Cistercian abbey in Glamorganshire, of which the de Braoses were patrons. William de Braose was privy to John's counsels during the months of Arthur's imprisonment, and this account may have come directly from him.[14]

According to these annals, at Rouen, 'after dinner on the Thursday before Easter', 3 April 1203, 'when he was drunk with wine and possessed of the Devil, [John] slew [Arthur] with his own hand and, tying a heavy stone to the body, cast it into the Seine. It was brought up by the nets of fishermen and, dragged to the bank, it was identified and secretly buried, for fear of the tyrant, in Notre-Dame des Prés, a priory of Bec.'[15]

After that Easter, according to several chronicles, Arthur was seen no more by any man with a tongue in his head or the ability to scrawl a message to the world, the implication being that John had those who might have talked silenced in one way or another. 'It was not safe to write of [Arthur] even when he was dead.'[16]

On 16 April, John wrote an open letter from Falaise to 'the Lady Queen his mother' and eight of her vassals, including the Archbishop of Bordeaux, the seneschals of Poitou and Gascony and Hubert de Burgh, which was witnessed by William de Braose: 'We send to you Brother John of Valesent [or Valerant], who has seen what is going forward with us, and who will be able to apprise you of our situation. Put faith in him respecting these things whereof he will inform you. Nevertheless, the grace of God is even more with us than he can tell you, and concerning the mission which we have made to you, rely upon what the same John shall tell you thereof.' A postscript, addressed to Robert of Thornham, seneschal of Poitou, commands him 'not to distribute the money we have transmitted to you, unless in the presence of our mother and William Cocus'.[17]

It is possible, as many historians[18] assert, that this letter refers to Arthur's death, and that the important news that Brother John was to impart, first to the Queen at Fontevrault and afterwards to her chief vassals in Poitou, was too sensitive to be committed to parchment. This theory presupposes that John knew Eleanor would welcome the news: it is obvious from the tone of the letter that whatever it was would be pleasing to her. It also assumes that the Queen was a willing accessory to the murder of her own grandson, unless John led her to believe that Arthur died of natural causes. This is more likely since, the previous year, Eleanor had strongly exhorted John to spare Arthur. It is indeed possible that she had since been persuaded of the political necessity of getting rid of him, yet hardly likely that she would impute the successful accomplishment of such a murder to 'the grace of God'. Considering how she had suffered, by her own admission, mental torture at the memory of the fate of Arthur's father Geoffrey, she surely cannot have consented to the murder of his son. She was, after all, now vowed to the religious life and, at her advanced age, expecting to be summoned to divine judgement at any time.

This is the only letter from John to his mother to survive, yet there must have been many others. Too much significance has perhaps been placed upon a document that may have related to an entirely different matter. The wording of the letter is insufficient to link it conclusively to Arthur's death, but if it was about this, then it is probable that John asserted that the boy died of natural causes and pointed out the very real advantages of his passing. After all, is it likely that John would have confided news of the murder to a monk, of all people, and referred obliquely to the deed in a letter addressed to nine people? It is far more plausible that the monk was sent to offer spiritual comfort for a natural bereavement, or indeed employed on an entirely unrelated errand.

Arthur's fate remained a mystery, and many rumours and apocryphal tales circulated in the years following his disappearance. The Bretons certainly believed John responsible for his death: some said he had been killed by a hired assassin, Peter of Malendroit; others that the King had pushed him over a cliff at Cherbourg.[19] The French chronicler Guillaume le Breton was perhaps nearer the truth, claiming that in the middle of the night on the eve of Good Friday, John sailed up the Seine to Rouen in a small boat – presumably returning from Molineux – and moored it by a small postern door at the base of the new tower. He ordered his nephew to be brought down to him, then dragged him into the boat and sailed away. Arthur begged for mercy, but the King seized him by the hair and ran him through with his sword. He then weighted the body and threw it into the Seine. This account tallies in many respects with that in the Annals of Margam.

A Breton tradition claims that John was denounced as Arthur's murderer by the lords of Brittany in a special assembly in 1203,[20] but there is no contemporary evidence for this. In 1204, Philip of France heard a rumour that Arthur had been drowned.[21] Twelve years later, after both John and Philip were dead, Louis VIII of France tried to make political capital out of the murder by claiming that Philip had called John to account and had his court condemn him for it.[22] Again, no contemporary source corroborates this assertion, and Pope Innocent in fact pointed out to Louis that Arthur had been a traitor who had been caught whilst harrying his grandmother.[23]

It is clear that Philip was for a time as ignorant of the boy's fate as everyone else. It has been claimed that he found out the truth after 1210, when William de Braose, after inexplicably incurring John's displeasure, was exiled and obliged to flee to the French court, but this seems unlikely, since he never made public what he was supposed to have found out, or exploited it for political advantage.

Fifty years after Arthur's disappearance, the great chronicler Matthew Paris still did not know what had happened to him, and could only voice the pious hope that John had not had him murdered.

In the spring of 1203, the rumours alone were sufficient to condemn John. 'Opinion about the death of Arthur gained ground, by which it seemed that John was suspected by all of having slain him with his own hand; for which reason many turned their affections from the King and entertained the deepest enmity for him.'[24]

In the eyes of his disillusioned vassals, John was a guilty man, and they began to desert him. The lords of Maine defected to Philip, and Le Mans fell to the French. In Brittany, Arthur's subjects rose in revolt at the assumed murder of their duke, and their defection cut Normandy off from Poitou, which had remained loyal, and left it more vulnerable to Philip's aggression.

Although they grumbled at the burdensome taxation imposed upon them, many of the Norman magnates held property on both sides of the Channel, and had every reason to support John. The duchy was well fortified along its frontiers and guarded by a ring of castles, chief of which was Château Gaillard. Had John bestirred himself at this time, he could have held on to Normandy, but he seemed to be in the grip of a strange inertia.

That spring, Philip advanced along the Loire and took the great fortress of Saumur. Chinon held out against him, so he swung north and marched unopposed into Normandy, taking town after town: Domfront, Coutances, Falaise, Bayeux, Lisieux, Caen and Avranches – those great bastions of Angevin power – all fell to him.[25] At the same time, the Bretons attacked the south-western borders of Normandy.

John asked for a truce, but Philip offered impossible terms, being determined only on conquest.[26] When messengers came in urgency to John, beseeching him to rise up and give the French King the trouncing he deserved, the King shrugged and said, 'Let him alone. Some day I will recover all I have lost.'[27] By then, many of his disgusted Norman vassals were willingly transferring their allegiance to Philip.

By August, most of the eastern reaches of the duchy were in Philip's hands, including Vaudreuil, which was only twelve miles from the capital, Rouen. In September, the French King cast covetous eyes on the mighty Château Gaillard, which held the key to Rouen's defences, and laid siege to it. 'In the meantime, King John was staying inactive with his queen at Rouen, so that it was said that he was infatuated by sorcery, for in the midst of all his losses and disgrace, he showed a cheerful countenance to all, as though he had lost nothing.'[28]

Late in September, he finally roused himself and attempted to relieve Château Gaillard by night, sailing with an armed force up the Seine from Rouen, but, having miscalculated the tides, he was forced to withdraw after suffering heavy casualties. Hoping to divert Philip, he harried the borders of Brittany, but without success. In desperation, he made erratic and inept attempts to recoup his losses in Normandy,[29] to no avail. After these failures, many hitherto loyal Norman barons lost faith in him entirely and decided that they would be better off under French rule.

By the autumn, Philip had made such inroads into Normandy that it was clear that John would never recover what had been lost. The defection of so many vassals had dramatically cut his revenues, and he could no longer afford to pay the mercenaries upon whom he had increasingly come to rely.[30] Belatedly, he became aware of the desperate reality of the situation, and when William the Marshal counselled him to abandon the struggle, he retorted, 'Whoso is afraid, let him flee. I myself will not flee.'[31] Tragically, it was months too late for such bullish heroism.

By the beginning of December, the only parts of Normandy remaining in John's hands were the capital Rouen, Château Gaillard (which was still holding out valiantly against Philip), the Côtentin, Mortain and the Channel coastline. Internally, these regions, deprived of firm leadership, were degenerating into anarchy. Yet on 6 December, giving his word that he would soon return to the war-torn duchy, the King sailed for England with the Queen and William the Marshal 'to seek aid and counsel of the English barons'[32] and to raise men and money.[33] The English, however, had learned of John's ineptitude, his capriciousness and his cruelties, and they had heard the rumours about his treatment of his nephew; many lords were therefore not prepared to support him. Some with Norman estates preferred to transfer their allegiance to Philip. In despair, John kept a miserable Christmas at Canterbury.

Virtually nothing is known of Eleanor's life during these terrible months. All that is recorded is her granting a charter to the city of Niort, perhaps with a view to securing its support against the French. Philip's advance through Maine and Anjou had left her isolated at Fontevrault, and John – to the detriment of his own interests in Normandy – had deployed his forces in Anjou, possibly with a view to preventing his mother from being cut off from him. It has been claimed that the old Queen took refuge in Poitiers at this time, yet the concentration of troops in Anjou suggests that she remained at Fontevrault.

On 6 March 1204, after holding out for six months, Château Gaillard, which King Richard had claimed was impregnable, fell to the French, cutting off Rouen. It was a bitter blow that signalled the beginning of the end of the struggle for Normandy, and news of it is said to have hastened Eleanor's death. Paulus Emilius, in his life of Philip II, claims that it was hastened by learning that John had murdered Arthur.

Neither claim is likely to have been true, for the annals of Fontevrault state that the Queen now existed as one already dead to the world. We may infer from this, not so much that she had renounced the world, but that she was no longer aware of her surroundings.

On 1 April 1204,[34] Eleanor 'passed from the world as a candle in the sconce goeth out when the wind striketh it'. She was eighty-two and her death went virtually unremarked in the chaos surrounding the collapse of the Angevin empire.

Such accounts as do exist differ in respect of where Eleanor died. Peter of Blois, her former secretary, states that she died at Fontevrault, where she was received for penance and put on the monastic habit. Other sources say she had donned the garb of a nun before dying at Fontevrault. The annals of Fontevrault clearly state that Eleanor was consecrated as a nun in 1202, a fact that may not have been widely known, which would account for the slight discrepancies in these reports. Half a century later, Matthew Paris recorded that 'the noble Queen Eleanor, a woman of admirable beauty and intelligence, died in Fontevrault'.

However, the *Chronique des églises d'Anjou* states that Eleanor died at Poitiers, as does the minor chronicle of St Aubin of Angers. It is more likely, however, that Peter of Blois, who knew her and may have kept in touch, was correct.

Eleanor's body was buried in the crypt of the abbey of Fontevrault in a fine tomb erected between those of her husband, Henry II, and her son, Richard I. It was surmounted by a painted stone *gisant*, or effigy, with a crown on its head, a hint of a smile on its lips and a book of devotions open in its hands. Such effigies were rare, and Eleanor's is one of the finest of the few that survive from this period. It was not by the same sculptor who worked on the effigies of Henry and Richard, which date from around 1200, and it has been suggested that it was made by the craftsman who helped build the transepts in Chartres Cathedral. Whether or not the Fontevrault effigies are attempts at portraiture is a matter for dispute, but they are very individualistic representations.

During the French Revolution the abbey of Fontevrault was sacked and the tombs were disturbed and vandalised. The bones of Eleanor, Henry, Richard, Joanna and Isabella of Angoulême[35] were exhumed and scattered, never to be recovered. The abbey was then converted into a prison.

Later, the desecrated tombs were cobbled together and rearranged in the crypt. In 1963, the prison was closed and the abbey, which is now a hotel, was restored to its former glory, with four of the tombs[36] being placed in the church. That and the nuns' kitchen date from Eleanor's time, but most of the conventual building were built in the sixteenth century or later. Today, after 800 years, the Plantagenet effigies bear the ravages of time and only traces of the paint remain.

Eleanor did not live to see the eventual destruction of the empire that both she and Henry had built. Her own death, in fact, removed an insuperable legal obstacle to Philip's ambitions. By June 1204, the whole of Normandy was in Philip's possession – lost by John, according to Roger of Wendover, under the quilts of the marriage bed – and at the end of that month, all that John had left of the duchy were the Channel Isles. Also gone were Anjou, Maine, Touraine and Brittany, leaving the English King in possession only of the vulnerable county of Poitou and the duchy of Aquitaine. In less than a year, Philip had quadrupled his territories and laid the basis for France's future greatness.

Not satisfied with this, immediately after Normandy fell, he sent a force under William des Roches to invade Poitou, which fell to him in 1205.

The nuns of Fontevrault recorded in their necrology[37] a glowing but conventional tribute to their late patroness, who had been a paragon among women, and 'who illuminated the world with the brilliance of her royal progeny. She graced the nobility of her birth with the honesty of her life, enriched it with her moral excellence, and adorned it with the flowers of her virtues; and by her renown for unmatched goodness, she surpassed almost all the queens of the world'.[38] No doubt they wrote in all sincerity, having known Eleanor during her venerable old age.

Others, who had known her in youth, could have told a different story, and after her death, as a direct consequence of the fall of the Angevin empire and King John's dire reputation, it was the scandals connected with his mother that were remembered and not her wise rule during the latter years of her life. 'By reason of her excessive beauty, she destroyed or injured nations,' asserted Matthew Paris, with some exaggeration. Even King John, he claimed, called his mother an 'unhappy and shameless woman'.

This may not have been true, since the evidence suggests that her memory was revered amongst her descendants. Her grandson, Henry III, who was born three years after her death, paid 'for the support of a chaplain to perform divine service for the soul of Queen Eleanor, our grandmother'.[39] In 1233, Henry also granted land to the brothers of the Holy Sepulchre in Jerusalem, 'for the safety of the soul of Queen Eleanor, the King's grandmother'.[40] Such intercessions were indiscriminately solicited for those whose sins had been great and for those whose lives were blameless, so we should not infer too much from it.

Desmond Seward, one of her modern biographers, has pointed out that Eleanor could, like Queen Victoria, be accurately described as 'the Grandmother of Europe': her sons and their descendants were kings of

England, her daughters queens of Sicily and Castile; among her grandsons were a Holy Roman Emperor and the kings of Castile and Jerusalem, while her great-grandson became king of France. Two saints, St Louis IX of France and St Ferdinand III of Castile, were also among her descendants. In England, the line of kings that she and Henry founded endured until 1485, and her blood flows in the veins of Britain's present queen, Elizabeth II.

Today, our knowledge of Eleanor is still clouded by the persistent legends that cling to her name. The myths that circulated after her death were through the ages increasingly accepted as fact, and are only now beginning to be disproved by objective scholarship.

Early thirteenth-century chroniclers compared her to the cruel Roman Empress Messalina, and some even confused her with the legendary Melusine. One French chronicler describes her asking the barons of France, after the dissolution of her marriage to Louis, 'Look at me, Sirs. Is not my body delightful? The King thought I was the Devil!'[41] This theme was echoed by the Minstrel of Rheims, who called Eleanor 'a very Devil'; and by the middle of the thirteenth century, many people were prepared to accept as fact his assertion that Eleanor intended to elope with Saladin. As time went by, the stories grew ever more fantastic: in one medieval ballad, 'Queen Eleanor's Confession', she was accused of having a bastard child by William the Marshal. And as we have seen, she was frequently accused of murder in the legends of Fair Rosamund.

Four hundred years after her death, Shakespeare, in *King John*, referred to Eleanor as a 'canker'd granddam, a monstrous injurer of Heaven and Earth' and compared her to Ate, the goddess of blind folly, while as late as the nineteenth century, Agnes Strickland, the Victorian biographer of the queens of England, was sufficiently shocked by the Rosamund legends and by contemporary accounts of Eleanor's dealings with men to call her a 'bad' and 'giddy Queen' who was given to 'disgusting levity'.

Only at the end of the nineteenth century was Eleanor at last given her due by the historian Bishop Stubbs, who wrote: 'This great lady deserves to be treated with more honour and respect than she has generally met with. She was a very able woman of great tact and experience, and still greater ambition; a most important adviser whilst she continued to support her husband; a most dangerous enemy when in opposition.'

In the twentieth century, Eleanor of Aquitaine has either been regarded as a romantic heroine — which has led several admiring biographers to exaggerate her achievements and write spirited defences of her failings – or has been relegated to the side-lines by male historians, who have focused on her husband and sons and greatly underestimated her own role. The result has been a distorted picture, which serious, but rarely publicised, academic studies have done little to correct. It has been my aim in this book to achieve a more balanced portrayal, based chiefly on contemporary sources.

In the final analysis, although Eleanor was important in her own day for who she was, her fame rests largely on what she did, and the controversial role she played during a long career on the political stage. Denied for so long the exercise of power, for which she had a natural aptitude, she came into her own at an age when most women were either dead or long in retirement, and ruled as capably as any man. She was no shrinking violet, but a tough, capable and resourceful woman who travelled widely throughout the known world and was acquainted with most of the great figures of the age. Remarkable in a period when females were invariably relegated to a servile role, she was, as Richard of Devizes so astutely claimed, an incomparable woman.

Notes on the Chief Sources

What follows is a brief description and evaluation of each of the main contemporary sources to which I have referred in the text and notes. They are arranged in alphabetical order according to forename. Full details of their works are given in the Bibliography that follows.

ADAM OF EYNSHAM wrote a laudatory biography of St Hugh of Lincoln, in which its author took care not to be too critical of Henry II.

The anonymous MONK OF BARNWELL, who flourished in the reign of King John, wrote a lively, relatively objective and elegant chronicle of his times.

GEOFFREY OF MONMOUTH (c. 1100–c. 1154) was a Welsh chronicler of possibly Breton origin, who became Archdeacon of Monmouth c. 1140 and Bishop of St Asaph in 1152. His fictitious *History of the Kings of Britain*, allegedly derived from ancient Welsh chronicles, is the first major English source for the legends of King Arthur.

GERVASE OF CANTERBURY (c. 1141–1210) was a monk of Christ Church Priory by Canterbury Cathedral from 1163, and sacrist from 1193. He wrote a chronicle of his times, a book on the deeds of kings and a history of the archbishops of Canterbury from St Augustine to Hubert Walter. An admirer of Becket, he dedicated his chronicles, which are among the finest of the age, to 'Brother Thomas and our humble community'. They are written in the traditional, generally uncritical monastic style, with the affairs of his priory as the dominant theme, yet are full of valuable information about the period.

GIRALDUS CAMBRENSIS, also known as Gerald of Wales and Gerald de Barri (c. 1146–c. 1220/23), was the youngest son of William de Barri, a Norman knight from Pembrokeshire, by Nesta, a Welsh princess. He was one of the foremost, most prolific and popular writers of his time, and his works include topographical accounts of Ireland (written c. 1188 and dedicated to Henry II) and Wales (1191), the latter – written after he had travelled through the principality in c. 1188 – being perhaps his most famous work. He also wrote the earliest autobiography to survive from the Middle Ages.

Gerald was educated at Gloucester Abbey and in the schools at Paris, and was one of the first to lecture at the new university at Oxford. He was personally acquainted with most of the important public figures of his time, and was an eye-witness to many great events. His style is grand and pompous, and he was a zealous critic of his times. However, he believed in the prophecies of Merlin and often failed to distinguish between history and legend.

An ambitious man, he was appointed Archdeacon of Brecon in 1172, and four years later was elected Bishop of St David's by the cathedral chapter, but after Henry II refused to confirm the appointment because he was suspicious of Gerald's royal Welsh blood, an embittered Gerald became very antagonistic towards the King, whom he had formerly admired, and wrote a waspish and hostile account of him in *Concerning the Instruction of a Prince*, which satirises the fate awaiting a sinful ruler.

Gerald was, however, later reconciled to Henry II and served as a royal chaplain from 1184 to 1189. In 1185, he accompanied the King's son John to Ireland.

His works are prejudiced in favour of the Welsh and the Normans and those in public life with whom he wished to curry favour; he despised the Saxon English, regarded the Irish as sub-human savages and disapproved of Eleanor of Aquitaine, whom he portrays as a sinister, shadowy figure. In fact, he sincerely believed that the Angevin family as a whole had, as they boasted, come from the Devil, as well as from corrupt stock, and would incur the wrath of God.

GUILLAUME LE BRETON was the chaplain of Philip II of France, and wrote the *Philippide*, a laudatory account of his master's reign.

THE ITINERARY OF RICHARD I was translated into Latin from an anonymous French eye-witness account by Richard, Prior of Holy Trinity, Aldgate. The original author stated that, in the midst of the din of war, he had written down things that were 'warm' in his memory.

JOHN OF SALISBURY (c.1115–80), one of the finest minds of the age, studied in Paris under Peter Abélard and was clerk to Pope Eugenius III before becoming secretary to Archbishop Theobald of Canterbury and then Thomas Becket, whose fervent supporter he remained. Estranged from Henry II, he retired in the 1160s to Rheims, where he wrote his *Historia Pontificalis*, amongst other works. Returning to England, he witnessed Becket's murder at Canterbury. In 1176, he was consecrated Bishop of Chartres. His works are rational, moderate and objective, and display a penetrating understanding of statesmanship.

JOSCELIN OF BRAKELOND (c. 1155–1215) was a Benedictine monk at Bury St Edmunds from 1173 and wrote a chronicle covering the period 1173 to 1202, focusing mainly on the history of his abbey.

LAYAMON was an English poet and a priest at Areley Regis near Bewdley in Worcestershire. He wrote *The Brut*, an alliterative history of the English based on the work of Robert Wace, between 1173 and 1207, 'to tell the noble deeds of Englishmen in their own tongue'. His work is the first surviving poem in Middle English. Both Sir Thomas Malory and Alfred, Lord Tennyson drew on his work as a source for their own versions of the Arthurian legends.

PETER OF BLOIS (1135–1205) came from a noble Breton family and, having been educated in the schools of Paris and then attached to the Norman court in Sicily, was invited to England by Henry II, who conferred upon him a succession of court offices, including that of secretary to the King and, later, to Archbishop Baldwin of Canterbury, then to Eleanor of Aquitaine herself. An impressively erudite man, Peter was eventually appointed Archdeacon of Bath, then Archdeacon of London. His surviving letters are distinguished by their sharp, acerbic wit and observation.

PIERS LANGTOFT (d. c.1307) came from Langtoft in Yorkshire and was an Augustinian canon at Bridlington Priory. He wrote a doggerel verse history of England covering the period up to the death of Edward I; his accounts of periods prior to Edward's reign are based on earlier chronicles and are not very reliable.

RALPH OF COGGESHALL (fl. 1207–24) was the Cistercian Abbot of Coggeshall in Essex, whose name has been attached to a chronicle covering the period 1066–1224; it is believed, however, that he wrote only the section from 1187 to 1224. He took pains to be accurate and made it his business to keep himself well informed as to the events of his time, which he was able to do through a wide network of contacts, built up through his monastic connections. For example, he learned about Richard I's battle against the Saracens in 1191 from a soldier who was present, and about Richard's capture by Leopold of Austria from the King's own chaplain, Anselm.

Nevertheless, like many otherwise reliable chroniclers, Ralph of Coggeshall was given to according miraculous events the same prominence as actual ones.

RALPH OF DICETO (d. 1201?) was Archdeacon of Middlesex, Canon and archivist of St Paul's Cathedral and, from 1180, its Dean. His *Images of History*, which covers the period up to 1201, is a concise and readable chronological account of his times. He was a conscientious researcher who took care to be accurate in his facts. His emphasis was on ecclesiastical history, but he used as sources a wealth of royal documents and contemporary letters, many of which he reproduced in his text. Remarkably for his time, he was an objective observer and made an attempt to analyse and evaluate events, such as the conflicts between Henry II and Becket, and between Henry II and his sons. Although Ralph of Diceto was appalled by Becket's murder, he nevertheless admired and respected Henry II.

RALPH NIGER (fl. 1170) was educated in Paris and became clerk to Henry, the Young King. The bulk of his output was religious works, but in later life he compiled two chronicles, drawn mainly from other sources but distinguished by an original, hostile and penetrating attack on Henry II.

RICHARD OF DEVIZES (fl. 1189–92) was a Benedictine monk of St Swithun's Abbey, Winchester, who wrote for his abbot a chronicle describing the deeds of Richard I, from his coronation in 1189 to the end of the Third Crusade in October 1192. His writing was, however, influenced by the romances and *chansons de geste* that were popular in his day, and is consequently dramatic and florid, and not always reliable. He could be acidic and sarcastic in his observations.

It has been suggested that Richard of Devizes, being resident in Winchester when Eleanor was kept a prisoner there in the 1170s and 1180s, would have had some personal knowledge of, and even acquaintance with, her, but there is no proof of this. Later, he was a loyal supporter of Richard I, and his praise of Eleanor for her wise rule during Richard's absence suggests that he had a genuine respect for her.

RICHARD FITZNIGEL was Bishop of London and Treasurer under Henry II, and a brilliant historian. In 1178, he began his great work, *Dialogue Concerning the Exchequer*, a comprehensive survey of the work and procedures of the Exchequer, giving details of the chequered cloth that gave it its name, and of record systems such as wooden tally-sticks and the Pipe Rolls.

ROBERT OF TORIGNI was Abbot of Mont-Saint-Michel in Normandy and knew Henry II personally, but left no description of his appearance or character. Very little else escaped Robert's notice: he meticulously researched his chronicle, which gives a year-by-year account of the period and is a valuable source for the otherwise poorly documented middle years of the twelfth century.

ROBERT WACE (c.1115–c.1183) was born in Jersey, studied in Paris and became a clerk at Caen in Normandy before being appointed Canon of Bayeux by Henry II in 1160/70. Around 1155, Wace wrote the *Roman de Brut*, a Norman-French verse history of England from the time of Brutus, then believed to have been the founder of the English people. It was in this work, based on the chronicle of Geoffrey of Monmouth, that the legend of the Round Table of King Arthur first appeared. Around 1160, Henry II commissioned from Wace the *Roman de Rou*, a metrical history in Norman-French of the dukes of Normandy commencing with Rollo (Rou).

ROGER OF HOVEDEN (d. 1201?) came from Howden in the East Riding of Yorkshire and became a civil servant, an itinerant justice and clerk of the Chapel Royal. He is known to have accompanied Henry II to France in the summer of 1174, and was present at the siege of Acre in 1191. Between 1192 and 1201, after retiring from his post, he is believed – although his authorship is unproven – to have written a massively detailed original account of the deeds of Henry II and Richard I, which was once attributed to Abbot Benedict of Peterborough, who is now thought merely to have commissioned or owned it. This work, which contains transcripts of original documents, is a major source for the period from 1171, despite its author's belief in miracles and supernatural intervention. It is generally favourable to Henry II and Richard I, although the author criticises Henry's dilatory approach to business. Because it was completed early in King John's reign, it is less biased against John than the works of later chroniclers who wrote retrospective studies.

Roger of Hoveden also wrote a chronicle history of England covering the period c. 732–1201.

ROGER OF WENDOVER (d. 1236) was a Benedictine monk at St Albans, and the first chronicler of that abbey. His chronicle, *Flowers of History*, dates from c.1215–35 and covers the period from 1188; he was therefore not an eye-witness to the life of Eleanor of Aquitaine, but drew much of his information from earlier sources, including Roger of Hoveden and Ralph of Diceto. Being resident in an abbey frequented by travellers on the Great North Road, Roger was in a good position to learn of events in the outside world. His work is relatively objective – he was not afraid to level criticism against great men – but not always reliable. His chronicle was later extended by the great thirteenth-century chronicler, Matthew Paris.

WALTER MAP (c.1137–c.1209/1210) came from a noble Anglo-Norman family who lived on the Welsh marches, and was educated in the schools at Paris; a friend of Giraldus Cambrensis, he became a courtier and Canon of St Paul's Cathedral. He served Henry II as a clerk from 1162, and wrote that he was 'dear and acceptable to the King, not for his own merits, but for those of his forebears who had been faithful and useful to the King, both before his accession and after it'. Map also served Henry as an itinerant justice, accompanying him to France in 1173 and 1183, and was later appointed Chancellor of Lincoln. In 1197, Map was made Archdeacon of Oxford.

He was famous in his day as a writer and humorist, and his style is lively, witty and satirical. *De Nugis Curialium* (*Courtiers' Trifles*) is the only one of his works to survive and was written in Latin prose in 1181–92; Map called it 'a little book I have jotted down by snatches at the court of King Henry', and it relates much indiscreet court gossip, as well as anecdotes and apocryphal stories. The sole extant copy is in the Bodleian Library, Oxford; it contains a detailed character sketch of Henry II and evidence that its author did not approve of Eleanor, who was Henry's prisoner at the time he was writing: he recounts with impunity gossip of her alleged affair with Geoffrey of Anjou. Among Map's lost works was, almost certainly, a version of the Arthurian legends, which is thought by some scholars to have been the first of its kind to link the Arthurian cycle of romances with the legend of the Holy Grail.

WILLIAM FITZSTEPHEN wrote, c.1177–80, an invaluable description of the London of his day as a preamble to his life of Thomas Becket, who was born in the city. He claimed that his was the best biography of the murdered Archbishop because he had served in Becket's household as his secretary and had been present at many of the great events of his life, including the confrontation with Henry II at Northampton. He was also an eye-witness to Becket's murder. His is certainly a lively and detailed account, valuable for its social commentary, although it is unashamedly prejudiced in favour of its subject. Nevertheless, FitzStephen was careful not to criticise Henry II.

WILLIAM OF NEWBURGH (c.1135–c.1200) was an Augustinian canon of Newburgh, Yorkshire, and another brilliant historian, whose work is one of the most important sources for Henry II's reign. His *History of English Affairs* covers the period 1066–1198 (at which latter date it was probably written). William of Newburgh wrote in a vivid, pacy style, and took an objective, judicious and relatively impartial approach. Like many chroniclers of the period, he included fantastic anecdotes and accounts of supernatural occurrences.

WILLIAM OF TYRE (c.1130–85) was probably born in Italy; he became an ecclesiastic in Syria, being appointed Archdeacon of Tyre in 1167 and Archbishop in 1175. He began writing 'A History of Deeds done beyond the Sea' – an account of the Second Crusade (1146–8) – around 1170, when he was Bishop of Palestine, where he spent much of his life. He may well have had some personal contact with the crusaders, although he was under twenty at the time. Nevertheless, his work, which covers the period 1095–1184, is well researched and fairly objective, thanks to his living at a distance from those he was writing about. However, it is pro-French in bias, and therefore takes a hostile view of Eleanor.

Bibliography

Primary Sources

Adam of Eynsham: *Magna Vita Sancti Hugonis Episcopi Lincolniensis* (*The Life of St Hugh, Bishop of Lincoln*) (ed. James F. Dimmock, Rolls Series; also ed. Decima L. Douie and David Hugh Farmer, 2 vols, London, 1961; Edinburgh, 1962; reprinted Oxford, 1985)

Addison, Joseph: *The Miscellaneous Works* (ed. A.C. Guthkelch, London, 1914)

Alan of Tewkesbury: *Materials for the History of Thomas Becket* (ed. J.C. Robertson, Rolls Series, 1875–85)

Ambrose: *The Crusade of Richard the Lion Heart* (trans. Morton Jerome Hubert, ed. John L. La Monte, New York, 1941)

Ambrose: *L'éstoire de la guerre sainte* (probably English, late thirteenth century; only exists in a single surviving manuscript in the Vatican Library; ed. G. Paris, Paris, 1897; also in *Three Old French Chronicles*, trans. Edward Noble Stone, Seattle, 1939; also trans. M.J. Hubert and J. La Monte as *The Crusade of Richard Lionheart*, New York, 1941)

Ancient Charters, Royal and Private, Prior to AD 1200 (ed. John Horace Round, Pipe Roll Society, London, 1888)

Andreas Capellanus (Andrew the Chaplain): *De Amore: The Art of Courtly Love* (trans. and ed. John Jay Parry, New York, 1941)

Anecdotes historiques d'Étienne de Bourbon (ed. A. Lecoy de la Marche, Paris, 1877)

The Anglo-Saxon Chronicle (trans. and ed. G.N. Garmonsway, London, 1954)

Annales Monastici (ed. H.R. Luard, 5 vols, Rolls Series, 1864–9)

Annals of Bermondsey (in *Annales Monastici*, ed. H.R. Luard, Rolls Series, 1864–9)

Annals of Margam/*Annales de Margam* (in *Annales Monastici*, ed. H.R. Luard, Rolls Series, 1864)

Annals of Waverley (in *Annales Monastici*, ed. H.R. Luard, Rolls Series, 1864–9)

Anthology of the Provençal Troubadours (ed. R.T. Hill and T.G. Bergin, Yale, 1941; reprinted 1973)

Archives historiques de Poitou (source for Philip of Cognac)

Arnulf of Lisieux: *The Letters of Arnulf of Lisieux* (ed. Frank Barlow, Camden Society, 1939)

The Barnwell Annals (anonymous, ed. William Stubbs in *The Historical Collections of Walter of Coventry*, Rolls Series, 1873)

Baudri de Bourgeuil: *Les oeuvres politiques* (ed. Phyllis Adams, Paris, 1926)

'Benedict of Peterborough': *Gesta Regis Henrici Secundi et Ricardi I: The Chronicle of the Reigns of Henry II and Richard I, known commonly under the name of Benedict of Peterborough*: see Roger of Hoveden: *Gesta Regis Henrici Secundi et Ricardi I*

Benedict/Benôit de Sainte-Maure: *Chronique des ducs de Normandie* (ed. F. Michel, Paris, 1938)

Benedict/Benôit de Sainte-Maure: *Le roman de Troie* (ed. Leopold Constans, Société des Anciens Textes Français, Paris, 1904–12)

Bernard of Clairvaux: *Epistolae: S. Bernardi, Opera Omnia* (ed. J. Mabillon, Vol. I, in *Patrologiae Latinae*, Vol. 182, ed. J.P. Migne, Paris, 1844–64)

Bernard of Clairvaux: *The Letters of St Bernard of Clairvaux* (trans. and ed. Bruno Scott James, Chicago, 1953)

Bernard of Clairvaux: *Oeuvres complètes de Saint Bernard* (Paris, 1873)

Bernard von Ventadour: *Bernard von Ventadour, seine Lieder* (ed. Carl Appel, Halle, 1915)

Bertran de Born; *The Poems of the Troubadour Bertran de Born* (ed. William D. Paden Jr, Tilde Sankovitch and Patricia H. Stablein, University of California, 1986)

Bertran de Born: *Poésies complètes de Bertran de Born* (ed. A. Thomas, Toulouse, 1888)

Bibliothèque des Croisades: History of the Crusades (ed. Joseph Michaud, 4 vols, Paris, 1829; trans. W. Robson, 3 vols, London, 1852)

Bohaddin: 'The Crusade of Richard I, 1189–1192' (in *English History from Contemporary Writers*, ed. D. Nutt, 1888)

Bohn's Antiquarian Library (ed. Henry G. Bohn, 44 vols, London, 1847–1913)

Bouchet, Jean: *Les annales d'Aquitaine* (Poitiers, 1644)

The Brut, or the Chronicles of England (ed. F.W.D. Brie, 2 vols, Early English Texts Society, London, 1906–8)

Calendar of Documents preserved in France illustrative of the History of Great Britain and Ireland, Vol. I, 918–1206 (ed. John Horace Round, London, 1899)

Carmina Burana (ed. A. Hilka and O. Schumann, Heidelberg, 1930–70)

Catalogue des actes de Philippe Auguste (ed. Léopold Delisle, Paris, 1856)

Les chansons de croisade avec leurs mélodies (ed. Joseph Bédier and Pierre Aubry, Paris, 1909; reprinted Geneva, 1974)

Charter Rolls: Rotuli Chartorum (ed. T.D. Hardy, Records Commissioners, London, 1837)

Child, Francis James: *English and Scottish Ballads* (8 vols, Boston, 1857–8)

Choix des poésies originales des troubadours (ed. F.J.M. Raynouard, Paris, 1816–21)

Chrétien de Troyes: *Arthurian Romances* (trans. D.D.R. Owen, London, 1987)

Chrétien de Troyes: *Philomena, conte raconte d'après Ovid par Chrétien de Troyes* (ed. Charles de Boer, Paris, 1909)

The Chronicle of Ernoul and the Continuations of William of Tyre (ed. M.R. Morgan, Oxford, 1973)

The Chronicle of Lanercost (ed. Joseph Stevenson, Edinburgh, 1839)

The Chronicle of Meaux (ed. E.A. Bond, 3 vols, Rolls Series 1866–8)

Chronicles and Memorials of the Reign of Richard I (ed. William Stubbs, 2 vols, Rolls Series, 1864–5)

Chronicles of the Reigns of Stephen, Henry II and Richard I (ed. Richard Howlett, 4 vols, Rolls Series, 1884–90)

The Chronicon of Battle Abbey (ed. J.S. Brewer, Anglia Christiana Society, 1846)

La chronique de Marigny (ed. Leon Mirot, Paris, 1912)

Chronique de Saint-Denis (in *Receuil des historiens des Gaules et de la France*, ed. Leopold Delisle, 24 vols, Paris, 1739–1904)

Chronique de Touraine (ed. A. Salmon, Tours, 1894)

Chroniques des comtes d'Anjou et des siegneurs d'Amboise (ed. L. Halphen and R. Poupardin, Collection des Textes, Paris, 1913)

Chroniques des églises d'Anjou (ed. P. Marchegay and E. Mabille, *Société de l'Histoire de France, Paris,* 1869)

Chronique de Londres (ed. G.J. Aungier, London, 1844)

Chroniques de Normandie (ed. Francisque Michel, Rouen, 1839)

Chroniques de St Martial de Limoges (ed. H. Duplès-Agier, Société de l'Histoire de France, Paris, 1874)

Collection des mémoires relatifs à l'histoire de France depuis la fondation de la monarchie française jusqu'au 13e siècle (ed. F.P.G. Guizot, 32 vols, Paris, 1823–36)

A Collection of all the Wills of the Kings and Queens of England (ed. John Nicholls, London, 1780)

Comnena, Anna: *The Alexiad of Anna Comnena* (trans. Elizabeth Davies, New York, 1967)

Coudrette: *Le roman de Mélusine ou histoire de Lusignan* (ed. Eleanor Roach, Paris, 1982)

Court, Household and Itinerary of King Henry II, instancing also the Chief Agents and Adversaries of the King in his Government, Diplomacy and Strategy (ed. Robert W. Eyton, London, 1878; reprinted New York, 1974)

The Crusade of Richard Lionheart: see Ambrose: *L'éstoire de la guerre sainte*

Curia Regis Rolls: Rotuli Curia Regis (ed. F. Palgrave, Records Commissioners, London, 1835)

Daniel, Samuel: *The Complete Works* (ed. A.B. Grosart, no provenance given, 1885)

Drayton, Michael: see under More, Sir Thomas, *et al.*

English Historical Documents, 1042–1189 (trans. and ed. D.C. Douglas and George W. Greenaway, London, 1953)
English History from Contemporary Writers (ed. D. Nutt, 1888)

Fantosme, Jordan: *Metrical Chronicle: Chronique de la guerre entre les Anglais et les Écossais en 1173 et 1174* (*Chronicle of the War between the English and the Scots in 1173 and 1174*) (in *Chronicles of the Reigns of Stephen, Henry II and Richard I*, ed. Richard Howlett, Rolls Series, 1884–90; also in *English Historical Documents, 1042–1189*, trans. and ed. D.C. Douglas and G.W. Greenaway, London, 1953)
FitzNigel/FitzNeale, Richard: *Dialogus de Scaccario: Dialogue concerning the Exchequer, or, The Course of the Exchequer, by Richard, son of Nigel* (trans. Charles Johnson, London, 1950; reprinted 1963)
FitzStephen, William: *A Description of London* (trans. H.E. Butler with 'A Map of London under Henry II' by Marjorie B. Honeybourne, Historical Association Pamphlets, Nos 93 and 94, 1934)
FitzStephen, William: *Materials for a History of Becket* (ed. J.C. Robertson, Rolls Series, 1875–85; also trans. W.H. Hutton: 'St Thomas from the Contemporary Biographies' in *English History from Contemporary Writers*, ed. D. Nutt, 1889)
FitzStephen, William: 'Vita Sancti Thomae: The Life of Thomas Becket' (trans. and ed. G.W. Greenaway in *The Life and Death of Thomas Becket, Chancellor of England and Archbishop of Canterbury*, The Folio Society, London, 1961)
Florence of Worcester: *Florenti Wigorniensis Monachi Chronicon ex Chronicis: The Chronicle of Florence of Worcester* (ed. B. Thorne, 2 vols, London, 1848–9; also trans. and ed. Thomas Forester, Bohn's Antiquarian Library, London, 1854)
Florilège des troubadours (trans. and ed. André Berry, Paris, 1930)
Foedera, Conventiones, Litterae et cujuscunque generis Acta Publica (ed. Thomas Rymer and Robert Sanderson, 20 vols, London, 1704–35; also ed. A. Clarke and F. Holbrooke, 7 vols, London, 1816–69)
Foliot, Gilbert: *The Letters and Charters of Gilbert Foliot* (ed. A. Morey and C.N.L. Brooke, Cambridge, 1967)
'A French Chronicle of London' (in *Chroniques de Londres*, ed. G.J. Aungier, London, 1844)
Fulcher of Chartres: *Chronicle of the First Crusade* (*Historia Hioerosolymitana* (trans. and ed. M.E. McGinty, Philadelphia, 1941)

Geoffrey of Monmouth: *Historia Regum Britaniae: The History of the Kings of Britain* (trans. and ed. A. Griscom and R.E. Jones, New York, 1929; also ed. J. Hammer, Cambridge, Massachussetts, 1951; also trans. Lewis Thorpe, London, 1966)
Geoffrey de Vigé/Vigeois: *Chronica Gaufredi Coenobitae Monasterii S. Martialis*

Lemovicensis ac Prioris Vosciensis Coenobbi: La chronique de Geoffrey, prieur de Vigeois (in *Nova Bibliotheca Manuscriptorum*, Vol. II, ed. P. Labbé, Paris, 1657; also in *Receuil des historiens des Gaules et de la France*, ed. Léopold Delisle and others, 24 vols, Paris, 1738–1904; also trans. and ed. F. Bonnélye, Tulle, 1864)

Gerald of Wales: see Giraldus Cambrensis

Gervase of Canterbury: *The Deeds of Kings* (ed. William Stubbs in *The Historical Works of Gervase of Canterbury*, Rolls Series, 1880; also in *English Historical Documents, 1042–1189*, trans. and ed. D.C. Douglas and G.W. Greenaway, London, 1953)

Gervase of Canterbury: *Opera Historica: The Historical Works of Gervase of Canterbury* (ed. William Stubbs, 2 vols, Rolls Series, 1879–80)

Gesta Abbatum Monasterii Sancti Albani: Chronici Monasterii S. Albani (Vol. I, ed. H.T. Riley, Rolls Series, 1867)

Gesta Francorum et Aliorum Hierosolimitanorum: The Deeds of the Franks and the Other Pilgrims to Jerusalem (ed. Rosalind Hill, London, 1962)

Gesta Henrici Secundi: The Deeds of Henry II (in *English Historical Documents 1042–1189*, trans. and ed. D.C. Douglas and G.W. Greenaway, London, 1953)

Gesta Regis Ricardi: The Deeds of King Richard (ed. William Stubbs, 2 vols, Rolls Series)

Gesta Stephani: The Deeds of Stephen (anonymous, trans. and ed. Thomas Forester in *Henry of Huntingdon*, Bohn's Antiquarian Library, 1853; also trans. and ed. K.R. Potter, London, 1955)

Giraldus Cambrensis: *The Autobiography of Giraldus Cambrensis/Gerald the Welshman* (trans. and ed. H.E. Butler, London, 1937)

Giraldus Cambrensis: *The First Version of the Topography of Ireland by Giraldus Cambrensis* (trans. J.J. O'Mara, Dundalk, 1951)

Giraldus Cambrensis: *The Journey through Wales, and the Description of Wales* (trans. Lewis Thorpe, London, 1978)

Giraldus Cambrensis: *Opera* (ed. J.S. Brewer, J.F. Dimmock and George F. Warner, 8 vols, Rolls Series, 1861–91)

Giraldus Cambrensis: *De Principis Instructione: Concerning the Instruction of Princes* (trans. J. Stevenson, London, 1858; also ed. George F. Warner, Rolls Series, 1861–91)

Giraldus Cambrensis: *De Vita Galfredi: The Life of Geoffrey* (ed. J.S. Brewer, Rolls Series, 1861–91)

Gottfried von Strasburg: *Tristan, with the Surviving Fragments of the Tristan of Thomas* (ed. A.T. Hatto, London, 1960)

The Great Rolls of the Pipe for the First Year of the Reign of King Henry II (in *The Red Book of the Exchequer*, Vol. II, ed. H. Hall, 3 vols, Rolls Series, 1896)

The Great Rolls of the Pipe for the Second, Third and Fourth Years of the Reign of King Henry II, 1155–1158 (ed. Joseph Hunter, Records Commission, London, 1844)

The Great Rolls of the Pipe of the Reign of Henry the Second, 5th to 34th Years (30 vols, Pipe Roll Society, London, 1884–1925)

The Great Roll of the Pipe for the Thirty-Third Year of the Reign of King Henry the Second, AD 1186–7 (ed. John Horace Round, Pipe Roll Society, London, 1915)

The Great Roll of the Pipe for the First Year of the Reign of Richard I, 1189–90 (ed. J. Hunter, London, 1844)

The Great Rolls of the Pipe for the Reign of Richard I (Pipe Roll Society, London, 1925–33)

Grim, Edward: *Materials for a History of Thomas Becket* (ed. J.C. Robertson, Rolls Series, 1875–85)

Guiart, Guillaume: *Branches des royaux lignages* (Fourteenth-century verse history; ed. J.A. Buchon, Paris, 1920)

Guillaume le Breton: *Gesta Philippe Augusti: Philippide* (ed. H.F. Delaborde, 2 vols, Paris, 1882–5)

Guillaume le Clerc: *The Romance of Fergus, or Fergus of Galloway, Knight of King Arthur* (ed. Wilson Frescoln, Philadelphia, 1983; also trans. D.D.R. Owen, London, 1991)

Guillaume de Nangis: *Chronique* (in *Collection des mémoires relatifs à l'Histoire de France . . .*, ed. F.P.G. Guizot, 32 vols, Paris, 1823–36)

Guy de Bazoches: *Éloge de Paris* (trans. Helen Waddell, undated)

Hearne, Thomas: see under More, Sir Thomas, *et al.*

Helinant de Froidmont: *Chronicon* (ed. J.P. Migne in *Patrologia Latinae*, Vol. 212, Paris, 1855)

Henry of Bracton: *De Legibus et Consuetudinibus Angliae* (ed. T. Twiss, 6 vols, Rolls Series, 1878–83)

Henry of Huntingdon: *The Chronicle of Henry of Huntingdon* (trans. and ed. Thomas Forester, Bohn's Antiquarian Library, London, 1853)

Henry of Huntingdon: *Historiae Anglorum: The History of the English* (ed. T. Arnold, Rolls Series, 1879)

Herbert of Bosham: *Materials for the History of Thomas Becket* (ed. J.C. Robertson, Rolls Series, 1875–85)

Higden, Ranulf: *Polychronicon* (fourteenth century, 9 vols, ed. Joseph Rawson Lumby, Rolls Series, 1882)

L'Histoire de Guillaume le Maréchale, Comte de Striguil et de Pembroke: The History of William the Marshal, Earl of Striguil and Pembroke (written c. 1225; trans. and ed. Paul Meyer, 3 vols, Société de l'Histoire de France, Paris, 1891–1901)

Histoire des ducs de Normandie et des rois d'Angleterre (ed. Francisque Michel, Société de l'Histoire de France, Paris, 1840)

The Icelandic Life of Becket: Thomas Saga Erkibyskups (trans. and ed. Eirikr Magnusson, Rolls Series, 1875–83)

Itinerarium et Peregrinorum et Gesta Regis Ricardi (ed. William Stubbs, Rolls Series, 1864)

The Itinerary of King Richard I (trans. in *Chronicles of the Crusades*, Bohn's Antiquarian Library, 1865; also ed. Lionel Landon, Pipe Roll Society, London, 1935)

Joffroi de Poitiers: *Roman d'aventures du XIIIe siècle* (ed. Perceval B. Fay and John L. Grigsby, Textes Littéraires Français, Geneva and Paris, 1972)

John de Marmoutier: *The Chronicles of the Counts of Anjou (and) Historia Gaufredi Ducis Normannorum et Comitis Andegavorum: The History of Geoffrey, Duke of Normandy and Count of Anjou* (ed. L. Halphen and R. Poupardin in *Chroniques des Comtes d'Anjou et d'Amboise*, Collection des Textes, Paris, 1913)

John of Salisbury: *Ioannis Saresberiensis Historia Pontificalis: John of Salisbury's Memoirs of the Papal Court* (trans. and ed. Marjorie Chibnall, London, 1956; reprinted Oxford, 1986)

John of Salisbury: *The Letters of John of Salisbury* (ed. W.J. Millor and H.E. Butler, revised (C.N.L. Brooke, 2 vols), London, 1955 and 1965)

John of Salisbury: *Materials for the History of Thomas Becket* (ed. J.C. Robertson, Rolls Series, 1875–85)

John of Salisbury: *Policraticus: The Statesman's Book* (trans. John Dickinson, New York, 1927)

Joscelin of Brakelond: *Chronica Jocelini de Brakelonde De Rebus Gestis Samsonis, Abbatis Monasteri Sancti Edmundi* (trans. and ed. H.E. Butler, Oxford, 1949)

Journey Through Wales/Description of Wales (trans. and ed. Lewis Thorpe, London, 1978)

Langtoft, Piers: *The Chronicle of Pierre de Langtoft*, in *French Verse from the Earliest Period to the Death of Edward I* (ed. T. Wright, 2 vols, Rolls Series, London, 1866–8)

Layamon: see under Wace

Letters of the Kings of England (ed. James O. Halliwell-Phillipps, Vol. I, London, 1848)

Letters of the Queens of England, 1100–1547 (ed. Anne Crawford, Stroud, 1994)

Letters of Royal and Illustrious Ladies of Great Britain (ed. Mary Anne Everett Wood, 3 vols, London, 1846)

Liberate Rolls (3 vols, Rolls Series, London, 1916–37)

The Life and Death of Thomas Becket, Chancellor of England and Archbishop of Canterbury (various accounts, trans. and ed. G.W. Greenaway, The Folio Society, London, 1961)

Lyrics of the Troubadours and Trouvères (ed. Frederick Goldin, New York, 1973)

Map, Walter: *De Nugis Curialium: Courtiers' Trifles* (ed. T. Wright, Camden Society, 1850; also trans. and ed. M.R. James, Oxford, 1914; revised C.N.L.

Brooke and R.A.B. Mynors, Oxford, 1983; also trans. and ed. Frederick Tupper and M.B. Ogle, London, 1924)

Marie de France: *Lais* (ed. A. Ewart, Oxford, 1944)

Materials for the History of Thomas Becket, Archbishop of Canterbury (various accounts, ed. J.C. Robertson, Vols 1–6, and J.B. Sheppard, Vol. 7, Rolls Series, 1875–85)

Minstrel of Rheims: *Récits d'un ménestrel de Reims, or, The Chronicle of Rheims* (thirteenth century, ed. Natalis de Wailly, Paris, 1876; also in *Three Old French Chronicles*, trans. Edward Noble Stone, Seattle, 1939)

Der Mittelenglische Versroman über Richard Löwenherz: The Middle English Romance of Richard the Lion Heart (thirteenth-century romance of the life of Richard I, now only surviving in a fourteenth-century Middle English version; trans. and ed. Karl Brunner in *Wiener Beiträge zur Englischen Philologie Vol. XLII*, Vienna and Leipzig, 1913)

More, Sir Thomas; Drayton, Michael; Hearne, Thomas, and others: *The Unfortunate Royal Mistresses, including Rosamund Clifford and Jane Shore, Concubines to King Henry the Second and Edward the Fourth, with Historical and Metrical Memoirs of those Celebrated Persons* (London, 1825?)

Niketas Choniates: *Die Krone de Komnenen: die Regierungszeit der Kaiser Joannes und Manuel Komnenos (1118–1180) aus dem Geschichtswerk des Niketas Choniates* (trans. Franz Grabler, Byzantine Geschichtzschreiber VII; Graz-Vienna-Cologne, 1958)

Niketas Choniates: *Nicetae Choniatae Historia: Corpus Scriptorum Historiae Byzantinae* (ed. Emmanuel Bekker, Bonn, 1835)

Niño, Pedro: *Sumario de los Reyes de España* (in *Colección de las crónicas de Castilla*, Madrid, 1782)

Nouvelle anthologie des Troubadours (ed. J. Audiau, Paris, 1928)

Odo de Deuil: *De Ludovici VII Francorum Regis, Profectione in Orientem* (trans. and ed. Virginia D. Berry, New York, 1948; also ed. H. Waquet, Paris, 1949)

Ordericus Vitalis: *Orderici Vitalis Angligenae Coenobi Uticensis Monachi, Historia Ecclesiae: The Ecclesiastical History of England and Normandy* (ed. A. le Prevost, 5 vols, Société de l'Histoire de France, Paris, 1838–55; also trans. and ed. Thomas Forester, 4 vols, Bohn's Antiquarian Library, London, 1853–6)

Oeuvres de Rigord et de Guillaume le Breton, historiens de Philippe Auguste (ed. H.F. Delaborde, 2 vols, Société de l'Histoire de France, Paris, 1882–5)

Paris, Matthew: *Chronica Major* (ed. H.R. Luard, 7 vols, Rolls Series, 1872–3)

Paris, Matthew: *Flores Historiarum* (once erroneously ascribed to Paris; see under Roger of Wendover)

Paris, Matthew: *Historia Anglorum, sive, ut vulgo dicitur, Historia Minor* (ed. Sir Frederick H. Madden, 3 vols, Rolls Series, 1866–9)

Patrologiae Latinae, Cursus Completus a Tertullian ad Innocentium III, Series Latinae (ed. J.P. Migne, 221 vols, Paris, 1844–64)

Percy, Thomas: *Reliques of Ancient English Poetry* (ed. R.A. Willmott, London, undated)

Peter of Blois: *Petri Blensis Archidiaconi Opera Omnia* (ed. J.A. Giles, 4 vols, Oxford, 1846–7; also in *Patrologiae Latinae*, Vol. CCVII, ed. J.P. Migne, Paris, 1855)

The Peterborough Chronicle: Chronicon Angliae Petriburgense, 1070–1154 (ed. J.A. Giles, London, 1945; also ed. Cecily Clark, Oxford, 1970)

The Pilgrimage of Charlemagne: Le Pèlerinage de Charlemagne and Aucassin and Nicolette: Aucassin et Nicolette (ed. Anne Elizabeth Cobby and Glyn S. Burgess, New York and London, 1988)

Pipe Rolls: see *The Great Rolls of the Pipe*

Ralph of Coggeshall: *Radulphi de Coggeshall Chronicon Anglicanum: The English Chronicle* (ed. Joseph Stevenson, Rolls Series, 1875)

Ralph of Diceto: *Imagines Historiarum: Images of History* (ed. William Stubbs in *The Historical Works of Master Ralph of Diceto*, Rolls Series, 1876)

Ralph of Diceto (Diss): *Radulfi de Diceto Decani Londoniensis Opera Historica: The Historical Works of Master Ralph of Diceto, Deacon of London* (ed. William Stubbs, 2 vols, Rolls Series, 1876)

Ralph Niger: *Radulphi Nigri Chronica* (ed. Robert Anstruther, Caxton Society, London, 1851)

Raoul de Cambrai (ed. Sarah Kay, Oxford, 1992)

The Receipt Roll of the Exchequer for Michaelmas Term 1185 (ed. Hubert Hall, London School of Economics, 1899)

Receuil des actes de Henri II, roi d'Angleterre et duc de Normandie, concernant les provinces françaises et les affaires de France (ed. Léopold Delisle and Elie Berger, 4 vols, Paris, 1906–27)

Receuil des actes de Philippe Auguste, roi de France (ed. H.F. Delaborde *et al.*, 3 vols, Paris, 1916–66)

Receuil d'annales Angevins et Vendômoises (ed. L. Halphen, Paris, 1903)

Receuil des historiens des croisades: Auteurs occidentaux (5 vols, Paris, 1872–1906) and *Auteurs orientaux* (5 vols, Paris, 1872–1906) (par les soins de l'Académie Impériale des Inscriptions et Belles-Lettres)

Receuil des historiens des Gaules at de la France: Rerum Gallicarum et Francicarum Scriptores (ed. Léopold Delisle, M. Bouquet *et al.*, 24 vols, Paris, 1738–1904)

The Red Book of the Exchequer (ed. H. Hall, 3 vols, Rolls Series, 1896)

Richard of Devizes: *Chronicon Richardi Divisensis de tempore Regis Richardi Primi: Richard of Devizes' Chronicle of the Times of King Richard the First* (in *Chronicles of the Reigns of Stephen, Henry II and Richard I*, ed. Richard Howlett, Rolls Series, 1884–90; also trans. and ed. John T. Appleby, London, 1963)

Richard of Hexham: *Historia Ricardi, Prioris Ecclesia Haugustaldensis, De Gesta Regis Stephani: Richard, Prior of Hexham's History of the Deeds of King Stephen*

(in *Chronicles of the Reigns of Stephen, Henry II and Richard I*, ed. Richard Howlett, Rolls Series, 1884–90)

Richard le Poitevin: *Ex Chronico* (in *Receuil des historiens des Gaules et de la France*, ed. Léopold Delisle *et al.*, 24 vols, Paris, 1738–1904)

Rigord: *Gesta Philippi Augusti: The Deeds of Philip Augustus* (ed. H.F. Delaborde in *Oeuvres de Rigord et de Guillaume le Breton*, Société de l'Histoire de France, 1882–5)

Rishanger William: *Chronica* (ed. H.T. Riley, Rolls Series, 1865)

Robert of Torigny: *Chronica Roberti de Torigneio, Abbatis Monasterii Sancti Michaelis in Periculo Maris* (in *Chronicles of the Reigns of Stephen, Henry II and Richard I*, ed. Richard Howlett, Rolls Series, 1884–90)

Roger of Hoveden (or Howden): *Annals* (trans. and ed. Henry T. Riley, 2 vols, Bohn's Antiquarian Library, London, 1853)

Roger of Hoveden: *Chronica Magistri Rogeri de Houedene* (ed. William Stubbs, 4 vols, Rolls Series, 1868–71)

Roger of Hoveden: *Gesta Regis Henrici Secundi et Gesta Ricardi I: The Deeds of King Henry the Second and the Deeds of Richard I* (previously attributed erroneously to Benedict of Peterborough; ed. William Stubbs, 2 vols, Rolls Series, 1867)

Roger of Pontigny: *Materials for the History of Thomas Becket* (ed. J.C. Robertson, Rolls Series, 1875–85)

Roger of Wendover: *Chronica Rogeri de Wendover liber qui dictus Flores Historiarum: Flowers of History* (formerly ascribed to Matthew Paris; ed. H.O. Coxe, English Historical Society, 1841–4; also trans. J.A. Giles, 2 vols, Bohn's Antiquarian Library, London, 1849; also ed. H.J. Hewlett, Rolls Series, 1886–9; also ed. H.R. Luard, 3 vols, Rolls Series, 1890)

The Rolls Series: *Rerum Britannicarum Medii Aevi Scriptores, or, Chronicles and Memorials of Great Britain and Ireland during the Middle Ages, published under the Authority of the Master of the Rolls* (198 vols, HMSO, London, 1858–99)

Le roman de Renart (trans. and ed. Jean Dufournet, 2 vols, Paris, 1985)

Rotuli Litterarum Patentium in Turri Londinensi Asservati (ed. T.D. Hardy, Record Commissioners, London, 1835)

Royal Writs in England from the Conquest to Glanville (ed. R.C. van Caenegem, Selden Society, London, 1959)

Shakespeare, William: *King John* (ed. E.A.J. Honigmann, The Arden Shakespeare, London, 1954)

Simeon of Durham: *Historical Works* (ed. T. Arnold, 2 vols, Rolls Series, 1882–5)

The Song of Roland (trans. D.D.R. Owen, London, 1972)

Suger: *Oeuvres de Suger* (ed. A. Lecoy de la Marche, Paris, 1867)

Suger: *Vie de Louis VI le Gros par Suger, suivie de l'histoire du roi Louis VII: Historia Ludovici VII* (ed. Auguste Molinier, Paris, 1887; also ed. Henri Waquet, Paris, 1929)

Thomas: *Les fragments du roman de Tristan, poème du XIIe siècle* (ed. Bartina H. Wind, Textes Littéraires Français, Geneva and Paris, 1960) (see also under Gottfried von Strasburg)

Thomas: *The Romance of Tristram and Ysolt by Thomas of Britain* (trans. Roger Sherman Loomis, New York, 1931)

Thomas Agnellus: *De Morte et Sepultura Henrici Regis Junioris* (ed. Joseph Stevenson in *Ralph of Coggeshall: The English Chronicle*, Rolls Series, 1875)

Three Old French Chronicles (trans. Edward Noble Stone, University of Washington, Seattle, 1939)

Vidal, Pierre: *Poésie* (ed. D.S. Avalle, Milan, 1960)

Wace, Robert: *Le roman de Brut* (ed. J. Arnold, 2 vols, Société des Anciens Textes Français, Paris, 1938–40)

Wace, Robert: *Le roman de Rou* (ed. A.J. Holden, Société des Anciens Textes Français, Paris, 1970)

Wace, Robert, and Layamon: *Arthurian Chronicles* (trans. Eugène Mason, London 1912, 1962)

Walter of Coventry: *Memoriale Walteri de Coventria: The Historical Collections of Walter of Coventry* (also contains the Barnwell Annals; ed. William Stubbs, Rolls Series, 1872–3)

Walter of Guisborough: *The Chronicle of Walter of Guisborough* (ed. H. Rothwell, London, 1957)

William IX, Duke of Aquitaine: *Les chansons de Guillaume IX* (ed. Alfred Jeanroy, Classiques Français du Moyen Age, Paris, 1927)

William of Canterbury: *Materials for the History of Thomas Becket* (ed. J.C. Robertson, Rolls Series, 1875–85)

William of Malmesbury: *De Gestis Regum Anglorum libri quinque* (ed. William Stubbs, 2 vols, Rolls Series, 1887–9)

William of Malmesbury: *Historia Novella* (ed. K.R. Potter, London, 1955)

William of Newburgh: *Historia Rerum Anglicarum: The History of English Affairs* (ed. Thomas Hearne, 3 vols, Oxford, 1719; also ed. Richard Howlett in *Chronicles of the Reigns of Stephen, Henry II and Richard I*, Rolls Series, 1844–90 also in *English Historical Documents, 1042–1189*, trans. and ed. D.C. Douglas and G.W. Greenaway, London, 1953; also trans. and ed. P.G. Walsh and M.J. Kennedy, Warminster, 1988)

William of Orange: *Les chansons de geste du cycle de Guillaume d'Orange* (ed. Jean Frappier, Paris, 1965)

William of Orange: *Four Old French Epics* (trans. D.G. Hoggan, ed. Glanville Price, London, 1975)

William of Poitiers: *Les chansons de Guillaume IX, duc d'Aquitaine* (ed. A. Jeanroy, Paris, 1927)

William of Tyre: *The Chronicle of Ernoul and the Continuations of William of Tyre* (ed. M.R. Morgan, Oxford, 1973)

William of Tyre: *Guillaume de Tyr et ses continuateurs* (ed. Paulin Paris, 2 vols, Paris, 1879–80)
William of Tyre: *A History of Deeds done beyond the Sea* (trans. and ed. E.A. Babcock and A.C. Krey, 2 vols, New York, 1943; reprinted 1976)

Secondary Sources

Abel, F.M.: *L'état de la cité de Jerusalem au XIIe siècle* (Publication of the Council of the Pro-Jerusalem Society, 1920–2)
Appel, C.: *Bertrand van Born* (Halle, 1931)
Appel, C.: *Provenzalische Chrestomathie* (Leipzig, 1912)
Appleby, John T.: *England Without Richard, 1189–1199* (London, 1965)
Appleby, John T.: *Henry II: The Vanquished King* (London, 1962)
Appleby, John T.: *The Troubled Reign of King Stephen* (London, 1969)
Arbellot, F.: *Vérité sur la mort de Richard Coeur de Lion* (Paris, 1878)
d'Arbois de Jubainville, M.H.: *L'histoire des ducs et des comtes de Champagne* (Paris, 1860)
L'Art de vérifier les dates (18 vols, Paris, 1818–19)
Ashdown, Dulcie M.: *Ladies in Waiting* (London, 1976)
Ashe, Geoffrey: *The Quest for Arthur's Britain* (London, 1968)
Ashley, Maurice: *The Life and Times of King John* (London, 1972)

Barber, Richard: *The Devil's Crown: Henry II, Richard I, John* (London, 1978)
Barber, Richard: *Henry Plantagenet: A Biography of Henry II of England* (London, 1964; reprinted 1972)
Barker, J.R.V.: *The Tournament in England, 1100–1400* (Woodbridge, 1986)
Barlow, Frank: *The Feudal Kingdom of England, 1042–1216* (London, 1955)
Beech, G.T.: *A Rural Society in Mediaeval France: The Gatine of Poitou in the Eleventh and Twelfth Centuries* (Baltimore, 1964)
Benton, John F.: 'The Court of Champagne as a Literary Centre' (*Speculum*, 36, 1961)
Bezzola, R.R.: *Les origines et la formation de la littéraire courtoise en occident, 500–1200* (5 vols, La Société Courtoise, Paris, 1944–63)
Bienvenu, Jean-Marc: 'Aliénor d'Aquitaine et Fontevraud' (*Cahiers de Civilisation Médiévale*, 29, 1986)
Bingham, Caroline: *The Crowned Lions: The Early Plantagenet Kings* (Newton Abbot, 1978)
Bloch, M.: *Les rois thaumaturges. Étude sur le caractère supernaturel attribué à la puissance royale particulièrement en France et Angleterre* (Strasburg, 1924)
Boase, T.S.R.: *Fontevraut and the Plantagenets* (*Journal of the British Archaeological Association*, 34, 1971)
Boissonade, Prosper: 'L'ascension, le déclin et la chute d'un grand état féodal due centre-ouest: les Taillefer et les Lusignans, comtes de la Marche et d'Angoulême et leurs relations avec les Capétiens et les Plantagenêts,

1137–1314' (*Bulletins et Mémoires de la Société Archéologiques de la Charente*, 1935)

Boissonade, Prosper: 'Les comtes d'Angoulême – les ligues féodales contre Richard Coeur de Lion et les poésies de Bertran de Born, 1176–1194' (*Annales du Midi*, 7, 1895)

Boissonade, Prosper: *Histoire de Poitou* (Paris, 1926)

Boussard, Jacques: *Le comté d'Anjou sous Henri Plantagenêt et ses fils, 1151–1204* (Paris, 1938)

Boussard, Jacques: *Le gouvernement d'Henri II Plantagenêt* (Paris, 1956)

Boussard, Jacques: *Nouvelle histoire de Paris de la fin du siège de 885–886 à la mort de Philippe August* (Paris, 1976)

Boutière, Jean, and Schutz, A.H.: *Biographies des troubadours: textes provençaux des XIIIe et XIVe siècles* (Paris, 1964)

Bregy, Katherine: *From Dante to Jeanne d'Arc: Adventures in Mediaeval Life and Letters* (New York, 1964)

Bridge, Anthony: *Richard the Lionheart* (London, 1989)

Brooke, Christopher: *From Alfred to Henry III* (Edinburgh, 1961)

Brooke, Christopher: *The Twelfth-Century Renaissance* (London, 1969)

Brooke, Christopher, and Keir, Gillian: *The History of London: London 800–1216: The Shaping of a City* (London, 1975)

Brooke, C.N.L.: 'The Marriage of Henry II and Eleanor of Aquitaine' (*The Historian*, 20, 1988)

Brooke, Z.N., and Brooke, C.N.L.: 'Henry II, Duke of Normandy and Aquitaine' (*English Historical Review*, 61, 1946)

Broughton, Bradford B.: *The Legends of King Richard I, Coeur de Lion* (The Hague, 1966)

Brown, E.A.R.: *The Monarchy of Capetian France and Royal Ceremonial* (Aldershot, 1991)

Bruce, J.C.: *The Evolution of Arthurian Romance from the Beginnings down to the Year 1300* (2 vols, Baltimore, 1928)

Brundage, James A.: *Richard Lion Heart* (New York, 1973)

Carducci, Giosuè: *Un poeta d'amore nel secolo XII* (in *Opere*, vol. III, Bologna, 1893)

De Castries, Duc: *The Lives of the Kings and Queens of France* (New York, 1979)

Chambers, F.W.: 'Some Legends Concerning Eleanor of Aquitaine' (*Speculum*, 16, 1941)

Chapman, Robert L.: 'Notes on the Demon Queen Eleanor' (*Modern Language Notes*, June 1955)

Chartrou, Josèphe: *L'Anjou de 1109 à 1151, Foulque de Jérusalem et Geoffroi Plantagenêt* (Paris, 1928)

Chayter, H.J.: *The Troubadours* (Cambridge, 1912)

Cheney, C.R.: *Hubert Walter* (London, 1967)

Chronicle of the Royal Family (ed. Derrik Mercer, London, 1991)

Churchill, Sir Winston S.: *A History of the English Speaking Peoples* (London, 1956)

Clédat, Léon: *Du rôle historique de Bertrand de Born, 1175–1200* (Paris, 1879)

Coulton, G.G.: *Life in the Middle Ages* (4 vols, London and New York, 1930)

Davis, H.W.C.: *England under the Normans and Angevins, 1066–1272* (London, 1905)

Davis, R.H.C.: *King Stephen, 1135–1154* (London, 1967)

Demimuid, Maurizio: *Jean de Salisbury* (Paris, 1873)

The Dictionary of National Biography (ed. Leslie Stephen and Sidney Lee, 63 vols, Oxford, 1885–1900)

Diehl, Charles: *La société byzantine à l'époque des Comnenes* (Paris, 1929)

Diener, Bertha: *Imperial Byzantium* (trans. Eden Paul and Cedar Paul, Boston, 1938)

Douie, D.L.: *Archbishop Geoffrey Plantagenet* (York, 1960)

Dronke, Peter: *Mediaeval Latin and the Rise of the European Love Lyric* (2 vols, Oxford, 1965–6)

Dufour, J.M.: *De l'ancien Poitou et de sa capitale* (Poitiers, 1826)

Duggan, Alfred: *Devil's Brood: The Angevin Family* (London, 1957)

Edwards, Cyril: 'The Magnanimous Sex Object: Richard the Lionheart in the Mediaeval German Lyric' (in *Courtly Literature: Culture and Context*, ed. Keith Busby and Erik Cooper, Amsterdam and Philadelphia, 1990)

Eleanor of Aquitaine: Patron and Politician (ed. W.W. Kibler, Austin, Texas, 1976)

Facinger, Marion: 'A Study in Mediaeval Queenship: Capetian France, 987–1237' (in *Studies in Mediaeval and Renaissance History*, Vol. 5, Nebraska, 1968)

Fawtier, Robert: *The Capetian Kings of France* (trans. L. Butler and J. Adam, London, 1960)

Foreville, R.: *L'église et la royauté en Angleterre sous Henri II Plantagenêt* (Paris, 1943)

Fowler, G.: 'Henry FitzHenry at Woodstock' (*English Historical Review*, 49, 1924)

Gervaise, F.A.: *Histoire de Suger* (3 vols, Nevers, 1721)

Gillingham, John: *The Life and Times of Richard I* (London, 1973)

Gillingham, John: 'Richard I and Berengaria of Navarre' (*Bulletin of the Institute of Historical Research*, 1980)

Gillingham, John: *Richard the Lionheart* (London, 1978)

Given-Wilson, Chris, and Curteis, Alice: *The Royal Bastards of Mediaeval England* (London, 1984)

Great Dynasties (various authors, New York, 1976)

Green, Mary Anne Everett: *Lives of the Princesses of England from the Norman Conquest* (6 vols, London, 1849–55)

Grousset, René: *Histoire des croisades et du royaume franc de Jérusalem* (3 vols, Paris, 1934–6)

Hall, Hubert: *Court Life under the Plantagenets* (London, 1890)

Hallam, E.M.: 'Royal Burial and the Cult of Kingship in France and England, 1060–1330' (*Journal of Mediaeval History*, 8, 1982)

Halphen, Louis: *Paris sous les premiers Capetiens* (Paris, 1909)

Hammond, Peter: *Her Majesty's Royal Fortress of the Tower of London* (HMSO, London, 1987)

Harvey, John: *The Plantagenets* (London, 1948)

Harvey, Ruth E.: *The Troubadour Marcabru and Love* (London, 1989)

Haskell, Daniel C.: *Provençal Literature and Language, including the Local History of Southern France* (New York, 1925)

Haskins, Charles Homer: *The Renaissance in the Twelfth Century* (Cambridge and Harvard, 1927; reprinted New York, 1957)

Hassall, W.O.: *They Saw It Happen, 55 BC–AD 1485* (Oxford, 1957)

Hassall, W.O.: *Who's Who in History, Vol. I, 55 BC–1485* (Oxford, 1960)

Heltzel, Virgil B.: *Fair Rosamund: A Study of the Development of a Literary Theme* (Evanston, Illinois, 1947)

Henderson, Philip: *Richard Coeur de Lion* (New York, 1959)

Heslin, Anne: 'The Coronation of the Young King in 1170' (in *Studies in Church History*, Vol. 2, ed. G.J. Cunning, London, 1968)

Hibbert, Christopher: *The Court at Windsor* (London, 1964)

Hibbert, Christopher: *The Tower of London* (London, 1971)

Hindley, Geoffrey: *The Book of Magna Carta* (London, 1990)

Hodgson, C.E.: *Jung Heinrich, König von England, Sohn König Heinrichs II, 1155–83* (Jena, 1906)

Holt, J.C.: *King John* (Cambridge, 1963)

Hope, W.H. St J.: 'On the Funeral Effigies of the Kings and Queens of England' (*Archaeologia*, 60, 1907)

Howard, Philip: *The Royal Palaces* (Boston, 1970)

Howitt, M.: *Biographical Sketches of the Queens of England* (London, 1866)

Imbert, Hughes: *Notice sur les vicomtes de Thouars* (Thouars, 1864)

Jenner, Heather: *Royal Wives* (London, 1967)

Joliffe, J.E.A.: *Angevin Kingship* (London, 1955)

Kelly, Amy: 'Eleanor of Aquitaine and her Courts of Love' (*Speculum*, 12, 1937)

Kelly, Amy: *Eleanor of Aquitaine and the Four Kings* (Harvard and London, 1950)

Kiessman, Rudolph: *Untersuchen über die Bedeutung Eleanorens von Poitou für die Litterature ihrer Zeit* (Bernberg, 1901)

Kirchhoff, Elisabeth: _Rois et reines de France_ (Paris, 1996)

Knowles, Dom. D.: _The Episcopal Colleagues of Thomas Becket_ (Cambridge, 1961)

Knowles, Dom. D.: _Thomas Becket_ (London, 1971)

Labande, Edmond-René: 'Les filles d'Aliénor d'Aquitaine: étude comparative' (_Cahiers de Civilisation Médiévale_, 29, 1986)

Labande, Edmond-René: 'Pour une image véridique d'Aliénor d'Aquitaine' (_Bulletin de la Société des Antiquaires de l'Ouest_, 4th Series, 2, Poitiers, 1952)

Lane, Henry Murray: _The Royal Daughters of England_ (2 vols, London, 1910)

De Larry, Isaac: _Histoire d'Eléonor de Guyenne_ (Rotterdam, 1691; London, 1788)

Legg, L.G.W.: _English Coronation Records_ (Westminster, 1901)

Lees, Beatrice A.: 'The Letters of Queen Eleanor of Aquitaine to Pope Celestine III' (_English Historical Review_, 21, 1906)

Leese, T. Anna: _Blood Royal: Issue of the Kings and Queens of Mediaeval England, 1066–1399_ (Bowie, Maryland, 1996)

Lejeune, R.: 'Le rôle littéraire de la famille d'Aliénor d'Aquitaine' (_Cahiers de Civilisation Médiévale_, 1, 1958)

The Lives of the Kings and Queens of England (ed. Antonia Fraser, London, 1977)

Lloyd, Alan: _King John_ (Newton Abbot, 1973)

Lofts, Norah: _Queens of Britain_ (London, 1977)

De Loi, Raimon: _Trails of the Troubadours_ (New York, 1926)

Loomis, Roger Sherman: _Arthurian Literature in the Middle Ages: A Collaborative History_ (Oxford, 1959)

Loomis, Roger Sherman: 'Tristram and the House of Anjou' (_Modern Language Review_, 17, 1922)

Louda, J., and Maclagan, M.: _Lines of Succession: Heraldry of the Royal Families of Europe_ (London, 1981)

Lyttelton, Lord George: _The History of the Life of King Henry the Second_ (4 vols, London, 1767–71)

Marlow, Joyce: _Kings and Queens of Britain_ (London, 1977)

Meade, Marion: _Eleanor of Aquitaine: A Biography_ (London, 1977)

Mediaeval Monarchs (ed. Elizabeth Hallam, London, 1990)

Michaud, Joseph: _A History of the Crusades_ (trans. W. Robson, 3 vols, New York, 1881)

Mitchell, Mairin: _Berengaria, Enigmatic Queen of England_ (London, 1986)

La Monte, J.L.: _Feudal Monarchy in the Latin Kingdom of Jerusalem, 1100–1291_ (Cambridge, Massachusetts, 1932)

Moore, Olin H.: 'The Young King, Henry Plantagenet (1155–1183)' in _History, Literature and Tradition_ (Ohio State University: _University Studies_, Vol. 2, No. 12, 1924)

Morby, John E.: _Handbook of Kings and Queens_ (London, 1989)

Munro, D.C.: _The Kingdom of the Crusaders_ (New York, 1935)

Nitze, W.A.: 'The Exhumation of King Arthur at Glastonbury' (*Speculum*, 9, 1934)

Norgate, Kate: *England under the Angevin Kings* (2 vols, London, 1887)

Norgate, Kate: *John Lackland* (London, 1902)

Norgate, Kate: *Richard the Lion Heart* (London, 1924)

De La Noy, Michael: *Windsor Castle, Past and Present* (London, 1990)

Owen, D.D.R.: *Eleanor of Aquitaine, Queen and Legend* (Oxford, 1993)

Owen, D.D.R.: *Noble Lovers* (London, 1975)

Owen, D.D.R.: 'The Prince and the Churl: The Traumatic Experience of Philip Augustus' (*Journal of Mediaeval History*, 17, 1992)

The Oxford Book of Royal Anecdotes (ed. Elizabeth Longford, Oxford, 1989)

Pacaut, Marcel: *Louis VII et son royaume* (Paris, 1964)

Pain, Nesta: *Empress Matilda, Uncrowned Queen of England* (London, 1978)

Pain, Nesta: *The King and Becket* (New York, 1967)

Painter, Sidney: 'The Houses of Lusignan and Chatellerault, 1150–1250' (*Speculum*, 30, 1955)

Painter, Sidney: 'The Lords of Lusignan in the Eleventh and Twelfth Centuries' (*Speculum*, 32, 1957)

Painter, Sidney: *The Reign of King John* (Baltimore, 1949)

Painter, Sidney: *William Marshal, Knight-Errant, Baron and Regent of England* (Baltimore, 1933; reprinted Toronto, 1982)

Parsons, John Carmi: *Eleanor of Castile: Queen and Society in Thirteenth-Century England* (New York, 1995)

Pernoud, Régine: *Blanche of Castile* (London, 1975)

Pernoud, Régine: *Eleanor of Aquitaine* (Paris, 1965; London, 1967)

Petit-Dutaillis, Charles E.: *Le déshéritement de Jean sans Terre et le meutre d'Arthur de Bretagne* (Paris, 1925)

Petit-Dutaillis, Charles E.: *Feudal Monarchy in France and England from the Tenth to the Thirteenth Century* (trans. E.D. Hunt, New York, 1964)

The Plantagenet Encyclopaedia (ed. Elizabeth Hallam, London, 1996) Plumb, J.H.: *Royal Heritage* (London, 1977)

Poole, Austin Lane: *From Domesday Book to Magna Carta, 1087–1216* (Oxford, 1951)

Poole, R.L.: 'Henry Plantagenet's Early Visits to England' (*English Historical Review*, 47, 1932)

Powicke, Sir F. Maurice: *The Loss of Normandy, 1189–1203* (Manchester, 1913; reprinted 1961)

Raby, F.J.E.: *A History of Christian-Latin Poetry from the Beginnings to the Close of the Middle Ages* (Oxford, 1953)

Ramsay, Sir J.H.: *The Angevin Empire, or the Three Reigns of Henry II, Richard I and John, 1154–1216* (Oxford, 1903)

Ramsay, Sir J.H.: *A History of the Revenues of the Kings of England, 1066–1399* (Oxford, 1925)

Richard, Alfred: *Histoire des ducs et des comtes de Poitou, 778–1204* (2 vols, Paris, 1903)

Richardson, Helen G.: 'The Letters and Charters of Eleanor of Aquitaine' (*English Historical Review*, 74, 1959)

Richardson, Helen G.: 'The Marriage and Coronation of Isabella of Angoulême' (*English Historical Review*, 61, 1946)

Riffault, Robert: *The Troubadours* (Indiana, 1965)

Robinson, J.A.: 'Peter of Blois' (in *Somerset Historical Essays*, London, 1921)

Rorimer, J.J.: *The Cloisters* (New York, 1938)

Rosenberg, Melrich V.: *Eleanor of Aquitaine, Queen of the Troubadours and of the Courts of Love* (Boston and New York, 1937)

Round, John Horace: *Feudal England: Historical Studies on the Eleventh and Twelfth Centuries* (London, 1895; reprinted London, 1964)

Runciman, Sir Stephen: *Byzantine Civilisation* (London, 1936)

Runciman, Sir Stephen: *A History of the Crusades* (Cambridge, 1951–4)

Salvini, J.: 'Aliénor d'Aquitaine' (in *Dictionnaire de biographie française* (Paris, 1933–67)

Schirmer, Walter F., and Broich, Ulrich: *Studiem zum literarischen Patronat im England des 12. Jahrhunderts* (Cologne and Opladen, 1962)

Schlight, John: *Henry II Plantagénet* (New York, 1973)

Schramm, P.E.: *A History of the English Coronation* (trans. G. Wickham-Legg, Oxford, 1937)

Seward, Desmond: *Eleanor of Aquitaine: The Mother Queen* (London, 1978)

Smith, C.E.: *Papal Reinforcement of some Mediaeval Marriage Laws* (Louisiana, 1940)

Softly, Barbara: *The Queens of England* (Newton Abbot, 1976)

Stenton, Frank M.: *Norman London* (includes a translation of William FitzStephen's *Description of London* by H.E. Butler) (Historical Association Pamphlet, London, 1934)

Stimming, Albert: *Bertran van Born* (Romanische Bibliothek, Halle, 1892)

Stothard, C.A.: *The Monumental Effigies of Great Britain* (ed. J. Hewitt, London, 1876)

Strickland, Agnes: *Lives of the Queens of England* (8 vols, London, 1852; reprinted Bath, 1974)

Stubbs, William: *The Early Plantagenets* (London, 1903)

Stubbs, William: *Historical Introduction to the Rolls Series* (London, 1902)

Swinburne, Algernon Charles: *The Tragedies, Vol. I* (London, 1905)

Tennyson, Alfred, Lord: *The Life and Works of Alfred, Lord Tennyson*, Vol. XI (London, 1899)

Thomas, Antoine: *Bertran van Born, poésies complètes* (Toulouse, 1888)

Treece, Henry: *The Crusades* (New York, 1964)

Turner, Ralph V.: 'Eleanor of Aquitaine and her Children: An Inquiry into Mediaeval Family Attachment' (*Journal of Mediaeval History*, 14, 1988)

Vaissete, Joseph: *Abrégé de l'histoire générale de Languedoc* (5 vols, Paris, 1799)
De Villepreux, L.: *Eléonore de Guyenne* (Paris, 1862)

Waddell, Helen: *The Wandering Scholars* (London, 1954)
Walker, Curtis: *Eleanor of Aquitaine* (Richmond, Virginia, 1950)
Ward, P.L.: 'The Coronation Ceremony in Mediaeval England' (*Speculum*, 14, 1939)
Warren, W.L.: *Henry II* (London, 1973)
Warren, W.L.: *King John* (London, 1961)
Webb, G.: 'Fontevrault' (*Life of the Spirit*, January, 1962)
Weir, Alison: *Britain's Royal Families: The Complete Genealogy* (London, 1989)
White, Freda: *Ways of Aquitaine* (London, 1968)
Winston, Richard: *Becket* (London, 1967)
Women and Power in the Middle Ages (ed. M. Erler and M. Kowaleski, Athens, Georgia, 1988)

Notes and References

1 'Opulent Aquitaine'

1 *Chroniques des églises d'Anjou*
2 For the history of the Counts of Poitou and Dukes of Aquitaine, and in particular for the life of William IX, see Ordericus Vitalis; see also Alfred Richard: *Histoire des ducs et des comtes de Poitou*, which draws heavily on original sources (hereafter referred to as Richard).
3 Gervase of Canterbury
4 *Chroniques des comtes d'Anjou*
5 William of Malmesbury
6 Ibid.
7 Ordericus Vitalis
8 William of Malmesbury
9 Giraldus Cambrensis
10 William of Malmesbury
11 Ibid.
12 Giraldus Cambrensis
13 Geoffrey de Vigeois
14 Bernard of Clairvaux: *Letters*
15 Bernard of Clairvaux: *Epistolae*
16 Richard le Poitevin
17 For William X's will and death, see Ordericus Vitalis
18 Ordericus Vitalis; Suger: *Vie de Louis VI*
19 Suger

2 'A Model of Virtue'

1 Suger; Richard
2 Suger
3 Ibid.

4 Ibid.
5 Walter Map
6 Suger; he is the chief source for the early life of Louis VII
7 Suger
8 Geoffrey de Vigeois
9 Ibid.
10 Suger
11 Ibid. Geoffrey de Vigeois; Richard
12 *La chronique de Marigney, Chronicle of Montierneuf Abbey*
13 *Chronique de Touraine*
14 Suger; Richard; *Chronique de Touraine*
15 Suger; Richard
16 Ordericus Vitalis
17 Ibid.
18 Ibid.
19 Richard
20 Guy de Bazoches: *Éloge de Paris* (quoted in Amy Kelly, 'Eleanor of Aquitaine').
21 Stephen of Paris, chronicler; Giraldus Cambrensis
22 Richard
23 Ibid.
24 For this episode, see Suger

3 'Counsel of the Devil'

1 For the Toulouse campaign, see Ordericus Vitalis
2 For the summer in Poitou, see Richard
3 *Historia Francorum* (in *Receuil des historiens des Gaules et de la France*); *Chronico Mauriniacensi*
4 *Historia Francorum*
5 For the holocaust at Vitry, see *Historia Francorum*
6 *Receuil des historiens*
7 Ibid.
8 F. A. Gervaise: *Histoire de Suger*
9 Ibid.; Suger
10 Ibid.
11 *Vita Tertia, fragments of a life of Bernard of Clairvaux* by Galfredas Claras Vallensis (in *Patrologiae Latinae*, ed. Migne)
12 Ibid. Migne cites several other contemporary accounts of this meeting, but all are third-hand and vary slightly in detail.
13 Odo de Deuil
14 William of Tyre
15 Ibid.
16 Odo de Deuil
17 Ibid.

18 Ibid.; see also *La chronique de Marigny*
19 Suger
20 Odo de Deuil
21 Ibid.
22 William of Newburgh
23 *Bibliothèque des croisades*
24 This tale is repeated as fact by many later writers, notably de Larry: *Histoire d'Eléonor de Guyenne*; Michaud: *A History of the Crusades*; and Strickland: *Lives of the Queens of England*.
25 Niketas Choniates (see Chapter 4)
26 Odo de Deuil
27 *Chronique des églises d'Anjou*
28 Odo de Deuil
29 Ibid.
30 John of Salisbury: *Historia Pontificalis*
31 Odo de Deuil
32 Henry of Huntingdon

4   'To Jerusalem!'

1 *Gestes de Louis VII* (in *Bibliothèque des Croisades*)
2 Odo de Deuil
3 Ibid.
4 Ibid.
5 Ibid.
6 Ibid.
7 Ibid.; William of Tyre
8 Odo de Deuil
9 Ibid.
10 Ibid.
11 William of Tyre
12 Odo de Deuil
13 William of Tyre
14 Ibid.
15 Ibid.
16 Ibid.
17 Ibid.; Odo de Deuil
18 The chief sources for this episode and its aftermath are William of Tyre, Odo de Deuil and the *Gestes de Louis VII* (see note 1).
19 Odo de Deuil; Guillaume de Nangis
20 Odo de Deuil
21 Ibid.
22 William of Tyre
23 For descriptions of Antioch, see William of Tyre and Fulcher of Chartres.

24 William of Tyre
25 Ibid.
26 Ibid.
27 Ibid.
28 John of Salisbury; his account of the rift between Louis and Eleanor appears in his *Historia Pontificalis*, written in the 1160s. All his subsequent quotations in this chapter are taken from this work.
29 William of Tyre
30 Ibid.
31 Quoted in Harvey: *The Troubadour Marcabru and Love*
32 John of Salisbury
33 Ibid.
34 Ibid.
35 Guillaume de Nangis
36 John of Salisbury; William of Newburgh; Suger
37 John of Salisbury
38 Ibid.
39 Ibid.
40 Ibid.
41 Ibid.
42 His letter is lost, but its contents may be inferred from Suger's reply, which is printed in *Receuil des historiens*.
43 William of Tyre
44 For Louis' reception in Jerusalem, see William of Tyre and the *Chronique de Saint-Denis* (in *Receuil des historiens*).
45 William of Tyre
46 Henry of Huntingdon
47 William of Tyre
48 Ibid.
49 John of Salisbury
50 For this episode, see John of Salisbury, Guillaume de Nangis and a letter from Louis to Suger in *Receuil des historiens*.
51 William of Tyre
52 Letter in *Receuil des historiens*.
53 John of Salisbury
54 Ibid.
55 This is inferred from the fact that the Pope made them share a bed (see the following paragraph). Some writers assert that Eleanor was pregnant when she arrived in Tusculum, but this is highly unlikely.
56 John of Salisbury
57 Ibid.
58 Ibid. (all quotes)
59 Ibid.
60 Gervaise: *Histoire de Suger*

5 'A Righteous Annulment'

1 Ralph of Coggeshall; Ralph of Diceto
2 Gervase of Canterbury
3 William of Newburgh
4 The dating is inferred from the fact that sexual relations between Louis and Eleanor were resumed in October 1149
5 *Chronique de Saint-Denis* (in *Receuil des historiens*)
6 Matthew Paris
7 Giraldus Cambrensis
8 Ibid.
9 The palace of the Plantagenets at Angers was demolished in the reign of Louis IX of France and rebuilt in 1228–30
10 The chief sources for the history of the counts of Anjou are the *Chronicles* (or the *Deeds*) of the counts of *Anjou* (Chroniques des comtes d'Anjou), which exists in several versions and was compiled in the twelfth century by various writers, among them Odo, Abbot of Marmoutier in the Loire Valley, and Thomas of Loches, who flourished around 1130. John, a monk of Marmoutier, wrote a new version of the chronicle in 1164–73, which includes a laudatory life of Count Geoffrey the Fair and was dedicated to Geoffrey's son, Henry II of England, who was patron of the abbey of Marmoutier. The *Chronicle* recounts the history of the counts of Anjou from the tenth to the twelfth centuries, and is a mixture of fact and myth: most of the passages dealing with the early counts are based on legend.
11 Ibid.
12 Ibid.
13 Ibid.; abridged from John of Marmoutier
14 Ralph of Diceto
15 His work is now lost
16 William of Malmesbury
17 *Gesta Stephani*
18 *Chroniques des comtes d'Anjou*
19 Ibid.
20 William of Conches: *Dragmaticon*, dedicated to Geoffrey of Anjou
21 Giraldus Cambrensis
22 *The Anglo-Saxon Chronicle*
23 Walter Map
24 Ibid.
25 Ibid.
26 Ibid.
27 Giraldus Cambrensis
28 Gervase of Canterbury; Master Matthew may perhaps be identified with Henry's future chancellor and Bishop of Angers

29 Giraldus Cambrensis
30 Walter Map
31 Henry of Huntingdon
32 Giraldus Cambrensis
33 Walter Map
34 Giraldus Cambrensis
35 Ibid.
36 Henry of Huntingdon
37 Giraldus Cambrensis
38 Henry of Huntingdon
39 Peter of Blois
40 Ralph Niger
41 Ibid.
42 Giraldus Cambrensis
43 Peter of Blois
44 Giraldus Cambrensis
45 Walter Map
46 Ibid.
47 Robert of Torigni
48 During the tenth century the Vexin had been partitioned: the northern part, with the city and castle of Gisors, was absorbed into Normandy, and the southern area became part of France. Ever since then, the Norman Vexin had been a bone of contention between the kings of France and the dukes of Normandy.
49 Robert of Torigni
50 Ibid.
51 John of Marmoutier
52 Robert of Torigni
53 John of Marmoutier. The enamel plaque is now in the municipal museum at Le Mans. The inscription translates as: 'By your sword, Seigneur, the troop of brigands has been put to flight, and through the restoration of peace, repose given to the Church.'
54 *Chronique de Touraine;* Geoffrey of Vigeois; Guillaume de Nangis; Richard
55 See, for example, Helinand of Froidmont, poet and chronicler at the court of Philip II of France (his *Chronicon* is in *Patrologiae Latinae*); also the Minstrel of Rheims and later sources quoted by Pacaut.
56 Bouchet: *Les Annales d'Aquitaine*

6 *'A Happy Issue'*

1 *Chronique de Touraine*
2 Ibid.
3 Gervase of Canterbury
4 *Chronique de Touraine*; Gervase of Canterbury; Robert of Torigni; William of Newburgh

5 Richard

6 cf. Richard of Devizes, who called her 'a common English whore who scorned no filthiness'.

7 Giraldus Cambrensis

8 Gervase of Canterbury

9 Giraldus Cambrensis

10 Robert of Torigni

11 Ibid.

12 Ibid.

13 Ibid.; *Gesta Stephani*; Gervase of Canterbury

14 Robert of Torigni

15 Richard

16 Ibid.

17 Ibid.

18 This biography was by Uc of Saint-Circ, who is quoted in *Choix des poésies originales des troubadours*, ed. Raynouard; see also *Bernard von Ventadour, seine Lieder*, ed. Appel; *Florilège des troubadours*, ed. Berry; Carducci: *Un poeta d'amore nel secolo XII*; and *Anthology of the Provençal Troubadours*, ed. Hill and Bergin.

19 Henry of Huntingdon

20 Ibid.

21 *Gesta Stephani*

22 Gervase of Canterbury

23 Ibid.; Robert of Torigni

24 Ralph of Diceto

25 William, who had secured the rich earldom of Surrey by marrying the heiress Isabella de Warenne, had taken no part in the civil war, or expressed any desire to become king.

26 Robert of Torigni

27 *English Historical Documents*

28 Henry of Huntingdon

29 Ibid.

30 Walter Map

31 His reign would not officially begin until the day of his coronation. Until then he would be styled *dominus*, or the Lord Henry. As was customary in early medieval times, his regnal years would be dated from the day of his coronation.

32 Henry of Huntingdon

33 Robert of Torigni

34 *Choix des poésies originales des troubadours*, ed. Raynouard; Boutière and Schutz: *Biographies des troubadours*

35 *Les origines . . . de la littéraire courtoise*, ed. Bezzola

36 Henry of Huntingdon

37 *The Anglo-Saxon Chronicle*

38 Ralph of Diceto

39 Henry of Huntingdon
40 Ibid.
41 Gervase of Canterbury
42 The *Chronicon* of Battle Abbey
43 Gervase of Canterbury
44 Henry of Huntingdon; for the coronation, see also Gervase of Canterbury, Robert of Torigni and William of Newburgh
45 Henry of Huntingdon
46 Ibid.
47 William of Newburgh

7 *'All the Business of the Kingdom'*

1 *The Anglo-Saxon Chronicle*
2 Richard FitzNigel
3 Giraldus Cambrensis
4 Walter Map
5 Ibid
6 William of Malmesbury
7 Roger of Hoveden
8 Peter of Blois

8 *'Eleanor, by the Grace of God, Queen of England'*

1 *The Anglo-Saxon Chronicle*
2 William of Newburgh
3 Ibid.
4 Ibid.
5 Walter Map
6 William of Newburgh
7 Ibid.
8 Pipe Rolls
9 Richard FitzNigel
10 Adam of Eynsham
11 Walter Map
12 Ibid.
13 Adam of Eynsham
14 William of Newburgh
15 *Rotuli Curiae Regis* (ed. F. Palgrave, Records Commissioners, 1835)
16 Peter of Blois
17 Ralph of Diceto
18 William of Newburgh
19 Ralph of Diceto
20 Ibid.
21 Peter of Blois

22 Translation by Owen in *Eleanor of Aquitaine*

23 Pipe Rolls

24 *Court, Household and Itinerary of King Henry II*

25 Peter of Blois

26 Layamon

27 See Owen: *Eleanor of Aquitaine*

28 Giraldus Cambrensis

29 Ibid.

30 Ibid. Although the tomb was destroyed and the bones dispersed during the Reformation, the site is still marked in the abbey ruins.

31 Peter of Blois

32 Ibid.

33 Ibid.

34 Ibid.

35 Ibid.

36 *Constitutio Domus Regis* (see C. Johnson: 'The System of Account in the Wardrobe of Edward I' (Transactions of the Royal Historical Society, 4th series, 6, 1923)

37 *Court, Household and Itinerary*; *The Red Book of the Exchequer*

38 Ibid.

39 Ibid.

40 John of Salisbury: *Policraticus*

41 Giraldus Cambrensis

42 Pipe Rolls

43 Ibid.

44 Ibid.

9   *'The King Has Wrought a Miracle'*

1 Gervase of Canterbury

2 For the life, career and character of Becket, see chiefly *Materials for the History of Thomas Becket*; *The Icelandic Life of Becket*; John of Salisbury; Edward Grim; William of Canterbury; William FitzStephen; and Herbert of Bosham.

3 Henry of Huntingdon

4 William FitzStephen

5 Roger of Hoveden

6 William FitzStephen

7 Ibid.

8 Ibid.

9 Ralph of Diceto

10 Gervase of Canterbury

11 Robert of Torigni

12 William FitzStephen; *Court, Household and Itinerary*; J.H. Ramsay: *A History of Revenues of the Kings of England*

13 William of Newburgh
14 Roger of Hoveden; Robert of Torigni
15 Pipe Rolls
16 Robert of Torigni
17 Founded by Matilda of Scotland, first queen of Henry I
18 Gervase of Canterbury; *Court, Household and Itinerary*; charters in *Receuil des actes de Henri II*; Richard
19 Jacques Boussard
20 William of Newburgh
21 Ralph of Diceto
22 Ibid. The significance of this act is still not understood by historians.
23 *Receuil des historiens*
24 For details of Becket's visit to Paris, see William FitzStephen
25 Robert of Torigni
26 Ralph of Diceto
27 Ibid.
28 Robert of Torigni is the main source for the Toulouse campaign; see also *Materials for the History of Thomas Becket.*
29 Robert of Torigni
30 Ralph of Diceto
31 William FitzStephen
32 Ibid.
33 Robert of Torigni
34 Pipe Rolls
35 Ibid.
36 Ralph of Diceto; Gervase of Canterbury
37 Robert of Torigni
38 Pipe Rolls
39 Ralph of Diceto
40 Ibid.
41 Roger of Hoveden
42 William of Newburgh
43 Ibid.
44 Roger of Hoveden
45 Robert of Torigni
46 Gervase of Canterbury
47 Not 1162, the date incorrectly given in some modern history books.
48 *Patrologiae Latinae*
49 Ralph of Diceto
50 Herbert of Bosham
51 Ibid.; William of Canterbury; John of Salisbury
52 Pipe Rolls
53 John of Salisbury
54 Ralph of Diceto
55 Herbert of Bosham

56 William FitzStephen
57 Ibid.; Herbert of Bosham
58 Herbert of Bosham

10 *'Conjectures which Grow Day by Day'*

1 Herbert of Bosham
2 *Materials for the History of Thomas Becket*
3 Ibid.
4 Roger of Pontigny; Herbert of Bosham
5 J.H. Ramsay: *A History of the Revenues of the Kings of England*
6 *Court, Household and Itinerary*
7 Ibid.
8 Roger of Pontigny
9 Letter of Gilbert Foliot
10 Roger of Pontigny
11 Roger of Hoveden; Gervase of Canterbury; Edward Grim; Herbert of Bosham
12 Herbert of Bosham
13 William FitzStephen
14 William of Canterbury
15 Gervase of Canterbury
16 Roger of Pontigny
17 Pipe Rolls
18 Roger of Pontigny
19 *Materials for the History of Thomas Becket*; John of Salisbury
20 William of Newburgh
21 Ibid.; Herbert of Bosham; William FitzStephen
22 *Court, Household and Itinerary*
23 Robert of Torigni
24 *Materials for the History of Thomas Becket*
25 Roger of Hoveden
26 Ralph of Diceto
27 Robert of Torigni; William of Newburgh; Ralph of Diceto
28 For a full discussion of these legends and the literary tradition surrounding Rosamund de Clifford, see Owen: *Eleanor of Aquitaine*.
29 Translation by John of Trevisa, 1387
30 Ralph of Diceto
31 Pipe Rolls
32 Pipe Rolls
33 Roger of Hoveden
34 John of Salisbury
35 *Court, Household and Itinerary*
36 1167 is the date given by Robert of Torigni, but it must be inaccurate: in

1167 Henry was on the continent and Eleanor in England at the time when she would have conceived, and both spent Christmas in Normandy.

37 Ralph of Diceto; *Court, Household and Itinerary*, quoting the chronicler Matthew of Westminster, who also gives the date as 1166

38 *Court, Household and Itinerary*

39 Pipe Rolls

40 Her remains were later removed to Rouen Cathedral

41 Ralph of Diceto

42 *Court, Household and Itinerary*

43 Ibid.

44 Ibid.

45 Robert of Torigni; Gervase of Canterbury

46 Some writers claim that Eleanor stayed in Lusignan Castle, but she could not have done, because it was then occupied by the rebel Lusignans.

47 Bibliothèque Nationale MSS. Latin 5480, Paris

48 Robert of Torigni; *Chronique des églises d'Anjou*

49 *L'Histoire de Guillaume le Maréchale*

50 For this episode, see *L'Histoire de Guillaume le Maréchale*; Gervase of Canterbury; Roger of Hoveden

51 *L'Histoire de Guillaume le Maréchale*

52 William FitzStephen; Ralph Niger

53 See below, Chapter 13

54 Ralph Niger

55 *Court, Household and Itinerary*

56 Giraldus Cambrensis

57 Ralph Niger

11 'The Holy Martyr'

1 Gervase of Canterbury

2 Robert of Torigni; John of Salisbury. The office of seneschal of France had previously been bestowed by Louis on another son-in-law, Theobald of Blois.

3 William of Canterbury

4 Robert of Torigni

5 William of Canterbury

6 Giraldus Cambrensis; Richard

7 Herbert of Bosham

8 Ibid.

9 Robert of Torigni

10 Ralph of Diceto

11 Ibid.; William FitzStephen

12 He was a son of Earl Robert of Gloucester, Henry I's bastard son.

13 Ralph of Diceto

14 William FitzStephen

15 *Court, Household and Itinerary*
16 Ibid.
17 Robert of Torigni
18 Ibid.
19 Ralph of Diceto; the date is sometimes given erroneously as 24 May
20 A few twelfth-century chroniclers refer to him as Henry III
21 William of Canterbury; Matthew Paris
22 *L'Histoire de Guillaume le Maréchale*
23 Walter Map
24 Geoffrey of Vigeois
25 Walter Map
26 Ambrose
27 Giraldus Cambrensis
28 Walter Map
29 *L'Histoire de Guillaume le Maréchale*
30 Roger of Hoveden
31 Robert of Torigni
32 Walter Map
33 William of Newburgh
34 *L'Histoire de Guillaume le Maréchale*
35 Giraldus Cambrensis
36 Ibid.
37 Adam of Eynsham
38 Geoffrey of Vigeois
39 Ibid.; Gervase of Canterbury
40 Ralph of Diceto
41 William FitzStephen
42 *Materials for the History of Thomas Becket*
43 Roger of Hoveden
44 Robert of Torigni
45 Richard
46 Ralph of Diceto
47 Ibid.
48 William FitzStephen
49 Herbert of Bosham
50 Ralph of Diceto
51 Roger of Hoveden
52 William FitzStephen
53 Ibid.
54 William of Newburgh
55 Edward Grim; he knew Becket personally and wrote a biography of him around 1175–7. There are two other versions of the King's speech in *Materials for the History of Thomas Becket*, the version given in this text being an amalgamation of all three.
56 William of Newburgh

57 There are nine contemporary accounts of the murder of Becket, four of them by eye-witnesses. The account given here is by one of the latter, Edward Grim.
58 Edward Grim
59 *Materials for the History of Thomas Becket*
60 Ibid.
61 William FitzStephen
62 Edward Grim
63 William FitzStephen
64 Edward Grim; Ralph of Diceto

12   'The Cubs Shall Awake'

 1 Roger of Hoveden
 2 Ibid.
 3 William of Newburgh
 4 Roger of Hoveden
 5 Edward Grim
 6 *English Historical Documents*; see also Ralph of Diceto
 7 Ralph of Diceto
 8 Ibid.
 9 William FitzStephen
10 *Materials for the History of Thomas Becket*
11 Ralph of Diceto
12 Roger of Hoveden
13 Ibid.; Gervase of Canterbury; William of Newburgh
14 Roger of Hoveden
15 Geoffrey of Vigeois; some sources give the date of Richard's investiture as Duke of Aquitaine as 1170 or 1179, but it is clear that Geoffrey of Vigeois is correct.
16 Richard
17 *Itinerary of Richard I*
18 Ralph of Coggeshall
19 Ralph of Diceto
20 Charter of Eleanor to the abbey of Fontevrault, 1199
21 *Itinerary of Richard I*
22 Ibid.
23 Giraldus Cambrensis
24 *Chronique de Touraine*
25 Ralph of Diceto; Roger of Hoveden
26 Ralph of Diceto
27 Roger of Hoveden; Gervase of Canterbury
28 Jordan Fantosme
29 Robert of Torigni
30 William of Newburgh

31 Roger of Hoveden

13 *'Beware of Your Wife and Sons'*

1 Ralph of Diceto
2 Geoffrey of Vigeois
3 Ibid.
4 Ralph of Diceto; Robert of Torigni
5 William of Newburgh; Ralph of Diceto; Robert of Torigni
6 Ralph of Diceto
7 Roger of Hoveden; Gervase of Canterbury; Ralph of Coggeshall
8 Roger of Hoveden
9 William of Newburgh
10 Ibid.
11 For the rebellion of 1173–4, see chiefly William of Newburgh; Gervase of Canterbury; Roger of Hoveden; *Gesta Henrici Secundi*; Peter of Blois; Robert of Torigni, and Ralph of Diceto
12 Giraldus Cambrensis
13 *Patrologiae Latinae*; *Receuil des historiens*
14 Gervase of Canterbury. Gervase is the only chronicler to mention Eleanor's arrest, and then only to express shock at the fact that she was wearing male attire, which was then considered a serious offence against good order in society and was virtually heresy, as far as the Church was concerned. Gervase does not specify when or where the arrest of the Queen took place, but since he places it between his accounts of the princes' departure for Paris and the outbreak of hostilities in May, it is likely that it occurred in the spring, rather than the autumn of 1173, as some historians have suggested.
15 Richard
16 *Gesta Henrici Secundi*
17 Roger of Hoveden
18 Gervase of Canterbury
19 Roger of Hoveden; Ralph of Diceto
20 Ralph of Diceto
21 Ibid.
22 Richard le Poitevin; Robert of Torigni
23 *Gesta Henrici Secundi*
24 Roger of Hoveden
25 Ralph of Diceto
26 Ibid.
27 Roger of Hoveden
28 Ralph of Diceto
29 Jordan Fantosme
30 Ralph of Diceto; Roger of Hoveden
31 Roger of Hoveden

32 Ralph of Diceto

33 Ibid.

34 Ralph of Diceto, Gervase of Canterbury and the *Gesta Henrici Secundi* all state that Eleanor was taken to Winchester; only Geoffrey de Vigeois says she was first taken to Salisbury.

35 Ralph of Diceto

36 Giraldus Cambrensis; Roger of Hoveden

37 Gervase of Canterbury

38 Roger of Wendover

39 Ibid.

40 Gervase of Canterbury

41 Jordan Fantosme

42 Gervase of Canterbury

43 For this episode, see Jordan of Fantosme; Roger of Hoveden; and William of Newburgh

44 Ralph of Diceto

45 Ibid.

46 Scotland remained a fief of England until 1189, when Richard I, in need of money for his crusade, revoked the Treaty of Falaise in return for 10,000 marks.

47 Ralph of Diceto

48 Ibid.

49 The figure usually quoted is £15,000 in Angevin pounds, which is equivalent to £3,750 in English pounds.

50 For the Treaty of Montlouis, see Ralph of Diceto: Roger of Hoveden; and William of Newburgh.

51 Roger of Hoveden

52 Ralph of Diceto

53 Giraldus Cambrensis

14   'Poor Prisoner'

1 Gervase of Canterbury

2 Pipe Rolls

3 Roger of Hoveden; Ralph of Diceto

4 Giraldus Cambrensis

5 Roger of Hoveden; Ralph of Diceto

6 Roger of Hoveden

7 Ralph of Diceto

8 Ibid.

9 Ibid.

10 Ibid.

11 Ibid.

12 Roger of Hoveden

13 Ibid; Ralph of Diceto

14 Adam of Eynsham
15 Roger of Hoveden
16 Ibid.
17 Bertran de Born
18 Roger of Hoveden
19 *L'Histoire de Guillaume le Maréchale*
20 Ralph of Diceto
21 Roger of Hoveden
22 Roger of Wendover
23 This is inferred from the fact that Eleanor was at Winchester for Michaelmas in September.
24 Ralph of Diceto
25 Pipe Rolls
26 Her name is variously given as Hawise, Hawisa, Avise, Avisa or Isabella
27 See Owen: *Eleanor of Aquitaine*; T.A. Archer's article on Rosamund Clifford in the *Dictionary of National Biography*; and Chambers; 'Some Legends concerning Eleanor of Aquitaine'.
28 Roger of Hoveden
29 For Rosamund's reburial, see Ranulf Higden's *Polychronicon*
30 Roger of Hoveden
31 Ralph of Diceto; Pipe Rolls
32 Roger of Hoveden
33 Ibid.
34 Ibid.
35 Ibid.
36 Ibid.
37 Ibid.
38 Ibid.
39 *The Chronicle of Meaux*
40 Roger of Hoveden
41 Ralph of Diceto
42 Ibid.
43 Ibid.
44 Roger of Hoveden
45 Ibid.
46 Ibid.; Ralph of Diceto
47 Giraldus Cambrensis
48 Ralph of Diceto
49 Ibid.
50 William of Tyre
51 Robert of Torigni; Roger of Hoveden
52 Roger of Hoveden; *Choix des poésies originales des troubadours*; Antoine Thomas: *Bertran van Born*; Clédat: *Du rôle historique de Bertran de Born*; Stimming: *Bertran van Born*
53 Robert of Torigni; Roger of Hoveden

54 Ralph of Diceto
55 Roger of Hoveden
56 Ibid.
57 Robert of Torigni
58 Roger of Hoveden
59 *Histoire de Guillaume le Maréchale*
60 Gervase of Canterbury
61 Ralph of Diceto
62 Ibid.
63 Ibid.; Roger of Hoveden; Gervase of Canterbury
64 Ralph of Diceto
65 For the rising in Aquitaine, see Roger of Hoveden and Geoffrey of Vigeois.
66 Roger of Hoveden
67 Gervase of Canterbury
68 Geoffrey of Vigeois
69 Walter Map
70 Roger of Hoveden; *Patrologiae Latinae*
71 Walter Map; Geoffrey of Vigeois
72 Roger of Hoveden
73 Ralph of Diceto
74 Geoffrey of Vigeois
75 Ibid.
76 Geoffrey of Vigeois is the principal source for the Young King's death.
77 *L'Histoire de Guillaume le Maréchale*
78 Ralph of Coggeshall
79 William of Newburgh
80 Geoffrey of Vigeois
81 Roger of Hoveden
82 Ralph of Diceto
83 Ibid.
84 Ralph of Coggeshall
85 *Foedera, Conventiones*
86 *Gesta Henrici Secundi*
87 Ralph of Diceto
88 Roger of Hoveden
89 Ralph of Diceto

15   Shame, 'Shame on a Conquered King!'

1 William of Newburgh
2 Roger of Hoveden
3 Ibid.
4 Gervase of Canterbury
5 *Chronique de Saint-Denis*

6 When his tomb in Worcester Cathedral was opened in 1797, John's skeleton was found to measure five feet five inches.

7 Richard of Devizes

8 *The Chronicle of Meaux*

9 William of Newburgh

10 Ralph of Diceto

11 Matthew Paris

12 Roger of Wendover; Matthew Paris

13 Matthew Paris

14 Roger of Hoveden

15 Ibid.

16 *The Chronicle of Meaux*

17 Roger of Hoveden

18 Giraldus Cambrensis

19 Pipe Rolls

20 Ralph of Diceto

21 Ibid.

22 Pipe Rolls

23 Ibid.

24 Roger of Hoveden; Geoffrey of Vigeois

25 Roger of Hoveden

26 Her birthdate is given as 1184 or 1186, but 1184 is the date accepted by most historians.

27 Roger of Hoveden

28 Henry also declined to accept the crown of Jerusalem for himself.

29 Roger of Hoveden

30 It would be rebuilt in the Gothic style by Bishop Hugh of Avalon from 1192.

31 *Gesta Henrici Secundi*; Roger of Hoveden

32 Roger of Hoveden

33 *Gesta Henrici Secundi*

34 Roger of Hoveden

35 William of Newburgh

36 Ibid.

37 Ralph of Diceto

38 Roger of Hoveden; Ralph of Diceto

39 Ralph of Diceto

40 *Gesta Henrici Secundi*; Giraldus Cambrensis

41 Ralph of Diceto

42 William of Newburgh

43 Giraldus Cambrensis; Ralph of Diceto

44 Giraldus Cambrensis

45 Pipe Rolls

46 William of Newburgh

47 Ralph of Diceto
48 Ibid.
49 Roger of Hoveden
50 Ibid.
51 Ralph of Diceto
52 Ibid.
53 Giraldus Cambrensis
54 Ralph of Diceto
55 This is inferred from Gervase of Canterbury's statement that she was released from prison on Henry's death, and from references in the Pipe Rolls that suggest she stayed at Winchester for long periods towards the end of the reign.
56 Ralph of Diceto
57 Gervase of Canterbury
58 Ralph of Diceto
59 Ibid.
60 *L'Histoire de Guillaume le Maréchale*
61 Guillaume le Breton
62 *L'Histoire de Guillaume le Maréchale*
63 Ibid.; Giraldus Cambrensis
64 Ibid.
65 *L'Histoire de Guillaume le Maréchale*
66 Giraldus Cambrensis; Roger of Hoveden; Roger of Wendover
67 *L'Histoire de Guillaume le Maréchale*
68 Giraldus Cambrensis
69 Ibid.
70 Ibid.
71 Ibid.
72 Roger of Hoveden
73 *L'Histoire de Guillaume le Maréchale*
74 William of Newburgh
75 Roger of Hoveden; *Gesta Henrici Secundi*; Giraldus Cambrensis
76 Gervase of Canterbury
77 William of Newburgh

16 'The Eagle Shall Rejoice in Her Third Nesting'

1 *Itinerary of Richard I*
2 *L'Histoire de Guillaume le Maréchale*
3 *Ingulf's Chronicles of the Abbey of Croyland* (trans. H. T. Riley, 1854)
4 *L'Histoire de Guillaume de Maréchale*
5 Ralph of Diceto; Gervase of Canterbury
6 Ralph of Diceto
7 Ibid.

8 *Gesta Regis Ricardi*
9 Roger of Hoveden
10 Roger of Wendover
11 Roger of Hoveden; Ralph of Diceto
12 The English coinage had hitherto been subject to regional variations.
13 Roger of Hoveden
14 *Gesta Regis Ricardi*
15 Roger of Hoveden
16 Ralph of Diceto
17 Roger of Hoveden
18 Ralph of Diceto
19 *L'Histoire de Guillaume le Maréchale*
20 Ralph of Diceto
21 Ibid.
22 Glanville later died on crusade
23 Giraldus Cambrensis
24 Ibid.
25 Gervase of Canterbury
26 *Gesta Regis Ricardi*
27 Roger of Hoveden
28 *Itinerary of Richard I*
29 Ibid.
30 Ibid.
31 Pipe Rolls
32 *Itinerary of Richard I*
33 Roger of Wendover
34 Ralph of Diceto
35 Ibid.
36 Roger of Hoveden states it was 100,000 marks, but the *Gesta Regis Ricardi* claims that it was as much as 900,000.
37 *Gesta Regis Ricardi*
38 Richard of Devizes; William of Newburgh
39 Joscelin of Brakelond
40 Ralph of Diceto
41 Roger of Hoveden
42 William of Newburgh
43 Richard
44 Ibid.
45 Richard of Devizes; Ambrose; *Itinerary of Richard I*; Richard
46 This should read 'daughters', since Berengaria's father Sancho VI did not die until 1194.
47 Quoted in Mitchell: *Berengaria, Enigmatic Queen of England*
48 Roger of Hoveden; *Itinerary of Richard I*
49 Ambrose

17 *'The Admiration of Her Age'*

1 Roger of Hoveden; *Itinerary of Richard I*
2 The date of her death is not recorded, but is presumed to have been during or after 1230, when she is last mentioned in the records.
3 Most other reports of her beauty are found in the works of later chroniclers, viz. Ranulf Higden, Piers Langtoft, Walter of Guisborough and Henry Knighton.
4 Richard of Devizes
5 Ralph of Diceto; Roger of Hoveden
6 Peter of Blois
7 Ralph of Diceto
8 Ibid.
9 Roger of Hoveden
10 Roger of Wendover
11 Ralph of Diceto; Richard of Devizes
12 *Itinerary of Richard I*
13 Richard of Devizes
14 Roger of Hoveden
15 Ralph of Diceto
16 Roger of Hoveden
17 Giraldus Cambrensis; Roger of Hoveden; Piers Langtoft
18 Piers Langtoft
19 Roger of Hoveden
20 Philip's position is made clear in a *sirvents* by Bertran de Born entitled '*S'ieu fos aissi*'.
21 Roger of Hoveden; *The Chronicle of Meaux*; Giraldus Cambrensis
22 Roger of Hoveden
23 Ibid.; Ralph of Diceto; *Itinerary of Richard I*
24 Ralph of Diceto
25 Ibid.
26 Roger of Hoveden
27 Ibid.; Richard
28 Roger of Hoveden; Ralph of Diceto; *Itinerary of Richard I*
29 Pipe Rolls; *Itinerary of Richard I*
30 The chapel may still be visited today, along with various other sites connected with Richard and Berengaria in Cyprus, among them the ruined Berengaria Tower (of which the royal couple laid the foundations) on the outskirts of Kolossi, and Little Berengaria Village near Pannicon, north of Limassol.
31 Geoffrey de Vinsauf: *The Art of Poetry* (quoted in Mitchell: *Berengaria, Enigmatic Queen of England*). Vinsauf was a loyal subject and companion of Richard I.
32 Ambrose
33 Gervase of Canterbury

34 Roger of Hoveden

35 Some modern writers claim that the horror Berengaria felt on witnessing the massacre caused her to miscarry, but I can find no contemporary evidence for this.

36 *Gesta Henrici Secundi*

37 Richard of Devizes

38 William of Newburgh

39 Ibid.

40 Ibid.

41 For this episode, see Giraldus Cambrensis; Roger of Hoveden; and William of Newburgh.

42 William of Newburgh

43 Roger of Hoveden

44 Richard of Devizes

45 Roger of Hoveden

46 Richard of Devizes

47 William of Newburgh

48 Roger of Hoveden; Richard of Devizes

49 Richard of Devizes

50 Ibid.

51 Roger of Hoveden; Gervase of Canterbury; Roger of Wendover; Guillaume le Breton; William of Newburgh; Rigord

52 Bertran de Born (see note 20 above) makes it clear that Philip's sense of honour required him to avenge the slight to his sister.

53 Roger of Hoveden

54 Ibid.

55 Ibid.

56 Richard of Devizes

57 Ibid.

58 Roger of Hoveden

59 Richard of Devizes

60 Roger of Hoveden

61 Richard of Devizes

62 Ibid.

63 Ibid.

64 *Charter Rolls*

65 Richard of Devizes

66 Ibid.

67 Giraldus Cambrensis; Roger of Hoveden

68 Richard of Devizes

69 Ibid.

70 Ibid.

71 Ibid.

72 Ibid.

73 Ralph of Diceto

74 Ambrose
75 Gervase of Canterbury; Roger of Hoveden
76 Roger of Hoveden
77 Ibid.

18 *'The Devil is Loosed!'*

1 Letter from Henry VI to Philip II, quoted by Roger of Hoveden
2 Ibid.
3 Ibid. For Richard's adventures and capture, see also the account of his chaplain Anselm, in Ralph of Coggeshall.
4 Letter of Henry VI to Philip II, quoted by Roger of Hoveden
5 Ibid.
6 *L'Histoire de Guillaume le Maréchale*
7 For Eleanor's state of mind, see the letters to the Pope quoted later in this chapter (*Foedera*, Richard).
8 Roger of Hoveden
9 Ibid.
10 *Foedera*; Richard
11 Roger of Hoveden
12 Matthew Paris
13 William of Newburgh; *L'Histoire de Guillaume le Maréchale*
14 Ibid.
15 Ralph of Diceto
16 Roger of Hoveden
17 Ralph of Diceto
18 William of Newburgh
19 Ralph of Coggeshall
20 Ralph of Diceto
21 William of Newburgh
22 Ralph of Diceto
23 Roger of Hoveden
24 Ralph of Diceto
25 William of Newburgh
26 I have omitted repetitious passages and some of those citing scripture
27 Some historians erroneously translate this as 'Châteauroux', but it is clear that the Latin reference to the Castle of Ralph refers to the Castello Radulphi, where Eleanor had met the Pope during her visit to Rome in 1191. There is no record of her ever having met Celestine at Châteauroux. The Castle of Ralph is also mentioned (in a passage not quoted in this text) in her second letter to the Pope, where it is obvious that the Roman palace is being referred to.
28 *Foedera*; Richard
29 Rigord
30 Roger of Hoveden

31 Ibid.

32 Gervase of Canterbury

33 This is sometimes taken as the first of the three letters, but the explanatory detail in the first, and the angrier salutation in this, strongly suggest that it was the second.

34 This was an exaggeration, as Louis VII had already given Alexander III his support. Eleanor had not been present when these matters were discussed by Louis and Henry II.

35 *Foedera*; Richard

36 A mark was not a coin but a unit of account equivalent to 120 silver pennies or 8 oz of silver.

37 Roger of Hoveden

38 Ralph of Diceto

39 William of Newburgh

40 Roger of Hoveden

41 Ralph of Coggeshall

42 Ralph of Diceto; Roger of Hoveden

43 Ralph of Coggeshall

44 Roger of Hoveden

45 William of Newburgh

46 Ralph of Diceto; *Annals of Margam*

47 *Chroniques de St Martial*

48 Roger of Hoveden

49 *Foedera*; Richard

50 Roger of Hoveden

51 Giraldus Cambrensis

52 Roger of Hoveden

53 Ibid.; *L'Histoire de Guillaume le Maréchale*

54 William of Newburgh

55 Roger of Hoveden

56 Ibid.

57 Ibid.

58 William of Newburgh

59 Roger of Hoveden

60 Letter from Walter of Coutances to Ralph of Diceto; Roger of Hoveden

61 Ibid.

62 Roger of Hoveden

63 Letter from Walter of Coutances to Ralph of Diceto

64 Roger of Hoveden

65 Ibid.

66 Ralph of Diceto

67 Gervase of Canterbury

68 Roger of Hoveden

69 Ralph of Diceto; Roger of Hoveden

70 Roger of Hoveden

71 William of Newburgh; he refers to this port as 'Sweyne'
72 Roger of Hoveden; Ralph of Coggeshall
73 Ralph of Diceto; Gervase of Canterbury
74 Roger of Wendover
75 William of Newburgh
76 Roger of Hoveden
77 Ralph of Diceto
78 Ibid.
79 Roger of Wendover
80 Gervase of Canterbury
81 *Itinerary of Richard I*
82 Roger of Hoveden
83 William of Newburgh
84 Ralph of Diceto
85 Roger of Hoveden; for this ceremony, see also Gervase of Canterbury and *L'Histoire de Guillaume le Maréchale*
86 Gervase of Canterbury
87 Roger of Hoveden
88 Pipe Rolls
89 Roger of Hoveden

19 *'The Staff of My Old Age'*

1 Gervase of Canterbury; *L'Histoire de Guillaume le Maréchale*
2 *L'Histoire de Guillaume le Maréchale*
3 Ralph of Diceto; Roger of Wendover
4 Roger of Hoveden
5 Ralph of Diceto
6 For this episode, see *L'Histoire de Guillaume le Maréchale*
7 Roger of Hoveden
8 Pipe Rolls; Richardson: *The Letters and Charters of Eleanor of Aquitaine*
9 Pipe Rolls
10 *Calendar of Documents*, ed. Round
11 Giraldus Cambrensis
12 Adam of Eynsham
13 Roger of Hoveden
14 *Oxford Etymological Dictionary*
15 Rigord
16 Roger of Hoveden
17 See *Early Blazon. Heraldic Terminology in the Twelfth and Thirteenth Centuries* by Gerard J. Brault (Oxford, 1972); also *A European Armorial*, edited by Rosemary Pinches and Anthony Wood (Heraldry Today, 1971), *Armorial Bearings of the Sovereigns of England* by William Petchey (London, 1977), *Royal Beasts* by H. Stanford London (The Heraldry Society, East Knoyle, 1956), *European Civic Coats of Arms* by Jiri Louda (London, 1966) and *The*

Oxford Guide to Heraldry by Thomas Woodcock and John Martin Robinson (Oxford, 1988), amongst many other authorities. See also Nurith Kenaan-Kedar: *Aliénor d'Aquitaine conduite en captivité. Les peintures commémoratives de Sainte-Radegonde de Chinon* (Cahiers de civilisation médiévale, University of Poitiers, December 1998).

18 His name is subject to dispute: Gervase of Canterbury calls him John Sabroz, while Ralph of Diceto calls him Peter Basili.

19 Roger of Hoveden

20 Ibid.

21 Ibid.

22 *Annales Monastici*, ed. Luard

23 Ralph of Coggeshall

24 *Calendar of Documents*, ed. Round; *Itinerary of Richard I*

25 Ralph of Coggeshall

26 Ibid.

27 Ibid.; Ralph of Diceto

28 Charter of Queen Eleanor to the Abbey of Our Lady of Turpenay

29 Adam of Eynsham

30 Ibid.

31 Ralph of Diceto

32 Roger of Wendover

20 'The Most Reverend Eleanor'

1 Richard

2 His name is variously given in the sources as Aimery, Aimeri, Amaury and Adhemar

3 Adam of Eynsham

4 Ibid.

5 Ibid.

6 Ibid.

7 Ibid.

8 Roger of Hoveden; Richard

9 Roger of Hoveden

10 *Charter Rolls*

11 Roger of Hoveden

12 Richard

13 Calendar of Documents, ed. Round; Charter Rolls

14 Charter Rolls

15 She had borne a daughter, Mary or Wilhelmina, the previous year; this daughter later married Bernard of Elbine, Prince of Orange.

16 *Calendar of Documents*, ed. Round

17 *Charter Rolls*; Richard

18 *Charter Rolls*

19 Ibid.

20 Richard
21 Roger of Hoveden
22 *L'Histoire de Guillaume le Maréchale*
23 Roger of Hoveden; Ralph of Coggeshall
24 Ralph of Coggeshall
25 Ralph of Diceto
26 Ibid.; Ralph of Coggeshall; Roger of Hoveden; *L'Histoire de Guillaume le Maréchale*
27 Ralph of Diceto
28 Richard; Rigord; *Foedera*
29 Charter Rolls
30 Ibid.
31 Ibid.
32 Ibid.
33 Ibid.
34 Ibid.
35 For Joanna's veiling and death, see Roger of Hoveden.
36 Some genealogical works give his name as Betrand, perhaps confusing him with Count Raymond's illegitimate son Bertrand. It is far more likely that he was named after the late King Richard.
37 Charter Rolls
38 Ibid.; Richard
39 For this episode, see Roger of Hoveden
40 Roger of Hoveden
41 Gervase of Canterbury
42 Roger of Hoveden
43 Gervase of Canterbury
44 Richard
45 Roger of Hoveden; some modern writers assert that Eleanor left before the truce was concluded, but it is clear from this account that she did not.
46 Some books state that there were three unmarried daughters, including the eldest, Berengaria, but she had married Alfonso IX of Leon, as his second wife, in 1198.
47 Pierre Vidal: *Poésie*; Queen Eleanor of Castile lived until 1214; she and King John were the only two of Eleanor's children to survive her.
48 Quoted in Appel, *Provenzalische Chrestomathie*
49 Roger of Hoveden
50 Ibid.

21 *'The Brood of the Wicked Shall Not Thrive'*

1 Charter Rolls
2 Roger of Hoveden; Ralph of Diceto; Rigord. Hugh of Lincoln bore witness to this hatred when he visited Arthur in Paris and advised him to show himself friendly towards John in order to preserve the peace.

3 Roger of Hoveden; Ralph of Diceto; Rigord
4 Roger of Hoveden
5 *Foedera*
6 Ralph of Diceto; Richard
7 Ralph de Lusignan had acquired the county of Eu by marriage to its Norman heiress.
8 Roger of Hoveden
9 Guillaume le Breton
10 Roger of Hoveden
11 Aymer died in the summer of 1202, whereupon John succeeded him as Count of Angoulême.
12 Roger of Hoveden
13 Ibid.; *L'Histoire de Guillaume le Maréchale*; *Chronique de Touraine*; *Annals of Bury St Edmunds* (in *Annales Monastici*)
14 Ralph of Coggeshall
15 Roger of Wendover
16 Matthew Paris
17 Ibid.; Matthew Paris claimed he was told this by an eyewitness.
18 After King John's death in 1216, Isabella of Angoulême married Hugh X de Lusignan, the son of her former betrothed.
19 Ralph of Diceto
20 Adam of Eynsham
21 Roger of Wendover; Ralph of Diceto; Roger of Hoveden
22 *Foedera*
23 Charter Rolls
24 Ibid.
25 Roger of Wendover
26 Roger of Hoveden; Rigord
27 Rigord
28 Her body remained unburied until the church at Villeneuve was completed in 1225, when she was interred there beside Guy of Thouars and their daughter Alice.
29 Gervase of Canterbury
30 Ralph of Coggeshall
31 Ibid.
32 Ibid. Marie, Philip's daughter by Agnes of Méran, was five years old.
33 Rigord; Guillaume le Breton; Roger of Wendover
34 Roger of Wendover
35 *Calendar of Documents*, ed. Round
36 Ralph of Coggeshall
37 Ibid.; Guillaume le Breton; *Chronique des églises d'Anjou*; Roger of Wendover
38 Ralph of Coggeshall
39 *L'Histoire des ducs de Normandie*

40 Letter from King John to the English barons, quoted by Ralph of Coggeshall
41 Ralph of Coggeshall
42 *L'Histoire des ducs de Normandie*
43 Guillaume le Breton; Ralph of Coggeshall
44 Roger of Wendover
45 Ralph of Coggeshall
46 *L'Histoire des ducs de Normandie*
47 Ralph of Coggeshall
48 Ibid.
49 Roger of Wendover
50 Ibid.
51 Ibid.
52 John's quarrel with the Lusignans was not resolved until 1214, when Hugh's son, the future Hugh X, was betrothed to Joanna, the daughter of John and Isabella. After John's death, the betrothal was broken and Isabella herself married Hugh X.
53 Roger of Wendover
54 Ralph of Coggeshall; Matthew Paris
55 Ralph of Coggeshall
56 Roger of Wendover
57 *Chronique des églises d'Anjou*

22   'A Candle Goeth Out'

1 Ralph of Coggeshall
2 Roger of Wendover
3 Ralph of Coggeshall
4 Ibid.
5 Ibid.
6 *L'Histoire de Guillaume le Maréchale*
7 Ibid.
8 Roger of Wendover
9 *Rotuli Litterarum Patentium*; Ralph of Coggeshall
10 *Rotuli Litterarum Patentium*
11 Roger of Wendover
12 Guillaume le Breton
13 Ibid.
14 *Annals of Margam* (in *Annales Monastici*)
15 Ibid.
16 Matthew Paris
17 *Rotuli Litterarum Patentium*
18 Most notably Richard and Powicke
19 Ralph of Coggeshall; *Chronicle of Lanercost*
20 Referred to in Powicke: *The Loss of Normandy*

21 Ralph of Coggeshall
22 *Annals of Margam*
23 Matthew Paris
24 Roger of Wendover
25 Rigord; Guillaume le Breton
26 *L'Histoire de Guillaume le Maréchale*
27 Roger of Wendover
28 Ibid.
29 *L'Histoire de Guillaume le Maréchale*
30 Ibid.
31 Ibid.
32 Ralph of Coggeshall
33 Ibid.
34 *Annals of Waverley* (in *Annales Monastici*); some later sources, notably, *L'art de vérifier les dates*, give the date of Eleanor's death incorrectly as 31 March.
35 Isabella was buried at Fontevrault on her death in 1246. Drawings of all the effigies prior to restoration were produced by C.A. Stothard in *The Monumental Effigies of Great Britain*, 1876.
36 Joanna's tomb was irrevocably damaged during the French Revolution
37 A record of all those souls to be prayed for by the community.
38 Quoted in Bienvenu: *Aliénor d'Aquitaine et Fontevraud*
39 Liberate Rolls
40 Charter Rolls
41 Philippe Mouskès: *Chronique Rimée* (quoted by Marion Meade in *Eleanor of Aquitaine.*)

Genealogical Tables

HOUSE OF
RAZÈS

Bernard "Hairyfoot"
Count of Auvergne

William I
Duke of Aquitaine by 898
d.918

HOUSE OF
POITIERS
(distant
cousins)

Eubalus "the Bastard"
Count of Poitou 890-2 & 902-34
Duke of Aquitaine 927-34

William III "Towhead"   m.
Duke of Aquitaine
d.963

William IV "Fierebras"   m.
Duke of Aquitaine
abdicated 996. d.996

William V "the Great"   m.
Duke of Aquitaine
d.1030

William VI "the Fat"   Eudes
Duke of Aquitaine   Duke of Aquitaine
d.1038   d.1039

Aimery I   m.   Dangerosa
de Rochefoucauld
Viscount of Châtellerault

Hugh   Raoul   Aenor   m. William X
Viscount of   de Faye   d. c1130   Duke of Aquitaine
Châtellerault   1099-1137

                ELEANOR   m.1. Louis VII
                DUCHESS OF AQUITAINE   ↓   King of France
                1122-1204   1121-80

                                         m.2. Henry II,
                                         ↓   King of England
                                              1133-89

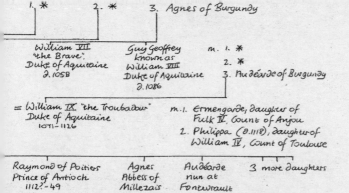

Adelinde m. Acfrid, Count of Razès

William II "the Younger"
Duke of Aquitaine
d. 926

Acfrid
Duke of Aquitaine
fl. 977

Adela,
daughter of William Longsword, Duke of Normandy

Emma (d. 1004)
daughter of Hugh Capet, Count of Paris

1. *   2. *   3. Agnes of Burgundy

William VII
"the Brave",
Duke of Aquitaine
d. 1058

Guy Geoffrey
known as
William VIII
Duke of Aquitaine
d. 1086

m. 1. *
2. *
3. Audéarde of Burgundy

= William IX "the Troubadour"
Duke of Aquitaine
1071–1126

m. 1. Ermengarde, daughter of
Fulk IV, Count of Anjou
2. Philippa (d. 1118), daughter of
William IV, Count of Toulouse

Raymond of Poitiers
Prince of Antioch
1112?–49

Agnes
Abbess of
Millezais

Audéarde
nun at
Fontevrault

3 more daughters

William Aiget
c.1247–1130

Petronilla m. Raoul,
c.1125–?   ↓   Count of
Vermandois

William Jocelin
(bastard sons of
William IX)

    * name not recorded

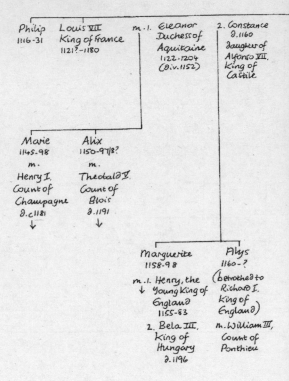

Louis VI "the Fat"
King of France
1081-1137

Philip
1116-31

Louis VII
King of France
1121?-1180

m.1. Eleanor
Duchess of
Aquitaine
1122-1204
(div.1152)

2. Constance
d.1160
daughter of
Alfonso VII.
King of
Castile

Marie
1145-98
m.
Henry I.
Count of
Champagne
d.c1181
↓

Alix
1150-97/8?
m.
Theobald V.
Count of
Blois
d.1191
↓

Marguerite
1158-98
m.1. Henry, the
↓ Young King of
England
1155-83
2. Bela III,
King of
Hungary
d.1196

Alys
1160-?
(betrothed to
Richard I.
King of
England)
m. William III,
Count of
Ponthieu

m. Adelaide
1092?–1154
daughter of Humbert II, Count of Maurienne and Savoy

3. Adela d.1206 daughter of Theobald IV, Count of Blois	Henry Archbishop of Rheims d.1175	Robert Count of Dreux d.1188 ↓	Peter, Infant of Courtenay d.1183?	Constance m.1. d.1176	Eustace Count of Boulogne 1127?–1153 2. Raymond V, ↓ Count of Toulouse d.1194

Philip II
Augustus
King of France
1165–1223

m.1. Isabella of Hainault
1170–90

2. Ingiborg of Denmark
d.1236 (div.)

3. Agnes of Meran
↓   d.1201

Agnes m.1. Alexius II
Comnenus,
Emperor of
Constantinople
d.1183

2. Emperor Andronicus
Comnenus
d.1185

3. Theodore Branas

Louis VIII
King of France
1187–1226

m. Blanche
↓ 1183–1253,
daughter of
Alfonso VIII,
King of Castile

Table Two: The Capetian Kings of France in
the Twelfth and early Thirteenth Centuries

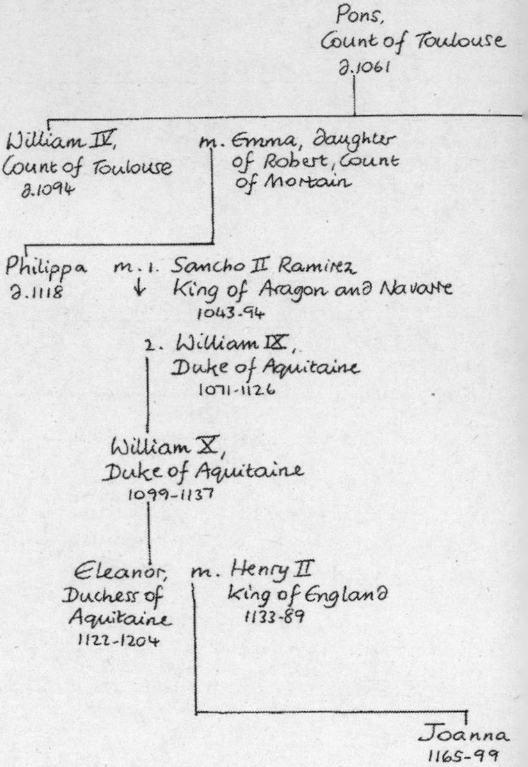

Pons,
Count of Toulouse
d.1061

William IV,
Count of Toulouse
d.1094

m. Emma, daughter
of Robert, Count
of Mortain

Philippa
d.1118

m . 1. Sancho II Ramirez
King of Aragon and Navarre
1043-94

2. William IX,
Duke of Aquitaine
1071-1126

William X,
Duke of Aquitaine
1099-1137

Eleanor,
Duchess of
Aquitaine
1122-1204

m. Henry II
King of England
1133-89

Joanna
1165-99

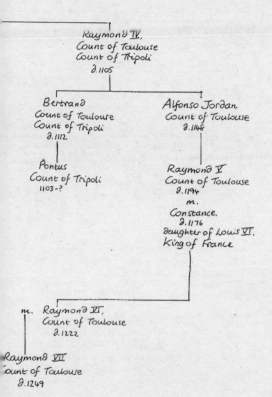

Raymond IV,
Count of Toulouse
Count of Tripoli
d. 1105

Bertrand
Count of Toulouse
Count of Tripoli
d. 1112

Alfonso Jordan
Count of Toulouse
d. 1148

Pontus
Count of Tripoli
1103 - ?

Raymond V
Count of Toulouse
d. 1194
m.
Constance.
d. 1176
daughter of Louis VI,
King of France

m. Raymond VI,
Count of Toulouse
d. 1222

Raymond VII
Count of Toulouse
d. 1249

Stephen
Count of Blois
d. 1102

William,   m. Agnes   Theobald IV   m. Matilda
Lord of Sulli   de Sulli   "the Great"   of
(disinherited   ↓   Count of Blois   Carinthia
due to lunacy)   and
      Champagne

Henry I   m. Marie   Theobald V   m. Alix
Count of Champagne   1145-98   Count of Blois   1150-47/8
d. 1181   daughter of   d. 1191   daughter
   Louis VII,   of
   King of France   Louis VII,
      King of
      France

Henry II,   m. Isabella   Theobald,   m.
Count of Champagne   daughter of   Count of
King of Jerusalem   Almaric I,   Champagne
d. 1196   King of Jerusalem   d. 1201

Louis   Theobald
Count of Blois   Count of Blois
Count of Chartres   Count of Chartres
d. 1205   d. 1219

m. Adela
1062?-1138
daughter of William I, King of England

Stephen,　　　　m. Matilda　　　Eleanor 1. m. Raoul　m. 2. Petronilla
King of England　　of Boulogne　　(div.)　　↓ Count of　　daughter of
1097?-1154　　　　d. 1152　　　　　　　　　Vermandois　　William X
　　　　　　　　　　　　　　　　　　　　　　　　　　　　Duke of
　　　　　　　　　　　　　　　　　　　　　　　　　　　　Aquitaine

　　　　　Eustace　　　　m. Constance
　　　　Count of Boulogne　　d. 1176
　　　　1127?-1153　　　　daughter of Louis VI,
　　　　　　　　　　　　　King of France

Stephen　　　　　　William　　　　Adela m. Louis VII,
Count of Sancerre　　Archbishop of　　b. 1208 ↓ King of France
　　　　　　　　　　Rheims　　　　　　　　　　1121?-1180

Blanche　　　Marie m. Baldwin VI,
daughter of　　　　　Count of
Garcia V,　　　　　Flanders,
King of Navarre　　Emperor of
　　　　　　　　　Constantinople

Isabella　　　　　　Daughter,　　　Margaret m. Otto I,
Countess of Blois　　un-named　　　　　　　Palatine of Burgundy,
m.　　　　　　　　m.　　　　　　　　　　youngest son of the
John of Châtillon,　Gauthier,　　　　　　German Emperor,
Lord of Avesnes,　Lord of Avesnes,　　Frederick Barbarossa
Count of Blois　　Count of Blois
d. 1201　　　　　　↓

Tortulf "the Woodman"
(semi-mythical)

Ingelgar of Anjou   m.
flourished 880

Fulk I "the Red",   m.
Count of Anjou 865
d.941/2

Fulk II "the Good"   m.
Count of Anjou
d.960/1

Geoffrey I "Greygown" m. Adela of Châlon-sur-Sâone
Count of Anjou
d.987

Maurice
Count of Anjou d.987

Fulk III "Nerra" ("the Black") m.1.
Count of Anjou 972-1040

Geoffrey II "Martel" m. Agnes of Burgundy
Count of Anjou
1006-60

Geoffrey III "Martel"   Fulk IV "Rechin" ("the Surly")
Count of Anjou   Count of Anjou
1040-98   abdicated 1103, d.1109

Ermengarde
m.1. William IX,   Geoffrey IV "Martel"
   Duke of Aquitaine   Count of Anjou
   1071-1126 (div.)   d.1106
2. Alan IV Fergant,
↓ Count of Brittany
   d.1112

Geoffrey V "the Fair" m. Matilda
"Plantagenet".   1102?-67
Count of Anjou,   daughter of
Duke of Normandy   Henry I, King of
1113-51   England

Henry II,   m.
King of England   ↓
1133-89

Alendis, heiress of Amboise

Roscilla, daughter of Warner, Lord of Loches

Gerberga

Guy
Bishop of Le Puy

Drogo
Bishop of Le Puy

Elizabeth, heiress of Vendôme   2. Hildegarde
burned as a witch, 1000

Adela   Hermengarde m. Geoffrey, Count of the Gatinais

m.1. Hildegarde,   2. Hermengarde   3. *   4. Bertrade de   5. *
daughter of   div. 1075   Montfort
Lancelin of   daughter of   (eloped with
Beaugency   Archenbaud the Strong   Philip I, King of
of Bourbon   France, 1101)

Aremburga   1. m.   Fulk V,   m.2. Melisende,
d.1126, daughter   Count of Anjou   ↓   Queen of
of Hélias de la Flèche,   King of Jerusalem   Jerusalem, d.1161,
Count of Maine   1131-43   daughter of
(resigned Anjou to his son)   Baldwin II.
King of Jerusalem

Isabella   m. William the Atheling,   Sybilla m.1. William Clito,
1073-54   Duke of Normandy   Count of Flanders
Abbess of   1103?-1120 (drowned)   1101-28 (div.)
Fontevrault   son of Henry I, King of England   2. Thierry of Alsace,
↓   Count of Flanders
d. 1168

Eleanor,   Geoffrey   William
Duchess of Aquitaine   Count of Nantes   1136-63
1122-1204   1135-57

* name not known.

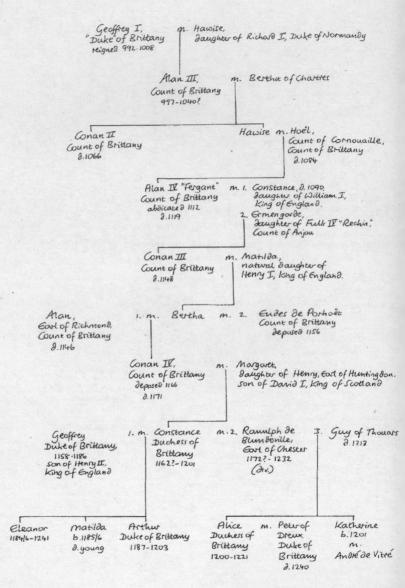

Geoffrey I,   m. Hawise,
"Duke" of Brittany   daughter of Richard I, Duke of Normandy
reigned 992-1008

Alan III,   m. Bertha of Chartres
Count of Brittany
997-1040?

Conan II   Hawise m. Hoël,
Count of Brittany   Count of Cornouaille,
d.1066   Count of Brittany
                                   d.1084

Alan IV "Fergant"   m. 1. Constance, d.1090,
Count of Brittany   daughter of William I,
abdicated 1112   King of England.
d.1119   2. Ermengarde,
                        daughter of Fulk IV "Rechin",
                        Count of Anjou

Conan III   m. Matilda,
Count of Brittany   natural daughter of
d.1148   Henry I, King of England.

Alan,   1. m.   Bertha   m. 2. Eudes de Porhoët
Earl of Richmond,   Count of Brittany
Count of Brittany   deposed 1156
d.1146

Conan IV,   m. Margaret,
Count of Brittany   daughter of Henry, Earl of Huntingdon,
deposed 1166   son of David I, King of Scotland
d.1171

Geoffrey   1. m. Constance   m.2. Ranulph de   3. Guy of Thouars
Duke of Brittany,   Duchess of   Blundeville,   d.1213
1158-1186   Brittany   Earl of Chester
son of Henry II,   1162?-1201   1172?-1232
King of England   (div.)

Eleanor   Matilda   Arthur   Alice   m. Peter of   Katherine
1184/6-1241 b.1185/6 Duke of Brittany   Duchess of   Dreux   b.1201
          d.young   1187-1203   Brittany   Duke of   m.
                                   1200-1221   Brittany   André de Vitré
                                           d.1240

Table Six: The Duchy of Brittany

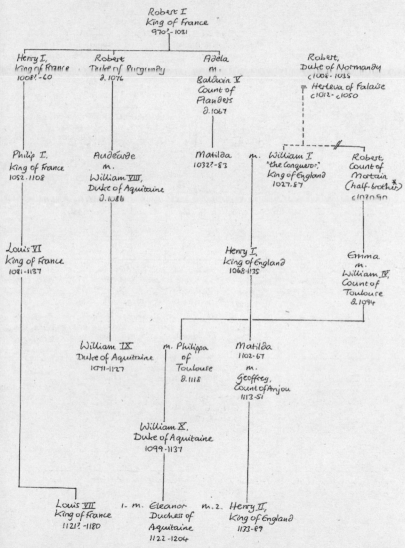

Table Seven: Eleanor of Aquitaine's Relationships to her Husbands

Robert I
King of France
970?-1031

Henry I,
King of France
1008?-60

Robert
Duke of Burgundy
d. 1076

Adela
m.
Baldwin V
Count of
Flanders
d. 1067

Robert,
Duke of Normandy
c1008-1035
= Herleva of Falaise
c1012-c1050

Philip I,
King of France
1052-1108

Audéarde
m.
William VIII,
Duke of Aquitaine
d. 1086

Matilda
1032?-83

m.

William I
"the Conqueror."
King of England
1027-87

Robert,
Count of
Mortain
(half-brother) *
c1030-90

Louis VI
King of France
1081-1137

Henry I,
King of England
1068-1135

Emma
m.
William IV,
Count of
Toulouse
d. 1094

William IX
Duke of Aquitaine
1071-1127

m. Philippa
of
Toulouse
d. 1118

Matilda
1102-67
m.
Geoffrey,
Count of Anjou
1113-51

William X,
Duke of Aquitaine
1099-1137

Louis VII
King of France
1121?-1180

1- m. Eleanor
Duchess of
Aquitaine
1122-1204

m.2. Henry II,
King of England
1133-89

* Son of Herleva by her husband, Herluin, Viscount of Conteville

William I "the Conqueror"
King of England
1027-87

William II "Rufus"   Henry I.
King of England   King of England
c1056 -1100   1068-1135

Geoffrey,   2 . m . Matilda   m.1. Henry V,
Count of Anjou   1102-67   German
1113-1151   Emperor
                                          d.1125

            Henry II,   m. Eleanor,
            King of England   Duchess of Aquitaine
            1133-1189   1122-1204

William   Henry,   Matilda   Richard I
Count of   the Young king, 1156-1189   King of England
Poitiers   Duke of   m.   1157-1199
1153 -1156   Normandy   Henry the Lion, m.
             1155-1183   Duke of Saxony   Berengaria
             m.   and   1163?-aft.1230,
             Margaret   Bavaria   daughter of
             1158-98,   1129-1195   Sancho VI,
             daughter of   King of
             Louis VII,   10 children   Navarre
             King of France

             William
             b. & d. 1177

m. Matilda
1032?-83
daughter of Baldwin V, Count of Flanders

Adela   m. Stephen,
c1062-1137/8   Count of Blois
                        d. 1102

Stephen,
King of England
c1097-1154

Eustace,
Count of Boulogne
c1127-1153

| Geoffrey. of Brittany ?-1186 m. Constance, duchess of Brittany ??-1201 children | Eleanor 1161-1214 m. Alfonso VIII, King of Castile 1156-1214 12 children | Joanna 1165-1199 m.1. William II, King of Sicily 1154-1189 m.2. Raymond VII Count of Toulouse 1156-1222 1 child by (1) 3 children by (2) | John, King of England 1166-1216 m.1. Hawise, d.1217 daughter of William, Earl of Gloucester (div.) 2. Isabella c1187-1246 daughter of Aymer, Count of Angoulême 5 children |

Index

www.vintage-books.co.uk